Reprints of Economic Classics

# POLITICAL ECONOMY
## AND POLITICS

THOMAS DE QUINCEY

# POLITICAL ECONOMY

## AND POLITICS

BEING VOLUME IX OF HIS COLLECTED WRITINGS
EDITED BY DAVID MASSON
[ 1897 ]

*THE LOGIC OF POLITICAL ECONOMY,*
*DIALOGUES OF THREE TEMPLARS,* ETC.

REPRINTS OF ECONOMIC CLASSICS

AUGUSTUS M. KELLEY · PUBLISHERS
*NEW YORK 1970*

First Published In This Edition 1897
( London: A. & C. Black, *Soho Square*, 1897 )

Reprinted 1970 by
AUGUSTUS M. KELLEY · PUBLISHERS
REPRINTS OF ECONOMIC CLASSICS
*New York New York 10001*

*I S B N 0 678 00680 6*
*L C N 66 21670*

PRINTED IN THE UNITED STATES OF AMERICA
*by* SENTRY PRESS, NEW YORK, N. Y. 10019

# CONTENTS

# EDITOR'S PREFACE

Among De Quincey's various readings and studies during the period of his settled residence at the Lakes from 1809 onwards there had been some attention to Political Economy. Especially in 1811, when he was in the twenty-sixth year of his age, he had been led, he tells us, "to look into loads of books and pamphlets on many branches of Economy"; and the taste for such readings had continued with him through the rest of his bachelor life, and the first year of his married life, in the Grasmere cottage. With no great admiration, it appears, however, for what were then the more recent writings, English or French, in Adam Smith's new science! "I saw," he says, "that these were generally the very dregs and "rinsings of the human intellect, and that any man of sound "head, and practised in wielding logic with a scholastic "adroitness, might take up the whole academy of modern "economists and throttle them between heaven and earth "with his finger and thumb, or bray their fungus heads to "powder with a lady's fan." He was still in this caustic mood on that subject when there ensued those two dreadful years, from 1817 to 1819, of which he has left record in his *Confessions* as having been the time of his most complete intellectual prostration, his indifference to the claims of any subject, consequent upon his first disastrous lapse into absolute besottedness with excess of opium. But, suddenly, in this time of gloomy torpor, broken only by intermittent agonies of opium-nightmare, his faculties, he tells us, seemed to be roused afresh, as if recovering themselves, under the influence of one particular book. It was a copy, sent him by an Edinburgh friend late in 1818, of Ricardo's *Principles of Political Economy and Taxation*, which had been published in the preceding year. "Wonder and curiosity," he says, "were emotions that had long been dead in me. Yet I "wondered once more,—wondered at myself that could once "again be stimulated to the effort of reading; and much "more I wondered at the book. Had this profound work "been really written during the tumultuous hurry of the "nineteenth century? Could it be that an Englishman, and "he not in academic bowers, but oppressed by mercantile and "senatorial cares, had accomplished what all the universities "of Europe, and a century of thought, had failed even to "advance by one hair's-breadth? Previous writers had been "crushed and overlaid by the enormous weights of facts, "details, and exceptions; Mr. Ricardo had deduced, *a priori*, "from the understanding itself, laws which first shot arrowy "light into the dark chaos of materials, and had thus con-"structed what hitherto was but a collection of tentative discus-"sions into a science of regular proportions, now first standing "upon an eternal basis." From that hour, in short, Ricardo was one of the great names in De Quincey's select list of eminent thinkers. As Kant had been his master for the previous twelve or fourteen years in the general domain of Abstract Logic and Metaphysics, so now Ricardo became his master in the special field of Social Economics. Nay, in the first fluttering back of his faculties to something like their normal use, it was to the new economic teachings of Ricardo, rather than to the medley of general philosophic meditations with which his mind had gradually filled itself under the prior teaching of Kant and others, that he was anxious to give immediate effect. Whereas his main literary project before his illness had been that of a great and all-comprehensive work of Abstract Philosophy to be entitled *De Emendatione Humani Intellectus* ("Of the Amendment of the Human Intellect"), that project was now postponed in favour of a shorter pamphlet or treatise, to be entitled *Prolegomena to all future Systems of Political Economy*. As his recovery advanced, he had actually begun such a pamphlet, had made arrangements for the printing of it in a town eighteen miles distant from Grasmere, and had advertised it as about to appear. Domestic straits, however, were too much for him; the umbrage of his opium-lethargy closed round him again; and, when he did escape from it into clear possession of his faculties and power of exerting them for his household needs, the exertion was to be neither in a *De Emendatione Humani Intellectus* nor in *Prolegomena to all Future Systems of Political Economy*, but,—O Pegasus roped to a cart!—in the shabbily-paid editorship of a provincial Tory newspaper.[1]

A year or two more, and the *Westmoreland Gazette* had found another editor, while De Quincey, famous as "The English Opium-Eater" by the publication of his "Confessions" in 1821 in the *London Magazine*, had the full command of that periodical for whatever further contributions he cared to offer. How frequent and various these were from 1821 to the end of 1824 we have already seen. It would have been strange if Political Economy and Ricardo had not now benefited by the chance. Accordingly, in the number of the *London Magagine* for October 1823, containing a continuation of a series of miscellaneous odds and ends which De Quincey had begun in the preceding number under the title "Notes from the Pocket-Book of a Late Opium-Eater," one of the odds and ends was a short article entitled *Malthus*, pointing out what the writer regarded as a serious flaw in Malthus's Theory of Population. Among the readers of this short article was William Hazlitt, then forty-five years of age,—*i.e.* seven years De Quincey's senior. As Hazlitt also was a valued member of the staff of contributors to the *London Magazine*, and as it chanced that in Hazlitt's *Political Essays*, published in 1819 and republished in 1822, there had been a criticism of Malthus of similar purport to that in De Quincey's short paper, the editor of the *London Magazine* felt himself bound to insert in the next, or November, number of the magazine a letter from Hazlitt, calling attention to this coincidence. As the letter, though not explicitly charging De Quincey with plagiarism, seemed to imply that

[1] For the authority for the facts in this paragraph see the enlarged edition of the *Confessions* (*ante*, Vol. III, pp. 431-433); but some of the quoted phrases are from the first or 1822 edition.

charge, there followed a reply from De Quincey in the December number. It was scrupulously polite to Hazlitt, but with a gleam of menace, as from a rapier half-unsheathed. So that matter ended; but in the same December number there was another short paper by De Quincey of an independent kind, entitled *Measure of Value*, in which, while Malthus was again the principal object, there was a defence of Ricardo against Malthus. Though this little paper did not appear till December 1823, it had been written, as a prefatory note explained, before the author had heard of Ricardo's death,—which had occurred on the 11th of the preceding September, when the great Economist was but in the fifty-second year of his age, and in the prime of his Parliamentary influence and reputation. One of De Quincey's cherished hopes had been for an opportunity of becoming acquainted with Ricardo personally and testifying his allegiance by discipleship to the living man. That hope having been disappointed, it remained for him to do what he could in honour of the deceased by some systematic exposition of the Ricardian views,—the rather because, in the first place, Ricardo himself had not been the best of expositors in matters so abstruse, and because, in the second place, there were points in which even Ricardo's views required correction or modification. Thus it happened that, amid all De Quincey's industry for the *London Magazine* on miscellaneous topics, literary, historical, or philosophical (as many as three or four separate articles of his sometimes in one number), he found time for one express effort of some length towards a full account of what was most essential in Ricardo's new doctrines in Political Economy. In the number of the magazine for March 1824 there appeared, with De Quincey's customary signature of X. Y. Z., a paper entitled *On the Services of Ricardo to Political Economy*, intimating that this was the first of a series in which Ricardo's principles should be clearly and succinctly expounded; and this promised exposition took the shape, in the next two numbers, of *Dialogues of Three Templars on Political Economy, chiefly in Relation to the Principles of Mr. Ricardo.* At the end of the seventh dialogue in May 1824 the series stopped, still not quite complete, but sufficiently complete perhaps for those magazine readers who wanted Ricardo only in moderation.

Yet a few years more, and *Blackwood's Magazine* had succeeded the *London Magazine* as the receptacle for the best that De Quincey's brain could produce, and he had entered on that long portion of his career which, beginning with contributorship to *Blackwood* from his Grasmere abode, was to end in his permanent transference of himself to Edinburgh, not only for continued facilities with *Blackwood*, but also for extension of his literary connexions to whatever else in periodical guise existed or might spring up in the northern metropolis. It is marvellous to observe, through all this portion of his career, when a poor modicum of guineas every month was all that one of the finest and most scholarly minds in Britain asked or expected for its teeming products, his fidelity in the main to his own ideal in the nature and the quality of those products, his adherence in the main to his own private standard of what constituted real literature, as distinct from the mere marketable matter known now as "padding." One observes this even in his choice of subjects. In that particular, indeed, he does not seem to have had much difficulty with editors,—either because the subjects he offered were in many cases popular enough, or because, being a privileged contributor, there might be a licence for him as to range and abstruseness of subjects that could not be accorded to others. All the more one is surprised that, in the time of the full swing of his contributorship to *Blackwood*, when he did not shrink from taxing the editor's indulgence and trying the public patience with occasional articles on Kant and other subjects similarly light and feathery, he abstained so long from his favourite Ricardo. But he did break out on Ricardo at last. In the volume of *Blackwood's Magazine* for the latter half of the year 1842 will be found a series of three papers,—the first in the September number, the second in the October number, and the third in the December number,—under the general title *Ricardo made Easy; or, What is the Radical Difference between Ricardo and Adam Smith? With an Occasional Notice of Ricardo's Oversights.* That these *Blackwood* papers of De Quincey should have been all but forgotten, and should have hardly been thought worth registering by De Quincey himself in any retrospective list of his writings, is accounted for by the fact that in the very next year he recast them, redigested them, expanded them, and rearranged them into a separate volume published by Messrs. Blackwood under the title *The Logic of Political Economy by Thomas De Quincey.* The *Blackwood* articles of 1842 were absorbed into this treatise of 1844 and superseded by it.

Those of De Quincey's hitherto known writings on Political Economy which demand reproduction in the present volume are, therefore, in chronological order, these :—(1) His brief criticism in 1823 of Malthus's theory of Population ; (2) his briefer criticism of Malthus in the same year in the scrap entitled *Measure of Value* ; (3) his exposition of Ricardo in 1824 in his *Dialogues of Three Templars on Political Economy* ; (4) his complete little treatise of 1844 entitled *The Logic of Political Economy.* Of these only No. 3,—to wit *The Templars' Dialogues,*—was reproduced by De Quincey himself in his Collective Edinburgh Edition of his writings. They formed part of volume iv of that edition, as published in 1854. If he meant to include also Nos. 1, 2, and 4 in his Collective Edition, he had not overtaken them at his death in 1859. The defect was to a great extent remedied in the revised reissue of the Collective Edition by Messrs. Black. *The Logic of Political Economy* was included in volume xiii of that reissue, by leave from Messrs. Blackwood ; and the short papers originally entitled *Malthus* and *Measure of Value* were recovered for insertion in volume xvi of the reissue. So far De Quincey's contributions to the Science of Political Economy were made collectively accessible ; but something has still had to be done for the proper exhibition of this class of his writings in the present volume. Chronological order being always of importance where development of opinion is part of the interest, that order has been reverted to. But, further, in the cases of Nos. 1, 3, and 4 individually, more has seemed necessary. In order to complete No. 1, both historically and in expository effect, Hazlitt's letter and De Quincey's reply to that letter have been extracted from the old pages of the *London Magazine* and added to the original little criticism of Malthus which occasioned both,—the triad forming together a kind of unity, for which *Malthus on Population* is the most suitable title. Then, though De Quincey reprinted only the last two of his three *London Magazine* papers of 1824 in exposition of Ricardo, omitting the prior paper specially entitled *On the Services of Ricardo to Political Economy*, it has been deemed advantageous to restore that paper to its proper historical place, as actually the introduction to the Dialogues and the announcement of them as forthcoming. This too is an addition of matter direct from the old columns of the magazine. Finally, though, as has been said, De Quincey's little treatise of 1844 called *The Logic of Political Economy* substantially absorbed and superseded the three *Blackwood* articles on Ricardo of 1842,—much of their very phraseology, as well as their matter, being repeated in the treatise,—yet, as, on examination, some paragraphs of the first of those three articles did seem to retain an independent interest, and to be entitled to preservation on that account, this has been managed by excerpting these paragraphs from *Blackwood's* columns of September 1842, and inserting them as a separate short article under the heading *Ricardo and Adam Smith.*

De Quincey's contributions to the science of Political Economy are represented, therefore, in this volume by five reprints instead of the four which have hitherto served the purpose, while two of the former four are given for the first time in complete form, and the whole series is arranged for the first time in proper order and coherence. Opinions, we believe, differ as to the value of some of those doctrines in Political Economy which De Quincey made it his special business to advocate, and as to his consequent title to rank among original authorities in the science; but competent judges have been unanimous in admiring his power of lucid exposition of the most difficult economic conceptions, his dialectical keenness in detecting fallacies, and the constant felicity and beauty of his illustrations.

In the next three papers of the volume we pass from Political Economy into General British Politics. These three papers have also a certain coherence among themselves, and may be read as a series. That entitled *Falsification of*

*English History* appeared first in the *London Magazine* for December 1824, as the last of De Quincey's "Notes from the Pocket-Book of a late Opium-Eater," and was in fact the last of all his contributions to that magazine. It was then entitled "Falsifications of the History of England"; and the slight change of title was made in 1859, when De Quincey detached the paper from its original connexion, and reprinted it in independent form in vol. xii of his Collected Writings. It is one of the bravest little papers he ever wrote. Avowing himself in the very first sentence to be, and to have always been, a loyal son of the Church of England, he proceeds, not the less openly, to administer a sharp rebuke to the English Clergy collectively as chiefly responsible, by the all but uniform character and style of their contributions to English Historical Literature through the whole of the two centuries that had elapsed since the Restoration of 1660, for a vitiation and degradation of historical scholarship in all that appertained to the great Puritan Revolution of the preceding twenty years. Maintaining those twenty years between 1640 and 1660 to have been the most heroic time in English annals, the fullest of great spirits and of noble agitations,—the time of the working out of important political results which not even the Restoration could repeal, which the Revolution of 1688 recapitulated and re-expressed only in part, and all of which are virtually permanent in the British body-politic to this day,—he accuses the English clergy of having, by persistence in official sycophancy to the Restoration itself, fostered systematically that gross ignorance of the real history of those twenty years, that habit of reference to some of their most memorable personalities and events only for sneers and vilification, which had disgraced and still disgraced British Literature. As the disgrace, if it was one, is not yet wholly removed,—as there is too much still in our literature of the unscholarly habit of treating one side of the Revolutionary struggle of those twenty years as an entirely disreputable series of ongoings in the past history of the British islands,—De Quincey's thesis of 1824 is not quite out of date, and may be still recommended. There is more of connexion with it in the next paper, entitled *A Tory's Account of Toryism, Whiggism, and Radicalism*, than the difference of the dates of the two papers, and the title of the latter, might suggest. It was in the pages of *Tait's Magazine*, in the numbers for December 1835 and January 1836, that De Quincey ventured on this second general essay of his on British Politics. As the politics of the magazine itself were strongly Whig or Whig-Radical, it was a boldness on the editor's or proprietor's part to admit such an exposition from so pronounced a Tory; but he conceded the liberty in most handsome fashion. To save himself, however, from undue responsibility, he announced each article as "By the English Opium-Eater," and took the precaution also of subjoining editorial footnotes commenting on the views expressed, and sometimes pretty sarcastically. These footnotes having somewhat nettled De Quincey, he wrote another paper, though not till after a year's interval, replying to the editorial censures of the first, and further developing the thesis he had then maintained. He was extremely anxious that this paper too should appear in *Tait's Magazine*; but the proprietor would not continue the controversy, and refused. Details of the story of this little affair between De Quincey and Mr. Tait are reserved for a special note on the subject; enough to say here that the rejected additional paper, written in 1837, and entitled *On the Political Parties of Modern England*, remained in manuscript till 1863, when it was published by Messrs. Black in one of the supplementary volumes to their revised Collective Edition of De Quincey. It was annexed there to a reprint of the paper to which it was properly the sequel, and which De Quincey had not overtaken in the process of his own reprints. The two papers, in fact, have a common aim and purpose, which might be best indicated by abandoning the names which De Quincey affixed to them, and describing them as "Essays on the History and Philosophy of British Party Politics." Their main doctrine, deduced from a review of British History from the Revolution of 1688 onwards, is that neither Toryism nor Whiggism is complete in itself, or a summary in itself of all political virtue, but that both are necessary forces in the British Constitution, working by a transmitted polar antagonism, always honourable and beneficial when each of the two representative parties keeps to the strict law of conduct prescribed by its historical origin. It is perhaps a pity that in essays the purport of which is thus so far purely scientific there should be occasional outbreaks of De Quincey's violent personal antipathy to modern Radicalism and all its designs and belongings. These particular passages of gratuitous insult to one class of his political opponents cannot fail to be irritating to some ; but, where no such irritation is felt, or where it can be got over, the essays are pretty sure to be valued as among De Quincey's best. A more subtle, and in some respects more instructive, insight into the history and philosophy of British Party Politics may be obtained from them than from anything in Hallam or Macaulay.

The paper entitled *California and the Gold-Digging Mania* was first published in 1852, and first republished in 1871, in the last supplementary volume of Messrs. Black's revised edition of the Collected Writings. From its nature, it might have been added to the Political Economy papers which form the first part of the volume ; but, as there are political implications in it, in the shape of suggestions as to some of the duties of mother nations to their colonies, it comes properly enough where we have placed it. To the present volume also, though for reasons of a more profoundly speculative kind, belongs the Translation of Kant's "*Idea of a Universal History on a Cosmopolitical Plan.*" This highly-important Essay on what may be called Transcendental Politics or World-Politics had attracted De Quincey's attention in the course of his readings in Kant ; and his Translation of it, though published so long ago as 1824, may still have an interest of novelty for many.

D. M.

# MALTHUS ON POPULATION[1]

"Go, my son,"—said a Swedish chancellor to his son,—"go and see with how little cost of wisdom this world is governed."[2] "Go," might a scholar in like manner say after a thoughtful review of literature, "go and see how little logic is required to the composition of most books." Of the many attestations to this fact, furnished by the history of opinions in our hasty and unmeditative age, I know of none more striking than the case of Mr. Malthus, both as regards himself and his critics. About a quarter of a century ago Mr. Malthus wrote his Essay on Population, which soon rose into great reputation.[3] And why? Not for the truth it contained; *that* is but imperfectly understood even at present; but for the false semblance of systematic form with which he had invested the truth. Without any necessity he placed his whole doctrine on the following basis: man increases in a geometrical ratio—the food of man in an arithmetical ratio. This proposition,

[1] Printed first in the *London Magazine* for October 1823, as one of the series of odds and ends contributed by De Quincey to that periodical under the running title, "Notes from the Pocket-Book of a late Opium-Eater." Reprinted in 1871 in the last volume of Messrs. Black's sixteen-volume edition of De Quincey's Collective Writings.—M.

[2] "*Nescis, mi fili, quantilla prudentia homines regantur*" ("You know not, my son, with what a very small quantity of wisdom men are governed") was the original form of this famous saying of the Swedish statesman Oxenstiern (1583-1654) in a letter sent in 1648 to his son, then one of the Swedish envoys negotiating the Treaty of Westphalia.—M.

[3] The first edition of Malthus's *Essay on Population* was in 1798; and it had passed through several editions before 1823.—M.

though not the main error of his work, is *one*; and therefore I shall spend a few lines in exposing it. I say, then, that the distinction is totally groundless: both tend to increase in a geometric ratio; both have this tendency checked and counteracted in the same way. In everything which serves for the food of man, no less than in man himself, there is a *positive* ground of increase by geometrical ratios; but, in order that this positive ground may go on to its effect, there must in each case be present a certain *negative* condition (*i.e. conditio sine qua non* [1]). For the food, as suppose for wheat, the negative condition is soil on which it may grow and exert its virtue of self-multiplication; for man the negative condition is food: *i.e.* in both cases the negative condition is the same, *mutatis mutandis*; for the soil is to the wheat what the wheat is to man. Where this negative condition is present, both will increase geometrically; where it is absent, neither. And so far is it from being true that man has the advantage of the wheat, or increases according to any other law, as Mr. Malthus affirms, that, on the contrary, the wheat has greatly the advantage of man (though both increase according to the same law). But, says Mr. Malthus, you would find it impossible to increase the annual supply of wheat in England by so much as the continual addition even of the existing quantity; whereas man might, on a certain supposition, go on increasing his species in a geometric ratio. What is that supposition? Why, this—that the negative condition of increase, the absence of which is the actual resistance in both cases to the realization of a geometric increase, is here by supposition restored to man but *not* restored to the wheat. It is certainly true that wheat in England increases only by an arithmetic ratio; but then so does man: and the inference thus far would be that both alike were restricted to this law of increase. "Ay, but then man," says Mr. Malthus, "will increase by another ratio, if

[1] Once for all let me say to the readers of these memoranda that I use the term *negative condition* as equivalent to the term *conditio sine qua non*, and both in the scholastic sense. The negative condition of X is that which being absent X can*not* exist, but which being present X will not *therefore* exist unless a positive ground of X be co-present. Briefly,—If not, not: if yes, not therefore yes.

you allow him an unlimited supply of food." Well, I answer, and so will the wheat: to suppose this negative condition (an unlimited supply of food) concurring with the positive principle of increase in man, and to refuse to suppose it in the wheat, is not only contrary to all laws of disputing, but is also on this account the more monstrous, because the possibility and impossibility of the negative concurring with this positive ground of increase is equal, and (what is still more to the purpose) is identical, for both: wheresoever the concurrence is realised for man, there of necessity it is realised for the wheat. And, therefore, you have not only a right to demand the same concession for the wheat as for the man, but the one concession is actually involved in the other. As the soil (S) is to the wheat (W), so is the wheat (W) to man (M); *i.e.* S : W : : W : M. You cannot even by way of hypothesis assume any cause as multiplying the third term which will not also presuppose the multiplication of the first: else you suffer W as the third term to be multiplied, and the very same W as the second term not to be multiplied. In fact, the coincidence of the negative with the positive ground of increase must of necessity take place in all countries during the early stages of society for the food of man no less than for man: this coincidence must exist and gradually cease to exist for both simultaneously. The negative condition, without which the positive principle of increase in man and in the food of man is equally inefficient, is withdrawn *in fact* as a country grows populous: for the sake of argument, and as the basis of a chain of reasoning, it may be restored *in idea* to either; but not more to one than to the other. That proposition of Mr. Malthus, therefore, which ascribes a different law of increase to man and to the food of man (which proposition is advanced by Mr. Malthus and considered by most of his readers as the fundamental one of his system) is false and groundless. Where the positive principle of increase meets with its complement the negative ground, there the increase proceeds in a geometrical ratio—alike in man and in his food: where it fails of meeting this complement, it proceeds in an arithmetical ratio, alike in both. And I say that, wherever the geometrical ratio of increase exists for man, it exists of necessity for the food of man: and I say that, wherever the arithmetical ratio exists for the food of man, it exists of necessity for man.

Lastly, I repeat that, even where the food of man and man himself increase in the same *ratio* (viz. a geometrical ratio), yet the food has greatly the advantage in the *rate* of increase. For assume any cycle of years (suppose 25) as the period of a human generation and as corresponding to the annual generations of wheat, then I say that, if a bushel of wheat and a human couple (man and woman) be turned out upon Salisbury plain,—or, to give them more area and a better soil for the experiment, on the stage of Canada and the uncolonized countries adjacent,—the bushel of wheat shall have produced its cube—its 4th—10th—Mth power in a number of years which shall always be fewer than the number of periods of 25 years in which the human pair shall have produced its cube—its 4th—10th—Mth power, etc. And this assertion may be easily verified by consulting any record of the average produce from a given quantity of seed corn.

II. The famous proposition, therefore, about the geometrical and arithmetical ratios as applied to man and his food is a radical blunder. I come now to a still more remarkable blunder, which I verily believe is the greatest logical oversight that has ever escaped any author of respectability. This oversight lies in Mr. Malthus's view of population considered not with reference to its own internal coherency but as an answer to Mr. Godwin. That gentleman, in common with some other philosophers,—no matter upon what arguments,—had maintained the doctrine of the "perfectibility" of man. Now, says Mr. Malthus, without needing any philosophic investigation of this doctrine, I will overthrow it by a simple statement drawn from the political economy of the human race: I will suppose that state of perfection towards which the human species is represented as tending to be actually established: and I will show that it must melt away before the principle which governs population. How is this accomplished? Briefly, thus:—In every country the food of man either goes on increasing simply in an arithmetical ratio, or (in proportion as it becomes better peopled) is rapidly tending to such a ratio. Let us suppose this ratio everywhere established, as it must of necessity be as soon as no acre of land remains untilled which is susceptible of tillage; since no revolutions in the mere science of agriculture can be supposed capable of transmuting an arithmetic into a geometric ratio of increase. Food then increasing under this law can never go on *pari passu* with any population which should increase in a geometric ratio. Now, what is it that prevents population from increasing in such a ratio? Simply the want of food. But how? Not directly, but through the instrumentality of vice and misery in some [1] shape or other. These are the repressing forces which everywhere keep down the increase of man to the same ratio as that of his food—viz. to an arithmetic ratio. But vice and misery can have no existence in a state of perfection; so much is evident *ex vi termini.* If, then, these are the only repressing forces, it follows that in a state of perfection there can be none at all. If none at all, then the geometric ratio of increase will take place. But, as the arithmetic ratio must still be the law for the increase of food, the population will be constantly getting ahead of the food. Famine, disease, and every mode of wretchedness will return; and thus out of its own bosom will the state of perfection have regenerated the worst form of imperfection by necessarily bringing back the geometric ratio of human increase unsupported by the same ratio of increase amongst the food. This is the way in which Mr. Malthus applies his doctrine of population to the overthrow of Mr. Godwin. Upon which I put this question to Mr. Malthus,—In what condition must the human will be supposed if, with the clear view of this fatal result (such a view as must be ascribed to it in a state of perfection), it could nevertheless bring its own acts into no harmony with reason and conscience? Manifestly it must be in a most diseased state. Ay, says Mr. Malthus, but "I take it for granted" that no important change will ever take place in that part of human nature. Be it so, I answer: but the

[1] What is the particular shape which they put on in most parts of the earth furnishes matter for the commentary of Mr. Malthus on his own doctrine, and occupies the greater part of his work. The materials are of course drawn from voyages and travels; but from so slender a reading in that department of literature that the whole should undoubtedly be re-written and more learnedly supported by authorities.

question here is not concerning the *absolute* truth,—Is there any hope that the will of man can ever raise itself from its present condition of weakness and disorder? The question is concerning the formal or logical truth—concerning the truth *relatively* to a specific concession previously made. Mr. Malthus had consented to argue with Mr. Godwin on the supposition that a state of perfection might be and actually was attained. How comes he then to "take for granted" what in a moment makes his own concession void? He agrees to suppose a perfect state; and at the same time he includes in this supposition the main imperfection of this world—viz. the diseased will of man. This is to concede and to retract in the same breath; explicitly to give, and implicitly to refuse. Mr. Godwin may justly retort upon Mr. Malthus—You promised to show that the state of perfection should generate out of itself an inevitable relapse into that state of imperfection: but *your* state of perfection already includes imperfection, and imperfection of a sort which is the principal parent of almost all other imperfection. Eve, after her fall, was capable of a higher resolution than is here ascribed to the children of perfection; for she is represented by Milton as saying to Adam

——miserable it is
To be to others cause of misery,
Our own begotten, and of our loins to bring
Into this cursed world a woeful race,
That after wretched life must be at last
Food for so foul a monster: in thy power
It lies, yet ere conception, to prevent
The race unblest, to being yet unbegot.
Childless thou art; childless remain.

*P. L.*, Book x. 981-989.

What an imperfect creature could meditate, a perfect one should execute. And it is evident that, if ever the condition of man were brought to so desirable a point as that, simply by replacing itself, the existing generation could preserve unviolated a state of perfection, it would become the duty (and, if the duty, *therefore* the inclination of perfect beings) to comply with that ordinance of the reason.[1]

[1] Mr. Malthus has been charged with a libel on human nature for denying its ability, even in its present imperfect condition, to practise

III. Thus far on the errors of Mr. Malthus: now let me add a word or two on the errors of his critics. But first it ought in candour to be acknowledged that Mr. Malthus's own errors, however important separately considered, are venial as regards his system; for they leave it unaffected, and might be extirpated by the knife without drawing on any consequent extirpations or even any alterations. That sacrifice once made to truth and to logic,—I shall join with Mr. Ricardo (Pol. Econ. p. 498, 2d ed.) in expressing my persuasion "that the just reputation of the Essay on Population will spread with the cultivation of that science of which it is so eminent an ornament." With these feelings upon Mr. Malthus's merits, it may be supposed that I do not regard his critics with much sympathy: taking them generally, they seem to have been somewhat captious, and in a thick mist as to the true meaning and tendency of the doctrine. Indeed I question whether any man amongst them could have begun his own work by presenting a just analysis of that which he was assailing; which, however, ought always to be demanded peremptorily of him who assails a systematic work, for the same reason that in the old schools of disputation the respondent was expected to repeat the syllogism of his opponent before he undertook to answer it. Amongst others, Mr. Coleridge, who probably contented himself *more suo* with reading the first and last pages of the work, has asserted that Mr. Malthus had written a 4to volume (in which shape the second edition appeared) to prove that man could not live without eating. If this were the purpose and amount of the Malthusian doctrine, doubtless an infraduodecimo would have been a more becoming size for his speculations. But I, who have read the 4to,

the abstinence here alluded to—provided an adequate motive to such abstinence existed. But this charge I request the reader to observe that I do not enter into. Neither do I enter into the question whether any great change for the better in the moral nature of the man is reasonably to be anticipated. What I insist on is simply the *logical* error of Mr. Malthus in introducing into the hypothesis which he consents to assume one element which is a contradiction *in terminis* to that hypothesis. Admit that Mr. Malthus is right in denying the possibility of a perfect state of man on this earth; he cannot be right in assuming an enormous imperfection (disorder of the will) as one constituent of that perfect state.

must assure Mr. Coleridge that there is something more in it than *that.* I shall also remind him that, if a man produces a body of original and eminently useful truths, in that case, the more simple, the more elementary, the more self-evident is the proposition on which he suspends the chain of those truths, the greater is his merit. Many systems of truth which have a sufficient internal consistency have yet been withheld from the world, or have lost their effect, simply because the author has been unable to bridge over the gulph between his own clear perceptions and the universal knowledge of mankind—has been unable to deduce the new truths from the old *precognita.* I say therefore that our obligations to Mr. Malthus are the greater for having hung upon a postulate so simple as that which Mr. Coleridge alleges so much valuable instruction, both theoretic and practical, as his work contains. Is it nothing for our theoretic knowledge that Mr. Malthus has taught us to judge more wisely of the pretended depopulations from battle, pestilence, and famine, with which all history has hitherto teemed? Is it nothing for our practical knowledge that Mr. Malthus has taught the lawgivers and the governors of the world to treat with contempt the pernicious counsels of political economists from Athenian days down to our own—clamouring for direct encouragements to population? Is it nothing for England that he first has exposed the fundamental [1] vice of our Poor Laws (viz. that they act as a bounty on population), and placed a lighthouse upon the rocks to which our course was rapidly carrying us in darkness? Is it nothing for science and the whole world that, by unfolding the laws which govern population, he has given to political economy its complement and sole desideratum; which wanting, all its movements were insecure and liable to error; which added, political economy (however imperfect as to its development) has now become, as to the *idea* of its parts, perfect and orbicular? Is this, and more that might be alleged, nothing? I say, Mr. Coleridge,

[1] Fundamental, I mean, for the political economist: otherwise for the philosopher they have a still profounder vice, in their obvious tendency to degrade the moral character of their objects in their best elements of civic respectability.

Is this nothing?
Why then the world, and all that's in't, is nothing:
The covering sky is nothing, Bohemia nothing.
*Winter's Tale.*

Others, who have been more just to Mr. Malthus than Mr. Coleridge, and have admitted the value of the truths brought forward, have disputed his title to the first discovery. A fuller development and a more extensive application of these truths they concede to him; but they fancy that in the works of many others before him they find the outlines of the same truths more or less distinctly expressed. And doubtless in some passages of former economists, especially of Sir James Steuart, and in one work of Wallace (Views of Providence, &c.) there is so near an approach made to the Malthusian doctrine[1] that at this day, when we are in possession of that doctrine, we feel inclined to exclaim in the children's language of blind-man's-buff—Lord! how he *burns!* But the best evidence that none of these writers did actually touch the central point of the doctrine is this: that none of them deduced from it those corollaries as to the English poor laws, foundling-hospitals, endowments of cottages with land, and generally of all artificial devices for stimulating population, which could not have escaped a writer of ability who had once possessed himself of the entire truth. In fact, such is the anarchy of thought in most writers on subjects which they have never been led to treat systematically that it is nothing uncommon to meet with a passage written apparently under Malthusian views in one page of a writer who in the next will possibly propose a tax on celibacy, a prize for early marriages, or some other absurdity not less outrageously hostile to those views. No! let the merit of Mr. Malthus be otherwise what it may, his originality is incontestable—unless an earlier writer can be adduced who has made the same oblique applications of the doctrine, and in general who has shown with what consequences that doctrine is pregnant; separate from which consequences the mere naked doctrine, in and for itself, is but a meagre truth.

[1] *An Enquiry into the Principles of Political Œconomy*, 1767, by Sir James Steuart, Bart.; *Various Prospects of Mankind, Nature,*

## Letter of William Hazlitt respecting the foregoing Article[1]

*To the Editor of the London Magazine.*

Sir,—Will you have the kindness to insert in the Lion's Head[2] the two following passages from a work of mine published some time since? They exhibit rather a striking coincidence with the reasonings of the "Opium-Eater" in your late number on the discoveries of Mr. Malthus; and as I have been a good deal abused for my scepticism on that subject, I do not feel quite disposed that any one else should run away with the credit of it. I do not wish to bring any charge of plagiarism in this case: I only beg to put in my own claim of priority. The first passage I shall trouble you with relates to the geometrical and arithmetical series, and is as follows:—

> Both the principle of the necessary increase of the population beyond the means of subsistence, and the application of that principle as a final obstacle to all Utopian perfectibility schemes, are borrowed (whole) by Mr. Malthus from Wallace's work ("*Various Prospects of Mankind, Nature, and Providence*," 1761). This is not very stoutly denied by his admirers; but, say they, Mr. Malthus was the first to reduce the inequality between the possible increase of food and population to a mathematical certainty, or to the arithmetical and geometrical ratios. In answer to which we say that those ratios are, in a strict and scientific view of the subject, entirely fallacious—a pure fiction. For a grain of corn or of mustard-seed has the same or a greater power of propagating its species than a man, till it has overspread the whole earth, till there is no longer any room for it to grow or to spread farther. A bushel of wheat will sow a whole field: the produce of that field will sow twenty fields, and produce twenty

---

*and Providence*, 1761, by Dr. Robert Wallace of Edinburgh, author also of a *Dissertation on the Numbers of Mankind*, published in 1752. —M.

[1] The following letter appeared in the *London Magazine* for November 1823, *i.e.* in the number immediately following that which had contained De Quincey's article. We reprint it direct from an old copy of the Magazine.—M.

[2] "The Lion's Head" was the running name of the first page or two in every number of the Magazine, containing editorial notices, communications from correspondents, &c. Hazlitt's letter *was* inserted there.—M.

harvests. Till there are no longer fields to sow,—that is, till a country or the earth is exhausted,—the means of subsistence will go on increasing in more than Mr. Malthus's geometrical ratio, will more than double itself in every generation or season, and will more than keep pace with the progress of population: for this is supposed only to double itself, where it is unchecked, every twenty years. Therefore, it is not true as an abstract proposition, that of itself, or in the nature of the growth of the produce of the earth, food can only increase in the snail-pace progress of an arithmetical ratio while population goes on at a swinging geometrical rate: for the food keeps pace, or more than keeps pace, with the population, while there is room to grow it in, and after that room is filled up it does not go on even in that arithmetical ratio,—it does not increase at all, or very little. That is, the ratio (laid down by Mr. Malthus), instead of being always true, is never true at all: neither before the soil is fully cultivated, nor afterwards. Food does not increase in an arithmetical series in China, or even in England; it increases in a geometrical series, or as fast as the population in America. The rates at which one or the other increases naturally, or can be made to increase, have no relation to an arithmetical and geometrical series. They are co-ordinate till the earth or any given portion of it is occupied and cultivated, and after that they are quite disproportionate: or rather, both stop practically at the same instant—the means of subsistence with the limits of the soil, and the population with the limits of the means of subsistence. All that is true of Mr. Malthus's doctrine, then, is this:—that the tendency of population to increase remains after the power of the earth to produce more food is gone: that the one is limited, the other unlimited. This is enough for the morality of the question: his mathematics are altogether spurious. *Political Essays*, p. 403. See also *Reply to Malthus*, Longmans, 1807.

This passage, allowing for the difference of style, accords pretty nearly with the reasoning in the *Notes from the Pocket-Book of an Opium-Eater*. I should really like to know what answer Mr. Malthus has to this objection if he would deign one, or whether he thinks it best to impose upon the public by his silence? So much for his mathematics: now for his logic, which the Opium-Eater has also attacked, and with which I long ago stated my dissatisfaction in manner and form following:—

The most singular thing in this singular performance of our author is that it should have been originally ushered into the world as the most complete and only satisfactory answer to the speculations of Godwin, Condorcet, and others, or to what has been called the modern philosophy. A more complete piece of wrong-headedness, a more strange perversion of reason, could hardly be devised by the wit of man. Whatever we may think of the doctrine of the progressive improvement of the human mind, or of a state of society in which every thing will be subject to the absolute control of reason; however absurd, unnatural, or impracticable we may conceive such a system to be: certainly it cannot without the grossest inconsistency be objected to it that such a system would necessarily be rendered abortive, because, if reason should ever get the mastery over all our actions, we shall then be governed entirely by our physical appetites and passions, and plunged into evils far more insupportable than any we at present endure in consequence of the excessive population which would follow, and the impossibility of providing for its support. This is what I do not understand. It is, in other words, to assert that the doubling the population of a country, for example, after a certain period, will be attended with the most pernicious effects, by want, famine, bloodshed, and a state of general violence and confusion; and yet that at this period those who will be most interested in preventing these consequences and the best acquainted with the circumstances that lead to them, will neither have the understanding to foresee, nor the heart to feel, nor the will to avert, the sure evils to which they expose themselves and others; though this advanced state of population, which does not admit of any addition without danger, is supposed to be the immediate result of a more general diffusion of the comforts and conveniences of life, of more enlarged and liberal views, of a more refined and comprehensive regard to our own permanent interests as well as those of others, of correspondent habits and manners, and of a state of things in which our gross animal appetites will be subjected to the practical control of reason. If Mr. Malthus chooses to say that men will always be governed by the same gross mechanical motives that they are at present, I have no objection to make to it; but it is shifting the question: it is not arguing against the state of society we are considering from the consequences to which it would give rise, but against the possibility of its ever existing. It is very idle to alarm the imagination by deprecating the evils that must follow from the practical adoption of a particular scheme, yet to allow that we have no reason to dread those consequences but because the scheme itself is impracticable."—See *Reply to Malthus*, *passim*, or *Political Essays*, p. 421.

This, Mr. Editor, is the writer whom "our full senate call all-in-all sufficient." There must be a tolerably large *bonus* offered to men's interests and prejudices to make them swallow incongruities such as that here alluded to; and I am glad to find that our ingenious and studious friend the *Opium-Eater* agrees with me on this point too, almost in so many words.

I am, Sir, your obliged friend and servant,

W. HAZLITT.

## De Quincey's Reply to Hazlitt's Letter[1]

*To the Editor of the London Magazine.*

Westmoreland, *November* 4, 1823.

My dear Sir,—This morning I received your parcel, containing amongst other inclosures the two last numbers of your journal. In the first of these is printed a little paper of mine on Mr. Malthus; and in the second I observe a letter from Mr. Hazlitt—alleging two passages from the 403d and 421st pages of his "Political Essays" as substantially anticipating all that I had said. I believe that he *has* anticipated me: in the passage relating to the geometric and arithmetic ratios, it is clear that he has: in the other passage, which objects to Mr. Malthus's use of the term *perfection* that he has represented it under contradictory predicates, it is not equally clear; for I do not find my own meaning so rigorously expressed as to exclude another[2] in-

[1] This appeared as the first article in the "Lion's Head" part of the *London Magazine* for December 1823; from an old copy of which we reprint it here.—M.

[2] What other interpretation? An interpretation which makes Mr. Hazlitt's argument coincide with one frequently urged against Mr. Malthus—viz. "that in fact he himself relies practically upon *moral restraint* as one great check to Population, though denying that any great revolution in the moral nature of man is practicable." But, so long as Mr. Malthus means by a *great revolution* a revolution in the sense which he imputes to Mr. Godwin, to Condorcet, &c., viz. a revolution amounting to absolute perfection, so long there is no logical error in all this: Mr. Malthus may consistently rely upon moral restraint for getting rid, suppose, of 90 cases out of every 100 which at present tend to produce an excessive population, and yet maintain that even this tenth of the former excess would be sufficient, at a certain stage of population, to reproduce families, &c.,—*i.e.* to reproduce as much misery and vice as had been got rid of. Here there is an absolute increase of moral restraint, but still insufficient for the purpose of preventing misery, &c. For, as soon as the maximum of population is attained, even one single birth in excess (*i.e.* which does more than replace the existing numbers)—*a fortiori*, then, 1-10th of the present excess (though implying that the other 9-10ths had been got rid of by moral restraint)—would yet be sufficient to prevent the attainment of a state of perfection. And, if Mr. Malthus had so shaped his argument, whether wrong or right, he would not have

terpretation even now when I know what to look for; and, without knowing what to look for, I should certainly not have found it: on the whole, however, I am disposed to think that Mr. Hazlitt's meaning is the same as my own.

So much for the *matter* of Mr. Hazlitt's communication: as to the *manner*, I am sorry that it is liable to a construction which perhaps was not intended. Mr. Hazlitt says—"I do not wish to bring any charge of plagiarism in this case": words which are better fitted to express his own forbearance than to exonerate me from the dishonour of such an act. But I am unwilling to suppose that Mr. Hazlitt has designedly given this negative form to his words. He says also—"As I have been a good deal abused for my scepticism on that subject, I do not feel quite disposed that any one else should run away with the credit of it." Here

offended in point of *logic*: his logical error lies in supposing a state of perfection already existing and yet as brought to nothing by this excess of births: whereas it is clear that such an excess may operate to prevent, but cannot operate to destroy, a state of perfection; because in such a state no excess could ever arise; for, though an excess may co-exist with a vast increase of moral restraint, it cannot co-exist with entire and perfect moral restraint, and nothing less than *that* is involved in the term "perfection." A perfect state which allows the possibility of the excess here spoken of is already an imperfect state. Now, if Mr. Hazlitt says that this is exactly what he means, I answer that I believe it is; because I can in no other way explain his sixth sentence—from the words "but it is shifting the question" to the end of that sentence. Yet again the seventh sentence (the last) is so expressed as to be unintelligible to me. And all that precedes the sixth sentence, though very intelligible, yet seems the precise objection which I have stated above, and which I think untenable. Nay, it is still less tenable in Mr. Hazlitt's way of putting it than as usually put: for to represent Mr. Malthus as saying that, "if reason should ever get the mastery over all our actions, we shall then be governed *entirely* by our physical appetites" (which are Mr. Hazlitt's words), would be objected to even by an opponent of Mr. Malthus: why "*entirely*"? why more than we are at present? The utmost amount of the objection is this,—that, relying so much upon moral restraint *practically*, Mr. Malthus was bound to have allowed it more weight *speculatively*; but it is unreasonable to say that in his ideal case of perfection Mr. Malthus has allowed no weight at all to moral restraint: even he who supposes an increased force to be inconsistent with Mr. Malthus's theory has no reason to insist upon his meaning a diminished force.

again I cannot allow myself to think that Mr. Hazlitt meant deliberately to bring me before the reader's mind under the odious image of a person who was "running away" with the credit of another. As to "credit," Mr. Hazlitt must permit me to smile when I read that word used in that sense: I can assure him that not any abstract consideration of credit, but the abstract idea of a credi*tor* (often putting on a concrete shape, and sometimes the odious concrete of a dun), has for some time past been the animating principle of my labours. Credit, therefore, except in the sense of twelve months' credit where now, alas! I have only six, is no object of my search: in fact I abhor it: for to be a "noted" man is the next bad thing to being a "protested" man. Seriously, however, I sent you this as the first of four notes which I had written on the logical blunders of Mr. Malthus (the other three being taken not from his Essay on Population, but from works more expressly within the field of Political Economy): not having met with it elsewhere, I supposed it my own and sent it to complete the series: but the very first sentence, which parodies the words of Chancellor Oxenstiern—("Go and see—how *little* logic is required," &c.), sufficiently shows that, so far from arrogating any great merit to myself for this discovery, I thought it next to miraculous that it should have escaped any previous reviewer of Mr. Malthus.—I must doubt, by the way, whether Mr. Hazlitt has been "a good deal abused" for these specific arguments against Mr. Malthus; and my reason for doubting is this:—About ten or twelve years ago, happening to be on a visit to Mr. Southey, I remember to have met with a work of Mr. Hazlitt's on this subject—*not* that which he quotes, but another (*Reply to Malthus*) which he refers to as containing the same opinions (either *totidem verbis* or in substance). In Mr. Southey's library, and in competition with Mr. Southey's conversation, a man may be pardoned for not studying any one book exclusively: consequently, though I read a good deal of Mr. Hazlitt's "Reply," I read it cursorily: but, in all that I *did* read, I remember that the arguments were very different from those which he now alleges; indeed it must be evident that the two logical objections in question are by no means fitted to fill an octavo volume. My inference therefore is—that any "abuse" which Mr. Hazlitt may have met with must have been directed to something else in his Reply: and in fact it has happened to myself on several occasions to hear this book of Mr. Hazlitt's treated as unworthy of his talents; but never on account of the two arguments which he now claims. I would not be supposed, in saying this, to insinuate any doubt that these arguments are really to be found in the Reply; but simply to suggest that they do not come forward prominently or constitute the main argument of that book, and consequently, instead of being opposed, have been overlooked by those who have opposed him as much as they were by myself.

Finally, Mr. Hazlitt calls the coincidence of my objections with his own "striking," and thus (though unintentionally I dare say) throws the reader's attention upon it as a very surprising case. Now, in this there is a misconception which, apart from any personal question between Mr. Hazlitt and myself, is worth a few words on its own account for the sake of placing it in a proper light. I affirm then that, considering its nature, the coincidence is *not* a striking one, if by "striking" be meant surprising: and I affirm also that it would not have been the more striking if, instead of two, it had extended to two hundred similar cases. Supposing that a thousand persons were required severally to propose a riddle, no conditions or limitations being expressed as to the terms of the riddle, it would be surprising if any two in the whole thousand should agree: suppose again that the same thousand persons were required to solve a riddle, it would now be surprising if any two in the whole thousand should differ. Why? Because, in the first case, the act of the mind is an act of synthesis; and there we may readily conceive a thousand different roads for any one mind; but, in the second case, it is an analytic act; and there we cannot conceive of more than one road for a thousand minds. In the case between Mr. Hazlitt and myself there was a double ground of coincidence for any possible number of writers. First, the object was given,—*i.e.* we were not left to an unlimited choice of the propositions we were to attack, but Mr. Malthus had himself, by insisting on two in particular (however erroneously) as the capital propositions of his system, determined our attention to these two as the assailable points: secondly, not only was the object given—*i.e.* not only was it predetermined for us where [1] the error must lie, if there were an error ; but the nature of that error, which happened to be logical, predetermined for us the nature of the solution. Errors which are such *materialiter*, *i.e.* which offend against our *knowing*, may admit of many answers—involving more and less of truth. But errors which are such logically, *i.e.* which offend against the form (or internal law) of our *thinking*, admit of only one answer. Except by failing of any answer at all, Mr. Hazlitt and I could not *but* coincide : as long as we had the same propositions to examine (which were not of our own choice, but pointed out to us *ab extra*), and as long as we understood those propositions in the same sense, no variety was possible except in the expression and manner of our answers ; and to that extent a variety exists. Any other must have arisen from our understanding that proposition in a different sense.

My answer to Mr. Hazlitt therefore is—that in substance I think his claim valid ; and, though it is most true that I was not aware of any claim prior to my own, I now formally forgo any claim on my own part to the credit of whatsoever kind which shall ever arise from the two objections to Mr. Malthus's logic in his Essay on Population. In saying this, however, and acknowledging therefore a coincidence with Mr. Hazlitt in those two arguments, I must be understood to mean a coincidence only in what really belongs to them. Meantime Mr. Hazlitt has used two expressions in his letter to yourself which seem to connect with those propositions other opinions from which I dissent. That I may not therefore be supposed to extend my acquiescence in Mr. Hazlitt's views to these points, I add two short notes upon them : which, however, I have detached from this letter—as forming

[1] "Where the error must lie"—*i.e.* to furnish a sufficient answer *ad hominem* : otherwise it will be seen that I do not regard either of the two propositions as essential to Mr. Malthus's theory ; and therefore to overthrow those propositions is not to answer that theory. But still, if an author will insist on representing something as essential to his theory which is not so, and challenges opposition to it, it is allowable to meet him on his own ground.

no proper part of its business.—Believe me, my dear sir, your faithful humble servant. X. Y. Z.

1. Mr. Hazlitt represents Mr. Malthus's error in regard to the different ratios of progression as a *mathematical* error; but the other error he calls *logical*. This may seem to lead to nothing important: it is, however, not for any purpose of verbal cavil that I object to this distinction, and contend that both errors are logical. For a little consideration will convince the reader that he who thinks the first error mathematical will inevitably miss the true point where the error of Mr. Malthus arises; and the consequence of that will be that he will never understand the Malthusians, nor ever make himself understood by them. Mr. Hazlitt says, "A bushel of wheat will sow a whole field: the produce of that will sow twenty fields." Yes: but this is not the point which Mr. Malthus denies: this he will willingly grant: neither will he deny that such a progression goes on by geometrical ratios. If he did, then it is true that his error would be a mathematical one. But all this he will concede. Where then lies his error? Simply in this—that he assumes (I do not mean in words, but it is manifestly latent in all that he says) that the wheat shall be continually resown on the same area of land: he will not allow of Mr. Hazlitt's "twenty fields": keep to your original field, he will say. In this lies his error: and the nature of that error is—that he insists upon shaping the case for the wheat in a way which makes it no fair analogy to the case which he has shaped for man. That it is unfair is evident: for Mr. Malthus does not mean to contend that his men will go on by geometrical progression, or even by arithmetical, upon the *same* quantity of food: no! he will himself say the positive principle of increase must concur with the same sort of increase in the external (negative) condition, which is food. Upon what sort of logic therefore does he demand that his wheat shall be thrown upon the naked power of its positive principle, *not* concurring with the same sort of increase in the negative condition, which in this case is land? It is true that at length we shall come to the end of the land, because that is limited: but this has nothing to do with the race between

man and his food, so long as the race is possible. The race is imagined for the sake of trying their several powers: and the terms of the match must be made equal. But there is no equality in the terms as they are supposed by Mr. Malthus. The amount therefore is—that the case which Mr. Malthus everywhere supposes and reasons upon is a case of false analogy: that is, it is a logical error. But, setting aside the unfairness of the case, Mr. Malthus is perfectly right in his mathematics. If it were fair to demand that the wheat should be constantly confined to the same space of land, it is undeniable that it could never yield a produce advancing by a geometrical progression, but at the utmost by a very slow arithmetical progression. Consequently, taking the case as Mr. Malthus puts it, he is right in calling it a case of arithmetical progression: and his error is in putting that case as a logical counterpart to his other case.

2. Mr. Hazlitt says—"This, Mr. Editor, is the writer whom 'our full senate call all-in-all sufficient.'"—And why not? I ask. Mr. Hazlitt's inference is—that, because two propositions in Mr. Malthus's Essay are overthrown, and because these two are propositions to which Mr. Malthus ascribes a false importance in relation to his theory, therefore that theory is overthrown. But, if an architect, under some fancied weakness of a bridge which is really strong and self-supported, chooses to apply needless props, I shall not injure the bridge by showing these to be rotten props and knocking them away. What is the real strength and the real use of Mr. Malthus's theory of population cannot well be shown except in treating of Political Economy. But, as to the influence of his logical errors upon that theory, I contend that it is none at all. It is one error to affirm a different law of increase for man and for his food: it is a second error to affirm of a perfect state an attribute of imperfection: but in my judgment it is a third error, as great as either of the others, to suppose that these two errors can at all affect the Malthusian doctrine of Population. Let Mr. Malthus say what he will, the first of those errors is not the true foundation of that doctrine; the second of those errors does not contain its true application.

Two private communications on the paper which refuted Mr. Malthus, both expressed in terms of personal courtesy, for which I am bound to make my best acknowledgments, have reached me through the Editor of the London Magazine. One of them refers me to the number of the New Monthly Magazine for March or April 1821 for an article on Malthus, in which the view taken by myself of his doctrine as an answer to Godwin, "seems to have been anticipated." In reply to this I have only to express my regret that my present situation, which is at a great distance from any town, has not yet allowed me an opportunity for making the reference pointed out.—The other letter disputes the soundness of my arguments, not so much in themselves, as in their application to Mr. Malthus. I know not that I am authorized to speak of the author by name: his arguments I presume that I am at liberty to publish: they are as follows:—"The first objection appears untenable for this reason: Mr. Malthus treats of the abstract tendency to increase in Man, and in the Food of Man, relatively. Whereas you do not discuss the abstract tendency to increase, but only the *measure* of that increase, which is food. To the second objection I thus answer: Mr. Godwin contends, not (I presume) for abstract, essential, perfection, but for perfection relating to, and commensurate with, the capabilities of an earthly nature and habitation. All this Mr. Malthus admits *argumenti gratia*, and at the same time asserts that Mr. Godwin's estimate in his own terms is incompatible with our state. 8 October, 1823."—To these answers my rejoinder is this:—The first argument I am not sure that I perfectly understand; and therefore I will not perplex myself or its author by discussing it. To the second argument I reply thus:—I am aware that whatsoever Mr. Malthus admits from Mr. Godwin he admits only *argumenti gratia*. But, for whatsoever purpose he admits it, he is bound to remember that he *has* admitted it. Now, what is it that he has admitted? A state of perfection. This term, under any explanation of it, betrays him into the following dilemma: Either he means *absolute* perfection, perfection which allows of no degrees; or he means (in the sense which my friendly antagonist has supposed) *relative* perfection, *quoad* our present state—*i.e.* a continual approximation to the ideal of absolute perfection, without ever reaching it. If he means the first, then he is exposed to the objection (which I have already insisted on sufficiently) of bringing the idea of perfection under an inconsistent and destructory predicate. If he means the second, then how has he overthrown the doctrine of human perfectibility as he professes to have done? At this moment, though the earth is far from exhausted (and still less its powers), many countries are, according to Mr. Malthus, suffering all the evils which they could suffer if population had reached its maximum: innumerable children are born which the poverty of their parents (no less fatal to them than the limitation of the earth) causes to be thrown back prematurely into the grave. Now, this is the precise *kind* of evil which Mr. Malthus anticipates for the human species when it shall have reached its numerical maximum. But in *degree* the evil may then be much less—even upon Mr. Malthus's own showing: for he does not fix any limit to the increase of moral restraint, but only denies that it will ever become absolute and universal. When the principle of population, therefore, has done its worst, we may be suffering the same kind of evil—but, in proportion to an indefinitely *in*creasing moral restraint, an indefinitely *de*creasing degree of that evil: *i.e.* we may continually approximate to the ideal of perfection: *i.e.*, if the second sense of perfection be Mr. Godwin's sense, then Mr. Malthus has not overthrown Mr. Godwin.

X. Y. Z.[1]

[1] This was De Quincey's usual signature in the *London Magazine* when he did not sign himself "The English Opium-Eater."—M.

# MALTHUS ON THE MEASURE OF VALUE[1]

To the Reader.—This article was written and printed before the author heard of the lamented death of Mr. Ricardo.[2]

It is remarkable at first sight that Mr. Malthùs, to whom Political Economy is so much indebted in one chapter (viz. the chapter of Population), should in every other chapter have stumbled at every step. On a nearer view, however, the wonder ceases. His failures and his errors have arisen in all cases from the illogical structure of his understanding: his success was in a path which required no logic. What is the brief abstract of his success? It is this: *he took an obvious and familiar truth, which until his time had been a barren truism, and showed that it teemed with consequences.* Out of this position—*That in the ground which limited human food lay all the ground which limited human increase,* united with this other position, *That there is a perpetual nisus in the principle of population to pass that limit*—he unfolded a body of most important corollaries. I have remarked in another article on this subject how entirely these corollaries had escaped all Mr. Malthus's predecessors in the same track.[3]

[1] This paper appeared in the *London Magazine* for December 1823, in addition to De Quincey's Letter in Reply to Hazlitt, but as an independent contribution. It was reprinted in vol. xvi. of Messrs. Black's re-edited issue of De Quincey's Collected Writings, and annexed there to the paper on Malthus.—M.

[2] Ricardo died 11th September 1823.—M.

[3] In a slight article on Mr. Malthus, lately published [*ante*, pp. 11-19. —M.], I omitted to take any notice of the recent controversy between this gentleman, Mr. Godwin, and Mr. Booth; my reason for which was that I have not yet found time to read it. But, if Mr. Lowe has

Perhaps the most striking instance of this which I could have alleged is that of the celebrated French work "*L'Ami des Hommes, ou Traité de la Population*" (written about the middle of last century); which sets out deliberately from this principle, expressed almost in the very words of Mr. Malthus, *Que la mésure de la Subsistance est celle de la Population;* beats the bushes in every direction about it; and yet (with the exception of one corollary on the supposed depopulating tendency of war and famine) deduces from it none but erroneous and Anti-Malthusian doctrines. That from a truth apparently so barren any corollaries were deducible was reserved for Mr. Malthus to show. *As* corollaries, it may be supposed that they imply a logical act of the understanding. In some small degree, no doubt; but no more than necessarily accompanies every exercise of reason. Though inferences, they are not remote inferences, but immediate and proximate; and not dependent upon each other, but collateral. Not logic, but a judicious choice of his ground, placed Mr. Malthus at once in a station from which he commanded the whole truth at a glance, with a lucky dispensation from all necessity of continuous logical processes.

But such a dispensation is a privilege indulged to few other parts of Political Economy, and least of all to that which is the foundation of all Political Economy: viz. the Doctrine of Value. Having therefore repeatedly chosen to tamper with this difficult subject, Mr. Malthus has just

rightly represented this principle of Mr. Booth's argument in his late work on the Statistics of England, it is a most erroneous one: for Mr. Booth is there described as alleging against Mr. Malthus that, in his view of the tendencies of the principle of population, he has relied too much on the case of the United States—which Mr. Booth will have to be an extreme case, and not according to the general rule. But of what consequence is this to Mr. Malthus? And how is he interested in relying on the case of America rather than that of the oldest European country? Because he assumes a perpetual nisus in the principle of human increase to pass a certain limit, he does not therefore hold that this limit ever *is* passed either in the new countries or in old (or only for a moment, and inevitably to be thrown back within it). Let this limit be placed where it may, it can no more be passed in America than in Europe; and America is not at all more favourable to Mr. Malthus's theory than Europe. Births, it must be remembered, are more in excess in Europe than in America, though they do not make so much positive addition to the population.

made so many exposures of his intellectual infirmities,—which, but for this volunteer display, we might never have known. Of all the men of talents whose writings I have read up to this hour, Mr. Malthus has the most perplexed understanding. He is not only confused himself, but is the cause that confusion is in other men. Logical perplexity is shockingly contagious; and he who takes Mr. Malthus for his guide through any tangled question ought to be able to box the compass very well; or before he has read ten pages he will find himself (as the Westmoreland guides express it) "maffled,"—and disposed to sit down and fall a-crying with his guide at the sad bewilderment into which they have both strayed. It tends much to heighten the sense of Mr. Malthus's helplessness in this particular point that of late years he has given himself the air too much of teasing Mr. Ricardo, one of the "ugliest customers" in point of logic that ever entered the ring. Mr. Ricardo is a most "dangerous" man; and Mr. Malthus would do well not to meddle with so "vicious" a subject, whose arm (like Neate's) gives a blow like the kick of a horse. He has hitherto contented himself very goodnaturedly with gently laying Mr. Malthus on his back; but, if he should once turn round with a serious determination to "take the conceit" out of him, Mr. Malthus would assuredly be "put into chancery," and suffer a "punishment" that must distress his friends. Amongst those whom Mr. Malthus has perplexed by his logic, I am not one. In matter of logic I hold myself impeccable; and, to say nothing of my sober days, I defy the devil and all the powers of darkness to get any advantage over me even on those days when I am drunk, in relation to *Barbara*, *Celarent*, *Darii*, or *Ferio*. "Avoid, old Satanas!" I exclaim, if any man attempts to fling dust in my eyes by false syllogism, or any mode of dialectic sophism. And, in relation to this particular subject of Value, I flatter myself that in a paper expressly applied to the exposure of Mr. Malthus's blunders in his Political Economy,[1] I have made it impossible for Mr. Malthus, even though he should take to his assistance seven worse logicians than himself, to put down my light with their darkness. Meantime, as a labour of

[1] *Ante*, pp. 11-19, as before.—M.

shorter compass, I will call the reader's attention to the following blunder, in a later work of Mr. Malthus's—viz. a pamphlet of 80 pages, entitled, "The Measure of Value Stated and Applied" (published in the spring of the present year).[1] The question proposed in this work is the same as that already discussed in his Political Economy: viz. What is the measure of value? But the answer to it is different. In the Political Economy the measure of value was determined to be a mean between corn and labour; in this pamphlet Mr. Malthus retracts that opinion, and (finally, let us hope) settles it to his own satisfaction that the true measure is labour,—not the quantity of labour, observe, which will produce X, but the quantity which X will command. Upon these two answers, and the delusions which lie at their root, I shall here forbear to comment, because I am now chasing Mr. Malthus's *logical* blunders; and these delusions are not so much logical as economic. What I now wish the reader to attend to is the blunder involved in the question itself, because that blunder is not economic, but logical. The question is What is the measure of value? I say then that the phrase "measure of value" is an equivocal phrase, and, in Mr. Malthus's use of it, means indifferently that which determines value in relation to the *principium essendi* and that which determines value in relation to the *principium cognoscendi.* Here, perhaps, the reader will exclaim "Avoid, Satanas!" to me, falsely supposing that I have some design upon his eyes, and wish to blind them with learned dust. But, if he thinks *that*, he is in the wrong box. I must and will express scholastic notions by scholastic phrases; but, having once done this, I am then ready to descend into the arena with no other weapons than plain English can furnish. Let us therefore translate *measure of value* into *that which determines value*; and, in this shape, we shall detect the ambiguity of which I complain. For I say that the word *determines* may be taken subjectively for what determines X in relation to our knowledge, or objectively for what determines X in relation to itself. Thus, if I were to ask "What determined the length of the race-course?" and the answer were "The convenience of the

[1] 1823.

spectators, who could not have seen the horses at a greater distance," or "The choice of the subscribers,"—then it is plain that by the word "determined" I was understood to mean "determined objectively," *i.e.* in relation to the existence of the object; in other words, what *caused* the racecourse to be this length rather than another length. But, if the answer were "An actual admeasurement," it would then be plain that by the word "determined" I had been understood to mean "determined subjectively," *i.e.* in relation to our knowledge, — what ascertained it? Now, in the objective sense of the phrase "determiner of value," the measure of value will mean *the ground of value*: in the subjective sense, it will mean *the criterion of value.* Mr. Malthus will allege that he is at liberty to use it in which sense he pleases. Grant that he is, but not therefore in both. Has he then used it in both? He will perhaps deny that he has, and will contend that he has used it in the latter sense as equivalent to the *ascertainer* or *criterion of value.* I answer —No: for, omitting a more particular examination of his use in this place, I say that his use of any word is peremptorily and in defiance of his private explanation to be extorted from the use of the corresponding term in him whom he is opposing. Now, he is opposing Mr. Ricardo: his *labour which X commands* is opposed to Mr. Ricardo's *quantity of labour which will produce X.* Call the first A, the last B. Now, in making B the determiner of value, Mr. Ricardo means that B is the ground of value: *i.e.* that B is the answer to the question What makes this hat of more value than this pair of shoes? But, if Mr. Malthus means by A the same thing, then by his own confession he has used the term *measure of value* in two senses: on the other hand, if he does not mean the same thing, but simply the *criterion* of value, then he has not used the word in any sense which opposes him to Mr. Ricardo. And yet he advances the whole on that footing. On either ground, therefore, he is guilty of a logical error; which implies that, so far from answering his own question, he did not know what his own question was.

# DIALOGUES OF THREE TEMPLARS ON POLITICAL ECONOMY:

## CHIEFLY IN RELATION TO THE PRINCIPLES OF MR. RICARDO [1]

# INTRODUCTION

## THE SERVICES OF MR. RICARDO TO THE SCIENCE OF POLITICAL ECONOMY [2]

I DO not remember that any public event of our own times has touched me so nearly, or so much with the feelings belonging to a private affliction, as the death of Mr. Ricardo.[3] To me in some sense it *was* a private affliction—and no

[1] Appeared originally in the three successive numbers of the *London Magazine* for March, April, and May, 1824. In De Quincey's revised reprint in 1854 for vol. iv of the Collective Edition of his writings, he omitted the first or March instalment of the paper, in which the dialogue form had not been yet assumed, and confined himself to the April and May portions, where the dialogue form was in full play. The omitted portion, however, having a kind of necessary connexion with the rest, and possessing also some independent autobiographic interest, is here resuscitated from the old columns of the magazine, and placed as the "Introduction" to the Dialogues,—which, in fact, it properly was. By this means one of the most elaborate of De Quincey's early magazine performances is presented for the first time in complete form, and its history is made more intelligible.—M.

[2] The original magazine title of this instalment of the general paper was "*The Services of Mr. Ricardo to the Science of Political Economy briefly and plainly stated.*" It was evidently De Quincey's intention that this should be the running title of the series of articles which should together constitute the "brief and plain statement" so promised. How the intention came to be modified will appear presently: meanwhile the title is modified to suit.—M.

[3] The death of Ricardo was on the 11th of September 1823, not quite six months before the appearance of the present paper in the *London Magazine*. See *ante*, p. 32, and footnote.—M.

doubt to all others who knew and honoured his extraordinary talents. For great intellectual merit, wherever it has been steadily contemplated, cannot but conciliate some personal regard: and for my own part I acknowledge that, abstracting altogether from the use to which a man of splendid endowments may apply them, or even supposing the case that he should deliberately apply them to a bad one, I could no more on that account withhold my good wishes and affection from his person, than, under any consideration of their terrific attributes, I could forbear to admire the power and the beauty of the serpent or the panther. Simply on its own account, and without further question, a great intellect challenges, as of right, not merely an interest of admiration in common with all other exhibitions of power and magnificence, but also an interest of human love, and (where that is necessary) a spirit of tenderness to its aberrations.

Mr. Ricardo, however, stood in no need of a partial or indulgent privilege; his privilege of intellect had a comprehensive sanction from all the purposes to which he applied it in the course of his public life: in or out of parliament, as a senator or as an author, he was known and honoured as a public benefactor. Though connected myself by private friendship with persons of the political party hostile to his, I heard amongst them all but one language of respect for his public conduct. Those who stood neutral to all parties remarked that Mr. Ricardo's voice—though heard too seldom for the wishes of the enlightened part of the nation—was never raised with emphasis upon any question lying out of the province in which he reigned as the paramount authority, except upon such as seemed to affect some great interest of liberty or religious toleration. And, wherever a discussion arose which transcended the level of temporary and local politics (as that, for example, upon corporal punishments), the weight of authority—which mere blank ability had obtained for him in the House of Commons—was sure to be thrown into that view of the case which upheld the dignity of human nature.

Participating most cordially in these feelings of reverence for Mr. Ricardo's political character, I had besides a sorrow not unmixed with self-reproach arising out of some considerations more immediately relating to myself. In August and September 1821 I wrote *The Confessions of an English Opium-Eater*: and in the course of this little work I took occasion to express my obligations, as a student of Political Economy, to Mr. Ricardo's "Principles" of that science.[1] For this, as for some other passages, I was justly[2] attacked by an able

[1] For the passage in the *Confessions of an Opium-Eater* giving an account of De Quincey's first acquaintance in 1818 with Ricardo's *Principles of Political Economy* (published in 1817), and of the stirring effects of that book upon him in his then prostrated condition under opium excess, see *ante*, Vol. III, pp. 431-433. The passage as there given, though it belongs to De Quincey's greatly enlarged edition of his *Confessions* in 1856, is substantially, and all but verbally, the same as the corresponding passage in the original or 1821 form of the *Confessions*. One little difference is that it substitutes 1818 for 1819 as the date of De Quincey's first acquaintance with Ricardo's book. See, however, Editor's Preface to the present volume.—M.

[2] Not so, however, let me say in passing, for three supposed instances of affected doubt; in all of which my doubts were, and are at this moment, very sincere and unaffected; and, in one of them at least, I am assured by those of whom I have since inquired that my reviewer is undoubtedly mistaken. As another point which, if left unnoticed, might affect something more important to myself than the credit of my taste or judgment,—let me inform my reviewer that, when he traces an incident which I have recorded most faithfully about a Malay to a tale of Mr. Hogg's, he makes me indebted to a book which I never saw. In saying this I mean no disrespect to Mr. Hogg; on the contrary, I am sorry that I have never seen it: for I have a great admiration of Mr. Hogg's genius, and have had the honour of his personal acquaintance for the last ten years. [The *New Edinburgh Review* was started in Edinburgh in July 1821, in rivalry to its great namesake, and continued in existence till April 1823. Among the contributors to the numbers of it actually published was Carlyle, then between twenty-six and twenty-eight years of age, resident mainly in Edinburgh, and making his first experiments in literature. The article to which De Quincey refers was apparently a notice of his *Confessions* which appeared in one of the early numbers. In that notice it was suggested, as De Quincey notes, that the hint for the famous Malay story in the *Confessions* (see *ante*, Vol. III. pp. 402-406) had been furnished by one of the Ettrick Shepherd's tales. De Quincey's statement, while repudiating that original for the story, that he had been personally acquainted with Hogg for ten years before the date at which he was then writing,—*i.e.* since 1814,—is not uninteresting. It was in 1814 that De Quincey made his first visit to Edinburgh,—taken thither by his Lakist friend Wilson, and in fact as Wilson's guest. Among the notabilities of Edinburgh society whom he then came to know,—not a little impressed by

and liberal critic in the New Edinburgh Review—as for so many absurd irrelevancies: in that situation no doubt they were so; and of this, in spite of the haste in which I had written the greater part of the book, I was fully aware. However, as they said no more than was true, I was glad to take that or any occasion which I could invent for offering my public testimony of gratitude to Mr. Ricardo. The truth is—I thought that something might occur to intercept any more appropriate mode of conveying my homage to Mr. Ricardo's ear, which should else more naturally have been expressed in a direct work on Political Economy. This fear was at length realized—not in the way I had apprehended, viz. by my own death—but by Mr. Ricardo's. And now therefore I felt happy that, at whatever price of good taste, I had in some imperfect way made known my sense of his high pretensions—although unfortunately I had given him no means of judging whether my applause were of any value. For during the interval between September 1821 and Mr. Ricardo's death in September 1823 I had found no leisure for completing my work on Political Economy: on that account I had forborne to use the means of introduction to Mr. Ricardo which I commanded through my private connexions or simply as a man of letters: and in some measure therefore I owed it to my own neglect that I had for ever lost the opportunity of benefiting by Mr. Ricardo's conversation or bringing under his review such new speculations of mine in Political Economy as in any point modified his own doctrines—whether as corrections of supposed oversights, as derivations of the same truth from a higher principle, as further illustrations or proofs of anything which he might have insufficiently developed, or simply in the way of supplement to his known and voluntary omissions. All this I should have done with the utmost fearlessness of giving offence, and not for a moment believing that Mr. Ricardo would have regarded anything in the light of an undue liberty which in the remotest degree might seem to affect the interests of a science so eminently indebted to himself. In

some of them, as we chance to know independently, and greatly impressing them in return,—was, it seems, Hogg. De Quincey was then in his thirtieth year, Hogg in his forty-third.—M.]

reality candour may be presumed in a man of first-rate understanding—not merely as a moral quality, but almost as a part of his intellectual constitution *per se*; a spacious and commanding intellect being magnanimous in a manner *suo jure*, even though it should have the misfortune to be allied with a perverse or irritable temper. On this consideration I would gladly have submitted to the review of Mr. Ricardo, as indisputably the first of critics in this department, rather than to any other person, my own review of himself. That I have forfeited the opportunity of doing this is a source of some self-reproach to myself. I regret also that I have forfeited the opportunity of perhaps giving pleasure to Mr. Ricardo by liberating him from a few misrepresentations, and placing his vindication upon a firmer basis even than that which he has chosen. In one respect I enjoy an advantage for such a service, and in general for the polemic part of Political Economy, which Mr. Ricardo did not. The course of my studies has led me to cultivate the scholastic logic. Mr. Ricardo has obviously neglected it. Confiding in his own conscious strength, and no doubt participating in the common error of modern times as to the value of artificial logic, he has taken for granted that the Aristotelian forms and the exquisite science of distinctions matured by the subtilty of the schoolmen can achieve nothing in substance which is beyond the power of mere sound good sense and robust faculties of reasoning; or at most can only attain the same end with a little more speed and adroitness. But this is a great error: and it was an ill day for the human understanding when Lord Bacon gave his countenance to a notion which his own exclusive study of one department in philosophy could alone have suggested. Distinctions previously examined, probed, and accurately bounded, together with a terminology previously established, are the crutches on which all minds—the weakest and the strongest—must alike depend in many cases of perplexity: from pure neglect of such aids, which are to the unassisted understanding what weapons are to the unarmed human strength or tools and machinery to the naked hand of art, do many branches of knowledge at this day languish amongst those which are independent of experiment.

As the best consolation to myself for the lost opportunities with which I have here reproached myself,—and as the best means of doing honour to the memory of Mr. Ricardo,—I shall now endeavour to spread the knowledge of what he has performed in Political Economy. To do this in the plainest and most effectual manner, I shall abstain from introducing any opinions peculiar to myself, excepting only when they may be necessary for the defence of Mr. Ricardo against objections which have obtained currency from the celebrity of their authors, or, in the few cases where they may be called for, by the errors (as I suppose them to be) even of Mr. Ricardo. In using this language, I do not fear to be taxed with arrogance: we of this day stand upon the shoulders of our predecessors; and that I am able to detect any errors in Mr. Ricardo I owe, in most instances, to Mr. Ricardo himself. X. Y. Z.[1]

## ADVERTISEMENT TO THE DIALOGUES [2]

I have resolved to fling my analysis of Mr. Ricardo's system into the form of Dialogues. A few words will suffice to

[1] This was De Quincey's usual signature to his papers in the *London Magazine* when he did not appear expressly as "The Opium Eater": for which name, indeed, it was the understood equivalent in the magazine circle. There is special reason, as will be seen immediately, for retaining it in the present case.—M.

[2] It is at this point that the whole paper *begins* in De Quincey's own reprint in 1854 in vol. iv of his Collective Writings. As has been explained, *ante*, p. 37, footnote, he thought fit there to reproduce only the matter of those two of his articles on the subject which appeared in the numbers of the *London Magazine* for the months of April and May 1824, omitting the article which had appeared in the preceding March number, and which we have resuscitated in the last few pages as forming properly the "Introduction." The reason for the resuscitation will now be more apparent. In the article of March 1824, entitled "The Services of Mr. Ricardo to the Science of Political Economy briefly and plainly stated," De Quincey, while referring to the recent death of Ricardo, and expressing generally his sense of the almost unique importance of Ricardo's contributions to the science of Political Economy, and in particular his own grateful recollection of the effects upon himself of Ricardo's teachings in that science, had intimated his intention of trying to explain to the public, in a "brief

determine the principles of criticism which can fairly be applied to such a form of composition on such a subject. It cannot reasonably be expected that dialogues on Political Economy should pretend to the appropriate beauty of dialogues *as* dialogues, by throwing any dramatic interest into the parts sustained by the different speakers, or any characteristic distinctions into their style. Elegance of this sort, if my time had allowed of it, or I had been otherwise capable of producing it, would have been here misplaced. Not that I would say even of Political Economy, in the words commonly applied to such subjects, that "*Ornari res ipsa negat, contenta doceri*": for all things have their peculiar beauty and sources of ornament—determined by their ultimate ends, and by the process of the mind in pursuing them. Here, as in the processes of nature and in mathematical demonstrations, the appropriate elegance is derived from the simplicity of the means employed, as expressed in the "Lex Parcimoniæ" ("*Frustra fit per plura quod fieri fas erat per pauciora*"), and other maxims of that sort. This simplicity, however, must be looked for in the order and relation of the

and plain" manner, the substance of the special Ricardian doctrines. As he had not done this in the article then published, it is evident that he meant to do it in subsequent articles in the magazine. Accordingly, in the April number he resumed the subject. In the interval, however, he had made up his mind on a point which he had not settled with himself when he wrote the March article,—viz. the *form* of the promised exposition. He had concluded that the *dialogue* form would best answer his purpose, and had therefore schemed out an imaginary conversation on Ricardo and his merits, in which the speakers should be three Templars, or law students,—two of them sceptics or dubious inquirers, but one (De Quincey himself) a thorough and convinced Ricardian. It was to explain this exchange of the direct style of the preceding article for the dialogue style adopted in the remaining articles that De Quincey prefixed the present "Advertisement" to his article in the *London Magazine* for April 1824. When he reprinted it in 1854 he entitled it expressly "Original Advertisement in April 1824." Such particularity is now unnecessary. The resuscitation of the omitted article of March 1824 as the proper "Introduction" to the entire paper there begun, but continued in changed form in the two subsequent articles, re-establishes for present readers the literary coherence of the three articles as it was obvious to readers of the *London Magazine* in 1824, and makes "Advertisement to the Dialogues" a sufficient title for the little prefatory paragraph introduced at this point.—M.

thoughts, and in the steps through which they are trained to lead into each other, rather than in any anxious conciseness as to words; which, on the contrary, I have rather sought to avoid in the earlier Dialogues, in order that I might keep those distinctions longer before the reader from which all the rest were to be derived. For he who has fully mastered the Doctrine of Value is already a good political economist. Now, if any man should object that in the following Dialogues I have uniformly given the victory to myself, he will make a pleasant logical blunder: for the true logic of the case is this, Not that it is myself to whom I give the victory, but that he to whom I give the victory (let me call him by what name I will) is of necessity myself; since I cannot be supposed to have put triumphant arguments into any speaker's mouth unless they had previously convinced my own understanding. Finally, let me entreat the reader not to be impatient under the disproportionate length (as he may fancy it) of the opening discussions on Value. Even for its own sake, the subject is a matter of curious speculation; but in relation to Political Economy it is all in all; for most of the errors (and, what is much worse than errors, most of the perplexities) prevailing in this science take their rise from this source. Mr. Ricardo is the first writer who has thrown light on the subject; and even he, in the last edition of his book, still found it a "difficult" one (see the Advertisement to the Third Edition). What a Ricardo has found difficult cannot be adequately discussed in few words; but, if the reader will once thoroughly master this part of the science, all the rest will cost him hardly any effort at all.

## PRELIMINARY DIALOGUE[1]

(SPEAKERS THROUGHOUT THE DIALOGUES ARE PHÆDRUS, PHILEBUS, AND X. Y. Z.)

*Phædrus.* This, Philebus, is my friend X. Y. Z., whom I have long wished to introduce to you.[2] He has some busi-

[1] De Quincey's phrase is "Introductory Dialogue"; but, as we have already had an "Introduction," the word "Preliminary" is here preferable.—M.

[2] See *ante*, p. 42, footnote.

ness which calls him into this quarter of the town for the next fortnight; and during that time he has promised to dine with me; and we are to discuss together the modern doctrines of Political Economy; most of which he tells me are due to Mr. Ricardo. Or rather I should say that I am to become his pupil; for I pretend to no regular knowledge of Political Economy, having picked up what little I possess in a desultory way amongst the writers of the old school; and, out of that little, X. obligingly tells me that three-fourths are rotten. I am glad, therefore, that you are in town at this time, and can come and help me to contradict him. Meantime X. has some right to play the tutor amongst us; for he has been a regular student of the science. Another of his merits is—that he is a Templar as well as ourselves, and a good deal senior to either of us.[1]

*Philebus.* And for which of his merits is it that you would have me contradict him?

*Phœd.* Oh, no matter for his merits, which doubtless are past all computation; but generally as a point of hospitality. For I am of the same opinion as M——, a very able friend of mine in Liverpool, who looks upon it as criminal to concede anything a man says in the process of a disputation: the nefarious habit of assenting (as he justly says) being the pest of conversation, by causing it to stagnate. On this account he often calls aside the talking men of the party before dinner, and conjures them with a pathetic earnestness not to agree with him in anything he may advance during the evening; and at his own table, when it has happened that strangers were present who indulged too much in the habit of politely assenting to anything which seemed to demand no particular opposition, I have seen him suddenly pause with the air of the worst-used man in the world, and exclaim, "Good heavens! is there to be no end to this? Am I *never* to be contradicted? I suppose matters will soon come to that pass that my nearest relations will be perfidiously agreeing with me; the very wife of my bosom will refuse to contradict me; and I shall not have a friend left

[1] De Quincey did actually, after leaving Oxford, enter himself as a student of law in the Middle Temple; and he "kept terms" there for some time in 1808-9. See *ante*, Vol. III, p. 41.—M.

on whom I can depend for the consolations of opposition."

*Phil.* Well, Phædrus, if X. Y. Z. is so much devoted as you represent to the doctrines of Mr. Ricardo, I shall perhaps find myself obliged to indulge your wishes in this point more than my own taste in conversation would lead me to desire.

*X.* And what, may I ask, is the particular ground of your opposition to Mr. Ricardo?

*Phæd.* I suppose that, like the man who gave his vote against Aristides because it wearied him to hear any man surnamed *the just*, Philebus is annoyed by finding that so many people look up to Mr. Ricardo as an oracle.

*Phil.* No: for the very opposite reason; it is because I hear him generally complained of as obscure and as ambitiously paradoxical; two faults which I cannot tolerate: and the extracts from his writings which I have seen satisfy me that this judgment is a reasonable one.

*Phæd.* In addition to which, Philebus, I now recollect something which perhaps weighs with you still more, though you have chosen to suppress it; and *that* is that you are a disciple of Mr. Malthus, every part of whose writings since the year 1816 (I am assured) has had one origin—jealousy of Mr. Ricardo, quem si non aliqua nocuisset, mortuus esset."

*X.* No, no, Phædrus: we must not go so far as *that*; though undoubtedly it is true that Mr. Malthus has often conducted his opposition in a most vexatious and disingenuous manner.

*Phil.* How so? In what instance? In what instance?

*X.* In this, for one,—Mr. Malthus in his "Political Economy" (1820) repeatedly charged Mr. Ricardo with having confounded the two notions of "cost" and "value." I smile by the way when I repeat such a charge, as if it were the office of a Ricardo to confound, or of a Malthus to distinguish: but

"Non usque adeo permiscuit imis
Longus summa dies, ut non—si voce Metelli
Serventur leges—malint a Cæsare tolli."[1]

[1] For the sake of the unclassical reader, I add a prose translation:—"Not to such an extent has the lapse of time confounded things

*Phil.* "Imis!" Why, I hope, if Mr. Ricardo may do for the Cæsar of the case, Mr. Malthus is not therefore to be thought the Metellus. "Imis" indeed!

*X.* As to *this*, he is. His general merits of good sense and ingenuity we all acknowledge; but for the office of a distinguisher, or any other which demands logic in the first place, it is impossible to conceive any person below him. To go on, however, with my instance:—This objection of Mr. Malthus's about "cost" and "value" was founded purely on a very great blunder of his own—*so* great that (as I shall show in its proper place) even Mr. Ricardo did not see the whole extent of his misconception. Thus much, however, was plain,—that the meaning of Mr. Malthus was that the new doctrine of value allowed for wages, but did *not* allow for profits, and thus, according to the Malthusian terminology, expressed the cost but not the value of a thing. What was Mr. Ricardo's answer? In the third edition of his book (p. 46), he told Mr. Malthus that, if the word "cost" were understood in any sense which *excluded* profits, then he did not assert the thing attributed to him; on the other hand, if it were understood in a sense which *included* profits, then of course he did assert it; but then in that sense Mr. Malthus himself did not deny it. This plain answer was published in 1821. Will it be believed that two years after (viz. in the spring of 1823) Mr. Malthus published a pamphlet in which he repeats the same objection over and over again, without a hint that it had ever met with a conclusive explanation which it was impossible to misunderstand? Neither must it be alleged that Mr. Malthus might not have seen this third edition; for it is the very edition which he constantly quotes in that pamphlet.

*Phæd.* What say you to this, my dear Philebus? You seem to be in perplexity.

*X.* But an instance of far greater disingenuousness is this:—Mr. Ricardo, after laying down the general law of value, goes on to state three cases in which that law will be modified; and the extraordinary sagacity with which he

highest with things lowest as that—if the laws can be saved only by the voice of a Metellus—they would not rather choose to be abolished by a Cæsar."

has detected and stated these modifications, and the startling consequences to which they lead, have combined to make this one of the most remarkable chapters in his books. Now, it is a fact, gentlemen, that these very restrictions of his own law—so openly stated as restrictions by Mr. Ricardo—are brought forward by Mr. Malthus as so many objections of his own to upset that law. The logic, as usual, is worthy of notice: for it is as if, in a question about the force of any projectile, a man should urge the resistance of the air, not as a limitation of that force, but as a capital objection to it. What I here insist on, however, is its extreme disingenuousness. But this is a subject which it is unpleasant to pursue: and the course of our subject will of itself bring us but too often across the blunders and mis-statements of Mr. Malthus. To recur therefore to what you objected about Mr. Ricardo—that he was said to be paradoxical and obscure—I presume that you use the word "paradoxical" in the common and improper sense, as denoting what has a specious air of truth and subtlety, but is in fact false; whereas I need not tell *you* that a paradox is the very opposite of this—meaning in effect what has a specious air of falsehood, though possibly very true: for a paradox, you know, is simply that which contradicts the popular opinion—which in too many cases is the false opinion, and in none more inevitably than in cases as remote from the popular understanding as all questions of severe science. However, use the word in what sense you please, Mr. Ricardo is no ways interested in the charge. Are my doctrines true, are they demonstrable? is the question for him; if not, let them be overthrown; if *that* is beyond any man's power, what matters it to him that the slumbering intellect of the multitude regards them as strange? As to obscurity, in general it is of two kinds—one arising out of the writer's own perplexity of thought; which is a vicious obscurity: and in this sense the opponents of Mr. Ricardo are the obscurest of all economists. Another kind——

*Phæd.* Ay, now let us hear what is a virtuous obscurity.

*X.* I do not say, Phædrus, that in any case it can be meritorious to be obscure: but I say that in many cases it is very natural to be so, and pardonable in profound thinkers, and in some cases inevitable. For the other kind of obscurity which I was going to notice is that which I would denominate elliptical obscurity; arising, I mean, out of the frequent ellipsis or suppression of some of the links in a long chain of thought. These are often involuntarily suppressed by profound thinkers, from the disgust which they naturally feel at overlaying a subject with superfluous explanations. So far from seeing too dimly, as in the case of perplexed obscurity, their defect is the very reverse; they see too clearly, and fancy that others see as clearly as themselves. Such, without any tincture of confusion, was the obscurity of Kant (though in him there was also a singular defect of the art of communicating knowledge, as he was himself aware): such was the obscurity of Leibnitz (who otherwise was remarkable for his felicity in explaining himself): such, if any, is the obscurity of Ricardo; though for my own part I must acknowledge that I could never find any: to me he seems a model of perspicuity. But I believe that the very ground of his perspicuity to me is the ground of his apparent obscurity to some others, and *that* is his inexorable consistency in the use of words: and this is one of the cases which I alluded to in speaking of an "inevitable obscurity": for, wherever men have been accustomed to use a word in two senses, and have yet supposed themselves to use it but in one, a writer who corrects this lax usage, and forces them to maintain the unity of the meaning, will always appear obscure; because he will oblige them to deny or to affirm consequences from which they were hitherto accustomed to escape under a constant though unconscious equivocation between the two senses. Thus, for example, Mr. Ricardo sternly insists on the *true* sense of the word Value, and (what is still more unusual to most men) insists on using it but in *one* sense: and hence arise consequences which naturally appear at once obscure and paradoxical to M. Say, to Mr. Malthus, to the author of an Essay on Value,[1] and to all other lax thinkers, who easily bend their understandings to the infirmity of the popular usage. Hence it is not surprising to find Mr. Malthus complaining ("Polit.

[1] I forget the exact title; but it was printed for Hunter, St. Paul's Churchyard.

Econ.," p. 214) of "the *unusual* application of common terms" as having made Mr. Ricardo's work "difficult to be understood by many people": though, in fact, there is nothing at all unusual in his application of any term whatever, but only in the steadiness with which he keeps to the same application of it.

*Phil.* These distinctions of yours on the subject of obscurity I am disposed to think reasonable: and, unless the contrary should appear in the course of our conversations, I will concede them to be applicable to the case of Mr. Ricardo: his obscurity may be venial, or it may be inevitable, or even none at all (if you will have it so). But I cannot allow of the cases of Kant and Leibnitz as at all relevant to that before us. For the obscurity complained of in metaphysics, etc., is inherent in the very *objects* contemplated, and is independent of the particular mind contemplating, and exists in defiance of the utmost talents for diffusing light: whereas the objects about which Political Economy is concerned are acknowledged by all persons to be clear and simple enough, so that any obscurity which hangs over them must arise from imperfections in the art of arranging and conveying ideas on the part of him who undertakes to teach it.

*X.* This I admit: any obscurity which clouds Political Economy, unless where it arises from want of sufficient facts, must be subjective; whereas the main obscurity which besets metaphysics is objective, and such an obscurity is in the fullest sense inevitable. But this I did not overlook; for an objective obscurity it is in the power of any writer to aggravate by his own perplexities; and I alleged the cases of Kant and Leibnitz no further than as they were said to have done so; contending that, if Mr. Ricardo were at all liable to the same charge, he was entitled to the same apology—viz. that he is never obscure from any confusion of thought, but, on the contrary, from too keen a perception of the truth which may have seduced him at times into too elliptic a development of his opinions, and made him impatient of the tardy and continuous steps which are best adapted to the purposes of the teacher. For the fact is that the *labourers of the Mine* (as I am accustomed to call them), or those who dig up the metal of truth, are seldom fitted to be also *labourers of the Mint*—*i.e.* to work up the metal for current use. Besides which, it must not be forgotten that Mr. Ricardo did not propose to deliver an entire system of Political Economy, but only an investigation of such doctrines as had happened to be imperfectly or erroneously stated. On this account much of his work is polemic, and presumes therefore in the reader an acquaintance with the writers whom he is opposing. Indeed, in every chapter there is an under-reference, not to this or that author only, but to the whole current of modern opinions on the subject, which demands a learned reader who is already master of what is generally received for truth in Political·Economy.

*Phil.* Upon this statement it appears at any rate that Mr. Ricardo's must be a most improper book as an elementary one. But, after all, you will admit that even amongst Mr. Ricardo's friends there is a prevailing opinion that he is too subtle (or, as it is usually expressed, too theoretic) a writer to be safely relied on for the practical uses of legislation.

*X.* Yes. And, indeed, we are all so deeply indebted to English wisdom on matters where theories really *are* dangerous that we ought not to wonder or to complain if the jealousy of all which goes under that name be sometimes extended to cases in which it is idle to suppose any opposition possible between the *true* theory and the practice. However, on the whole question which has been moved in regard to Mr. Ricardo's obscurity or tendency to paradox or to over-refinement and false subtlety, I am satisfied if I have won you to any provisional suspension of your prejudices, and will now press it no further—willingly leaving the matter to be settled by the result of our discussions.

*Phæd.* Do so, X.; and especially because my watch informs me that dinner—an event too awfully practical to allow of any violation from mere sublunary disputes—will be announced in six minutes; within which space of time I will trouble you to produce the utmost possible amount of truth with the least possible proportion of obscurity, whether "subjective" or "objective," that may be convenient.

*X.* As the time which you allow us is so short, I think

that I cannot better employ it than in reading a short paper which I have drawn up on the most general distribution of Mr. Ricardo's book; because this may serve to guide us in the course of our future discussions:—

"Mr. Ricardo's Principles of Political Economy consisted in the second Edition of 31 chapters; to which, in the third edition, was added another, making 32. These 32 chapters fall into the following classification:—Fourteen are on the subject of Taxation,—viz. the 8th to the 18th[1] inclusively, the 22d, 23d, and 29th; and these may be entirely omitted by the student, and ought at any rate to be omitted on his first examination of the work. For, though Mr. Ricardo has really been not the chief so much as the sole author of any important truths on the subject of Taxation, and though his 14 chapters on that head are so many inestimable corollaries from his general doctrines, and could never have been obtained without them, yet these general doctrines have no sort of reciprocal dependency upon what concerns Taxation. Consequently, it will greatly lighten the burden to a student if these 14 chapters are sequestered from the rest of the work, and reserved for a separate and after investigation, which may furnish a commentary on the first. The chapters on Taxation deducted, there remain, therefore, 17 in the second edition, or 18 in the third. These contain the general principles, but also something more—which may furnish matter for a second subtraction. For in most speculations of this nature it usually happens that, over and above the direct positive communication of new truths, a writer finds it expedient (or perhaps necessary in some cases, in order to clear the ground for himself) to address part of his efforts to the task of meeting the existing errors: hence

[1] The 11th is on Tithes, and the 18th on Poor-Rates; but these of course belong to the subject of Taxation properly defined. The present Lord Chancellor (late Earl of Eldon) said, on some cause which came before him about a year ago, that Tithes were unjustly called a Tax; meaning only that Tithes were not any arbitrary imposition of the government, but claimed by as good a tenure as any other sort of property. In this doctrine no doubt the Chancellor was perfectly right; and only wrong in supposing that any denial of that doctrine is implied by the Political Economists in calling Tithes a Tax; which, on the true definition of a Tax (as I shall show hereafter), they certainly are.

arises a division of his work into the doctrinal or *affirmative* part and the polemic[1] or *negative* part. In Mr. Ricardo's writings all parts (as I have already observed) have a latent polemic reference ; but some, however, are more directly and formally polemic than the rest ; and these may be the more readily detached from the main body of the work because (like the chapters on Taxation) they are all corollaries from the general laws, and in no case introductory to them. Divided on this principle, the 18 chapters fall into the following arrangement :—

| Chap. | Affirmative Chapters. | Chap. | Negative (or Polemic) Chapters. |
|---|---|---|---|
| 1. 4. 30. | on Value ; | 20. | on Value and Riches : against Adam Smith, Lord Lauderdale, M. Say ; |
| 2. 3. | on Rent ; | 24. | Rent of Land : against Adam Smith ; |
| 5. | on Wages ; | 26. | Gross and Nett Revenue : against Adam Smith ; |
| 6. | on Profits ; | | |
| 7. | on Foreign Trade ; | 28. | Relations of Gold, Corn, and Labour, under certain circumstances: against Adam Smith ; |
| 19. | on Sudden Changes in Trade ; | | |
| 21. | on Accumulation ; | | |
| 25. | on Colonial Trade ; | | |
| 27. | on Currency and Banks ; | 32. | Rent : against Mr. Malthus. |
| 31. | on Machinery. | | |

---

[1] "*Polemic*":—There is an occasional tendency in the use and practice of the English language capriciously to limit the use of certain words. Thus, for instance, the word *condign* is used only in connexion with the word *punishment* ; the word *implicit* is used only (unless by scholars, like Milton) in connexion with *faith*, or *confidence*. So also *putative* is restricted most absurdly to the one sole word *father*, in a question of doubtful affiliation. These and other words, if unlocked from their absurd imprisonment, would become extensively useful. We should say, for instance, "condign honours," "condign rewards," "condign treatment" (treatment appropriate to the merits)—thus at once realising two rational purposes : viz., giving a useful function to a word which at present has none ; and also providing an intelligible expression for an idea which otherwise is left without means of uttering itself, except through a ponderous circumlocution. Precisely in the same circumstances of idle and absurd sequestration stands the term *polemic*. At present, according to the popular usage, this word has some fantastic inalienable connexion with controversial theology. There cannot be a more childish chimera. No doubt there is a polemic side or aspect of theology ; but so there is of *all* knowledge ; so there is of *every* science. The radical and characteristic idea concerned in this term *polemic* is found in our own Parliamentary distinction of *the*

Deducting the polemic chapters, there remain 13 affirmative or doctrinal chapters: of which one (the 27th), on Currency, &c., ought always to be insulated from all other parts of Political Economy. And thus, out of the whole 32 chapters, 12 only are important to the student on his first examination; and to these I propose to limit our discussions."

*Phœd.* Be it so; and now let us adjourn to more solemn duties.

## DIALOGUE THE FIRST

### ON THE ELEMENTARY PRINCIPLE OF POLITICAL ECONOMY.

*Phœd.* To cut the matter short, X.Y.Z.—and to begin as near as possible to the end—is there any one principle in Political Economy from which all the rest can be deduced? A principle, I mean, which all others presuppose, but which itself presupposes none.

*X.* There is, Phædrus: such a principle exists in the Doctrine of Value—truly explained. The question from which all Political Economy will be found to move—the question to which all its difficulties will be found reducible—is this: *What is the ground of exchangeable value?* My hat, for example, bears the same value as your umbrella; double the value of my shoes; four times the value of my gloves; one-twentieth of the value of this watch. Of these several relations of value what is the sufficient cause? If they were capricious, no such science as that of Political

*good speaker* as contrasted with *the good debater.* The good speaker is he who unfolds the whole of a question in its affirmative aspects, who presents these aspects in their just proportions, and according to their orderly and symmetrical deductions from each other. But *the good debater* is he who faces the negative aspects of the question, who meets sudden objections, has an answer for any momentary summons of doubt or difficulty, dissipates seeming inconsistencies, and reconciles the geometrical smoothness of *a priori* abstractions with the coarse angularities of practical experience. The great work of Ricardo is of necessity, and almost in every page, polemic; whilst very often the particular objections or difficulties to which it replies are not indicated at all—being spread through entire systems, and assumed as *precognita* that are familiar to the learned student.

Economy could exist; not being capricious, they must have an assignable cause: this cause—what is it?

*Phæd.* Ay, what is it?

*X.* It is this, Phædrus; and the entire merit of the discovery belongs to Mr. Ricardo. It is this; and listen with your whole understanding: *The ground of the value of all things lies in the quantity* (but mark well that word "quantity") *of labour which produces them.* Here is that great principle which is the corner-stone of all tenable Political Economy; which granted or denied, all Political Economy stands or falls. Grant me this one principle, with a few square feet of the sea-shore to draw my diagrams upon, and I will undertake to deduce every other truth in the science.

*Phæd.* Take it and welcome. It would be impossible for most people to raise a cabbage out of the sea-shore, though the sand were manured by principles the noblest. You therefore, my dear friend, that promise to raise from it, not a cabbage, but a system of Political Economy, are doubly entitled to your *modicum* of sand, and to your principle beside; which last is, I daresay, a very worthy and respectable principle, and not at all the worse for being as old as my great-grandfather.

*X.* Pardon me, Phædrus: the principle is no older than the first edition of Mr. Ricardo's book; and, when you make me this concession so readily under the notion that you are conceding nothing more than has long been established, I fear that you will seek to retract it as soon as you are aware of its real import and consequences.

*Phæd.* In most cases, X., I should hesitate to contradict you peremptorily upon a subject which you have studied so much more closely than myself; but here I cannot hesitate; for I happen to remember the very words of Adam Smith which are——

*X.* Substantially the same, you will say, as those which I have employed in expressing the great principle of Mr. Ricardo. This is your meaning, Phædrus; and excuse me for interrupting you. I am anxious to lose no time; and therefore let me remind you, as soon as possible, that "the words" of Adam Smith cannot prove any agreement with Mr. Ricardo, if it appears that those words are used as equivalent and convertible at pleasure with certain other words, not only irreconcilable with Mr. Ricardo's principle, but expressing the very doctrine which Mr. Ricardo does, and must in consistency, set himself to oppose. Mr. Ricardo's doctrine is that A and B are to each other in value as the *quantity* of labour is which produces A to the quantity which produces B; or, to express it in the very shortest formula by substituting the term *base* as synonymous with the term *producing labour*, *All things are to each other in value as their bases are in quantity.* This is the Ricardian law: you allege that it was already the law of Adam Smith; and in some sense you are right; for such a law is certainly to be found in the "Wealth of Nations." But, if it is *ex*plicitly affirmed in that work, it is also *im*plicitly denied: formally asserted, it is virtually withdrawn. For Adam Smith everywhere uses, as an equivalent formula, this,—that A and B are to each other in value as the *value* of the labour which produces A to the *value* of the labour which produces B.

*Phæd.* And the formula for Mr. Ricardo's law is, if I understand you, that A and B are to each other in value not as the *value*, but as the *quantity* of the labour which produces A to the *quantity* which produces B.

*X.* It is.

*Phæd.* And is it possible that any such mighty magic can lurk in the simple substitution of *quantity* for *value?* Surely, X., you are hair-splitting a little in this instance, and mean to amuse yourself with my simplicity, by playing off some logical legerdemain upon me from the "seraphic" or "angelic" doctors.

*X.* The earnestness and good faith of my whole logic and reasoning will soon become a pledge for me that I am incapable of what you call hair-splitting: and in this particular instance I might appeal to Philebus, who will tell you that Mr. Malthus has grounded his entire opposition to Mr. Ricardo on the very distinction which you are now treating as aërial. But the fact is, you do not yet perceive to what extent this distinction goes. You suppose me to be contending for some minute and subtle shades of difference; so far from *that*, I mean to affirm that the one law is the direct, formal, and diametrical negation of the other: I assert in the most peremptory manner that he who says "The value of A is to the value of B as the *quantity* of labour producing A is to the *quantity* of labour producing B," does of necessity deny by implication that the relations of value between A and B are governed by the *value* of the labour which severally produces them.

*Phil.* X. is perfectly right in his distinction. You know, Phædrus, or you soon will know, that I differ from X. altogether on the choice between the two laws: he contends that the value of all things is determined by the *quantity* of the producing labour; I, on the other hand, contend that the value of all things is determined by the *value* of the producing labour. Thus far you will find us irreconcilable in our difference; but this very difference implies that we are agreed on the distinction which X. is now urging. In fact, so far are the two formulæ from presenting merely two different expressions of the same law that the very best way of expressing negatively Mr. Ricardo's law (viz. A is to B in value as the *quantities* of the producing labour) would be to say, A is *not* to B in value as the *values* of the producing labour.

*Phæd.* Well, gentlemen, I suppose you must be right: I am sure you are by the logic of kings, and "according to the flesh"; for you are two to one. Yet, to my poor glimmering understanding, which is all I have to guide me in such cases, I must acknowledge that the whole question seems to be a mere dispute about words.

*X.* For once, Phædrus, I am not sorry to hear you using a phrase which in general is hateful to my ears. "A mere dispute about words" is a phrase which we hear daily; and why? Is it a case of such daily occurrence to hear men disputing about mere verbal differences? So far from it, I can truly say that I never happened to witness such a dispute in my whole life—either in books or in conversation; and, indeed, considering the small number of absolute synonymes which any language contains, it is scarcely possible that a dispute on words should arise which would not also be a dispute about ideas (*i.e.* about realities). Why, then, is the phrase in every man's mouth, when the actual occurrence must be so very uncommon? The reason is this, Phædrus:

such a plea is a "sophisma pigri intellectus," which seeks to escape from the effort of mind necessary for the comprehending and solving of any difficulty under the colourable pretext that it is a question about shadows, and not about substances, and one therefore which it is creditable to a man's good sense to decline: a pleasant sophism this, which at the same time flatters a man's indolence and his vanity! For once, however, I repeat that I am not sorry to hear such a phrase in your mouth, Phædrus: I have heard it from you before; and I will frankly tell you that you ought to be ashamed of such a plea, which is becoming to a slothful intellect, but very unbecoming to yours. On this account, it gives me pleasure that you have at length urged it in a case where you will be obliged to abandon it. If that should happen, remember what I have said; and resolve never more to shrink effeminately from the toil of an intellectual discussion under any pretence that it is a verbal dispute. In the present case, I shall drive you out of that conceit in less time than it cost you to bring it forward. For now, Phædrus, answer me to one or two little questions which I will put. You fancy that between the expressions "*quantity* of producing labour" and "*value* of producing labour" there is none but a verbal difference. It follows therefore that the same effect ought to take place whether the value of the producing labour be altered or its quantity.

*Phæd.* It does.

*X.* For instance, the production of a hat such as mine has hitherto cost (we will suppose) four days' labour at 3s. a-day: now, without any change whatsoever in the *quantity* of labour required for its production, let this labour suddenly increase in value by 25 per cent.—in this case four days' labour will produce a hat as heretofore; but, the value of the producing labour being now raised from 3s. a-day to 3s. 9d., the value of the total labour necessary for the production of a hat will now be raised from 12s. to 15s. Thus far you can have nothing to object?

*Phæd.* Nothing at all, X. But what next?

*X.* Next, let us suppose a case in which the labour of producing hats shall increase, not in value (as in the preceding case), but in quantity. Labour is still at its old value of

3s. a-day ; but, from increased difficulty in any part of the process, five days' labour are now spent on the production of a hat instead of four. In this second case, Phædrus, how much will be paid to the labourer ?

*Phæd.* Precisely as much as in the first case : that is, 15s.

*X.* True : the labourer on hats receives 15s. in the second case as well as in the first ; but in the first case for four days' labour, in the second for five : consequently, in the second case, wages (or the value of labour) have not risen at all, whereas in the first case wages have risen by 25 per cent.

*Phæd.* Doubtless : but what is your inference ?

*X.* My inference is as follows :—According to yourself and Adam Smith, and all those who overlook the momentous difference between the quantity and the value of labour, fancying that these are mere varieties of expression for the same thing, the price of hats ought in the two cases stated to be equally raised—viz. 3s. in each case. If then it be utterly untrue that the price of hats would be equally raised in the two cases, it will follow that an alteration in the value of the producing labour and an alteration in its quantity must terminate in a very different result ; and consequently the one alteration cannot be the same as the other, as you insisted.

*Phæd.* Doubtless.

*X.* Now then let me tell you, Phædrus, that the price of hats would *not* be equally raised in the two cases : in the second case the price of a hat will rise by 3s., in the first case it will not rise at all.

*Phæd.* How so, X. ? How so ? Your own statement supposes that the labourer receives 15s. for four days instead of 12s.,—that is, 3s. more. Now, if the price does not rise to meet this rise of labour, I demand to know whence the labourer is to obtain this additional 3s. If the buyers of hats do not pay him in the price of hats, I presume that the buyers of shoes will not pay him. The poor devil must be paid by somebody.

*X.* You are facetious, my friend. The man must be paid, as you say ; but not by the buyers of hats any more than by the buyers of shoes : for the price of hats cannot possibly rise in such a case, as I have said before. And, that I may demonstrate this, let us assume that, when the labour spent on a hat cost 12s., the rate of profits was 50 per cent,—it is of no consequence what rate be fixed on,—assuming this rate, therefore, the price of a hat would at that time be 18s. Now, when the *quantity* of labour rose from four to five days, this fifth day would add three shillings to the amount of wages; and the price of a hat would rise in consequence from 18s. to a guinea. On the other hand, when the *value* of labour rose from 12s. to 15s., the price of a hat would not rise by one farthing, but would still continue at 18s.

*Phæd.* Again I ask, then, who is to pay the 3s.?

*X.* The 3s. will be paid out of profits.

*Phæd.* What, without reimbursement?

*X.* Assuredly, without a farthing of reimbursement. It is Mr. Ricardo's doctrine that no variation in either profits or wages can ever affect price; if wages rise or fall, the only consequence is that profits must fall or rise by the same sum; so again, if profits rise or fall, wages must fall or rise accordingly.

*Phæd.* You mean then to assert that, when the value of the labour rises (as in the first of your two cases) by 3s., this rise must be paid out of the 6s. which had previously gone to profits.

*X.* I do; and your reason for questioning this opinion is, I am sure, because you think that no capitalist would consent to have his profits thus diminished, but would liberate himself from this increased expense by charging it upon the price. Now, if I prove that he cannot liberate himself in this way, and that it is a matter of perfect indifference to him whether the price rises or not, because in either case he must lose the 3s., I suppose that I shall have removed the sole ground you have for opposing me.

*Phæd.* You are right: prove this, X., "et eris mihi magnus Apollo."

*X.* Tell me then, Phædrus, when the value of labour rises —in other words, when wages rise—what is it that causes them to rise?

*Phæd.* Ay, what is it that causes them, as you say? I should be glad to hear your opinion on that subject.

*X.* My opinion is that there are only two[1] great cases in which wages rise or seem to rise:

1. When money sinks in value; for then, of course, the labourer must have more wages nominally, in order to have the same virtually. But this is obviously nothing more than an apparent rise.

2. When those commodities rise upon which wages are spent. A rise in port wine, in jewels, or in horses, will not affect wages, because these commodities are not consumed by the labourer; but a rise in manufactured goods of certain kinds, upon which perhaps two-fifths of his wages are spent, will tend to raise wages: and a rise in certain kinds of food, upon which perhaps the other three-fifths are spent, will raise them still more. Now, the first case being only an apparent rise, this is the only case in which wages can be said really to rise.

*Phæd.* You are wrong, X.; I can tell you of a third case, which occurs to me whilst you are speaking. Suppose that there were a great deficiency of labourers in any trade, as in the hatter's trade for instance, that would be a reason why wages should rise in the hatter's trade.

*X.* Doubtless, until the deficiency were supplied, which it soon would be by the stimulus of higher wages. But this is a case of *market* value, when the supply happens not to be on a level with the demand: now, throughout the present conversation I wish studiously to keep clear of any reference to market value, and to consider exclusively that mode of exchangeable value which is usually called natural value—*i.e.* where value is wholly uninfluenced by any redundancy or deficiency of the quantity. Waiving this third case, therefore, as not belonging to the present discussion, there remains only the second; and I am entitled to say that no cause can really and permanently raise wages but a rise in the price of those articles on which wages are spent. In the instance

[1] There is another case in which wages have a constant tendency to rise—viz. when the population increases more slowly than the demand for labour. But this case it is not necessary to introduce into the dialogue: first, because it is gradual and insensible in its operation; secondly, because, if it were otherwise, it would not disturb any part of the argument.

above stated, where the hatter's wages rose from 3s. to 3s. 9d. a day, some commodity must previously have risen on which the hatter spent his wages. Let this be corn, and let corn constitute one-half of the hatter's expenditure; on which supposition, as his wages rose by 25 per cent, it follows that corn must have risen by 50 per cent. Now tell me, Phædrus, will this rise in the value of corn affect the hatter's wages only; or will it affect wages in general?

*Phæd.* Wages in general, of course: there can be no reason why hatters should eat more corn than any other men.

*X.* Wages in general, therefore, will rise by 25 per cent. Now, when the wages of the hatter rose in that proportion, you contended that this rise must be charged upon the price of hats; and, the price of a hat having been previously 18s., you insisted that it must now be 21s.; in which case a rise in wages of 25 per cent would have raised the price of hats about 16½ per cent. And, if this were possible, two great doctrines of Mr. Ricardo would have been overthrown at one blow: 1st, that which maintains that no article can increase in price except from a previous increase in the quantity of labour necessary to its production,—for here is no increase in the *quantity* of the labour, but simply in its value; 2d, that no rise in the value of labour can ever settle upon price, but that all increase of wages will be paid out of profits, and all increase of profits out of wages. I shall now, however, extort a sufficient defence of Mr. Ricardo from your own concessions. For you acknowledge that the same cause which raises the wages of the hatter will raise wages universally, and in the same ratio—*i.e.* by 25 per cent. And, if such a rise in wages could raise the price of hats by 16½ per cent, it must raise all other commodities whatsoever by 16½ per cent. Now tell me, Phædrus, when all commodities without exception are raised by 16½ per cent, in what proportion will the power of money be diminished under every possible application of it?

*Phæd.* Manifestly by 16½ per cent.

*X.* If so, Phædrus, you must now acknowledge that it is a matter of perfect indifference to the hatter whether the price of hats rise or not, since he cannot under any circumstances escape the payment of the 3s. If the price should *not* rise (as assuredly it will not), he pays the 3s. directly; if the price were to rise by 3s., this implies of necessity that prices rise universally (for it would answer no purpose of your argument to suppose that hatters escaped an evil which affected all other trades). Now, if prices rise universally, the hatter undoubtedly escapes the direct payment of the 3s., but he pays it indirectly; inasmuch as £116 : 10s. is now become necessary to give him the same command of labour and commodities which was previously given by £100. Have you any answer to these deductions?

*Phæd.* I must confess I have none.

*X.* If so, and no answer is possible, then I have here given you a demonstration of Mr. Ricardo's great law—That no product of labour whatsoever can be affected in value by any variations in the *value* of the producing labour. But, if not by variations in its value, then of necessity by variations in its quantity, for no other variations are possible.

*Phæd.* But at first sight, you know, variations in the *value* of labour appear to affect the value of its product: yet you have shown that the effect of such variations is defeated, and rendered nugatory in the end. Now, is it not possible that some such mode of argument may be applied to the case of variations in the *quantity* of labour?

*X.* By no means. The reason why all variations in the *value* of labour are incapable of transferring themselves to the value of its product is this,—that these variations extend to all kinds of labour, and therefore to all commodities alike: now that which raises or depresses all things equally leaves their relations to each other undisturbed. In order to disturb the relations of value between A, B, and C, I must raise one at the same time that I do *not* raise another; depress one, and *not* depress another; raise or depress them unequally. This is necessarily done by any variations in the *quantity* of labour. For example, when more or less labour became requisite for the production of hats, that variation could not fail to affect the value of hats, for the variation was confined exclusively to hats, and arose out of some circumstance peculiar to hats; and no more labour was on that account requisite for the production of gloves, or wine, or carriages. Consequently, these and all other articles remaining unaffected, whilst hats required 25 per cent more labour, the previous relation between hats and all other commodities was disturbed —*i.e.* a *real* effect was produced on the value of hats. Whereas, when hats without requiring a greater quantity of labour were simply produced by labour at a higher value, this change could not possibly disturb the relation between hats and any other commodities, because they were all equally affected by it. If by some application of any mechanic or chemical discovery to the process of making candles the labour of that process were diminished by one-third, the value of candles would fall; for the relation of candles to all other articles, in which no such abridgment of labour had been effected, would be immediately altered: two days' labour would now produce the same quantity of candles as three days' labour before the discovery. But if, on the other hand, the wages of three days had simply fallen in value to the wages of two days—that is, if the labourer received only 6s. for three days instead of 9s.—this could not affect the value of candles; for the fall of wages, extending to all other things whatsoever, would leave the relations between them all undisturbed; everything else which had required 9s. worth of labour would now require 6s. worth; and a pound of candles would exchange for the same quantity of everything as before. Hence it appears that no cause can possibly affect the value of anything—*i.e.* its exchangeable relation to other things—but an increase or diminution in the quantity of labour required for its production: and the prices of all things whatsoever represent the quantity of labour by which they are severally produced; and the value of A is to the value of B universally as the quantity of labour which produces A to the quantity of labour which produces B.

Here, then, is the great law of value as first explained by Mr. Ricardo. Adam Smith uniformly takes it for granted that an alteration in the quantity of labour, and an alteration in wages (*i.e.* the value of labour), are the same thing, and will produce the same effects: and hence he never distinguishes the two cases, but everywhere uses the two expressions as synonymous. If A, which had hitherto required 16s. worth of labour for its production, should to-morrow require only 12s. worth, Adam Smith would have treated it as a matter of no importance whether this change had arisen from some discovery in the art of manufacturing A which reduced the quantity of labour required from four days to three, or simply from some fall in wages which reduced the value of a day's labour from 4s. to 3s. Yet in the former case A would fall considerably in price as soon as the discovery ceased to be monopolised; whereas in the latter case we have seen that A could not possibly vary in price by one farthing.

*Phæd.* In what way do you suppose that Adam Smith came to make so great an oversight, as I now confess it to be?

*X.* Mr. Malthus represents Adam Smith as not having sufficiently explained himself on the subject. "He does not make it quite clear," said Mr. Malthus, "whether he adopts for his principle of value the quantity of the producing labour or its value." But this is a most erroneous representation. There is not a chapter in the "Wealth of Nations" in which it is not made redundantly clear that Adam Smith adopts both laws as mere varieties of expression for one and the same law. This being so, how could he possibly make an election between two things which he constantly confounded and regarded as identical? The truth is, Adam Smith's attention was never directed to the question: he suspected no distinction; no man of his day, or before his day, had ever suspected it; none of the French or Italian writers on Political Economy had ever suspected it; indeed, none of them has suspected it to this hour. One single writer before Mr. Ricardo has insisted on the *quantity* of labour as the true ground of value, and, what is very singular, at a period when Political Economy was in the rudest state—viz. in the early part of Charles II's reign. This writer was Sir William Petty, a man who would have greatly advanced the science if he had been properly seconded by his age. In a remarkable passage, too long for quotation, he has expressed the law of value with a Ricardian accuracy: but it is scarcely possible that even he was aware of his own accuracy; for, though he has asserted that the reason why any two articles exchange for each other (as so much corn of Europe, suppose, for so much silver of Peru) is because the same quantity of labour has been employed on their production, and though he has certainly not vitiated the purity of this principle by the usual heteronomy (if you will allow me a learned word)—*i.e.* by the introduction of the other and opposite law derived from the *value* of this labour—yet it is probable that in thus abstaining he was guided by mere accident, and not by any conscious purpose of contradistinguishing the one law from the other ; because, had *that* been his purpose, he would hardly have contented himself with forbearing to affirm, but would formally have denied, the false law. For it can never be sufficiently impressed upon the student's mind that it brings him not one step nearer to the truth to say that the value of A is determined by the quantity of labour which produces it, unless by that proposition he means that it is *not* determined by the *value* of the labour which produces it.

To return to Adam Smith. Not only has he "made it quite clear" that he confounded the two laws, and had never been summoned to examine whether they led to different results ; but I go farther, and will affirm that, if he *had* been summoned to such an examination, he could not have pursued it with any success until the discovery of the true law of Profits. For, in the case of the hats as before argued, he would have said, "The wages of the hatter, whether they have been augmented by increased quantity of labour, or by increased value of labour, must in any case be paid." Now, what is the answer ? They must be paid, but from what fund ? Adam Smith knew of no fund, nor could know of any, until Mr. Ricardo had ascertained the true law of Profits, except Price : in either case, therefore, as Political Economy then stood, he was compelled to conclude that the 15s. would be paid out of the price—*i.e.* that the whole difference between the 12s. and the 15s. would settle upon the purchaser. But we now know that this will happen only in the case when the difference has arisen from increased labour, and that every farthing of the difference which arises from increased value of labour will be paid out of another fund — viz. Profits. But this conclusion could not be arrived at without the new theory of Profits (as will be seen more fully when we come to that theory) ; and thus one error was the necessary parent of another.

Here I will pause, and must beg you to pardon my long speeches, in consideration of the extreme importance of the subject; for everything in Political Economy depends, as I said before, on the law of value; and I have not happened to meet with one writer who seemed fully to understand Mr. Ricardo's law, and still less who seemed to perceive the immense train of consequences which it involves.

*Phœd.* I now see enough to believe that Mr. Ricardo is right; and, if so, it is clear that all former writers are wrong. Thus far I am satisfied with your way of conducting the argument, though some little confusion still clouds my view. But, with regard to the consequences you speak of, how do you explain that under so fundamental an error (as you represent it) many writers, but above all Adam Smith, should have been able to deduce so large a body of truth that we all regard him as one of the chief benefactors of the science?

*X.* The fact is that his good sense interfered everywhere to temper the extravagant conclusions into which a severe logician could have driven him.[1] At this very day a French

[1] The "Wealth of Nations" has never yet been ably reviewed, nor satisfactorily edited. The edition of Mr. Buchanan is unquestionably the best, and displays great knowledge of Political Economy as it stood before the revolution effected by Mr. Ricardo. But, having the misfortune to appear immediately before that revolution, it is already to some degree an obsolete book. Even for its own date, however, it was not good as an edition of Adam Smith, its value lying chiefly in the body of original disquisitions which composed the fourth volume; for the notes not only failed to correct the worst errors of Adam Smith (which indeed in many cases is saying no more than that Mr. Buchanan did not forestall Mr. Ricardo), but were also deficient in the history of English finance, and generally in the knowledge of facts. How much reason there is to call for a new edition, with a commentary adapted to the existing state of the science, will appear on this consideration:—The "Wealth of Nations" is the text-book resorted to by all students of Political Economy. One main problem of this science, if not *the* main problem (as Mr. Ricardo thinks), is to determine the laws which regulate Rent, Profit, and Wages; but everybody who is acquainted with the present state of the science must acknowledge that precisely on these three points it affords "very little satisfactory information." These last words are the gentle criticism of Mr. Ricardo; but the truth is that not only does it afford very little information on the great heads of Rent, Profits, and Wages, but (which is much worse) it gives very false and misleading information.

and an English economist have reared a Babel of far more elaborate errors on this subject; M. Say, I mean, and Mr. Malthus—both ingenious writers, both eminently illogical, especially the latter, with whose "confusion worse confounded" on the subject of value, if reviewed by some unsparing Rhadamanthus of logical justice, I believe that chaos would appear a model of order and light. Yet the very want of logic which has betrayed these two writers into so many errors has befriended them in escaping from their consequences; for they leap with the utmost agility over all obstacles to any conclusions which their good sense points out to them as just, however much at war with their own premisses. With respect to the confusion which you complain of as still clinging to the subject, this naturally attends the first efforts of the mind to disjoin two ideas which have constantly been regarded as one. But, as we advance in our discussions, illustration and proof will gradually arise from all quarters to the great principle of Mr. Ricardo which we have just been considering; besides which, this principle is itself so much required for the illustration and proof of other principles that the mere practice of applying it will soon sharpen your eye to a steady familiarity with all its aspects.[1]

## DIALOGUE THE SECOND

### REDUCTIO AD ABSURDUM

*Phil.* X., I see, is not yet come: I hope he does not mean to break his appointment, for I have a design upon him. I

P.S.—September 27, 1854—It is suggested to me by a friend that, in this special notice of Mr. Buchanan's edition, I shall be interpreted as having designed some covert reflection upon the edition of Adam Smith published by Mr. M'Culloch. My summary answer to any such insinuation is that this whole paper was written in the spring of 1824, *i.e.* thirty and a-half years ago; at which time, to the best of my knowledge, Mr. M'Culloch had not so much as meditated any such edition. Let me add that, if I had seen or fancied any reason for a criticism unfriendly to Mr. M'Culloch, or to any writer whatever, I should not have offered it indirectly, but openly, frankly, and in the spirit of liberal candour due to an honourable contemporary.

[1] To this point what one has been reading is the opening article of the *London Magazine* for April 1824, forming pp. 341-355 of the

have been considering his argument against the possibility of any change of price arising out of a change in the value of labour, and I have detected a flaw in it which he can never get over. I have him, sir—I have him as fast as ever spider had a fly.

*Phæd.* Don't think it, my dear friend : you are a dexterous *retiarius;* but a gladiator who is armed with Ricardian weapons will cut your net to pieces. He is too strong in his cause, as I am well satisfied from what passed yesterday. He'll slaughter you : to use the racy expression of a friend of mine in describing the redundant power with which one fancy boxer disposed of another, he'll slaughter you "with ease and affluence." But here he comes.—Well, X., you're just come in time. Philebus says that you are a fly, whilst *he* is a murderous spider, and that he'll slaughter you with "ease and affluence"; and, all things considered, I am inclined to think he will."

*Phil.* Phædrus does not report the matter quite accurately ; however, it is true that I believe myself to have detected a fatal error in your argument of yesterday on the case of the hat ; and it is this :—When the value of labour rose by 25 per cent, you contended that this rise would be paid out of profits. Now, up to a certain limit this may be possible ; beyond that it is impossible. For the price of the hat was supposed to be 18s. ; and, the price of the labour being assumed originally at 12s., leaving 6s. for profits, it is very possible that a rise in wages of no more than 3s. may be paid out of these profits. But, as this advance in wages increases, it comes nearer and nearer to that point at which

number ; but, by an unusual indulgence of the editor, the article, though it seemed to stop there, was resumed at p. 427 of the same April number, with this editorial explanation of the gap between the two portions of the article : "This dialogue [*i.e.* Dialogue the Second], which seems necessary for the elucidation of the principle advanced in Dialogue I, did not reach us sufficiently early to be placed in immediate connexion with it : we have, therefore, thought it advisable to print it here rather than to keep it for another month."—What follows as "Dialogue the Second" comes, in fact, as the eighteenth article (pp. 427-428) in that same number of the magazine in which what has preceded was the first article. Actually in the same number De Quincey had two *other* articles besides,—four articles in all in one number !—M.

it will be impossible for profits to pay it; since, let the advance once reach the whole 6s., all motives for producing hats will be extinguished; and, let it advance to 7s., there will in that case be no fund at all left out of which the seventh shilling can be paid, even if the capitalist were disposed to relinquish all his profits. Now, seriously, you will hardly maintain that the hat could not rise to the price of 19s.—or of any higher sum?

*X.* Recollect, Philebus, what it is that I maintain. Assuredly the hat may rise to the price of 19s., or of any higher sum, but not as a consequence of the cause you assign. Taking your case, I *do* maintain that it is impossible the hat should exceed or even reach 18s. When I say 18s., however, you must recollect that the particular sums of 12s. for labour, and 6s. for profits, were taken only for the sake of illustration. Translating the sense of the proposition into universal forms, what I assert is that the rise in the value of the labour can go no further than the amount of profits will allow it: profits swallowed up, there will remain no fund out of which an increase of wages can be paid, and the production of hats will cease.

*Phil.* This is the sense in which I understood you; and in this sense I wish that you would convince me that the hat could not, under the circumstances supposed, advance to 19s. or 20s.

*X.* Perhaps in our conversation on *Wages* you will see this more irresistibly; you yourself will then shrink from affirming the possibility of such an advance as from an obvious absurdity. Meantime, here is a short demonstration of it, which I am surprised that Mr. Ricardo did not use as the strongest and most compendious mode of establishing his doctrine:—Let it be possible that the hat may advance to 19s.; or, to express this more generally, from $x$ (or 18s.)—which it was worth before the rise in wages—to $x+y$; that is to say, the hat will now be worth $x+y$ quantity of money—having previously been worth no more than $x$. That is your meaning?

*Phil.* It is.

*X.* And, if in money, of necessity in everything else; because otherwise, if the hat were worth more money only, but more of nothing besides, that would simply argue that money had fallen in value; in which case undoubtedly the hat might rise in any proportion that money fell; but then without gaining any increased value, which is essential to your argument.

*Phil.* Certainly; if in money, then in everything else.

*X.* Therefore, for instance, in gloves; having previously been worth 4 pair of buckskin gloves, the hat will now be worth 4 pair $+ y$?

*Phil.* It will.

*X.* But, Philebus, either the rise in wages is universal or it is not universal. If not universal, it must be a case of accidental rise from mere scarcity of hands; which is the case of a rise in *market* value; and that is not the case of Mr. Ricardo, who is laying down the laws of *natural* value. It is therefore universal; but, if universal, the gloves from the same cause will have risen from the value of $x$ to $x + y$. Hence, therefore, the price of the hat, estimated in gloves, is $= x + y$. And, again, the price of the gloves, estimated in hats, is $= x + y$. In other words

$$H - y = x.$$

$$H + y = x.$$

That is to say, $H - y = H + y$.

*Phæd.* Which, I suppose, is an absurdity; and in fact it turns out, Philebus, that he has slaughtered you with "ease and affluence."

*X.* And this absurdity must be eluded by him who undertakes to show that a rise in the wages of labour can be transferred to the value of its product.[1]

[1] At this point we leave the number of the *London Magazine* for April 1824; and all that follows of the paper is from the May number (pp. 547-565).—M.

## DIALOGUE THE THIRD

[Et æquiori sane animo feres, cum hic de primis agatur principiis, si superstitiose omnia examinavi, viamque quasi palpando singulaque curiosius contrectando lente me promovi et testudineo gradu. Video enim ingenium humanum ita comparatum esse ut facilius longe quid *consequens* sit dispiciat quam quid in natura *primo* verum, nostramque omnium conditionem non multum ab illa Archimedis abludere—Δος που στω και κινησω την γην. Ubi primum figamus pedem invenire multo magis satagimus quam (ubi invenimus) ulterius progredi.—*Henricus Morus in Epist. ad Cartesium.*][1]

### PRINCIPLE OF VALUE CONTINUED

*Phæd.* In our short conversation of yesterday, X., you parried an objection brought forward by Philebus in a way which I thought satisfactory. You reduced him to an absurdity, or what seemed such. In fact, I did verily believe that you had slaughtered Philebus ; and so I told him. But we have since reconsidered the matter, and have settled it between ourselves that your answer will not do ; that your "absurdity," in fact, is a very absurd absurdity. Philebus will tell you why. I for my part shall have enough to do to take care of a little argument of my own, which is designed to meet something that passed in our first dialogue. Now, my private conviction is that both I and Philebus shall be cudgelled ; I am satisfied that such will be the issue of the business. And my reason for thinking so is this—that I already see enough to discern a character of boldness and determination in Mr. Ricardo's doctrines which needs no help from sneaking equivocations, and this with me is a high presumption that he is in the right. In whatever rough

[1] "You will bear it with more equanimity, since here one is dealing with first principles, if I have religiously examined everything, and, as if by feeling the way and handling each particular with the utmost curiosity, have advanced myself slowly and at a tortoise-like pace. For I see that the human intellect is so constituted that it discerns far more easily what is *consequent* than what in nature is *first* true, and that the condition of all of us is not much unlike that of Archimedes,—'Give me a spot to stand on, and I shall move the Earth.' Where first we plant our foot we busy ourselves much more in discovering than (where we have made a discovery) in advancing farther."—Henry More in letter to Des Cartes.

way his theories are tossed about, they seem always, like a cat, to light upon their legs. But, notwithstanding this, as long as there is a possibility that he may be in the wrong, I shall take it for granted that he is, and do my best to prove him so.

*X.* For which, Phædrus, I shall feel greatly indebted to you. We are told of Trajan that in the camp exercises he not only tolerated hard blows, but courted them,—"alacer virtute militum, et lætus quoties aut cassidi suæ aut clypeo gravior ictus incideret. Laudabat quippe ferientes, hortabaturque ut auderent." When one of our theatres let down an iron curtain upon the stage as a means of insulating the audience from any fire amongst the scenery, and sent men to prove the strength of this curtain by playing upon it with sledge-hammers in the sight and hearing of the public—who would not have laughed at the hollowness of the mummery if the blows had been gentle, considerate, and forbearing? A "make-believe" blow would have implied a "make-believe" hammer and a "make-believe" curtain. No!—hammer away, like Charles Martel; "fillip me with a three-man beetle"; be to me a *malleus hæreticorum*; come like Spencer's Talus—an iron man with an iron flail—and thresh out the straw of my logic; rack me; put me to the question; get me down; jump upon me; kick me; throttle me; put an end to me in any way you can.

*Phæd.* I will, I will, my dear friend; anything to oblige you; anything for peace. So now tie yourself to the stake, whilst we bait you. And you begin, Philebus; unmuzzle.

*Phil.* I shall be brief. The case of the hat is what I stand upon; and, by the way, I am much obliged to you, X., for having stated the question in that shape; it has furnished me with a very manageable formula for recalling the principle at issue. The wages alter from two different causes: in one case, because there is the same quantity of labour at a different rate; in another case, because there is a different quantity at the same rate. In the latter case it is agreed that the alteration settles upon price; in the former case you affirm that it will *not*: I affirm that it will. I bring an argument to prove it; which argument you attempt to parry by another. But in this counter-argument of yours it strikes me that there lurks a *petitio principii.* Indeed, I am sure of it. For observe the course of our reasoning. I charge it upon your doctrine as an absurd consequence that, if the increase of wages must be paid out of profits, then this fund will at length be eaten out, and, as soon as it is, there will be no fund at all for paying any further increase, and the production must cease. Now, what in effect is your answer? Why, that as soon as profits are all eaten up the production *will* cease. And this you call reducing me to an absurdity. But where is the absurdity? Your answer is in fact an identical proposition; for, when you say, "*As soon as* profits are absorbed," I retort, Ay, no doubt "*as soon*" as they are; but when will that be? It requires no Ricardo to tell us that, *when* profits are absorbed, they will be absorbed; what I deny is that they ever *can* be absorbed. For, as fast as wages increase, what is to hinder price from increasing *pari passu*? In which case profits will *never* be absorbed. It is easy enough to prove that price will not increase, if you may assume that profits will not remain stationary. For then you have assumed the whole point in dispute; and, after *that*, of course you have the game in your own hands; since it is self-evident that, if any body is made up of two parts, P and W, so adjusted that all which is gained by either must be lost by the other, then *that* body can never increase.

*Phæd.* Nor decrease.

*Phil.* No, nor decrease. If my head must of necessity lose as much weight as my trunk gains, and *vice versa,* then it is a clear case that I shall never be heavier. But why cannot my head remain stationary, whilst my trunk grows heavier? This is what you had to prove, and you have not proved it.

*Phæd.* Oh! it's scandalous to think how he has duped us; his "*reductio*" turns out to be the merest swindling.

*X.* No, Phædrus—I beg your pardon. It is very true I did not attempt to prove that your head might not remain stationary; I could not have proved this *directly* without anticipating a doctrine out of its place; but I proved it *indirectly*, by showing that, if it were supposed possible, an absurdity would follow from that supposition. I said, and

I say again, that the doctrine of wages will show the very supposition itself to be absurd ; but, until we come to that doctrine, I content myself with proving that, let that supposition seem otherwise ever so reasonable (the supposition, namely, that profits may be stationary whilst wages are advancing), yet it draws after it one absurd consequence—viz. that a thing may be bigger than that to which it is confessedly equal. Look back to the notes of our conversation, and you will see that this is as I say. You say, Philebus, that I prove profits in a particular case to be incapable of remaining stationary by assuming that price cannot increase; or, if I am called upon to prove that assumption—viz. that price cannot increase—I do it only by assuming that profits in that case are incapable of remaining stationary. But, if I had reasoned thus, I should not only have been guilty of a *petitio principii* (as you alleged), but also of a circle. Here then I utterly disclaim and renounce either assumption. I do not ask you to grant me that price must continue stationary in the case supposed ; I do not ask you to grant me that profits must recede in the case supposed. On the contrary, I will not have them granted to me ; I insist on your refusing both of these principles.

*Phil.* Well, I *do* refuse them.

*Phæd.* So do I. I'll do anything in reason as well as another. "If one might give a testril——"[1]

*X.* Then let us suppose the mines from which we obtain our silver to be in England.

*Phæd.* What for ? Why am I to suppose this ? I don't know but you have some trap in it.

*X.* No ; a Newcastle coal mine, or a Cornwall tin-mine, will answer the purpose of my argument just as well. But it is more convenient to use silver as the illustration ; and I suppose it to be in England simply to avoid intermixing any question about foreign trade. Now, when the hat sold for 18s., on Mr. Ricardo's principle why did it sell for that sum ?

*Phil.* I suppose, because the quantity of silver in that sum is assumed to be the product of four days' labour in a silver mine.

[1] Sir Andrew Aguecheek, in "Twelfth Night."

*X.* Certainly; because it is the product of the same quantity of labour as that which produced the hat. Calling 20s., therefore, 4 ounces of silver, the hat was worth 9-10ths of 4 ounces. Now, when wages advance from 12s. to 14s., profits (you allege) will not pay this advance, but price. On this supposition the price of the hat will now be—what?

*Phil.* Twenty shillings; leaving, as before, 6s. for profit.

*X.* Six shillings upon 14s. are not the same *rate* of profit as 6s. upon 12s.; but no matter; it does not affect the argument. The hat is now worth 4 entire ounces of silver, having previously been worth 4 ounces *minus* a tenth of 4 ounces. But the product of 4 days' labour in a silver mine must also advance in value for the same cause. Four ounces of silver, which is that product, will now have the same power or value as 22·22s. had before. Consequently the 4 ounces of silver, which had previously commanded in exchange a hat and the 9th of a hat, will now command a hat and 2-9ths, fractions neglected. Hence, therefore, a hat will, upon any Anti-Ricardian theory, manifestly buy 4 ounces of silver; and yet, at the same time, it will not buy 4 ounces by 1-5th part of 4 ounces. Silver and the denominations of its qualities being familiar make it more convenient to use that metal; but substitute lead, iron, coal, or anything whatsoever—the argument is the same, being in fact a universal demonstration that variation in wages cannot produce corresponding variations in price.

*Phæd.* Say no more, X.; I see that you are right; and it's all over with our cause, unless I retrieve it. To think that the whole cause of the Anti-Ricardian economy should devolve upon me! that fate should ordain me to be the Atlas on whose unworthy shoulders the whole system is to rest! This being my destiny, I ought to have been built a little stronger. However, no matter. I heartily pray that I may prove too strong for you; though at the same time I am convinced I shall not. Remember, therefore, that you have no right to exult if you toss and gore me, for I tell you beforehand that you will. And, if you do, that only proves me to be in the right—and a very sagacious person; since my argument has all the appearance of being irresistible, and yet such is my discernment that I foresee most acutely that it will turn out a most absurd one. It is this:—Your answer to Philebus issues in this—that a thing A is shown to be at once more valuable and yet not more valuable than the same thing B. Now this answer I take by the horns: it is possible for A to be more and yet not more valuable than the same thing. For example, my hat shall be more valuable than the gloves,—more valuable, that is, than the gloves were; and yet not more valuable than the gloves,—not more valuable, that is, than the gloves now are. So of the wages; all things preserve their former relations, because all are equally raised. This is my little argument. What do you think of it? Will it do?

*X.* No.

*Phæd.* Why, so I told you.

*X.* I have the pleasure then to assure you that you were perfectly right. It will *not* do. But I understand you perfectly. You mean to evade my argument that the increase of wages shall settle upon profits: according to this argument it will settle upon price, and not upon profits,—yet again on price in such a way as to escape the absurdity of two relations of value existing between the very same things. But, Phædrus, this rise will be a mere metaphysical ens, and no real rise. The hat, you say, has risen; but still it commands no more of the gloves, because they also have risen. How then has either risen? The rise is purely ideal.

*Phæd.* It is so, X.; but that I did not overlook; for tell me—on Mr. Ricardo's principle, will not all things double their value simultaneously, if the quantity of labour spent in producing all should double simultaneously?

*X.* It will, Phædrus.

*Phæd.* And yet nothing will exchange for more or less than before.

*X.* True; but the rise is not ideal for all that, but will affect everybody. A pound of wheat, which previously bought three pounds of salt, will still buy three pounds; but then the salt-maker and the wheat-maker will have only one pound of those articles where before he had two. However, the difference between the two cases cannot fully be understood without a previous examination of certain distinctions which I will make the subject of our next dialogue;

and the rather because, apart from our present question, at every step we should else be embarrassed, as all others have been, by the perplexity attending these distinctions. Meantime, as an answer to your argument, the following consideration will be quite sufficient :—The case which your argument respects is that in which wages are supposed to rise. Why ? In consequence of a *real* rise in corn or something else. As a means of meeting this rise, wages rise ; but the increased value of wages is only a means to an end, and the labourer cares about the rise only in that light. The end is—to give him the same quantity of corn, suppose. That end attained, he cares nothing about the means by which it is attained. Now, your ideal rise of wages does not attain this end. The corn has *really* risen ; this is the first step. In consequence of this an ideal rise follows in all things, which evades the absurdities of a real rise—and evades the Ricardian doctrine of profits ; but then only by also evading any real rise in wages, the necessity of which (in order to meet the real rise in corn) first led to the whole movement of price. But this you will more clearly see after our next dialogue.

## DIALOGUE THE FOURTH

### ON THE USE AND ABUSE OF TWO CELEBRATED DISTINCTIONS IN THE THEORY OF VALUE

*X.* Now, gentlemen, I come to a question which on a double account is interesting : first, because it is indispensable to the fluency of our future progress that this question should be once for all decided ; secondly, because it furnishes an *experimentum crucis* for distinguishing a true knowledge of Mr. Ricardo's theory from a spurious or half - knowledge. Many a man will accompany Mr. Ricardo thus far, and will keep his seat pretty well until he comes to the point which we have now reached,—at which point scarcely one in a thousand will escape being unhorsed.

*Phæd.* Which one most assuredly will not be myself. For I have a natural alacrity in losing my seat, and gravitate so determinately to the ground that (like a Roman of old) I ride without stirrups, by way of holding myself in constant readiness for projection ; upon the least hint, anticipating my horse's wishes on that point, and throwing myself off as fast as possible ; for what's the use of taking the negative side in a dispute where one's horse takes the affirmative ? So I leave it to Philebus to ride through the steeplechase you will lead him ; his be the honour of the day—and his the labour.

*X.* But *that* cannot be. Philebus is bound in duty to be dismounted, for the sake of keeping Mr. Malthus, with many others, in countenance. For at this point, Phædrus, more than at any other almost, there is a sad confusion of lords and gentlemen that I could name thrown out of the saddle pell-mell upon their mother earth.

*Phil.* "So they among themselves in pleasant vein
Stood scoffing."

I suppose I may add—

"Heightened in their thoughts beyond
All doubt of victory."

Meantime, what is it you allude to ?

*X.* You are acquainted, I doubt not, Philebus, with the common distinction between *real* and *nominal* value ; and in your judgment upon that distinction I presume that you adopt the doctrine of Mr. Malthus.

*Phil.* I do ; but I know not why you should call it the doctrine of Mr. Malthus ; for, though he has re-urged it against Mr. Ricardo, yet originally it belongs to Adam Smith.

*X.* Not so, Philebus ; *a* distinction between real and nominal value was made by Adam Smith, but not altogether *the* distinction of Mr. Malthus. It is true that Mr. Malthus tells us ("Polit. Econ," p. 63), that the distinction is "exactly the same." But in this he is inaccurate ; for neither is it exactly the same, nor, if it had been, could Mr. Malthus have urged it in his "Political Economy" with the same consistency as its original author. This you will see hereafter. But no matter : how do you understand the distinction ?

*Phil.* I continue to think, with Mr. Malthus, and in his words, "that the most proper definition of real value in exchange, in contradistinction to nominal value in exchange, is the power of commanding the necessaries and conveniences of life, including labour, as distinguished from the power of commanding the precious metals."

*X.* You think, for instance, that if the wages of a labourer should in England be at the rate of 5s. a-day, and in France of no more than 1s. a-day, it could not, therefore, be inferred that wages were at a high real value in England, or a low real value in France. Until we know how much food, etc., could be had for the 5s. in England, and how much in France for the 1s., all that we could fairly assert would be that wages were at a high *nominal* value in England and at a low *nominal* value in France; but the moment it should be ascertained that the English wages would procure twice as much comfort as the French, or the French twice as much as the English, we might then peremptorily affirm that wages were at a high *real* value in England on the first supposition, or in France on the second :—is this what you think ?

*Phil.* It is, and very fairly stated. I think this, in common with Mr. Malthus; and can hold out but little hope that I shall ever cease to think it.

*X.* "Why then, know this :
Thou think'st amiss ;
And, to think right, thou must think o'er again."[1]

*Phœd.* But is it possible that Mr. Ricardo can require me to abjure an inference so reasonable as this ? If so, I must frankly acknowledge that I am out of the saddle already.

*X.* Reasonable inference ? So far from *that*, there is an end of all logic if such an inference be tolerated. *That* man may rest assured that his vocation in this world is not logical who feels disposed (after a few minutes' consideration) to question the following proposition—viz. That it is very possible for A continually to increase in value—in *real* value, observe—and yet to command a continually decreasing quantity of B; in short, that A may acquire a thousand

[1] Suckling's well-known song.

times higher value, and yet exchange for ten thousand times less of B.

*Phæd.* Why then, "chaos is come again!" Is this the unparadoxical Ricardo?

*X.* Yes, Phædrus; but lay not this unction to your old prejudices,—which you must now prepare to part with for ever,—that it is any spirit of wilful paradox which is now speaking; for get rid of Mr. Ricardo if you can, but you will not, therefore, get rid of this paradox. On any other theory of value whatsoever, it will still continue to be an irresistible truth, though it is the Ricardian theory only which can consistently explain it. Here, by the way, is a specimen of paradox in the true and laudable sense—in that sense according to which Boyle entitled a book "Hydrostatical Paradoxes"; for, though it wears a *prima facie* appearance of falsehood, yet in the end you will be sensible that it is not only true, but true in that way and degree which will oblige him who denies it to maintain an absurdity. Again, therefore, I affirm that, when the labourer obtains a large quantity of corn, for instance, it is so far from being any fair inference that wages are then at a high real value that in all probability they are at a very low real value; and inversely I affirm that, when wages are at their very highest real value, the labourer will obtain the very smallest quantity of corn. Or, quitting wages altogether (because such an illustration would drive me into too much anticipation), I affirm universally of Y (that is, of any assignable thing whatsoever) that it shall grow more valuable *ad infinitum*, and yet by possibility exchange for less and less *ad infinitum* of Z (*i.e.* of any other assignable thing).

*Phæd.* Well, all I shall say is this—am I in a world where men stand on their heads or on their feet? But there is some trick in all this; there is some snare. And now I consider—what's the meaning of your saying "by possibility"? If the doctrine you would force upon me be a plain, broad, straightforward truth, why fetter it with such a suspicious restriction?

*X.* Think for a moment, Phædrus, what doctrine it is which I would force upon you. Not, as you seem to suppose, that the quantity obtained by Y is in the *inverse* ratio of the value of Y; on the contrary, if that were so, it would still remain true that an irresistible inference might be drawn from the quantity purchased to the value of the thing purchasing, and, *vice versa*, from the value of the thing purchasing to the quantity which it would purchase. There would still be a connexion between the two; and the sole difference between my doctrine and the old doctrine would be this—that the connexion would be no longer *direct* (as by your doctrine), but *inverse*. This would be the difference, and the sole difference. But what is it that I assert? Why, that there is no connexion at all or of any kind, direct or inverse, between the quantity commanded and the value commanding. My object is to get rid of your inference, not to substitute any new inference of my own. I put, therefore, an extreme case. This case ought by your doctrine to be impossible. If, therefore, it be *not* impossible, your doctrine is upset. Simply as a possible case, it is sufficient to destroy *you*. But, if it were more than a possible case, it would destroy *me*. For if, instead of demonstrating the possibility of such a case, I had attempted to show that it were a universal and necessary case, I should again be introducing the notion of a connexion between the quantity obtained and the value obtaining; which it is the very purpose of my whole argument to exterminate. For my thesis is that no such connexion subsists between the two as warrants any inference that the real value is great because the quantity it buys is great, or small because the quantity it buys is small; or, reciprocally, that, because the real value is great or small, therefore the quantities bought shall be great or small. From, or to, the real value in these cases, I contend that there is no more valid inference than from, or to, the nominal value with which it is contrasted.

*Phil.* Your thesis, then, as I understand it, is this: that, if A double its value, it will not command double the quantity of B. I have a barouche which is worth about 600 guineas at this moment. Now, if I should keep this barouche unused in my coach-house for five years, and at the end of this term it should happen from any cause that carriages had doubled in value, *my* understanding would lead me to expect double the quantity of any commodity for which I might then exchange it, whether *that* were money, sugar, besoms, or anything whatsoever. But *you* tell me —no. And, *vice versa*, if I found that my barouche at the end of five years obtained for me double the quantity of sugar, or besoms, or political economists, which it would now obtain, I should think myself warranted in drawing an inference that carriages had doubled their value. But you tell me—no ; "non valet consequentia."

*X.* You are in the right, Phædrus ; I *do* tell you so. But you do not express my thesis quite accurately,—which is that, if A double its value, it will not *therefore* command double the former quantity of B. It may do so ; and it may also command five hundred times more, or five hundred times less.

*Phæd.* O tempora ! O mores ! Here is my friend X., that in any other times would have been a man of incorruptible virtue ; and yet, in our unprincipled age, he is content to barter the interests of truth and the "majesty of plain-dealing" for a brilliant paradox, or (shall I say ?) for the glory of being reputed an accomplished disputant.

*X.* But, Phædrus, there could be little brilliancy in a paradox which in the way you understand it will be nothing better than a bold defiance of common sense. In fact, I should be ashamed to give the air of a paradox to so evident a truth as that which I am now urging, if I did not continually remind myself that—evident as it may appear—it yet escaped Adam Smith. This consideration, and the spectacle of so many writers since his day thrown out and at a fault precisely at this point of the chase, make it prudent to present it in as startling a shape as possible ; in order that, the attention being thoroughly aroused, the final assent may not be languid or easily forgotten. Suffer me, therefore, Phædrus, in a Socratic way, to extort an assent from your own arguments—allow me to drive you into an absurdity.

*Phæd.* With all my heart. If our father Adam is wrong, I am sure it would be presumptuous in me to be right ; so drive me as fast as possible.

*X.* You say that A, by doubling its own value, shall command a double quantity of B. Where, by A, you do not mean some one thing in particular, but generally any assignable thing whatever. Now, B is some assignable thing. Whatever, therefore, is true of A will be true of B?

*Phæd.* It will.

*X.* It will be true therefore of B that, by doubling its own value, it will command a double quantity of A?

*Phæd.* I cannot deny it.

*X.* Let A be your carriage; and let B stand for six hundred thousands of besoms,—which suppose to express the value of your carriage in that article in this present moment. Five years hence, no matter why, carriages have doubled in value; on which supposition you affirm that in exchange for your barouche you will be entitled to receive no less than twelve hundred thousands of besoms.

*Phæd.* I do; and a precious bargain I shall have of it, like Moses with his gross of shagreen spectacles. But sweep on, if you please; brush me into absurdity.

*X.* I will. Because barouches have altered in value, that is no reason why besoms should *not* have altered?

*Phæd.* Certainly; no reason in the world.

*X.* Let them have altered; for instance, at the end of the five years, let them have been doubled in value. Now, because your assertion is this—simply by doubling in value B shall command a double quantity of A—it follows inevitably, Phædrus, that besoms, having doubled their value in five years, will at the end of that time command a double quantity of barouches. The supposition is that six hundred thousand at present command one barouche; in five years, therefore, six hundred thousand will command two barouches?

*Phæd.* They will.

*X.* Yet at the very same time it has already appeared from your argument that twelve hundred thousand will command only one barouche; *i.e.* a barouche will at one and the same time be worth twelve hundred thousand besoms, and worth only 1-4th part of that quantity. Is this an absurdity, Phædrus?

*Phæd.* It seems such.

*X.* And therefore the argument from which it flows, I presume, is false?

*Phæd.* Scavenger of bad logic! I confess that it looks so.

*Phil.* You confess? So do not I. You die "soft,"

Phædrus; give me the cudgels, and I'll die "game" at least. The flaw in your argument, X., is this: you summoned Phædrus to invert his proposition, and then you extorted an absurdity from this inversion. But that absurdity follows only from the particular form of expression into which you threw the original proposition. I will express the same proposition in other terms, unexceptionable terms, which shall evade the absurdity. Observe. A and B are at this time equal in value; that is, they now exchange quantity for quantity. Or, if you prefer your own case, I say that one barouche exchanges for six hundred thousand besoms. I choose, however, to express this proposition thus: A (one barouche) and B (six hundred thousand besoms) are severally equal in value to C. When, therefore, A doubles its value, I say that it shall command a double quantity of C. Now, mark how I will express the inverted case. When B doubles its value, I say that it shall command a double quantity of C. But these two cases are very reconcilable with each other. A may command a double quantity of C at the same time that B commands a double quantity of C, without involving any absurdity at all. And, if so, the disputed doctrine is established—that a double value implies a doubled command of quantity; and, reciprocally, that from a doubled command of quantity we may infer a double value.

*X.* A and B, you say, may simultaneously command a double quantity of C, in consequence of doubling their value; and this they may do without absurdity. But how shall I know *that*, until I know what you cloak under the symbol of C? For, if the same thing shall have happened to C which my argument assumes to have happened to B (viz. that its value has altered), then the same demonstration will hold; and the very same absurdity will follow any attempt to infer the quantity from the value, or the value from the quantity.

*Phil.* Yes, but I have provided against *that*; for by C I mean any assignable thing which has *not* altered its own value. I assume C to be stationary in value.

*X.* In that case, Philebus, it is undoubtedly true that no absurdity follows from the inversion of the proposition as it is expressed by you. But then the short answer which I return is this: your thesis avoids the absurdity by avoiding the entire question in dispute. Your thesis is not only not the same as that which we are now discussing; not only different in essence from the thesis which is *now* disputed; but moreover it affirms only what *never* was disputed by any man. No man has ever denied that A by doubling its own value will command a double quantity of all things which have been stationary in value. Of things in that predicament it is self-evident that A will command a double quantity. But the question is whether universally, from doubling its value, A will command a double quantity; and, inversely, whether universally, from the command of a double quantity, it is lawful to infer a double value. This is asserted by Adam Smith, and is essential to his distinction of nominal and real value; this is peremptorily denied by us. We offer to produce cases in which from double value it shall not be lawful to infer double quantity. We offer to produce cases in which from double quantity it shall *not* be lawful to infer double value. And thence we argue that, *until* the value is discovered in some other way, it will be impossible to discover whether it be high or low from any consideration of the quantity commanded; and, again, with respect to the quantity commanded, that, *until* known in some other way, it shall never be known from any consideration of the value commanding. This is what we say. Now, your "C" contradicts the conditions—"*until* the value is discovered in some other way, it shall never be learned from the quantity commanded." But in your "C" the value is already discovered; for you assume it; you postulate that C is stationary in value; hence it is easy indeed to infer that, because A commands double quantity of "C," it shall therefore be of double value; but this inference is not obtained from the single consideration of double quantity, but from *that* combined with the assumption of unaltered value in C, without which assumption you shall never obtain that inference.

*Phæd.* The matter is clear beyond what I require; yet, X., for the satisfaction of my "game" friend Philebus, give us a proof or two *ex abundanti*, by applying what you have said to cases in Adam Smith or others.

*X.* In general it is clear that, if the value of A increases in a duplicate ratio, yet if the value of B increases in a triplicate ratio, so far from commanding a greater quantity of B, A shall command a smaller quantity; and, if A continually goes on squaring its former value, yet, if B continually goes on cubing its former value, then, though A will continually augment in value, yet the quantity which it will command of B shall be continually less, until at length it shall become practically equal to nothing.[1] Hence, therefore, I deduce,

1. That, when I am told by Adam Smith that the money which I can obtain for my hat expresses only its *nominal* value, but that the labour which I can obtain for it expresses its *real* value—I reply that the quantity of labour is no more any expression of the real value than the quantity of money; both are equally fallacious expressions, because equally equivocal. My hat, it is true, now buys me $x$ quantity of labour—and some years ago it bought $\frac{x}{2}$ quantity of labour. But this no more proves that my hat has advanced in real value according to that proportion than a double *money* price will prove it. For how will Adam Smith reply to him who urges the double money value as an argument of a double real value? He will say—No; non valet consequentia. Your proof is equivocal; for a double quantity of money will as inevitably arise from the sinking of money as from the rising of hats. And, supposing money to have sunk to 1-4th of its former value, in that case a double money value—so far from proving hats to have risen in real value—will prove that hats have absolutely fallen in real value by one-half; and they will be seen to have done so by comparison with all things which have remained stationary; otherwise they would obtain not double merely, but four times the quantity of money price. This is what Adam Smith will reply in effect. Now, the very same objection I make to labour as

[1] The reader may imagine that there is one exception to this case—viz. if the values of A and B were assumed at starting to be =1; because in that case the squares, cubes, and all other powers alike, would be =1; and thus, under any apparent alteration, the real relations of A and B would always remain the same. But this is an impossible and unmeaning case in Political Economy, as might easily be shown.

any test of real value. My hat now obtains $x$ labour; formerly it obtained only one-half of $x$. Be it so; but the whole real change may be in the labour; labour may now be at one-half its former value; in which case my hat obtains the same real price,—double the quantity of labour being now required to express the same value. Nay, if labour has fallen to 1-10th of its former value, so far from being proved to have risen 100 per cent in real value by now purchasing double quantity of labour, my hat is proved to have fallen to 1-5th of its former value; else, instead of buying me only $x$ labour, which is but the double of its former value $(\frac{x}{2})$, it would buy me $5x$, or 10 times its former value.

*Phil.* Your objection, then, to the labour price, as any better expression of the *real* value than the money price, would be that it is an equivocal expression, leaving it doubtful on which side of the equation the disturbance has taken place, or whether on both sides. In which objection, as against others, you may be right; but you must not urge this against Adam Smith; because on his theory the expression is not equivocal; the disturbance can be only on one side of the equation—viz., in your hat. For, as to the other side (the labour), *that* is secured from all disturbance by his doctrine that labour is always of the same value. When, therefore, your hat will purchase $x$ quantity of labour instead of half $x$, the inference is irresistible that your hat has doubled its value. There lies no appeal from this: it cannot be evaded by alleging that the labour may have fallen; for the labour cannot fall.

*X.* On the Smithian theory it cannot; and therefore it is that I make a great distinction between the error of Adam Smith and of other later writers. He, though wrong, was consistent. That the value of labour is invariable is a principle so utterly untenable that many times Adam Smith abandoned it himself implicitly, though not explicitly. The demonstration of its variable value indeed follows naturally from the laws which govern wages; and therefore, I will not here anticipate it. Meantime, having once adopted that theory of the unalterable value of labour, Adam Smith was in the right to make it the expression of real value. But this is not done with the same consistency by Mr. Malthus at the very time when he denies the possibility of any invariable value.

*Phil.* How so? Mr. Malthus asserts that there is one article of invariable value; what is more, this article is labour—the very same as that formerly alleged for such by Adam Smith; and he has written a book to prove it.

*X.* True, Philebus, he has done so; and he *now* holds that labour is invariable, supposing that his opinions have not altered within the last twelve months. But he was so far from holding this in 1820 (at which time it was that he chiefly insisted on the distinction between nominal and real value) that he was not content with the true arguments against the possibility of an invariable value, but made use of one, as I shall soon show you, which involves what the metaphysicians call a *non-ens*—or an idea which includes contradictory and self-destroying conditions. Omitting, however, the inconsistency in the idea of *real* value, as conceived by Mr. Malthus, there is this additional error engrafted upon the Smithian definition, that it is extended to "the necessaries and conveniences of life" in general, and no longer confined exclusively to labour. I shall therefore, as another case for illustrating and applying the result of our dispute,

2. Cite a passage from Mr. Malthus's "Political Economy" (p. 59):—"If we are told that the wages of day-labour in a "particular country are, at the present time, fourpence a-day, "or that the revenue of a particular sovereign, 700 or 800 "years ago, was £400,000 a-year, these statements of "nominal value convey no sort of information respecting the "condition of the lower class of people in the one case, or "the resources of the sovereign in the other. Without further "knowledge on the subject we should be quite at a loss to "say whether the labourers in the country mentioned were "starving or living in great plenty; whether the king in "question might be considered as having a very inadequate "revenue, or whether the sum mentioned was so great as "to be incredible.[1] It is quite obvious that in cases of this

[1] "Hume very reasonably doubts the possibility of William the Conqueror's revenue being £400,000 a-year, as represented by an ancient historian, and adopted by subsequent writers."—*Note of Mr. Malthus.*

" kind,—and they are of constant recurrence,—the value of " wages, incomes, or commodities estimated in the precious " metals will be of little use to us alone. What we want " further is some estimate of a kind which may be de- " nominated real value in exchange, implying the quantity " of the necessaries and conveniences of life which those wages, " incomes, or commodities will enable the possessor of them " to command."

In this passage, over and above the radical error about real value, there is also apparent that confusion which has misled so many writers between *value* and *wealth*,—a confusion which Mr. Ricardo first detected and cleared up. That we shall not be able to determine from the mere money wages whether the labourers were "starving or living in great plenty" is certain; and that we *shall* be able to determine this as soon as we know the quantity of necessaries, &c., which those wages commanded, is equally certain; for, in fact, the one knowledge is identical with the other, and but another way of expressing it; we must, of course, learn that the labourer lived in plenty, if we should learn that his wages give him a great deal of bread, milk, venison, salt, honey, &c. And, as there could never have been any doubt whether we should learn *this* from what Mr. Malthus terms the real value, and that we should *not* learn it from what he terms the money value, Mr. Malthus may be assured that there never can have been any dispute raised on that point. The true dispute is whether, after having learned that the labourer lived in American plenty, we shall have at all approximated to the appreciation of his wages as to real value: this is the question; and it is plain that we shall not. What matters it that his wages gave him a great deal of corn, until we know whether corn bore a high or a low value? A great deal of corn at a high value implies wages of a high value; but a great deal of corn at a low value is very consistent with wages at a low value. Money wages, it is said, leave us quite in the dark as to real value. Doubtless; nor are we at all the less in the dark for knowing the corn wages, the milk wages, the grouse wages, &c. *Given* the value of corn, *given* the value of milk, *given* the value of grouse, we shall know whether a great quantity of those articles implies a high value, or is compatible with a low value in the wages which commanded them ; but, *until* that is given, it has been already shown that the quantity alone is an equivocal test—being equally capable of co-existing with high wages or low wages.

*Phil.* Why, then, it passes my comprehension to understand what test remains of real value, if neither money price nor commodity price expresses it. When are wages, for example, at a high real value ?

*X.* Wages are at a high real value when it requires much labour to produce wages, and at a low real value when it requires little labour to produce wages ; and it is perfectly consistent with the high real value that the labourer should be almost starving, and perfectly consistent with the low real value that the labourer should be living in great ease and comfort.

*Phil.* Well, this may be true ; but you must allow that it sounds extravagant.

*X.* Doubtless it sounds extravagant to him who persists in slipping under his notion of value another and heterogeneous notion—viz. that of wealth. But, let it sound as it may, all the absurdities (which are neither few nor slight) are on the other side. These will discover themselves as we advance. Meantime, I presume that, in your use, and in everybody's use, of the word value, a high value ought to purchase a high value, and that it will be very absurd if it should not. But, as to purchasing a great quantity, that condition is surely not included in any man's idea of value.

*Phil.* No, certainly : because A is of high value, it does not follow that it must purchase a great quantity; that must be as various as the nature of the thing with which it is compared. But, having once assumed any certain thing, as B, it does seem to follow that, however small a quantity A may purchase of this (which I admit may be very small, though the value of A should be very great), yet it does seem to follow, from everybody's notion of value, that this quantity of B, however small at first, must continually increase, if the value of A be supposed continually to increase.

*X.* This may "seem" to follow ; but it has been shown

that it does not follow; for, if A continually double its value, yet let B continually triple or quadruple its value and the quantity of B will be so far from increasing that it will finally become evanescent. In short, once for all, the formula is this: let A continually increase in value, and it shall purchase continually more and more in quantity—than what? More than it did? By no means; but more than it would have done but for that increase in value. A has doubled its value. Does it *therefore* purchase more than it did before of B? No: perhaps it purchases much less; suppose only 1-4th part as much of B as it did before; but still the doubling of A's value has had its full effect; for B, it may happen, has increased in value eight-fold; and, but for the doubling of A, it would, instead of 1-4th, have bought only 1-8th of the former quantity. A therefore, by doubling in value, has bought not double in quantity of what it bought before, but double in quantity of what it would else have bought.

The remainder of this dialogue related to the distinction between "relative" value, as it is termed, and "absolute" value; clearing up the true use of that distinction. But, this being already too long, the amount of it will be given hereafter—with a specimen of the errors which have arisen from the abuse of this distinction.

## DIALOGUE THE FIFTH

### ON THE IMMEDIATE USES OF THE NEW THEORY OF VALUE

*X.* The great law which governs exchangeable value has now been stated and argued. Next, it seems, we must ask —What are its uses? This is a question which you or I should not be likely to ask; for with what colour of propriety could a doubt be raised about the use of any truth in any science? still less, about the use of a leading truth? least of all, about the use of *the* leading truth? Nevertheless, such a doubt *has* been raised by Mr. Malthus.

*Phæd.* On what ground or pretence?

*X.* Under a strange misconception of Mr. Ricardo's meaning. Mr. Malthus has written a great deal, as you may have heard, against Mr. Ricardo's principle of value: his purpose is to prove that it is a false principle; independently of which, he contends that, even if it were a true principle, it would be of little use.[1]

*Phæd.* Little use? in relation to what?

*X.* Ay, *there* lies the inexplicable mistake: of little use as a *measure* of value. Now, this is a mistake for which there can be no sort of apology; for it supposes Mr. Ricardo to have brought forward his principle of value as a standard or measure of value; whereas Mr. Ricardo has repeatedly informed his reader that he utterly rejects the possibility of any such measure. Thus (at p. 10, edit. 2d), after laying down the *conditio sine qua non* under which any commodity could preserve an unvarying value, he goes on to say—"Of such a commodity we have no knowledge, and consequently are unable to fix on any standard of value." And again (at p. 343 of the same edition), after exposing at some length the circumstances which disqualify "any commodity or all commodities together" from performing the office of a standard of value, he again states the indispensable condition which must be realised in that commodity which should pretend to such an office; and again he adds immediately—"Of such a commodity we have no knowledge." But what leaves this mistake still more without excuse is that in the third edition of his book Mr. Ricardo has added an express section (the sixth) to his chapter on value, having for its direct object to expose the impossibility of any true measure of value. Setting aside, indeed, these explicit declarations, a few words will suffice to show that Mr. Ricardo could not have consistently believed in any standard or measure of value. What does a standard mean?

*Phæd.* A standard is that which stands still whilst other things move, and by this means serves to indicate or measure the degree in which those other things have advanced or receded.

*X.* Doubtless; and a standard of value must itself stand

[1] *Vide* the footnote to p. 54 of "The Measure of Value." [*i.e.* the publication referred to *ante*, p. 35.—M.]

still or be stationary in value. But nothing could possibly be stationary in value upon Mr. Ricardo's theory unless it were always produced by the same quantity of labour; since any alteration in the quantity of the producing labour must immediately affect the value of the product. Now, what is there which can always be obtained by the same quantity of labour? Raw materials (for reasons which will appear when we consider Rent) are constantly tending to grow dearer[1] by requiring more labour for their production; manufactures, from the changes in machinery, which are always progressive and never retrograde, are constantly tending to grow cheaper by requiring less; consequently, there is nothing which, upon Mr. Ricardo's theory, can long continue stationary in value. If, therefore, he had proposed any measure of value, he must have forgotten his own principle of value.

*Phil.* But allow me to ask, if that principle is not proposed as a measure of value, in what character *is* it proposed?

*X.* Surely, Philebus, as the *ground* of value; whereas a measure of value is no more than a *criterion* or test of value. The last is simply a *principium cognoscendi*, whereas the other is a *principium essendi.*

*Phil.* But wherein lies the difference?

*X.* Is it possible that you can ask such a question? A thermometer measures the temperature of the air; that is, it furnishes a criterion for ascertaining its varying degrees

[1] "*Constantly tending to grow dearer*":—To the novice in Political Economy it will infallibly suggest itself that the direct contrary is the truth; since, even in rural industry, though more tardily improving its processes than manufacturing industry, the tendency is always in that direction: agriculture, as an art benefiting by experience, has never yet been absolutely regressive, though not progressive by such striking leaps or sudden discoveries as manufacturing art. But, for all *that*, it still remains true, as a general principle, that raw materials won from the soil are constantly tending to grow dearer, whilst these same materials as worked up for use by manufacturing skill are constantly travelling upon an opposite path. The reason is that in the case of manufacturing improvements no conquest made is ever lost. The course is never retrogressive towards the worst machinery, or towards the more circuitous process; once resigned, the inferior method is resigned for ever. But in the industry applied to the soil this is otherwise. Doubtless the farmer does not, with his eyes open, return to methods which have experi-

of heat; but you cannot even imagine that a thermometer furnishes any *ground* of this heat. I wish to know whether a day's labour at the time of the English Revolution bore the same value as a hundred years after at the time of the French Revolution; and, if not the same value, whether a higher or a lower. For this purpose, if I believe that there is any commodity which is immutable in value, I shall naturally compare a day's labour with that commodity at each period. Some, for instance, have imagined that corn is of invariable value; and, supposing one to adopt so false a notion, we should merely have to inquire what quantity of corn a day's labour would exchange for at each period, and we should then have determined the relations of value between labour at the two periods. In this case, I should have used corn as the *measure* of the value of labour; but I could not rationally mean to say that corn was the *ground* of the value of labour; and, if I said that I made use of corn to *determine* the value of labour, I should employ the word "determine" in the same sense as when I say that the thermometer determines the heat—viz. that it ascertains it, or determines it to my knowledge (as a *principium cognoscendi*). But, when Mr. Ricardo says that the quantity of labour employed on A determines the value of A, he must of course be understood to mean that it *causes* A to be of this value, that it is the *ground* of its value, the *principium essendi* of its value; just as when, being asked what determines a

mentally been shown to be inferior, unless, indeed, where want of capital may have forced him to do so; but, as population expands, he is continually forced into descending upon inferior soils; and the product of these inferior soils it is which *gives the ruling price for the whole aggregate of products.* Say that soils Nos. 1, 2, 3, 4, had been hitherto sufficient for a nation, where the figures express the regular graduation downwards in point of fertility; then, when No. 5 is called for (which, producing less by the supposition, costs therefore more upon any given quantity), the price upon this last No. 5 regulates the price upon all the five soils. And thus it happens that, whilst always progressive, rural industry is nevertheless always travelling towards an increased cost. The product of Nos. 1, 2, 3, 4, is continually tending to be cheaper; but, when the cost of No. 5 (and so on for ever as to the fresh soils required to meet a growing population) is combined with that of the superior soils, the quotient from the entire dividend 1, 2, 3, 4, 5, is always tending gradually to a higher expression. [This footnote is an addition in 1854.—M.]

stone to fall downwards rather than upwards, I answer that it is the earth's attraction, or the principle of gravitation, meaning that this principle *causes* it to fall downwards; and if, in this case, I say that gravitation "*determines*" its course downwards, I no longer use that word in the sense of *ascertain*; I do not mean that gravitation *ascertains* it to have descended, but that gravitation has *causatively* impressed that direction on its course; in other words, I make gravitation the *principium essendi* of its descent.

*Phæd.* I understand your distinction; and in which sense do you say that Mr. Malthus has used the term Measure of Value—in the sense of a ground, or of a criterion?

*X.* In both senses; he talks of it as "*accounting for*" the value of A, in which case it means a ground of value; and as "*estimating*" the value of A, in which case it means a criterion of value. I mention these expressions as instances: but the truth is that, throughout his essay entitled "The Measure of Value Stated and Illustrated," and throughout his "Political Economy" (but especially in the second chapter, entitled "The Nature and Measures of Value"), he uniformly confounds the two ideas of a ground and a criterion of value under a much greater variety of expressions than I have time to enumerate.

*Phil.* But, admitting that Mr. Malthus has proceeded on the misconception you state, what is the specific injury which has thence resulted to Mr. Ricardo?

*X.* I am speaking at present of the uses to be derived from Mr. Ricardo's principle of value. Now, if it had been proposed as a measure of value, we might justly demand that it should be "ready and easy of application," to adopt the words of Mr. Malthus ("Measure of Value," p. 54); but it is manifestly not so; for the quantity of labour employed in producing A "could not in many cases" (as Mr. Malthus truly objects) "be ascertained without considerable difficulty"; in most cases, indeed, it could not be ascertained at all. A measure of value, however, which cannot be practically applied is worthless; as a measure of value, therefore, Mr. Ricardo's law of value is worthless; and, if it had been offered as such by its author, the blame would have settled on Mr. Ricardo; as it is, it settles on Mr. Malthus, who has grounded an imaginary triumph on his own gross misconception. For Mr. Ricardo never dreamed of offering a standard or fixed measure of value, or of tolerating any pretended measure of that sort, by whomsoever offered.

Thus much I have said for the sake of showing what is *not* the use of Mr. Ricardo's principle in the design of its author,—in order that he may be no longer exposed to the false criticism of those who are looking for what is not to be found, nor ought to be found,[1] in his work. On quitting this part of the subject, I shall just observe that Mr. Malthus, in common with many others, attaches a most unreasonable importance to the discovery of a measure of value. I challenge any man to show that the great interests of Political Economy have at all suffered for want of such a measure, — which at best would end in answering a few questions of unprofitable curiosity; whilst, on the other hand, without a knowledge of the *ground* on which value depends, or without some approximation to it, Political Economy could not exist at all, except as a heap of baseless opinions.

*Phæd.* Now then, having cleared away the imaginary uses of Mr. Ricardo's principle, let us hear something of its real uses.

*X.* The most important of these I expressed in the last words I uttered: *That* without which a science cannot exist is commensurate in use with the science itself; being the fundamental law, it will testify its own importance in the changes which it will impress on all the derivative laws. For the main use of Mr. Ricardo's principle I refer you therefore to all Political Economy. Meantime I will notice here the immediate services which it has rendered by liberat-

[1] At p. 36 of "The Measure of Value" (in the footnote) this misconception as to Mr. Ricardo appears in a still grosser shape; for not only does Mr. Malthus speak of a "concession" (as he calls it) of Mr. Ricardo as being "quite fatal" to the notion of a standard of value—as though it were an object with Mr. Ricardo to establish such a standard; but this standard, moreover, is now represented as being gold. And what objection does Mr. Malthus make to gold as a standard? The identical objection which Mr. Ricardo had himself insisted on in that very page of his third edition to which Mr. Malthus refers.

ing the student from those perplexities which previously embarrassed him on his first introduction to the science. I mention two cases by way of specimen.

1. When it was asked by the student what determined the value of all commodities, it was answered that this value was chiefly determined by wages. When again it was asked what determined wages, it was recollected that wages must generally be adjusted to the value of the commodities upon which they were spent; and the answer was in effect that wages were determined by the value of commodities. And thus the mind was entangled in this inextricable circle—that the price of commodities was determined by wages, and wages determined by the price of commodities. From this gross Διαλληλος (as the logicians call it) or see-saw we are now liberated; for the first step, as we are now aware, is false: the value of commodities is *not* determined by wages; since wages express the value of labour, and it has been demonstrated that not the *value* but the *quantity* of labour determines the value of its products.

2. A second case in which Mr. Ricardo's law has introduced a simplicity into the science which had in vain been sought for before, is this:—All former economists, in laying down the component parts of price, had fancied it impossible to get rid of what is termed *the raw material* as one of its elements. This impossibility was generally taken for granted: but an economist of our times, the late Mr. Francis Horner, had (in the "Edinburgh Review") expressly set himself to prove it. "It is not true," said Mr. Horner, "that the "thing purchased in every bargain is merely so much labour: "the value of the raw material can neither be rejected as "nothing, nor estimated as a constant quantity."[1] Now, this refractory element is at once, and in the simplest way possible, exterminated by Mr. Ricardo's reformed law of value. Upon the old system, if I had resolved the value of my hat into wages and profits, I should immediately have been admonished that I had forgotten one of the elements:

[1] Francis Horner, born 1778, died 1817. He was one of the chief early contributors to the *Edinburgh Review*, along with Jeffrey, Sydney Smith, and Brougham.

"wages, profits, and raw material, you mean," it would have said. Raw material! Well, but on what separate principle can this raw material be valued? or on what other principle than that on which the hat itself was valued? Like any other product of labour, its value is determined by the quantity of labour employed in obtaining it; and the amount of this product is divided between wages and profits as in any case of a manufactured commodity. The raw material of the hat suppose to be beaver: if, then, in order to take the quantity of beavers which are necessary to furnish materials for a thousand hats, four men have been employed for twenty-five days, then it appears that the raw material of a thousand hats has cost a hundred days' labour,—which will be of the same value in exchange as the product of a hundred days' labour (previously equated and discounted as to its *quality*) in any other direction; as, for example, if a hundred days' labour would produce two thousand pairs of stockings of a certain quality, then it follows that the raw material of my hat is worth two pairs of such stockings. And thus it turns out that an element of value which Mr. Horner and thousands of others have supposed to be of a distinct nature, and to resist all further analysis, gives way before Mr. Ricardo's law, and is eliminated: an admirable simplification, which is equal in merit and use to any of the rules which have been devised from time to time for the resolution of algebraic equations.

Here, then, in a hasty shape, I have offered two specimens of the uses which arise from a better law of value,—again reminding you, however, that the main use must lie in the effect which it will impress on all the other laws of Political Economy. And, reverting for one moment, before we part, to the difficulty of Philebus about the difference between this principle as a *principium cognoscendi* or measure and a *principium essendi* or determining ground, let me desire you to consider these two *essential* marks of distinction: 1, that by all respectable economists any true measure of value has been doubted or denied as a possibility, but no man can doubt the existence of a ground of value; 2, that a measure is posterior to the value; for, before a value can be measured or estimated, it must exist, but a ground of value must be antecedent to the value, like any other cause to its effect.

## DIALOGUE THE SIXTH

### ON THE OBJECTIONS TO THE NEW LAW OF VALUE

*X.* The two most eminent economists[1] who have opposed the Ricardian doctrines are Mr. Malthus and Colonel Torrens. In the spring of 1820 Mr. Malthus published his "Principles of Political Economy," much of which was an attack upon Mr. Ricardo, and the entire second chapter of 83 pages, "On the Nature and Measures of Value," was one continued attempt to overthrow Mr. Ricardo's theory of value. Three years afterwards he published a second attack on the same theory in a distinct essay of 81 pages, entitled "The Measure of Value Stated and Illustrated." In this latter work, amongst other arguments, he has relied upon one in particular, which he has chosen to exhibit in the form of a table. As it is of the last importance to Political Economy that this question should be settled, I will shrink from nothing that wears the semblance of an argument; and I will now examine this table, and will show that the whole of the inferences contained in the seventh, eighth, and ninth columns are founded on a gross blunder in the fifth and sixth; every number in which columns is falsely assigned.

### MR. MALTHUS'S TABLE ILLUSTRATING THE INVARIABLE VALUE OF LABOUR AND ITS RESULTS

(From p. 38 of the "Measure of Value Stated and Illustrated." London: 1823.)

N.B.—The sole change which has been made in this reprint of the original Table is the assigning of names (*Alpha*, *Beta*, *&c.*) to the several cases for the purpose of easier reference and distinction.

---

[1] The reader must continue to remember that this paper was written in 1824.

| CASE. | 1 | 2 | 3 | 4 | 5 | 6 | 7 | 8 | 9 |
|---|---|---|---|---|---|---|---|---|---|
| | Quarters of Corn produced by Ten Men. | Yearly Corn Wages to each Labourer. | Yearly Corn Wages of the whole Ten Men. | Rate of Profits under the foregoing Circumstances. | Quantity of Labour required to produce the Wages of Ten Men. | Quantity of Profits on the Advances of Labour. | Invariable Value of the Wages of a given Number of Men. | Value of 100 Quarters of Corn under the varying Circumstances supposed. | Value of the Product of the Labour of Ten Men under the Circumstances supposed. |
| | | Qrs. | Qrs. | Per Ct. | | | | | |
| Alpha . | 150 | 12 | 120 | 25 | 8 | 2 | 10 | 8.33 | 12.5 |
| Beta . | 150 | 13 | 130 | 15.38 | 8.66 | 1.34 | 10 | 7.7 | 11.53 |
| Gamma | 150 | 10 | 100 | 50 | 6.6 | 3.4 | 10 | 10 | 15 |
| Delta . | 140 | 12 | 120 | 16.66 | 8.6 | 1.4 | 10 | 7.14[1] | 11.6 |
| Epsilon | 140 | 11 | 110 | 27.2 | 7.85 | 2.15 | 10 | 9.09 | 12.7 |
| Zeta . | 130 | 12 | 120 | 8.3 | 9.23 | 0.77 | 10 | 8.33 | 10.8 |
| Eta . . | 130 | 10 | 100 | 30 | 7.7 | 2.3 | 10 | 10 | 13 |
| Theta . | 120 | 11 | 110 | 9 | 9.17 | 0.83 | 10 | 9.09 | 10.9 |
| Iota . | 120 | 10 | 100 | 20 | 8.33 | 1.67 | 10 | 10 | 12 |
| Kappa . | 110 | 10 | 100 | 10 | 9.09 | 0.91 | 10 | 10 | 11 |
| Lambda | 110 | 9 | 90 | 22.2 | 8.18 | 1.82 | 10 | 11.1 | 12.2 |
| My . . | 100 | 9 | 90 | 11.1 | 9 | 1 | 10 | 11.1 | 11.1 |
| Ny . . | 100 | 8 | 80 | 25 | 8 | 2 | 10 | 12.5 | 12.5 |
| Xi . . | 90 | 8 | 80 | 12.5 | 8.88 | 1.12 | 10 | 12.5 | 11.25 |

[1] This is an oversight on the part of Mr. Malthus, and not an error of the press; for 7.14 would be the value of the 100 quarters on the supposition that the entire product of the ten men (viz. 140 quarters) went to wages; but, the wages in this case (Delta) being 120 quarters, the true value on the principle of this table is manifestly 8.33.

## SECTION I

*Phæd.* Now, X., you know that I abhor arithmetical calculations; besides which, I have no faith in any propositions of a political economist which he cannot make out readily without all this elaborate machinery of tables and figures. Under these circumstances, I put it to you, as a man of feeling, whether you ought to inflict upon me this alarming pile of computations; which, by your gloomy countenance, I see that you are meditating.

*X.* Stop, recollect yourself: not I it is, remember, that impose this elaborate "table" upon you, but Mr. Malthus. The yoke is his. I am the man sent by Providence to lighten this yoke. Surrender yourself, therefore, to my guidance, Phædrus, and I will lead you over the hill by so easy a road that you shall never know you have been climbing. You see that there are nine columns; *that*, I suppose, does not pass your skill in arithmetic. Now, then, to simplify the matter, begin by dismissing from your attention every column but the first and the last; fancy all the rest obliterated.

*Phæd.* Most willingly; it is a heavenly fancy.

*X.* Next look into the first column, and tell me what you see there.

*Phæd.* I see "lots" of 150s and 140s, and other ill-looking people of the same description.

*X.* Well, these numbers express the products of the same labour on land of different qualities. The quantity of labour is assumed to be always the same—viz. the labour of ten men for a year (or one man for ten years, or twenty men for half a-year, &c.) The producing labour, I say, is always the same; but the product is constantly varying. Thus, in the case Alpha the product is one hundred and fifty quarters; in the cases Delta and Epsilon, when cultivation has been compelled by increasing population to descend upon inferior land, the product of equal labour is no more than one hundred and forty quarters; and in the case Iota it has fallen to one hundred and twenty quarters. Now, upon Mr. Ricardo's principle of valuation, I demand to know what ought to be the price of these several products which vary so much in quantity.

*Phæd.* Why, since they are all the products of the same quantity of labour, they ought all to sell for the same price.

*X.* Doubtless; not, however, of necessity for the same money price, since money may itself have varied, in which case the same money price would be really a very different price; but for the same price in all things which have *not* varied in value. The Xi product, therefore, which is only ninety quarters, will fetch the same real price as the Alpha or Gamma products, which are one hundred and fifty. But, by the way, in saying this, let me caution you against making the false inference that corn is at the same price in the case Xi as in the case Alpha or Gamma; for the inference is the very opposite; since, if ninety quarters cost as much as one hundred and fifty, then each individual quarter of the ninety costs a great deal more. Thus, suppose that the Alpha product sold at £4 a-quarter, the price of the whole would be £600. £600, therefore, must be the price of Xi, or the ninety quarters; but *that* is £6 : 13 : 4 a-quarter. This ought to be a needless caution; yet I have known economists of great name stand much in need of it.

*Phæd.* I am sure *I* stand in need of it, and of all sort of assistance, for I am "ill at these numbers." But let us go on; what you require my assent to, I understand to be this: that all the different quantities of corn expressed in the first column will be of the same value, because they are all alike the product of ten men's labour. To this I *do* assent; and what next? Does anybody deny it?

*X.* Yes,—Mr. Malthus. He asserts that the value will *not* be always the same; and the purpose of the ninth column is to assign the true values; which, by looking into that column, you may perceive to be constantly varying: the value of Alpha, for instance, is twelve and 5-10ths; the value of Epsilon is twelve and 7-10ths; of Iota, twelve; and of Xi, eleven and 25-100ths.

*Phæd.* But of what? Twelve and 5-10ths of what?

*X.* Of anything which, though variable, has in fact happened to be stationary in value; or, if you choose, of anything which is not variable in value.

*Phæd.* Not variable! But there is no such thing.

*X.* No! Mr. Malthus, however, says there is; labour, he asserts, is of unalterable value.

*Phæd.* What! does he mean to say then that the labourer always obtains the same wages?

*X.* Yes, the same real wages; all differences being only apparently in the wages, but really in the commodity in which the wages are paid. Let that commodity be wheat; then, if the labourer receives ten quarters of wheat in 1800, and nine in 1820, that would imply only that wheat was about 11 per cent dearer in the latter year. Or let money be that commodity; then, if the labourer receives this century 2s., and next century 3s., this simply argues that money has fallen in value by 50 per cent.

*Phœd.* Why, so it may; and the whole difference in wages may have arisen in that way, and be only apparent. But then it may also have arisen from a change in the *real* value of wages; that is, on the Ricardian principle, in the quantity of labour necessary to produce wages. And this latter must have been the nature of the change, if Alpha, Iota, Xi, &c., should be found to purchase more labour; in which case Mr. Ricardo's doctrine is not disturbed; for he will say that Iota in 1700 exchanges for 12, and Kappa in 1800 for 11, not because Kappa has fallen in that proportion (for Kappa, being the product of the same labour as Iota, *cannot* fall below the value of Iota), but because the commodity for which they are exchanged has risen in that proportion.

*X.* He will; but Mr. Malthus attempts to bar that answer in this case, by alleging that it is impossible for the commodity in question (viz. labour) to rise or to fall in that or in any other proportion. If then the change cannot be in the labour, it must be in Alpha, Beta, &c.; in which case Mr. Ricardo will be overthrown; for they are the products of the same quantity of labour, and yet have not retained the same value.

*Phœd.* But, to bar Mr. Ricardo's answer, Mr. Malthus must not allege this merely; he must prove it.

*X.* To be sure; and the first seven columns of this table are designed to prove it. Now then we have done with the ninth column, and also with the eighth; for they are both mere corollaries from all the rest, and linked together under the plain rule of three. Dismiss these altogether; and we will now come to the argument.

## SECTION II

The table is now reduced to seven columns, and the logic of it is this: the four first columns express the conditions under which the three following ones are deduced as consequences; and they are to be read thus, taking the case Alpha by way of example:—Suppose that (by *column one*) the land cultivated is of such a quality that ten labourers produce me one hundred and fifty quarters of corn; and that (by *column two*) each labourer receives for his own wages twelve quarters; in which case (by *column three*) the whole ten receive one hundred and twenty quarters, and thus (by *column four*) leave me for my profit thirty quarters out of all that they have produced,—*i.e.* 25 per cent. Under these conditions, I insist (says Mr. Malthus) that the wages of ten men, as stated in column three, let them be produced by little labour or much labour, shall never exceed or fall below one invariable value expressed in column seven; and, accordingly, by looking down that column, you will perceive one uniform valuation of 10. Upon this statement, it is manifest that the whole force of the logic turns upon the accuracy with which column three is valued in column seven. If that valuation be correct, then it follows that, under all changes in the quantity of labour which produces them, wages never alter in real value; in other words, the value of labour is invariable.

*Phæd.* But of course you deny that the valuation is correct?

*X.* I do, Phædrus: the valuation is wrong, even on Mr. Malthus's or any other man's principles, in every instance; the value is not truly assigned in a single case of the whole fourteen. For how does Mr. Malthus obtain this invariable value of ten? He resolves the value of the wages expressed in column three into two parts; one of which, under the name "*labour*," he assigns in column five; the other, under the name "*profits*," he assigns in column six; and column seven expresses the sum of these two parts; which are always kept equal to ten by always compensating each other's excesses and defects. Hence, Phædrus, you see that—as column seven simply expresses the sum of columns five and six—if those columns are right, column seven cannot be wrong. Consequently it is in columns five and six that we are to look for the root of the error; which is indeed a very gross one.

*Phil.* Why, now, for instance, take the case Alpha; and what is the error you detect in that?

*X.* Simply this—that in column five, instead of 8, the true value is 6.4, and in column six, instead of 2, the true value is 1.6 ; the sum of which values is not 10 but 8 ; and that is the figure which should have stood in column seven.

*Phil.* How so, X. ? In column five Mr. Malthus undertakes to assign the quantity of labour necessary (under the conditions of the particular case) to produce the wages expressed in column three, which in this case Alpha are one hundred and twenty quarters. Now, you cannot deny that he has assigned it truly ; for, when ten men produce one hundred and fifty (by column one)—*i.e.* each man fifteen—it must require eight to produce one hundred and twenty ; for one hundred and twenty is eight times fifteen. Six men and 4-10ths of a man, the number you would substitute. could produce only ninety-six quarters.

*X.* Very true, Philebus ; eight men are necessary to produce the one hundred and twenty quarters expressed in column three. And now answer me : what part of their own product will these eight producers deduct for their own wages ?

*Phil.* Why (by column two), each man's wages in this case are twelve quarters ; therefore the wages of the eight men will be ninety-six quarters.

*X.* And what quantity of labour will be necessary to produce these ninety-six quarters ?

*Phil.* Each man producing fifteen, it will require six men's labour, and 4-10ths of another man's labour.

*X.* Very well ; 6.4 of the eight are employed in producing the wages of the whole eight. Now tell me, Philebus, what more than their own wages do the whole eight produce ?

*Phil.* Why, as they produce in all one hundred and twenty quarters, and their own deduction is ninety-six, it is clear that they produce twenty-four quarters besides their own wages.

*X.* And to whom do these twenty-four quarters go ?

*Phil.* To their employer, for his profit.

*X.* Yes ; and it answers the condition expressed in column four ; for a profit of twenty-four quarters on ninety-six is exactly 25 per cent. But, to go on—you have acknowledged that the ninety-six quarters for wages would be produced by the labour of 6.4 men. Now, how much labour will be required to produce the remaining twenty-four quarters for profits ?

*Phil.* Because fifteen quarters require the labour of one man (by column one), twenty-four will require the labour of 1.6.

*X.* Right ; and thus, Philebus, you have acknowledged all I wish. The object of Mr. Malthus is to ascertain the cost in labour of producing ten men's wages (or one hundred and twenty quarters) under the conditions of this case Alpha. The cost resolves itself, even on Mr. Malthus's principles, into so much wages for the labourers, and so much profit to their employer. Now, you or I will undertake to furnish Mr. Malthus the one hundred and twenty quarters, not (as he says) at a cost of ten men's labour (for at that cost we could produce him one hundred and fifty quarters by column one), but at a cost of eight. For six men and 4-10ths will produce the whole wages of the eight producers ; and one man and 6-10ths will produce our profit of 25 per cent.

*Phœd.* The mistake, then, of Mr. Malthus, if I understand it, is egregious. In column five he estimates the labour necessary to produce the entire one hundred and twenty quarters—which, he says, is the labour of eight men; and so it is, if he means by labour what produces both wages and profits ; otherwise not. Of necessity, therefore, he has assigned the value both of wages and profits in column five. Yet in column six he gravely proceeds to estimate profits a second time.

*X.* Yes ; and, what is still worse, in estimating these profits a second time over, he estimates them on the whole one hundred and twenty ; *i.e.* he allows for a second profit of thirty quarters ; else it could not cost two men's labour (as by his valuation it does) ; for each man in the case Alpha produces fifteen quarters. Now, thirty quarters added to one hundred and twenty are one hundred and fifty. But this is the *product* of ten men, and not the *wages* of ten men ; which is the amount offered for valuation in column three, and which is all that column seven professes to have valued.

SECTION III

*Phæd.* I am satisfied, X. But Philebus seems perplexed. Make all clear, therefore, by demonstrating the same result in some other way. With your adroitness, it can cost you no trouble to treat us with a little display of dialectical skirmishing. Show us a specimen of manœuvring; enfilade him; take him in front and rear; and do it rapidly, and with a light-horseman's elegance.

*X.* If you wish for variations, it is easy to give them. In the first argument what I depended on was this—that the valuation was inaccurate. Now, then, *secondly*, suppose the valuation to be accurate, in this case we must still disallow it to Mr. Malthus; for in columns five and six he values by the quantity of producing labour; but that is the Ricardian principle of valuation, which is the very principle that he writes to overthrow.

*Phæd.* This may seem a good *quoad hominem* argument. Yet surely any man may use the principle of his antagonist in order to extort a particular result from it?

*X.* He may; but in that case will the result be true, or will it not be true?

*Phæd.* If he denies the principle, he is bound to think the result *not* true; and he uses it as a *reductio ad absurdum.*

*X.* Right; but now in this case Mr. Malthus presents the result as a truth.

*Phil.* Yes, X.; but observe, the result is the direct contradiction of Mr. Ricardo's result. The quantities of column first vary in value by column the last; but the result, in Mr. Ricardo's hands, is—that they do *not* vary in value.

*X.* Still, if in Mr. Malthus's hands the principle is made to yield a truth, then at any rate the principle is itself true; and all that will be proved against Mr. Ricardo is that he applied a sound principle unskilfully. But Mr. Malthus writes a book to prove that the principle is *not* sound.

*Phæd.* Yes, and to substitute another.

*X.* True; which other, I go on *thirdly* to say, is actually employed in this table. On which account it is fair to say that Mr. Malthus is a *third* time refuted. For, if two inconsistent principles of valuation be employed, then the table will be vicious because heteronymous.

*Phil. Negatur minor.*

*X.* I prove the minor (viz. that two inconsistent principles *are* employed) by column the ninth; and thence also I deduce a *fourth* and a *fifth* refutation of the table.

*Phœd. Euge!* Now this is a pleasant skirmishing.

*X.* For in column the last I say that the principle of valuation employed is different from that employed in columns five and six. Upon which I offer you this dilemma: it is—or it is not; choose.

*Phil.* Suppose I say it is?

*X.* In that case, the result of this table is a case of *idem per idem*; a pure childish tautology.

*Phil.* Suppose I say it is not?

*X.* In that case, the result of this table is false.

*Phil.* Demonstrate.

*X.* I say that the principle of valuation employed in column nine is, not the quantity of *producing* labour, but the quantity of labour *commanded.* Now, if it is, then the result is childish tautology, as being identical with the premises. For it is already introduced into the premises as one of the conditions of the case Alpha (viz. into column two) that twelve quarters of corn shall command the labour of one man; which being premised, it is a mere variety of expression for the very same fact to tell us in column nine that the one hundred and fifty quarters of column the first shall command twelve men and 5-10ths of a man; for one hundred and forty-four, being twelve times twelve, will of course command twelve men, and the remainder of six quarters will of course command the half of a man. And it is most idle to employ the elaborate machinery of nine columns to deduce, as a learned result, what you have already put into the premises, and postulated amongst the conditions.

*Phœd.* This will therefore destroy Mr. Malthus's theory a fourth time.

*X.* Then, on the other hand, if the principle of valuation employed in column nine is the same as that employed in columns five and six, this principle must be the quantity of producing labour, and not the quantity of labour commanded.

But in that case the result will be false. For column nine values column the first. Now, if the one hundred and fifty quarters of case Alpha are truly valued in column first, then they are falsely valued in column the last; and, if truly valued in column the last, then falsely valued in column the first. For by column the last the one hundred and fifty quarters are produced by the labour of twelve and a-half men; but it is the very condition of column the first that the one hundred and fifty quarters are prodnced by ten men.

*Phæd.* (*Laughing.*) This is too hot at last. Here we have a fifth refutation. Can't you give us a sixth, X.?

*X.* If you please. Supposing Mr. Malthus's theory to be good, it shall be impossible for anything whatsoever at any time to vary in value. For how shall it vary? Because the *quantity* of producing labour varies? But *that* is the very principle which he is writing to overthrow. Shall it vary, then, because the *value* of the producing labour varies? But *that* is impossible on the system of Mr. Malthus; for, according to this system, the value of labour is invariable.

*Phil.* Stop, I've thought of a dodge. The thing shall vary because the *quantity* of labour commanded shall vary.

*X.* But how shall *that* vary? A can never command a greater quantity of labour, or of anything which is presumed to be of invariable value, until A itself be of a higher value. To command an altered quantity of labour,—which (*on any theory*) must be the *consequence* of altered value,—can never be the *cause* of altered value. No alterations of labour, therefore, whether as to quantity or value, shall ever account for the altered value of A; for, according to Mr Malthus, they are either insufficient on the one hand, or impossible on the other.

*Phil.* Grant this, yet value may still vary; for, suppose labour to be invariable, still profits may vary.

*X.* So that, if A rise, it will irresistibly argue profits to have risen?

*Phil.* It will; because no other element *can* have risen.

*X.* But now column eight assigns the value of a uniform quantity of corn—namely, one hundred quarters. In case

Alpha, one hundred quarters are worth 8.33. What are one hundred quarters worth in the case Iota?

*Phil.* They are worth ten.

*X.* And *that* is clearly more. Now, if A have risen, by your own admission I am entitled to infer that profits have risen; but what are profits in the case Iota?

*Phil.* By column four they are twenty per cent.

*X.* And what in the case Alpha?

*Phil.* By column four, twenty-five per cent.

*X.* Then profits have fallen in the case Iota, but, because A has risen in case Iota from 8.33 to ten, it is an irresistible inference, on your theory, that profits ought to have risen.

*Phæd.* (*Laughing.*) Philebus, this is a sharp practice. Go on, X., and skirmish with him a little more in this voltigeur style.

## POSTSCRIPT IN 1854[1]

With respect to the "Templars' Dialogues," it may possibly be complained that this paper is in some measure a fragment. My answer is that, although fragmentary in relation to the entire *system* of Ricardo, and that previous *system* which he opposed, it is no fragment in relation to the radical *principle* concerned in those systems. The conflicting systems are brought under review simply at the *locus* of collision: just as the reader may have seen the chemical theory of Dr. Priestley, and the counter-theory of his anti-phlogistic opponents, stated within the limits of a single page. If the

[1] What is here printed as a Postscript was De Quincey's brief parting notice of the paper in the volume of his Collected Writings which contained the reprint of it. It suggests,—what indeed is suggested by the closing words of the dialogue,—that De Quincey had not quite finished in May 1824 the "plain and brief statement" of Ricardo's services to Political Economy which he had promised in the previous March to readers of the *London Magazine*, but contemplated another article or two. The Postscript is his apology for having broken off after the Sixth Dialogue. As it was, he says, the paper of the Six Dialogues was complete enough within itself.—M.

principle relied on by either party can be shown to lead into inextricable self-contradiction, *that* is enough. So much is accomplished in that case as was proposed from the beginning —namely, not to exhaust the *positive* elements of this system or that, but simply to settle the central logic of their several polemics ; to settle, in fact, not the matter of what is evolved, but simply the principle of evolution.

# RICARDO AND ADAM SMITH[1]

EXACTLY two years later than Waterloo, and therefore exactly twenty-five years earlier than this current summer of 1842, David Ricardo made the first and the last effort that ever can be made to revolutionize that science which, for nations, professes to lay bare the grounds of their prosperity, and for individuals, as distributed by nature into three great orders of proprietors, the grounds of their expectations.[2] These three orders are—1. That vast majority whose property lies in their natural endowments, whether intellectual powers, or physical powers, or mixed accomplishments between skill and strength: all these people, under some name or other—"salary," "appointments," "fees," or however the phrase may be courteously varied to suit the liberal quality of the service—receive WAGES. 2. Owners of capital, which (whether fixed or circulating) means any accumulated fund or materials whatever applied to reproduction and not to consumption: these people, if they are themselves the direct employers of the industry put in motion, receive PROFITS; but, if they act by proxy,—simply advancing funds to others who employ them,—they receive INTEREST, which

[1] From *Blackwood's Magazine* for September 1842. See explanation in Editor's Preface to this volume.—M.

[2] The "first and last effort" so referred to by De Quincey was Ricardo's work *On the Principles of Political Economy and Taxation*, published in 1817. Ricardo had previously published several pamphlets on subjects of Finance and Banking; but this was his one great work. He was forty-five years of age at the date of its publication; he entered Parliament in 1819 as member for an Irish borough; and he died 11th September 1823.—M.

must always sympathise with PROFITS, as being unavoidably an integral part of the same fund. 3. Owners of land, mines, quarries, fisheries, turbaries, of which the peculiar privilege is to yield two separate funds; and these funds are pretty generally vested in two separate classes. The case is that not one of these great engines, as we may call them, can be worked without capital. The mine, for instance, the land, the fishery, are all alike useless, in the same sense as artillery is useless without ammunition, unless so far as they are combined with the money requisite for paying wages, and the apparatus, whether in preparations or mechanic power, which gives effect to labour: that is, unless so far as they are *endowed* with capital both circulating and fixed. But hence arises a twofold fund; one upon the capital, another upon the mine, or whatever else may be the original subject to which the capital is applied. These two funds are in the most rigorous sense divided from each other; and the test of that division is, that they obey different laws—one tending slowly to increase, the other slowly to decline. The fund arising on the capital is *Profit*: the fund arising on the mine itself is RENT. The latter is always in correspondence to a scale of *differences* arising upon the several mines worked in co-existence with each other; the former obeys no such scale, for there *are* no differences: on the contrary, after allowing for a few cases of extra profits under special circumstances of hazard, or other repulsive accidents, it is pretty evident that profits must always be gravitating towards a general uniformity; because the first notorious inequality of profits raises a public temptation to that transfer of capital which immediately redresses it.

These, then, are the "functions," to adopt a philosophic term, of all property. There can be no other. All men who breathe, allowing for the mixed case of mendicants, depend upon one or other of these three funds:—upon, 1, wages; upon, 2, profits; or, 3, upon rent. For annuitants, public or private, fall under No. 2, since the receivers of interest and of profit are but joint dividers of the same fund.

Such being the case, is it not a marvellous thing that, according to the allegation of the new economy, No. 3 had not been so much as discovered twenty-eight years ago? We need not add, secondly, that its laws could not have been ascertained whilst the elementary idea had not been developed. But, thirdly, it may be necessary to add that even No. 1 and No. 2, radiating in fact from a central principle common to all the three modes of income, are challenged peremptorily by the new economy as falsely expounded in every preceding theory. . . .

Ricardo is brief; but brevity is not always the parent of obscurity. The obscurity, where any exists in Ricardo, is rather permitted than caused by his style of exposition: in part it adheres to the subject, and in part it grows out of the lax colloquial application which most men have allowed to the words *value*, *labour*, and *rent*; so that, when they find these words used with a stern fidelity to one sole definition, they are confounded. Pulled up sharply by the curb-chain of Ricardo, they begin to fret, plunge, and grow irritated. But the true account, and it is also the true justification, of Ricardo's brevity, both where it *does* and where it does *not* involve any slight obscurity, lies in the separate nature of his duties,—in the peculiar relation of that service which *he* offered to Political Economy, as compared with the service previously offered by Adam Smith.

What was the difference? It was the *system*, the aggregate of doctrines, which Smith undertook to develop. He did not so much propose to innovate in separate parts of the science as to organize the whole. What he said was, "*Given* the many parts already accumulated, I propose to exhibit their relations, to unfold their connexions." But did Ricardo promise a *system* in the same sense? Not at all. Whatever seemed to him correct, that he adopted silently; there was no need to say anything, for he had nothing to amend. But upon the great basis which supported the whole, *there* it was only that he disturbed the old settlements. The phenomena had been truly stated: generally their relations had been truly exposed. It was in the grounds, the causes, the conditions, of these phenomena, that Ricardo saw or imagined a series of errors: under such data he attempted to show that these phenomena could not have followed. His business therefore was to indicate these *fontal* errors, and to draw them into light. Further he was not required to go. He stood in the situation of Kepler; who, because he introduced new laws of motion and new forces into the mechanism of the heavens, was not in debt to any disciple of Tycho or of Ptolemy for a perfect scheme of the heavenly appearances. It was enough that such of these as were most intricate could be explained by his principles, and that by the old principles sometimes they could *not.* To carry out the new principles in the form of a comprehensive economic system, such as Adam Smith had accomplished, was a distinct labour, having no necessary connexion with the original objects of Ricardo. The Scottish philosopher, it must be remembered, had himself been the first man in Europe to complete an entire system. No other person, except Sir James Steuart and one Italian, had ever attempted such a thing. For, if it is objected that a peculiar hypothesis in Political Economy was actually known technically amongst its French supporters by so presumptuous a title as that of "*the* system"—apparently pretending not only to systematic completeness, but to that in some exclusive sense —we reply that the word *système* in that case was not used with any view to its philosophic meaning. Theory, hypothesis, system, are terms distributed in England and France as mere fancy distinctions; nor have they ever been so defined, still less so applied, as in all logic they ought to be. The French did not imply by *le système* the comprehensiveness and integrity of the doctrines concerned, but mysteriously they meant to hint at their profundity—a profundity like that in *Don Quixote*, where all night long master and man, hardly daring to draw their breath freely, have been sitting with their legs awfully pendulous (as they believe) over an unfathomable abyss; and lo! upon the light of dawn returning, they find their feet within twelve inches of the ground. The French *système* rested upon a blunder inevitable to all understandings at a certain stage of advance in these speculations. In the sense of a comprehensive aggregate, gathering into the unity of one edifice the total architecture of Political Economy, there are even at this day but few systems besides the *Wealth of Nations,*—none which approaches it in philosophic beauty; and, as to Ricardo's work in particular, it was not even an essay or overture in that direction. It was a work *de principiis*, a searching inquiry into principles, or first beginnings, as the golden rings from which all the rest is suspended; and, agreeably to that object, it was entitled "*Principles* of Political Economy." That title explains its office, and that office explains the unaccommodating brevity of its exposition.

Whatsoever, therefore, may be found either too rapid or too obscure in the delivery of Ricardo is a natural result from the very plan of the work: nobody is entitled to expect a *didactic* treatise on Natural Philosophy in a severe essay reviewing sceptically the elementary laws of motion and mechanism. Secondly, an equal justification might be drawn from the character of audience which the author proposed to himself: it was the *clerus*, not the *populus*, whom Ricardo addressed: he did not call attention from the laity who seek to learn, but from the professional body who seek to teach. To others, to uninitiated students, he needs a commentary.[1]

[1] The "commentary" which De Quincey proceeded to offer in the rest of the *Blackwood* article of September 1842, and which he continued in two subsequent articles in the October and December numbers of *Blackwood* for the same year, was completely superseded by De Quincey's *Logic of Political Economy*, published as an independent little treatise in 1844, but consisting really of an expansion and recast of the matter of the three *Blackwood* articles.—M.

# THE LOGIC OF POLITICAL ECONOMY[1]

## PREFACE

THAT the reader may not seek in this little work anything other or more than was designed, I will briefly state its primary object.

Political Economy does not advance. Since the revolution effected in that science by Ricardo (1817), upon the whole it has been stationary. But why? It has always been my own conviction that the reason lies not in any material defect of facts (except as to the single question of money), but in the laxity of some amongst the distinctions which are elementary to the science. For example, that one desperate enormity of vicious logic which takes place in the ordinary application to price of the relation between supply and demand has secured more arguments dispersed through speeches, books, journals, than a long life could fully expose. Let us judge by analogy from mathematics. If it were possible that but three elementary definitions, or axioms, or postulates in geometry should be liable to controversy and to a *precarious* use (a use dependent upon petition and momentary consent), what would follow? Simply this,—that the whole vast aerial synthesis of that science, at present towering upwards

[1] Published as a separate treatise of 260 octavo pages in 1844 by Messrs. Blackwood of Edinburgh, with the title "*The Logic of Political Economy, by Thomas De Quincey*"; but really a recast and enlargement of three papers which had appeared in *Blackwood's Magazine* for September, October, and December, 1842. See *ante*, Editor's Preface to this Volume, and footnote at p. 117. A reprint of the treatise formed part of volume xiii of Messrs. Black's reissue of De Quincey's Edition of his Collected Writings.—M.

towards infinity, would exhibit an eclipse eternally, perhaps, renewing itself by parts, but eternally tottering in some parts, and in other parts mouldering eternally into ruins. That science, which now holds "acquaintance with the stars" by means of its inevitable and imperishable truth, would become as treacherous as Shakspeare's "stairs of sand"; or, like the fantastic architecture which the winds are everlastingly pursuing in the Arabian desert, would exhibit phantom arrays of fleeting columns and fluctuating edifices, which, under the very breath that had created them, would be for ever collapsing into dust. Such, even to this moment, as regards its *practical* applications, is the science of Political Economy. Nothing can be postulated—nothing can be demonstrated; for anarchy, even as to the earliest principles, is predominant. Under this conviction, about twenty-two years ago, I sketched a fragment of this science, entitled "*The Templars' Dialogues*."[1] The purpose of this fragment was to draw into much stronger relief than Ricardo himself had done that one radical doctrine as to value by which he had given a new birth to Political Economy. My little sketch had the merit of drawing from an author, to this day anonymous, the "*Critical Dissertation upon Value*."[2] Naturally, it is gratifying to have called forth, whether in alliance or in opposition, so much of ingenuity and of logical acuteness. But, with all his ability, that writer failed to shake any of my opinions. I continue to hold my original ideas on the various aspects of this embarrassing doctrine; and I continue to believe that a much severer investigation of this doctrine is indispensable at the outset. In prosecution of that belief I now go on, without again travelling over the ground which possibly I had won in "The Templars' Dialogues," to investigate some further perplexities in the general doctrine of Value, and particularly such as these which I now specify, in the view of intercepting any misdirected expectations as to the nature of the book.

1. With respect to what is called *value in use* I endeavour to expose the total misapprehension by Adam Smith of the

[1] In 1823. See *ante*, p. 37, footnote.—M.

[2] The author was Samuel Bailey; and this book of his was published in 1825.—M.

word "*use*," as though any opposition were here indicated between the *useful* and the *ornamental* or *pleasurable*. Not what is useful, but what is used, here forms the *nodus* of the antithesis, and regulates conformably the mode of appreciation.

2. With respect to the same term, *value in use*, I endeavôur to establish another distinction as against another perplexity much more important. We sit on a summer day by the side of a brook, and, being thirsty, drink from its waters. Now, this beverage has confessedly a value in use; but in England it is so far from bearing a value in exchange that such a case expresses the very abnegation and antithesis of exchange value. On the other hand, there is by possibility a very different value in use; there is such a value (that is, a value determined altogether and simply on the scale of uses or teleologic aptitudes) arising under circumstances which will not range it *against* exchange value as its polar antithesis, but will range it *under* exchange value as one of its two modes. In the first acceptation, *value in use* is made co-ordinate with exchange value—ranges over against it, as its adequate contradiction; in the second acceptation, value in use is made subordinate to exchange value, as one of its two modifications. Here lies a source of confusion which never has been exposed, and which, at the very vestibule, has hitherto defeated all attempt at a systematic Theory of Value.

3. I endeavour to expose the confusion between "market value" as a fact and "market value" as a law. The term "market value," in *popular* use, expresses only a barren fact—the value of an article, for instance, in Liverpool as opposed to Glasgow; to-day as opposed to yesterday. It means no more than existing value as opposed to value past or future; actual value as opposed to possible value. But, in the *technical* use, "market value" points to no idle matter of fact (*idle*, I mean, because uninfluential on the price),—but it points to a law modifying the price, and derived from the market. In this use, the term "market" does not indicate the mere *ubi* or the *quando* of the sale, but is a shorthand expression for the relation between the quantity offered for sale and the quantity demanded. That is certainly a dis-

tinction old enough to be clearly apprehended; and often it *is* clearly apprehended. Yet also, in the practical use, too often it is utterly misapplied. Even by those who parade the distinction in their theoretical statements, even by him who introduced this distinction,—lastly, even by that Ricardo who favours us with a separate chapter on this distinction, —practically the two senses contemplated by the distinction are confounded, inferences being derived from one sense which apply only to the other.

4. I endeavour to expose the metaphysical confusion involved in "market value" when it is supposed by possibility to constitute an *original* value. This is an error which has led to worse consequences than any of the others here noticed. People fancy that the relation of Supply to Demand could by possibility, and that in fact it often *does*, determine separately *per se* the selling price of an article. Within a few months this monstrous idea has been assumed for true by Colonel Torrens, in an express work on Economic Politics; by Lord Brougham, in relation to the foreign corn trade; and by almost every journal in the land that has fallen under my own eye. But it is a metaphysical impossibility that Supply and Demand, the relation of which is briefly expressed by the term "market value," could ever affect price except by a *secondary* force. Always there must be a *modificabile* (*i.e.* an antecedent price, arising from some other cause), before any modification from Supply against Demand can take effect. Consequently, whilst "*natural* price" (the contradiction of "*market* price") is always a mononomial, price founded on the relation of Supply to Demand must always be a binomial.

The latter chapters, as a sort of *praxis* on the law of value applied to the leading doctrines of Ricardo, were added for the sake of the student in Political Economy. They are not absolutely required; but they may have a use in tracing the descent of a pure theory into consequences connected on the one side with theory and on the other side with practice.

*8th February* 1844.

# CHAPTER I—VALUE

## SECTION I.—VALUE IN THE GENERIC SENSE

THAT natural distinction which takes place from the very beginnings of society between value as founded upon some serviceable quality in an object too largely diffused to confer any power of purchasing other objects and value as founded upon some similar quality in an object so limited as to become *property*, and thus having a power to purchase other objects, has long been familiar to the public ear under the antithetic expressions of "*value in use*" and "*value in exchange*." Who first noticed pointedly a distinction which must always obscurely have been moving in the minds of men, it would now be idle to inquire: such an inquiry would too much resemble that Greek question, "Who first invented sneezing?" For my own part, the eldest author in whom I remember to have traced this distinction formally developed is Plautus—contemporary with Hannibal. He, in his "*Asinaria*," has occasion to introduce a lively scene on a question of prompt payment between *Argyrippus*, a young man then occupied in sowing wild-oats, and *Cœlereta*, a prudent woman settled in business on her own account. She is in fact *a lena*—which name, however, did not bear so horrid a construction under Pagan morals as most justly it does under Christian; and in that professional character she is mistress of a young beauty with whom Argyrippus had celebrated a left-handed marriage some time back, which connexion he now seeks to renew on a second contract. But for this a price is asked of sixty guineas. The question which arises between the parties respects the propriety of the household economy for the present going on upon tick; which Argyrippus views as the sublimest of philosophical discoveries, whilst the *lena* violently resists it as a vile one-sided policy, patronised by all who happened to be buyers, but rejected universally by sellers. The following is the particular passage which concerns the present distinction between *value in use* and *value in exchange*:—

> "ARGYR. Ubi illæc quæ dedi ante?
> "CÆLER. Abusa: nam, si ea durarent mihi,
> Mulier mitteretur ad te: nunquam quicquam poscerem.
> *Diem, aquam, solem, lunam, noctem,—hæc argento non emo:*
> *Cætera, quæque volumus uti, Græca mercamur fide.*
> *Quum a pistore panem petimus, vinum ex œnoplio,*
> *Si æs habent, dant mercem: eadem nos disciplina utimur.*
> Semper oculatæ nostræ sunt manus, credunt quod vident.
> Vetus est—nihili cocio est."

ARG. What has become of those sums which in times past I gave you?

CÆL. All spent, sir — all consumed; for, believe me, if those moneys still survived, the young woman should be despatched to your house without another word: once paid in full, I'm not the woman that would trouble you for a shilling. Look here:—*The successions of day and night, water, sunlight, moonlight—all these things I purchase freely without money; but that heap of things beside which my establishment requires, those I pay for on the old terms of Grecian credit.*[1] *When I send for a loaf to the baker's, for wine to the vintner's, certainly the articles are delivered; but when? Why, as soon as those people have touched the cash.* Now, that same practice is what I in my turn apply to others. My hands have still eyes at their finger-ends: their faith is strong in all money which actually they see. For "caution," as you call it—for guarantees—they are nothing: security be d——d; and that's an old saying.

The latter part of the speech wanders off into the difference between the system of prompt payment on the one hand

[1] Meaning—no credit at all, but ready money. One incomprehensible old commentator pretends that Plautus, in this phrase, designed a compliment to Greek integrity! He is obliged, however, to confess, as the true ground of the saying, that "Fluxæ fuerunt olim admodum fidei Græci: idcirco Græcus Græco non fidebat, nisi præsenti et numerata pecunia." Meantime, though the *fluxa fides* of the unprincipled Greek was quite undeniable, and, in fact, ruinous to the fiscal service, yet, doubtless, the general want of capital amongst sellers contributed to this absence of credit almost as much as the universal want of probity in the buyers.

and of credit on the other. But the part in italics confines itself to the difference between value in use and value in exchange—between the class of things valuable which could be had for nothing and that other class of things valuable which must be paid for ; secondly, which must also be paid for on the spot. The former class is a limited class ; the latter so extensive that she makes no attempt to enumerate the items : she simply selects two, bread and wine, as representative items—one of which is the more striking because it represents a necessity already provided for by nature in the gratuitous article of water.

Here, then, already two centuries before the Christian era, in the second or chief Punic war, is the great distinction brought out into broad daylight between the things useful to man which are too multiplied and diffused to be raised into property and the things useful to man which are *not* so multiplied and diffused, but which, being hard to obtain, support the owner in demanding a price for them. Many people fancy that these two ideas never are, nor could be, confounded ; and some people fancy, amongst whom was Mr. Malthus, that in the intercourse of real life the word *value* or *valuable* never is employed at all, rightly or not rightly, in the original sense as implying mere value in use, but that (except amongst affected or pedantic talkers) this word "*value*" must always indicate some sort of value in exchange. We never, therefore, according to Mr. Malthus, use or could use such a phrase as—"a valuable friend," or "a valuable doctrine." It would be impossible to say that "we ascribed great value to any deliberate judgment of such a judge"; or that "the friendship of a wise elder brother had proved of the highest value to a young man at Cambridge"; or that "the written opinion which we had obtained from Mr. Attorney-General was eminently valuable." Literally, it is terrific to find blank assertions made by men of sense so much in defiance of the truth, and on matters of fact lying so entirely within an ordinary experience. Full fifty times in every month must Mr. Malthus himself have used the word "value" and "valuable" in this very natural sense which he denounces as a mere visionary sense suggested by the existing books. Now, to show by a real and a recent case how possible it is for a sensible man to use the words *value* or *valuable* in this original sense—not merely where a pure generic usefulness is concerned, but even in cases which must forcibly have pointed his attention to the other sense (the exchange sense) of the words,—I cite in the note below a striking instance of such a use[1] from this day's paper (the *London Standard* for February 27th, 1843).

[1] "*A striking instance of such a use*":—It occurs in a very useful letter (under date of Dantzic, January 21, 1843) on the Baltic corn-trade, from a writer evidently familiar with the subject, and authenticating his statements by a real signature. The object of the writer, M. J. L. Stoddart, is to expose the true and ultimate operation of all fixed duties considered as protections to the home-grower, under those dreadful fluctuations in price which not man but nature causes, and which "cannot be avoided, in spite of the philosophers who dream they have discovered the philosopher's stone for steadying prices." The purpose and the execution of this gentleman's letter are equally excellent; but the use which he makes of the word *value* was so perplexing to me in its particular position and connexion that at first I apprehended some gross misprint. After one introductory sentence, in which he describes himself as a neutral observer under the advantage of being "removed from the excitement of the struggle between manufacturer and agriculturist," Mr. Stoddart goes on to say that "the value of Dantzic wheat, on an average of export, varies from 5s. to 8s. per quarter ABOVE the value of British average wheat"; and after this astounding statement he adds another not at all less so, viz. that Baltic wheat collectively (by which is not meant wheat opposed to the Dantzic wheat, but so understood as to include the Dantzic wheat) may with safety "be estimated on an average to be 5s. ABOVE the value of the growth of the British Islands." Could I trust my own eyes? Undoubtedly I was aware, and had repeatedly used that conviction in print, that the extreme difference between English wheat and foreign would never turn out such experimentally as to justify the monstrous delusions of the Corn-Law agitators. Well I knew that the working poor man would find the ultimate *bonus* upon his bread to be next to nothing under whatsoever changes of the Corn-Law; assuming even the stationariness of wages, and assuming also that no such reaction of evil should arise from the injury to our domestic agriculture as unavoidably would arise. All this I knew. But still, though pretty doubtful, and in the issue liable to be dangerously disturbed, any difference which *did* exist between the prices of Baltic and English wheat was undeniably in favour of the first. *That* was notoriously the cheaper; if not, how should importation need any legal restraint? Here was the perplexity; but one moment cleared it up. It was a verbal *equivoque*. Mr. Stoddart had pronounced the Baltic wheat by 5s. on a quarter ABOVE the English wheat in value. Ay, but in *what* value? Did he mean value in

Value in use, therefore, is an idea lurking by possibility under the elliptical term "*value*" quite as naturally, though not so frequently, as the idea of value in exchange. And, in any case of perplexity arising out of the term *value* employed absolutely, it may be well for the reader to examine closely if some such equivocation does not in reality cause the whole demur. One moment's consideration will convince the student that the second form of value—viz. value in exchange—does not exclude the first form, value in use; for, on the contrary, the second form could not exist without presupposing the first. But, in the inverse case, the logic is different: value in use, where it exists antithetically to the other form, not only may but must exclude it.

This leads to another capital distinction:—Value in exchange is an idea constructed by superadding to the original element of serviceableness (or value in use) an accessary element of power (howsoever gained) to command an equiva-

exchange, value as expressed by the market price? On the contrary, he meant value in use. From the tenor of what follows, it is evident that he does not dispute the usual intervaluations of Baltic and English grain. He assumes that in Poland, before it is loaded with a long list of expenses, the wheat would be very considerably cheaper than English wheat. Why, then, had he said that already in Poland it was *above* the English in value by 5s.? He meant that intrinsically, as a thing to be used, it was above the English: superior (1) in its capacity of being baked; or (2) in its capacity of being kept; or (3) in its capacity of yielding nutriment; or (4) in its flavour to the palate: in some one, or some two, or some three, or in all four of these advantages, he claims for it a superiority to the English; and, what must add to the reader's perplexity, he measures this superiority by money—meaning the 5s. (as one-eighth of 40s.) simply to indicate that the quality of Baltic wheat was superior in that precise ratio; better by a proportion answering to one-eighth part on any given quantity.——One single exemplification, drawn from a case of actual occurrence, is worth twenty which are artificially framed. And this decisive passage, from an excellent essay in a journal of high character, falling into my hands without search, at the very moment of writing the passage which it illustrates, seems effectual for the proof of what Mr. Malthus thought next to impossible: viz. that men can and do, without any system to serve, naturally fall into this use of "value" as representing the mere serviceableness of an article quite apart from its exchange-rating in the market. Let the extreme importance of the subject, and the necessity of weighing every turn in the dispute, for one who comes after a world of failures with the promise of setting them all to rights, apologise for the length of this note.

lent. It follows, therefore, that the original element, value in use, may be viewed in two states: 1*st*, as totally disengaged from the secondary element; 2*dly*, as *not* disengaged from that element, but as necessarily combining with it. In the second state we have seen that it takes the name of "*value in exchange.*" What name does it take in the first state, where it is wholly disengaged from the power of purchasing? *Answer*—(and let the reader weigh this well)—It takes the name of "*wealth.*"

Mr. Ricardo was the first person who had the sagacity to see that the idea of wealth was the true polar antagonist to the idea of value in exchange, and that without this regulative idea it is impossible to keep the logic of political economy true to its duties. This doctrine, so essentially novel, he first explained in his celebrated chapter (numbered xviii in his first edition) which bears for its title "*Value and Riches: their distinctive Properties.*" And in the early part of it he remarks most truly that "many of the errors in political economy have arisen from errors on this subject, from considering an increase of riches and an increase of value as meaning the same thing."

But it is singular enough that even Ricardo did not consciously observe the exact coincidence of riches, under this new limitation of his own, with "value in use." This was an accident likely enough to arise under the absence of any positive occasion for directing his eye to that fact. It was, no doubt, a pure case of inadvertence. But there is the same sort of danger from holding two ideas radically identical to be different, or in opposition to each other, as there is from confounding two ideas radically opposed. Meantime, no chapter in Ricardo's book (with the single exception of the first) has been so much singled out for attack, or for special admiration,[1] as this particular chapter which rectifies the idea of wealth. Even amongst the leading supporters of Ricardo it will be seen further on (in the brief

[1] "*Special admiration*":—For example, Mr. Prinsep (in his translation of "Say's Political Economy"), a man of great acuteness and information, has noticed this eighteenth chapter of Ricardo as peculiarly profound; whilst, on the other hand, to the able author of "A Critical Dissertation on Value," to Mr. Malthus, and to others, it is a mere scandal and rock of offence.

commentary upon this eighteenth chapter) that some have unconsciously surrendered it. Not only have they been unaware of their own revolt in this particular instance from that theory which they had professed to adopt; but they have been equally unaware that simultaneously with the collapse of this doctrine concerning wealth collapses the entire doctrine of Ricardo concerning value; and, if that basis should ever seriously be shaken, all the rest of Ricardo's system, being purely in the nature of a superstructure, must fall into ruins. These questions, however, with respect to the truth of particular doctrines, and their power to resist such assaults as have menaced them, will come forward by degrees, in proportion as their development ripens under our advance. For the present, my office is, not to defend them, but to state them, and to trace their logical deduction; by which word, borrowed from a case strictly analogous in the modern expositions of the civil law, I understand a process such as, by a more learned term, would be called a systematic "*genesis*" of any complex truth—the act, namely, of pursuing the growth which gradually carries that truth to its full expansion through all its movements, and showing of each separately how it arose, and in what change or movement of the principal idea, under what necessity supervening at that point, or on the suggestion of what occasional falling in with some other and kindred truth.

I have now traced the generic idea of "value," taken absolutely and without further limitation, into the two subordinate modes of—1*st*, Value resting exclusively on a power to serve the purpose, and, 2*d*, Of value resting on that power, but combined with the accessary power of commanding an equivalent—into value which *does* and value which does *not* involve the idea of property. The simpler mode of value I have announced to be identical with the Ricardian idea of *wealth*; and under that head it will come round for consideration in its proper place. But the other mode of value—viz. Exchange Value—which is far more important to political economy, being no longer a regulative but a constitutive idea,[1] now steps naturally into the place

[1] "*No longer regulative but constitutive*":—This is a great distinction heretofore applied to great purposes by Kant; and a general

standing next in order for investigation; and I warn the young student that at this point he steps forward upon perilous gronnd, of which every inch is debatable. Here it is that the true struggle takes place, that unavoidable combat between principles originally hostile which into every subsequent section carries forward its consequences, and which, upon *every* system past or to come, impresses that determinate character, exposes that determinate tendency or *clinamen*, eventually decisive of its pretensions.

## SECTION II.—VALUE IN EXCHANGE.

What is value in exchange? What is its foundation? Most remarkable it seems that up to a certain point all systems of modern economy answer this question correctly; yet, after passing that point, that all are wrong. In the vast accumulation of books on this subject, English, French, or Italian (for German books go for nothing here), I have not met with one which sustains the truth to the end;

reader might fancy reason for complaint in finding thus presupposed the knowledge of philosophy,—which in England is but slightly extended. To presume anything of the kind would indeed be eminently offensive, and an instance of affectation quite inconsistent with the simplicities of good sense. But in this case the two terms opposed almost explain themselves. As an example of a regulative idea one might allege any idea of pure abstract geometry. For instance, the want of parts or partibility in a geometrical point; the absolute equality of all the radii drawn from a common centre; or, in philosophy, the assumption of an ideal man as a normal type towards which we may conceive a perpetual tendency in the actual man of our experience: all these are *regulative* ideas. Nobody pretends for a moment that a true and actual equality of the semidiameters ever was, or could be, realised; the hand does not exist that could draw such lines, nor the eye that could judge of them, *if* drawn. But what then? They are most useful—nay, they are indispensable as initial postulates for the guidance of the mind in developing other ideas; without them, although in themselves often fugitive, and never to be overtaken in practice, we could not advance at all. And such is the precise benefit from Ricardo's idea of "*wealth*," technically so called: it is an artificial idea, which, though inert, keeps in their proper places other ideas more tangible and constitutive. On the other hand, the counterpole of this idea—viz. Value in Exchange—enters largely, and as a constituent element, into all the cardinal ideas of political economy.

whilst, on the other hand, it would be hardly less difficult to point out one which fails at the opening. Verbal inaccuracies might indeed be cited from all; for in an age of hasty reading, and of contempt for the whole machinery of scholastic distinctions, it cannot be expected that authors will spend much energy upon qualities which have ceased to be meritorious, upon nicety of distinction which perishes to the flying reader, or upon a jealous maintenance of consistency which, unless it were appreciated by severe study, could not benefit the writer. In this way, there arises at once a natural explanation of that carelessness in the mode of exposition which has everywhere disfigured the modern science of political economy.

Almost all writers have agreed substantially, and have rightly agreed, in founding exchangeable value upon two elements: power in the article valued to meet some natural desire or some casual purpose of man, in the first place; and, in the second place, upon difficulty of attainment. These two elements must meet, must come into combination, before any value in exchange can be established. They constitute the two co-ordinate conditions of which where either is absent no value in the sense of exchange value can arise for a moment. Indeed, it is evident to common sense that any article whatever, to obtain that artificial sort of value which is meant by exchange value, must begin by offering itself as a means to some desirable purpose, and, secondly, that, even though possessing incontestably this preliminary advantage, it will never ascend to an exchange value in cases where it can be obtained gratuitously and without effort—of which last terms both are necessary as limitations. For often it will happen that some desirable object may be obtained gratuitously; stoop, and you gather it at your feet: but still, because the continued iteration of this stooping exacts a laborious effort, very soon it is found that to gather for yourself virtually is *not* gratuitous. In the vast forests of the Canadas, at intervals, wild strawberries may be gratuitously gathered by ship-loads; yet such is the exhaustion of a stooping posture, and of a labour so monotonous, that everybody is soon glad to resign the service into mercenary hands. The same idea, the same demand of a twofold *con-*

*ditio sine qua non* as essential to the composition of an exchange value, is otherwise expressed (and in a shape better fitted for subsequent reference) by the two following cases, marked *Epsilon* and *Omicron*:—

*Case Epsilon.*—A man comes forward with his overture, "Here is a thing which I wish you to purchase; it has cost me in labour five guineas, and that is the price I ask." "Very well," you reply; "but tell me this,—What desire or purpose of mine will the article promote?" Epsilon rejoins, "Why, as candour is my infirmity, none at all. But what of *that*? Useful or not, the article embodies five guineas' worth of excellent labour." This man, the candid Epsilon, you dismiss.—*Case Omicron.*—Him succeeds Omicron, who praises your decisive conduct as to the absurd family of the Epsilons. "That man," he observes, "is weak—candid, but weak; for what was the cost in your eyes but so much toil to no effect of real service? But *that* is what nobody can say of the article offered by myself; it is serviceable always—nay, often you will acknowledge it to be indispensable." "What is it?" you demand. "Why simply, then, it is a pound of water, and as good water as ever you tasted." The scene lies in England, where water bears no value except under that machinery of costly arrangements which delivers it as a permanent and guaranteed succession into the very chambers where it is to be used. Omicron accordingly receives permission to follow the candid Epsilon. Each has offered for sale one element of value out of two,—one element in a state of insulation, where it was indispensable for any operative value, *i.e.* price, to offer the two in combination; and without such a combination it is impossible (neither does any economist deny this by his principles) that value in exchange, under the most romantic or imaginary circumstances, ever should be realised.

Thus far all is right; all is easy and all is harmonious; thus far, no hair-splitter by profession can raise even a verbal quillet against so plain a movement of the understanding, unless it were by some such cavil as is stated below.[1] It is in the next step that a difficulty arises, to

[1] "*By such a cavil as is stated below*":—When hay, for instance, is cited as an article uniting the two conditions laid down, and for

all appearance insurmountable. It is a difficulty which seems, when stated, to include a metaphysical impossibility. You are required to do *that* which, under any statement, seems to exact a contradiction in terms. The demand is absolute and not to be evaded, for realising an absurdity and extracting a positive existence out of a nonentity or a blank negation. To this next step, therefore, let us now proceed, after warning the reader that even Ricardo has not escaped the snare which is here spread for the understanding; and that, although a masculine good sense will generally escape in practice from merely logical perplexities (that is, will cut the knot for all immediate results of practice which it cannot untie), yet errors "in the first intention" come round upon us in subsequent stages, unless they are met by their proper and commensurate solutions. Logic must be freed by logic: a false dialectical appearance of truth must be put down by the fullest exposure of the absolute and hidden truth, since also it will continually happen (as it *has* happened in the present case) that a plausible sophism, which had been summarily crushed for the moment by a strong appeal to general good sense upon the absurd consequences arising, will infallibly return upon us when no such startling consequences are at hand. Now, therefore, with this sense of the critical step which next awaits us, let us move forward.

The idea of value in exchange having thus been analytically decomposed, the question which offers itself next in order concerns the subdivision of this idea. How many modes are possible of value in exchange? The general answer is—two; and the answer is just: there *are* two. But how are these two distinguished? How is it that they

that reason as obtaining exchangeable value, it might be alleged that hay meets no human desire, but only a bestial desire. True; and, with a view *inter alia* to this particular form of cavil, I have enlarged the definition by saying "human desire or *purpose*." A man has no direct gratification from hay, but indirectly he may have a good deal. The hay may be nothing to the man who buys it; but his horse, who is a connoisseur in hay, may be indispensable to his daily happiness, or even to his safety; and that which in some proportion is essential to the desires of his horse becomes secondarily a purpose to the man.

arise? Now here it is, in the answer to this question, that an infirm logic has disturbed the truth. Even Ricardo has not escaped the universal error. Suspensory judgments are painful acts. It is fatiguing to most readers that a provisional view of the truth should be laid before them, upon which all the pains taken to appropriate and master it are by agreement to be finally found worthless. This refutation of error is better so placed as to *follow* the establishment of the truth; in which position the reader may either dismiss it unread, as a corollary which already he knows to be too much—as an offshoot in excess—or, on the other hand, choosing to read it, will do so under the additional light obtained through the true doctrine now restored to its authority.

The difficulty which strikes us all upon the possibility of raising any subdivision under that generic idea of exchange value already stated is this:—The two elements are: 1*st*, Intrinsic utility; 2*d*, Difficulty of attainment. But these elements must concur. They are not reciprocating or alternating ideas; they are not, to borrow a word from Coleridge, inter-repellent[1] ideas, so that room might be made for a double set of exchange values, by supposing alternately each of the elements to be withdrawn, whilst the other element was left paramount. This is impossible; because, by the very terms of the analysis, each element is equally indispensable to the common idea which is the subject of division. Alike in either case, if No. 1, or if No. 2, should be dropped

[1] "*Inter-repellent*":—The late Mr. Coleridge suggested, and by his own example sanctioned, the use of the preposition *inter* for expressing cases of reciprocal action, or, in his language, of inter-action. Thus the verb *interpenetrate*, when predicated of the substances A and B, implied that, by an equal action and reaction, each penetrated the other; to *interaid* (though strictly a Latin preposition should not coalesce with a word not Latin) would express the case where aid in different modes is lent by each of two parties interchangeably. The same complex function is sustained by the French prefix *s'entre*. But, even as a justifiable English usage, it may be found occasionally in Shakspere, and much more frequently in Daniel, a writer of the same age, unusually meditative and philosophic, both in his prose and in his verse. The word *interview*, though now tamed into a lower cast of ideas, originally arose upon this application of interchangeable or reciprocating actions.

out of the composition, instantly the whole idea of exchange value falls to the ground like a punctured bladder. But this seems to preclose the road to any possible subdivision of the generic idea, because immediately it occurs to the student that, when no element can be withdrawn, *then* it is not possible that the subdivisions can differ except as to degree. In one case of exchange value there might, for instance, be a little more of the element A, and a little less of the element B. In some other case these proportions might be reversed. But all this is nothing. When we subdivide the genus *animal*, we are able to do so by means of an element *not* common to the two subdivisions: we assign man as one subdivision — brutes as the other — by means of a great differential idea, the idea of rationality ; consequential upon which are tears, laughter, and the capacity of religion. All these we deny to brutes ; all these we claim for man ; and thus are these two great sub-genera or species possible. But, when all elements are equally present to both of the subdividing ideas, we cannot draw any bisecting line between them. The two ideas lie upon one continuous line—differing, therefore, as higher and lower, by more and by less, but not otherwise ; and any subdividing barrier, wheresoever it is made to fall between them, must be drawn arbitrarily, without any reasonable foundation in real or essential differences.

These considerations are calculated to stagger us ; and at this precise stage of the discussion I request the reader's most vigilant attention. We have all read of secret doors in great cities so exquisitely dissembled by art that in what seemed a barren surface of dead wall, where even the eye forewarned could trace no vestige of a separation or of a line, simply by a simultaneous pressure upon two remote points, suddenly and silently an opening was exposed which revealed a long perspective of retiring columns—architecture the most elaborate, where all had passed for one blank continuity of dead wall. Not less barren in promise, not less abrupt in its transition, this speculation at the very vestibule of political economy, at the point where most it had appeared to allow of no further advance or passage, suddenly opens and expands before an artifice of logic which almost impresses the feelings as a trick of legerdemain—not by anything unsound in its own nature, but by the sudden kind of pantomime change which it effects. The demand is that you shall subdivide exchange value into two separate modes. You are to do this without aid from any new idea that has arisen to vary the general idea; you are to work with the two already contained in that general idea—consequently with ideas that *must* be common to both the subdivisions—and yet you are to differentiate these subdivisions. Each is to be opposed to the other,—each is to differ,—and yet the elements assigned to you out of which this difference is to be created are absolutely the same. Who can face such conditions as these—Given a total identity, and out of that you are to create a difference?

Let not the reader complain of the copious way in which the difficulty is exposed. After many hundreds of failures, after endless efforts with endless miscarriages, it is no time for refusing his own terms to the leader of a final assault. So many defeats have naturally made us all angry. I am angry—the reader is angry; and that offer is entitled to consideration, even though it should seem needlessly embarrassed or circuitous, which terminates in the one object that can be worth talking about—viz. in "doing the trick," and carrying by a summary effort that obstacle which (whether observed or not observed) has so long thwarted the power of perfecting and integrating the theory of value. Once being convinced that it is a mere contradiction to solve the problem, the reader may be relied on for attending to anything offered as a solution by one who has almost demonstrated its impossibility.

Out of nothing, nothing is generated. This is pretty old ontology; and apparently our case at present is of that nature; for by no Laputan process of extracting sunbeams from cucumbers does it appear how we can hope, out of two samenesses, to extract one difference; yet do it we must, or else farewell to the object before us. And, in order that we *may* do it, let us disembarrass our problem of all superfluous words; and, by way of sharpening the eye to the point of assault, let us narrow it to the smallest possible area.

What we have to do is to consider whether (and now) it is feasible so to use a sameness as to make it do the office of a difference. With one single sameness this would peremptorily *not* be possible; for we could vary it no otherwise than by varying its degrees. Now, a difference in degrees is no substantial difference in logic; and the pretended subdivisions would melt and play into each other, so as to confound the attempt at sustaining any subdivisions at all. But, on the other hand, with two samenesses it is possible to move. A little reflection will show that there *is* a resource for making them alternately act as differences. In physics we see vast phenomena taking place all day long which *a priori* might have been stated as paradoxes not less startling than that of extracting a difference out of a sameness. One gravity rises through another gravity. True, it is specifically lighter; but still it *has* a specific gravity: and thus we find as the result, with the usual astonishing simplicity of nature, that the same machinery serves for sinking objects and for raising them. By gravity they fall; by gravity they rise. So also, again, that same ocean which to nations populous and developed by civilisation offers the main high-road of intercourse was to the same nations, when feeble, the great wall of separation and protection. And, again, in the case before us, monstrous as really is the paradox,[1] yet it is true that, by a dexterous management of two elements absolutely identical, all the effects and benefits may be obtained of two elements essentially different.

Let us look more closely. The two elements are U and D. If both elements are to be present, and both are to be operative, then indeed we have a contradiction in terms such

[1] "*As really is the paradox*":—Some readers will here admonish me to say—not "*is*" the paradox, but "*seems*" the paradox; or rather, they will require me to omit the word paradox altogether, under the prevailing notion that a paradox implies something really extravagant, and something eventually hostile to the truth. In these circumstances it will scarcely be sufficient for me to remind them of the original Grecian meaning attached to this word, which implied no more than what was off-lying from the high-road of popular opinion, or what contradicted the tenor of popular expectation—all which might surely be found in some great truth as well as in some notorious falsehood. The objector will retort upon me that the original Grecian use may have been effectually disturbed and defeated by a long and

as never will be overcome. But how if both be uniformly present, one only being at any time operative? How if both be indispensably present, but alternately each become inert? How if both act as motives on the buyer for buying at all, but one only (each in turn under its own circumstances) as a force operating on the price?

This is the real case—this is the true solution; and thus is a difference obtained—such a difference as will amply sustain a twofold subdivision from elements substantially the same. Both are co-present, and always. Neither *can* be absent; for, if so, then the common idea of exchange value would vanish, the case *Epsilon* or the case *Omicron* would be realised. But each of the two is suspended alternately. Thus, by way of illustration, walk into almost any possible shop; buy the first article you see: what will determine its price? In ninety-nine cases of a hundred, simply the element D—difficulty of attainment. The other element, U, or intrinsic utility, will be perfectly inoperative. Let the thing (measured by its uses) be, for your purposes, worth ten guineas, so that you would rather give ten guineas than lose it; yet, if the difficulty of producing it be only worth one guinea, one guinea is the price which it will bear. But still not the less, though U is inoperative, can U be supposed absent? By no possibility; for, if it *had* been absent, assuredly you would not have bought the article even at the lowest price: U acts upon *you*, though it does not act upon the price. On the other hand, in the hundredth case, we will suppose the circumstances reversed. You are on Lake Superior in a steamboat, making your way to an unsettled region 800 miles ahead of civilisation, and con-

steady English abuse. Meantime the fact is that the original sense of the *paradoxical* has maintained itself not less in our language than in the ancient Greek. I remember once to have placed this under a clear light by the following antithetic form of words: "Not *that* is paradoxical, or not that chiefly, which, being false, puts on the semblance of truth; but, on the contrary, that which, being true, puts on the semblance of falsehood." Therefore it was that Boyle most accurately entitled some striking cases in statical physics *Hydrostatical Paradoxes*. Did he mean to advertise these startling facts of science as splendid falsehoods? No, but as great truths, which counterfeited the extravagant. [On this subject of the proper meaning of *paradox* De Quincey enlarges several times in other places.—M.]

sciously with no chance at all of purchasing any luxury whatsoever, little luxury or big luxury, for a space of ten years to come. One fellow-passenger, whom you will part with before sunset, has a powerful musical snuff-box; knowing by experience the power of such a toy over your own feelings, the magic with which at times it lulls your agitations of mind, you are vehemently desirous to purchase it. In the hour of leaving London you had forgot to do so: here is a final chance. But the owner, aware of your situation not less than yourself, is determined to operate by a strain pushed to the very uttermost upon U, upon the intrinsic worth of the article in your individual estimate for your individual purposes. He will not hear of D as any controlling power or mitigating agency in the case; and, finally, although at six guineas[1] apiece in London or Paris

[1] "*Six guineas*":—It is not a matter of much importance in a case which concerns us only by its principle, and where the principle would remain unaffected by any variation in the actual circumstances, what might be the price of a hypothetic snuff-box, in the hands of a hypothetic Jew, on the deck of a hypothetic steamboat. However, as a case within my own experience, it may be interesting to state the *known* extremes of price upon this class of trinkets. At present (1843) such boxes, coarsely mounted (in horn or mock tortoise-shell) are offered in London for one guinea apiece. Each box contains only two airs, which condition applies often indeed to boxes of seven, eight, or nine times the price; and a more important feature of inferiority lies in the slender volume of sound which the cheap ones emit. In a small room the music is sweet and sonorous, with the mimicry of an orchestric fulness; but, unless confined and concentrated, its power is too much on a miniature scale. On the other hand, in the opposite extreme, about twenty-seven years ago, I had an opportunity of seeing (or, more appropriately, of hearing) a musical snuff-box which had cost a thousand guineas. Inclosing a much profounder compass of harmonies, unavoidably it was inconveniently large,—that was its fault; and perhaps fifty guineas of the price might have been spent on the mounting, which was of gold ornamented. The interest of this toy lay in its history. Like a famous sword in the elder days of paganism, which gave occasion to the Greek proverb, *τα δωρα των πολεμιων ἀδωρα*, *bootless are the gifts of enemies*, or like a more famous horse in days a little later, both of which carried death and ruin through a long series of owners, this trinket was supposed to have caught in a fatal net of calamity all those whom it reached as proprietors. The box was a twin box (same time of making, same maker, same price) with one presented as a bribe to Napoleon. Amongst those who had once possessed it was a Jew—not our Jew on Lake

you might have loaded a waggon with such boxes, you pay sixty rather than lose it when the last knell of the clock has sounded which summons you to buy now or to forfeit for ever. Here, as before, only one element is operative: before it was D, now it is U. But, after all, D was not absent, though inoperative. The inertness of D allowed U to put forth its total effect. The practical compression of D being withdrawn, U springs up like water in a pump when released from the pressure of air. Yet still that D was present to your thoughts, though the price was otherwise regulated, is evident; both because U and D must co-exist in order to found any case of exchange value whatever, and because undeniably you take into very particular consideration this D, the extreme difficulty of attainment (which here is the

Superior, but another of London and Amsterdam, vulgarly reputed of immense wealth, who died unhappily. Him slightly I knew, and valued his acquaintance, for he had known intimately and admired, as "the foremost man of all this earth," Lord Nelson; and it illustrates the fervour of his veneration that always on reaching a certain point in Parliament Street he used to raise his hat, and bowed as to some shadowy presence, in memory that there for the last time he had met the great admiral on the day next but one before he left London for ever; viz. in the brief interspace between his return to Portsmouth from chasing the French fleet to the West Indies and his sailing to take the command of Cadiz. To Lord Nelson this perilous snuff-box had been offered repeatedly as an expression of idolatrous affection; but, as the fatal legend connected with it had not been concealed, Lord Nelson laughingly declined the gift. To laugh was inevitable in our age of weak faith for such superstitions; but, as a sailor,—who is generally credulous in such matters, and, if at all a man of feeling, must be so, considering the many invitations to superstition connected with that world of solitary wildernesses through which he roams for ever,—Lord Nelson was almost confessedly afraid of the box. Indeed, at that stage of its history, the owner would have found as much difficulty in transferring what he called his "pocket consoler" as the man who owned the bottle imp in ridding himself of that little pestilent persecutor. Here, however, so far as my own knowledge has extended, lay the higher extreme of costliness for such an article—one thousand guineas; whilst the lower extreme, in a tin or horn case, is offered, as I have said, for one guinea. But in the East Indies, amongst the native princes, such trinkets are found in abundance, and some perhaps even of higher value—musical clocks by the score, all chiming at once; and musical snuff-boxes by the hundred. They are naturally of European workmanship, as is perceived at once by the choice of the music.

greatest possible, viz. an impossibility), before you consent to have the price racked up to U. The special D has vanished, but it is replaced in your thoughts by an unlimited D. Undoubtedly you have submitted to U in extremity as the regulating force of the price; but it was under the sense of D's latent presence. Yet D is so far from exerting any positive force that the retirement of D from all agency whatever on the price—this it is which creates, as it were, a perfect vacuum, and through that vacuum U rushes up to its highest and ultimate graduation.

This is the foundation of any true solution applied to the difficulty of subdividing exchange value; and this statement of the case is open to a symbolical expression of its principle; which principle, let the reader not forget, is—that, under an eternal co-presence of two forces equally indispensable to the possibility of any exchange value at all, one only of those forces (and each alternately as the ultimate circumstances take effect) governs and becomes operative in the price. Both must concur to raise any motive for purchasing; but one separately it is which rules the price. Let not the reader quarrel beforehand with illustrations by geometrical symbols: the use which will be made of them is not of a kind to justify any jealousies of a surreptitious logic. It is a logic in applying which we abstract altogether from the qualities of objects, and consider them only in so far as they are liable to the affection of more and less. Simply the most elementary of geometrical ideas will be used; and the object is this—sometimes to render the student's apprehension of the case more definite, but sometimes also to show him that the same difficulty, or one analogous, might arise and be representable in the austere simplicities of geometry; in which case, by parity of argument, the explanation of the difficulty as represented in space will become inversely the explanation for the original difficulty.

Here the line U represents the utility value to the purchaser of any article whatever: that is, the very ultimate value to which, by possibility, it could ascend in the case that a screw were made to operate upon the purchaser's secret appreciation of its serviceable qualities. But in ordinary circumstances this cannot happen; and under such ordinary circumstances what will be the price? It will be the price determined by D—(difficulty of attainment)—and this difficulty is expressed by the line D. But mark how it acts. From the summit of the line D, standing on the same base as U, draw at right angles the dotted line which cuts U; that is to say, D, which is at present the operative force. The true determining force as regards the price takes up from U precisely as much (and no more at any time) as corresponds to itself. D is, in this case, the true and sole operating force. U, which must indeed be co-present (because else the purchaser would *not* be a purchaser—he would have no motive for purchasing—case *Epsilon*), yet, for all that, is inert *quoad* the price; itself submits to an action of D, but it exerts none, it reflects none the very smallest.

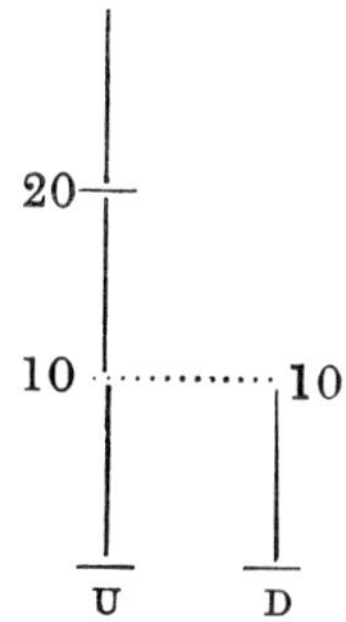


Now, suppose the case reversed: suppose not D, but U, to become suddenly the ruling force,—D has become infinite (as in the case of the musical toy in Canada): that is, the difficulties in the way of supplying the market by a continued reproduction of the article (in one word, the resistance) must be supposed so vast as to be quite beyond the power of any individual to overcome. Instantly, under these circumstances, U springs up to its utmost height. But what *is* the utmost? Because D, by ceasing to be finite and measurable, has caused U to come into play—will U therefore follow D, so as also to become infinite? Not at all: once called into action as the operating principle, U will become the sole principle; D will be practically extinct for any action that it can exert upon the price. The rare holders of the article, as surviving from past times or regions now inaccessibly distant, will fix a strain upon the few purchasers by means of the intrinsic or U value; each of the candidates must submit to see his own outside or extreme esteem for the article made operative against himself as the law of the price. He must ascend to the very *maximum* of what he will pay, under the known alternative of losing the article for ever if he will *not* pay it. U is therefore governed by no recollection of the past D, by no consideration of the present unlimited D,[1] but simply thrown back upon its own potential force; *i.e.* upon each purchaser's appreciation of the article for his own purposes—which can have *no* connexion whatever with the D, or variable resistance to the reproduction of that article in any particular place or time. If you submit to pay £30 of income-tax, doubtless the power of the state determines the general result of your paying at all; but it is not *that* which determines the how much: this is a mixed result from the Exchequer ratio on the one hand and the amount of your income on the other.

And that this is really so,—that both U and D, under the alternate circumstances, will become passive, latent, nugatory, as regards the price—may be shown *ex abundanti*; viz. by showing that, under any possible changes either to U or to D, no beginning, no initial moment, of action will arise for the one so long as the other is operative. Figure to yourself, as the object concerned in such a valuation, some powerful drug. Suppose it the Peruvian or Jesuit's bark, and that suddenly, by applying to it the agency of sulphuric acid, some new product (the sulphate of this foreign bark) arises with prodigiously greater powers—not only greater by far when applied to the common cases open equally to the old medicine and the new, but also in another respect greater: viz. that it is applicable to a set of cases from which the old medicine, by its bulk, or by its tendency to febrile symptoms, had found itself excluded. Suppose, under this enlarged power for the basis of the medicine, that the line U, expressing its utility value, should run up to triple or decuple of its present altitude, would that change disturb the present appreciation under D? Not by an iota. Nay, to press the principle to an excess, suppose U to become infinite—still, in all the cases where D is at all the regulative force, D will continue even under this change to be the sole force. Nay, suppose that,—even concurrently with this increase to

[1] "*By no consideration of the present* D":—*i.e.* in the appreciation which is thrown entirely upon U; but otherwise, in submitting to have the price thrown upon U—in submitting to purchase at all at a price so vastly exalted—doubtless he is governed by the existing D as a negative condition.

U,—D, by some cheaper or briefer process for obtaining the sulphate, should descend; still, even in such a compound case (vast increase for U—sudden decrease for D), not the less U would still continue inert—potentially capable, under the proper circumstances, of exerting an action which might centuple the price, and pitted against a decreasing force in D: nevertheless, so long as U was not in circumstances to exert the whole action, it could exert none at all; so long as D exerted any force, it would exert the whole.

In the opposite case, where U, or the utility value, is suddenly called into action as the controlling force, it will generally be found that this force, in its extremity, has not only been latent previously as regards any effect upon the price, but latent as regards even the consciousness of the individual appreciator. This we saw in the case of the musical toy on the Canadian lake. The buyer had not, until a certain moment, been aware of the potential U which really existed to his own contingent appreciation. No necessity had ever arisen that he should enquire rigorously how much he would submit to give in the case of U becoming the operative force. So much of U as was requisite to sustain D, so much as corresponded to D, had always been within the consciousness of the purchaser; and how much further it was capable of ascending had been hitherto a mere question of useless curiosity. But, when a sudden and violent revolution in all the circumstances has arisen for the purchaser, when D is felt to have become infinite, the difficulty of obtaining the article (except by one sole anomalous chance) being now greater than any *finite* expression could measure,—what follows? Does the price become infinite, as it would do if it were supposed at all to follow D? No; but D, though vexatiously present to the calculations of the purchaser, is no longer operative: it has become silent; and the alternate force U (now when the case has taken effect that either U screwed up to its maximum must rule, or else the article must be lost) instantly steps into the place of D, and becomes *exclusively* operative. The

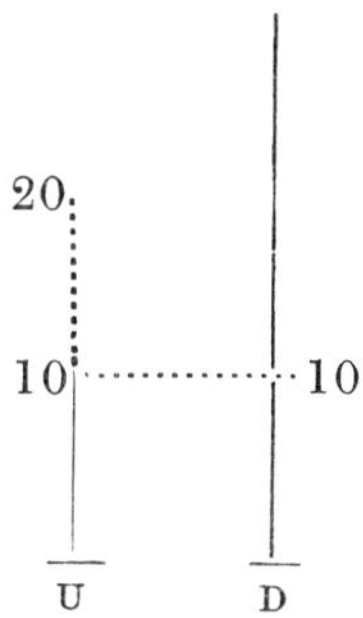

dotted perpendicular line represents the sudden ascent of U to double of its preceding altitude. How much further it would ascend must depend entirely upon the feeling and taste of the individual as regulating his wishes, and upon his disposable money as regulating his power.

Now, under this symbolic expression we may see at once the hyperbolic extravagance of that notion which has so often been cited with praise from Adam Smith, as though an object might be very great by its capacity in respect of D, and yet very little (or indeed nothing) by its capacity in respect of U. Diamonds, it is asserted, are trivial in respect of U, but enormously high on the scale measured by D. This is a blank impossibility. The mistake arises under a total misconception of what U indicates, as will be shown in a succeeding section. The countervailing proposition in Adam Smith,—viz. that other and ordinary objects, such as water, may reverse these conditions, being trivial in respect of D, but vast in respect of U,—is also false; false in the mode and principle of valuation. But this latter proposition is false only in fact; it is, at the same time, a very conceivable case: whereas the former proposition is false as to the very ideal possibility—it is inconceivable and monstrous. U may outrun D in any extent, and generally *does* so to some extent. It is rare that the whole potential utility value is exhausted by the cost or difficulty value. But the inverse case is monstrous; D can never outrun U by the most fractional increment. A man who would, in a case of necessity, give fifty guineas for an article rather than absolutely miss it, may habitually buy it for no more than three, simply because such is the price as squared to the scale of D. But it is impossible that a man, valuing the article (under the very ultimate pressure of U) at eight guineas, should consent to give twelve because D could not be overcome for less.

This latter part of the present section, viz. the symbolic illustration of the principles which control exchange value, may seem to the reader too long. Perhaps it is so; but he cannot pronounce it positively "de trop," for it enforces and explains this law,—viz. that the two eternally co-present forces essential to the idea of exchange nevertheless govern alternately one by one: each alternately becoming inert, and neither modifying the other by the smallest fraction, when that "other" is raised by circumstances into the true controlling principle. Now, this explanation never can be held useless so long as it shall be remembered that Adam Smith, in a passage not seldom cited as a proper basis for a whole system of dependent political economy, has absolutely declared it possible for a man to pay, by any assignable sum, a greater price for a commodity than that same man conceives its uttermost intrinsic value to justify: he will give more than the *maximum* which he *would* give. Not by one iota less extravagant is the proposition fairly deducible from his words. Diamands have no U value, he assures us—no use (which is the one sole ground upon which, at any price, a man buys anything at all); and yet, because the D value is great, in spite of this "no use," many a man will give an enormous price for diamonds: which proposition is a fierce impossibility. And although, as will be seen in the proper section, the word "use" is here employed most abusively, and in a sense unphilosophically limited, yet, in the same proportion by which this distinction as to the word "use" will redress some of the extravagant consequences deducible from the Smithian doctrine, in that same proportion will the famous antithesis upon diamonds and water, from which these consequences flow, vanish like a vapour; and thus will become available (against a party not within that writer's contemplation) a remark made by the critical dissertationist on value (as well as by the late Mr. Coleridge): viz. that oftentimes these plausible paradoxes on that side which offers any brilliancy will be found quite unsustainable; whilst on that side which can be sustained they will be found empty truisms—brilliant so far as they throw up a novel falsehood, but, where they reverberate a truth, utterly without either novelty or force. This remark was levelled by the dissertationist at others—chiefly (I believe) at Ricardo; but there is a luxury in seeing the engineer of so keen a truth, either in his own person or that of his friends, "hoist by his own petard."

## Section III.—On the True Relations in Logic of the Expressions U and D

There is no one manifestation of imbecile logic more frequent than the disposition to find in all controversies merely *verbal* disputes. Very early in life I came to be aware that this compendious mode of dismissing weighty questions—by alleging that in fact they seemed rather to offer a dispute about words than about things—had been always one regular and conscious resource of cant with the feeble and the indolent.[1] And amongst the first conclusions drawn from my own reading experience was this,—that for one known dispute seeming to concern things but ultimately evaporating in verbal cavils (supposing even *that one* to exist in any recorded form), there might be cited many hundreds of disputes which seemed, or had been declared, to be verbal, whilst by all their consequences they set in violently towards things.[2] The tendencies of men are altogether towards that error. In private companies where the tone of society is so underbred as to allow of two people annoying the rest by disputation such things as verbal disputes may possibly occur; but in public, where men dispute by the pen, or under ceremonial restraints, giving time for consideration, and often with large consequences awaiting the issue, such

[1] See *ante*, pp. 57-58.—M.

[2] This remark, made by myself in a spirit of youthful scorn for shallow thinkers, I shall not complain on finding imputed to others. Some years after, I met with it in one of the smaller philosophic essays, varying so much in merit, of Immanuel Kant. Fortunately it is of little consequence who first uttered a weighty truth: it is of the greatest that every truth be received for what it really is. The very feeblest amongst the "sons of the feeble" must be roused to the sense that they are canting when they find themselves challenged to the proof that ever any dispute, that so much as one which in any generation could be said properly to have existed by any test of books produced or passions excited, has turned at all upon words. And the daily experience in society, that all distinctions difficult to manage or to appraise are pronounced to *be* "*more verbal* than real," should open our eyes to the true origin of such pretences; they are the desperate resource of conscious weakness—the readiest evasion of a conflict for which the disputant feels that he has no strength and no preparation.

follies are out of the question: the strong natural instinct attached to the true and substantial, the practical results at hand, and the delays interposed for reflection, bar all opening to such visionary cases—possibilities indeed *in rerum natura*, but which no man has ever witnessed; and accordingly at this hour, throughout all our vast European libraries, no man can lay his hand upon one solitary book which argues a verbal question as if it were a real one, or contends for a verbal issue.[1]

The same capital mistake of false logic, mistaking its own greatest imbecility for conspicuous strength, has often alighted upon changes in terminology, or upon technical improvements of classification, as being in virtue no more than verbal changes. Here, again, we find Kant, though not the man meant by nature for clearing up delusions in the popular understanding, rightly contending that, in the science of algebra for instance, to impose new denominations

[1] Every man knows to what quarter the apologist for the cry of verbal disputes will address himself, viz. to the schoolmen; and, if we were to believe Locke, or many another of the same unsubtilising understanding, whose propensities to the tangible and the ponderable were a guarantee that they had never looked into such books, naturally we must suppose the whole vast product from those looms to be one tissue of moonshine and verbalism. Now, it is no part of my intention in this place to undertake a defence of the Scholastic Philosophy. But one error I must remark, as tending to sustain that delusive judgment on the schoolmen. It is popularly imagined that the scholastic philosophy was proved to be false in the decisive collision with another philosophy, more sound and practical; a regular conflict (it is imagined) came on between the two, and the issue was that the one triumphed while the other retired into obscurity. This is not true. The scholastic philosophy decayed simply because the scholastic divinity, to which it had been applied, and *for* which it had been originally created, was a Popish divinity. Thence came the first shock; and, after the Reformation, even the Papal Church was thrown upon such tactics and arms not as might be the best in a court of philosophy, but which could meet and parry the new practical and popular warfare of their opponents. Losing its *professional* use, scholasticism lost its main functions and occupation. The case was precisely as if special pleading were suddenly abolished in England by law. In one day the whole subtilties of that science would perish; but it would not therefore have been undermined in its pretensions, nor shown to be less than an exquisite system of casuistry, and a most elaborate machinery for keeping law up to the level of civilisation.

was often enough to reveal new relations which previously had not been suspected. In reality, we might go much further ; and of some changes in algebraic terminology (as particularly the invention of negative exponents) I should say that they had a value which could be adequately expressed only by such an analogy as might be drawn from the completion of a galvanic circle, where previously it had been interrupted. Not merely an addition of new power, but the ratification of all the previous powers yet inchoate, had been the result. It was impossible to use adequately the initial powers of the science until others had been added which distributed the force through the entire cycle of resistances.

In the present case, although the reader may fancy that such excessive solicitude for planting the great distinctions of value upon a true basis is not likely to reap any corresponding harvest of results in subsequent stages of the science, further experience will satisfy him that in all cases of dispute already existing, with the exception only of such as are still waiting for facts, and in all cases of efforts for the future progress of the science, it is really the ancient confusion overhanging this difficult theme of value which has been, or which will be, the sole retarding force. The question of value is that into which every problem finally resolves itself ; the appeal comes back to that tribunal, and for that tribunal no sufficient code of law has been yet matured which makes it equal to the calls upon its arbitration. It is a great aggravation of the other difficulties in the science of Economy that the most metaphysical part comes first. A German philosopher, who in that instance was aiming at anything but truth, yet with some momentary show of truth, once observed, with respect to the catechism of our English Church, that it was the most metaphysical of books in a case which required the simplest. "I," said he, "with all my philosophy, cannot swim where these infants are to wade." For my own part, I utterly deny his inference. To be simple, to be easy of comprehension, is but the second condition for a good elementary statement of Christian belief—the first is to be faithful. There is no necessity that all things should be at the earliest stage understood — in part they will never be understood in a human state, because they relate to what is infinite for an intellect which is finite. But there is a high necessity that, early in life, those distinctions should be planted which foreclose the mind, by a battery of prejudication and prepossession, against other interpretations, having perhaps the show of intelligibility, but terminating in falsehood,—which means contradiction to Scripture. Now, the condition of political economy is in this point analogous. Left to our own choice, naturally, none of us could wish to commence with what is most of all subtle, metaphysical, and perplexing. But no choice is allowed. Make a beginning at any other point, and the first explanation you attempt will be found to presuppose and involve all that you are attempting to evade ; and in such a case, after every attempt to narrow the immediate question into a mere occasional skirmish, you will find yourself obliged to bring on the general conflict, under the great disadvantage of being already engaged with a separate question—that is, on the most embarrassed ground you could possibly have selected. The great conflict, the main struggle, comes on at the very opening of the field ; and simply because *that* is too hastily and insufficiently fought out are all students forced, at one point or other, to retrace their steps—nay, simply from that cause, and no other, it is possible at this day to affirm with truth that, amongst many other strange results, no statesman in our British senate, and no leading critical review, has escaped that error in particular, that grossest and largest of errors, which is exposed in the 4th chapter upon market value. It is because men are impatient of the preliminary cares, efforts, and cautions, such as unavoidably they submit to in mathematics, that upon what is known in Economy there is perpetual uncertainty, and for any inroads into what is yet unknown perpetual insecurity.

The object of this section is to obtain a better, a more philosophic, and a more significant expression for the two modes of exchange value than those of U and D, employed hitherto, and, at the same time, to explode the expressions adopted by previous writers, as founded upon a false view of their relations.

In any exchange value whatsoever it has been agreed by all parties that both U and D must be present; there must be a real utility or serviceableness before a man will submit to be affected by D—*i.e.* before he will pay a price adjusted to the difficulty of attainment; and, *versa vice*, there must be this real difficulty of attainment before the simple fact of utility in the object will dispose him to pay for it, not by D in particular, but by anything at all. Now, though this is indispensable, yet, in the preceding section it has been shown that, whilst both alike are present, one only governs. And a capital error has been in fancying that value in use (value derived from U) is necessarily opposed to value in exchange; whereas, being one horn of the two into which value in exchange divides, as often as the value in use becomes operative at all it does itself become, it constitutes, value in exchange, and is no longer co-ordinate to exchange value (in which case it is wealth), but subordinate,—one subdivision of exchange value.

Now, then, having shown, under two different sets of circumstances, that the one element and the other will with equal certainty take effect and become dominant, I will request the student to consider what, after all, is the true, sole, and unvarying consideration which acts upon the mind of the purchaser in the first intention of wishing to possess. As regards the price, what acts is alternately U and D; sometimes one, sometimes the other. But not so with regard to the general purpose of buying. Here only one thing acts. No man ever conceived the intention of buying upon any consideration of the difficulty and expense which attend the production of an article. He wishes to possess, he resolves to buy, not on account of these obstacles—far from it—but in spite of them. What acts as the positive and sole attraction to him is the intrinsic serviceableness of the article towards some purpose of his own. The other element may happen to affect the price, and, generally speaking, *does* affect it as the sole regulating force, but it can never enter at all into the original motive for seeking to possess the article; uniformly, it is viewed in the light of a pure resistance to that desire.

Here, then, present themselves two reasonable designations

for supplanting U and D, which are far better—as being, 1*st*, in true logical opposition, and, 2*dly*, as pointing severally each to its own origin and nature. U may be called *affirmative*, D *negative*. The latter represents the whole resistance to your possession of the commodity concerned; the former represents the whole benefit, the whole positive advantage, the whole power accruing to you from possession of this commodity. There is always an affirmative value, there is always a negative value, on any commodity bearing an exchange value—that is, on any which can enter a market; but one only of these values takes effect at one time: under certain circumstances, the affirmative value; under other and more ordinary circumstances, the negative. And, accordingly, as one or other becomes operative, as it ceases to be latent and rises into the effectual force, we may say of it that it has passed into the corresponding price,—affirmative value into affirmative price, negative value into negative price. For price is value ratified or made effectual—the potential raised into the actual.

Many years ago, in a slight and unfinished sketch of what is most peculiar to Ricardo (bearing the title of "The Templars' Dialogues"),[1] I made it my business to show that a general confusion had pervaded Political Economy between two cardinal ideas—a *measure* of value, and a *ground* of value; that no writer within my knowledge had escaped this confusion; that the former idea was demonstrably a chimera, an *ens rationis*, which never could be realised; that, except in one instance[2] (viz. when needed as a test of the

[1] In connexion with the word "unfinished" here, see *ante*, pp. 111-112 and footnote there.—M.

[2] "*Except in one instance*":—Whether I remembered to make this exception, it is out of my power to say positively, having no copy of the little sketch in question [see *ante*, pp. 94-97.—M.]; but certainly I ought to have made it. At this moment there are men of great ability who believe that the whole relief from the war taxation of 1814 and 1815 now accumulated (say in round numbers the difference annually between eighty and fifty millions sterling) is made nugatory by an alleged rise in the value of money, as contrasted with the supposed depreciation (so eternally asserted) upon the national currency during the seven last years of the great war. What the taxpayer has gained by the relief he has lost in the higher value of what he continues to pay. Such is the allegation.

variations, whether real or only apparent, between successive stages of a paper currency), no practical benefit would be derived from the realisation of such a measure; whereas, on the other hand, a *ground* of value is so indispensable an idea that without it not one step can be taken in advance.

The author of "A Critical Dissertation on Value," who does me much honour in saying (p. xxv of Preface) that this little sketch of mine it was which "first suggested" his own work, gives two different opinions in the same page (p. 171) as to the original delivery of this broad distinction. In the text he says—"The author of the 'Templars' Dialogues on "Political Economy' is the only writer who appears to me "to have been fully aware of this confusion of two separate "and distinct ideas. He traces it partly to an ambiguity in "the word *determine*." But in a footnote on this same sentence he thus corrects himself:—"This was written "before I had seen the second edition of Mr. Mill's 'Elements,' "in which the distinction is for the first time introduced. "His language on this point, however, is not uniformly con-"sistent, as will be shown in the next chapter." I apprehend that, if any such distinction has been anywhere insisted upon *consciously* by Mr. Mill, it will be difficult to establish a priority for *him*. The fragment called "The Templars' Dialogues" was written at the end of 1821, and, to the best of my recollection, printed in the spring of 1822. Having never seen any edition whatsoever of Mr. Mill's "Elements" until this present return to the subject (spring of 1843), I obtained a copy from a public library. This happens to be the first edition (which is clear from the fact that no attempt occurs in this work at any distinction whatever between a "measure" and a "ground" of value); and this bears the date of 1821 upon the title-page. It seems probable, therefore, that the date of the second edition would be, at the earliest, 1822—a question, however, which I have no means of deciding.[1] But, be that as it may, two facts seem to discredit such a claim: 1*st*, that Mr. Mill, at p. iv of the

[1] If the second edition of James Mill's *Elements of Political Economy* was published in 1822, it *had* a priority to De Quincey's *Templars' Dialogues*; which were not published till 1823, though De Quincey misrecollects the date as 1822.—M.

Preface, says, "I profess to have made no discovery"; whereas, beyond all doubt, a distinction which exposes suddenly a vast confusion of thought affecting the great mob of books upon this subject *is* a discovery, and of very extensive use. *2dly*, it turns out, from a charge alleged at p. 204 by the Dissertator on Value, that Mr. Mill "confounds the *standard* with the *cause* of value." I understand him to mean, not that constructively Mr. Mill confounds these ideas, not that such a confusion can be extorted from his words though against his intention, but that formally and avowedly he insists on the identity of the two ideas. If so, there is an end of the question at once; for "a standard of value" is but a variety of the phrase "*measure* of value." The one, according to a scholastic distinction (most beneficially revived by Leibnitz), is a mere *principium cognoscendi*; the other (a *ground* of value) is a *principium essendi.*[1] What

[1] Both of these *principia* (the *esse* and the *scire*) meet and are confounded by our word "*determine.*" This was a former remark of my own in the "Templars' Dialogues," which I am enabled to quote indirectly through a quotation from that little sketch made at p. 171 by the Dissertator on Value:—"The word *determine* may be taken "subjectively for what determines $x$ in relation to our knowledge, or "objectively for what determines $x$ in relation to itself. Thus, if I "were to ask what determined the length of the racecourse?—and "the answer were, 'The convenience of the spectators,' or 'The choice "of the subscribers,' then it is plain that by the word *determined* I "was understood to mean *determined objectively*, in relation to the "existence of the object; in other words, what *caused* the racecourse "to be this length rather than another length. But, if the answer were, "*An actual admeasurement*, it would then be plain that by the word "*determined* I had been understood to mean *determined subjectively*— "*i.e.* in relation to our knowledge—what ascertained it." [See the passage, *ante*, pp. 35-36.—M.] Thus, again, it may be said, in one sense, that men determined the exact length of a degree in latitude, that is, of the interspace divided by 90 between either pole of our earth and its equator. But this is merely the *ratio cognoscendi.* Men determined it in the sense of rigorously measuring it. But the length of a degree could be determined causatively (in the sense of first establishing such a quantity) by no power less than that which could first form a planet having the shape of an oblate spheroid, combined with such and such dimensions, arising out of an axis about seven thousand miles long. This is the *ratio essendi.*—How necessary it is that this great distinction should be recalled might be exemplified by a large volume of cases where the failure of philosophic attempts has been due exclusively to its neglect. A greater failure, for example, there

qualifies an object to be a standard of value,—that is, to *stand* still when all other objects are moving,—and thus by consequence qualifies it to measure all changes of value between any two objects, showing, as on a delicate scale, how much of the change has belonged to the one object, how much to the other, or whether either has been stationary: this is a thing which we shall never learn, because no such qualification can arise for *any* object—none can be privileged from change affecting itself. And, if liable to change itself, we need not quote Aristotle's remark on the Lesbian rule to prove that it can never measure the changes in other objects. A measure of value is therefore not by accident impossible, but impossible by the very constitution of its idea ; precisely as the principle of perpetual motion is not accidentally impossible (by failure of all efforts yet made to discover it), but essentially impossible so long as this truth remains in force —that it is impossible to propagate motion without loss. On the other hand, to seek for the cause or ground of value is not only no visionary quest, speculatively impossible and practically offering little use, but is a *sine qua non* condition for advancing by a single step in political economy. Everything that enters a market we find to have some value or other. Everything in every case is known to be isodynamic with some fraction, some multiple, or some certain proportion, of everything else. For this universal scale of relations, for this vast table of equations, between all commodities concerned in human traffic, a ground, a sufficient reason, must exist. What is it? Upon examination it is found that there are two grounds, because there are two separate modes of exchange value for which I have deduced, as the adequate designations, the antithetic terms *affirmative* and *negative*. And, if the reader will look forward to Section IV, which arrays before him a considerable list of cases under each form, he will perceive (what in fact is my object in exposing those

cannot be than in Paley's Moral Philosophy as to its grounds, and in Lord Shaftesbury's Doctrine of Ridicule as a Criterion of Truth. But in both cases the true vice of the theories lay in this common confusion between the two *rationes*—the *ratio essendi* (accounting causatively for the existence), the *ratio cognoscendi* (accounting in the way of proof for the certainty of the knowledge). As regards the doctrine of value, such a distinction was at this point indispensable.

cases) simultaneously a proof of the necessity that such cases should exist and an illustration of the particular circumstances under which each arises. But first, and before all other remarks which he will be likely to make on this ζευγος—this two-headed system of cases—I anticipate the remark which follows: viz. that, such and so broad being the distinction between this double system of cases, it is not possible that former economists should have overlooked it. "Under some name or other," he will say, "I am satisfied that these distinctions must have been recognised." He will be right. The distinction *has* been recognised—*has* been formally designated. And what are the designations? Everywhere almost the same: the price which corresponds to the difficulties has been properly called the cost price, as representing in civilised societies the total resistance which is usually possible to the endless reproduction of an article. So far there is no blame; but go forward; go on to the opposite mode of price—to that which I have called the affirmative price. By what name is it that most economists designate *that*? They call it "*monopoly price*," or "*scarcity price*." But monopoly, but scarcity—these are accidents; these are impertinences—*i.e.* considerations not pertinent, not relevant to the case; or, to place the logic of the question under the clearest light, these express only the *conditio sine qua non*, or negative condition. But is *that* what we want? Not at all; we want the positive cause—technically, the *causa sufficiens*—of this antagonist price. That cause is found, not in the scarcity or the monopoly—Aristotle forbid such nonsense! (how could a pure absence or defect of importation, how could a mere negation, produce a robust *positive* ens—a price of sixty guineas?) No; but in something that has existed antecedently to all monopoly or scarcity; in a strong affirmative attraction of the article concerned; in a positive adaptation of this article to each individual buyer's individual purposes. True, the accidental scarcity brings this latent affirmative cause into play; but for that scarcity this latent cause might have concealed itself for generations—might never have acted. The scarcity it is—the absolute stoppage to all further receipts of the article from its regular reproduction—which has enabled *something* to rise into action as the regulator of price. But what *is* that something? You say, popularly, that the absence of a sentinel caused the treasury to be robbed; and this language it would be pedantic to censure, because the true meaning is liable to no virtual misconstruction. But everybody *would* censure it if the abstraction of "absence" were clothed with the positive attributes of a man, and absence were held responsible for the larceny to the exculpation of the true flesh-and-blood criminal. The case is in all respects the same as to scarcity: the scarcity creates the opening or occasion for "something" to supersede the D or negative value; but that something is the U value—the affirmative value.

This must be too self-evident to require any further words: the technical term of "scarcity value," adopted as the antithesis of "cost value" by Ricardo, by Mr. M'Culloch, and many beside, will not be defended by anybody, except under the idea that the false logic which it involves is sure to undergo a correction from the logical understanding. But it is unsafe trusting too much to *that*. In the hurry of disputation it would be too late to revise our terms, to allow for silent errors, and to institute *pro hac vice* rectifications. It is indispensable to the *free* movement of thought that we should have names and phrases for expressing our ideas upon which we can rely at all hours as concealing no vestige of error. Now, against the technical term in possession, besides the conclusive reasons already exposed, there may be alleged these two sufficient absurdities as consequences to which it is liable:—

1*st*, That, in any case of such scarcity actually realised, the scarcity could not be imagined to create a price; because neither as an absolute scarcity nor as graduated to any particular point could it have more relation to one price than to any other—to a shilling than to a thousand guineas. As rationally might it be said that the absence of the sentinel, according to the degrees of its duration, had created the costliness of the articles robbed from the treasury.

2*d*, That, if such a shadow as a blank negation *could* become a positive agency of causation, still there would arise many monstrous absurdities. One case will suffice as an illustration of all. Suppose the scarcity as to two articles to be absolute—in other words, the greatest possible, or beyond any finite degree—then, if the scarcity were the acting cause of the new price, which has superseded the old D price, being the same in both cases, this scarcity must issue in producing the same price for both articles: whereas the true cause, which has been brought into action by the scarcity and the consequent abolition of D, being in reality the U or utility value (pushed to its *maximum*), will soon show decisively that the one article may not reach the price of half-a-crown, whilst the other may run up to a thousand guineas.

It is useless to talk of "words" and "names" as being shadows, so long as words continue to express ideas, and names to distinguish actual relations. Verbalism it is in fact, and the merest babble of words, which can substitute a pure defect—so aerial an abstraction as a want or an absence—for a positive causal agency. *That* is really scholastic trifling. The true agencies in the case under discussion are eternally and alternately D and U—the resistance to the reproduction of the article, or the power in use of that article. Finally, it has been shown why these should be termed the affirmative and negative values of the article, and, from the moment when either value takes effect (ceases to be latent, and become operative upon the market), should be termed severally affirmative and negative price.[1]

[1] In the text of this section it did not seem requisite to pause for any distinction between monopoly and scarcity. But it may be right to add a few lines in a note for the sake of novices, who will naturally feel perplexed by the confused relations between two ideas approaching to each other, yet not identical; and still more perplexed by a case growing out of the two, viz. this:—They have heard the policy of creating an artificial scarcity by a partial destruction sometimes ridiculed as an extravagance too monstrous to be entertained, except by the most credulous of starving mobs, and sometimes solemnly attested by historical records. Where lies the truth? Is such a policy conceivable, or is it an absurd romance?

There are scarcities which imply no monopoly, as the occasional scarcity in England (every ten years less possible) of corn or hay; and inversely there are monopolies which imply no original scarcity, as that of spices in the hands of the Old Dutch East India Company. A monopoly does not necessarily act through any factitious or counterfeit scarcity. The English East India Company, that wisest and most princely of commercial institutions, long held a monopoly of tea; but there was no more of artificial scarcity ever created for the sake of giving effect to this monopoly during its long existence than we have

## Section IV.—On the Two Modes of Exchange Value, Affirmative and Negative

The business of this present section is chiefly to illustrate by cases the two possible modes of exchange value: viz. the alternate modes as founded on a negative principle and as founded on an affirmative principle. Any reader, therefore, who is already satisfied with this distinction and its grounds may pass on (without disturbing the *nexus* or logical dependency of the parts) to Section V.

That general principle which governs the transition under the appropriate circumstances from negative to affirmative value, might be brought forcibly before the reader by a political case drawn from the civil administration of ancient Rome. Any foreigner coming to Rome before the democratic basis of that republic had given way, would have found some difficulty (when reviewing the history of Rome) in accounting

experienced since the period of its abolition. On the other hand, the Dutch did confessedly destroy, at times, one ship-load of spices out of three, in order to sustain the prices of the other two in the markets of Europe. This fact is, I believe, historically certain, and might oftentimes become a very prudent policy. Yet, in opposition to this known precedent, what seems a parallel case of destruction on the part of English farmers has been loudly rejected as ridiculous; and certainly with justice. "But why"; the novice will ask—"in what lies the difference?" It lies in this:—For any party under any circumstances to create a beneficial scarcity, what he has to do is this:—1*st*, To destroy so largely as materially to raise the price on all which remains; 2*d*, To leave so large a remainder as may much more than compensate (by the higher price upon a reduced quantity) that original price which might have been received upon the whole quantity whilst unreduced. But to take the first step with any effect demands a conspiracy amongst all the sellers. Now, the Dutch East India Company were always in a conspiracy; they, from their common interest and unity of federation, stood constantly "*in procinctu*" for such a measure. But to the English farmers, dispersed so widely and thinking so variously, the initial steps towards a conspiracy, of whatever nature it might be, are impossible. No man can count upon any sacrifice but his own; yet even a conspiracy along a whole district or country-side (all impossible as it is) would not affect the national price of grain more than by a quantity equal to the consumption of one regiment or one line-of-battle ship fully manned; and we all know how trivial in its effects on the national markets is the sailing on foreign service of many regiments and of many ships. Such a removal of troops or seamen is, however,

for the principle which had governed the award of triumphs. "I am at a loss," he would say, "to reconcile the rule which in some instances appears to have prevailed with that which must have prevailed at others. In one case I see a rich province overrun, and no triumph granted to the conqueror; in another, I see a very beggarly (perhaps even a mutinous and unmanageable) province—no source of strength, but rather of continual anxiety to Rome—made the occasion of a most brilliant triumph, and even of a family title, such as 'Macedonicus' or 'Isauricus,' the most gratifying personal distinction which Rome had to confer." Here would seem a contradiction; but the answer could dispel it.—"We regard," it would be said on behalf of Rome, "two separate and alternate considerations. No province, whether poor or rich, has ever been annexed to our republic which had not this primary condition of value—that it tended to complete our arch of empire. By mere locality, as one link in a chain, it has tended to the *arrondissement* of our dominions, the orb

the case realised (as to its uttermost effect) of a conspiracy far beyond any that ever will be practicable. In the final result, therefore, the Dutchman, who is the person to suffer by the first step, is the same who will reap the whole indemnity and profit in the second. But the Englishman will find himself unable to create any such second stage in the case: his utmost sacrifices will not come near to the effect of raising the price; and, if they could, it will not be himself, with a reduced quantity, who can reap the compensation for his own sacrifices, but others who have made no such sacrifices, and who retain their undiminished stock to benefit by the new prices.

Yet how, it may be asked by the novice, can even the Dutchman be sure of receiving a balance of gain upon the case?—of not losing more by the quantity destroyed than can always be fetched back by a higher price upon the quantity which remains? Simply under his experience of the average, annual or triennial, demand for spices in Europe—under this, taken in combination with that notorious principle first consciously remarked by Sir Richard Steele in an age almost ignorant of political economy: viz. that upon any article of primary demand a deficiency to the extent of one-tenth will not enhance the price simply by a corresponding one-tenth, but say by one-fourth; whilst a deficiency of one-fourth will not, in its reaction upon price, confine itself to that proportion, but will frequently go near to double the price. Such are the circumstances of fact and principle which make that experiment ludicrously impossible for the English farmer which for the Dutch farmer of Java or the Moluccas was, in years of redundant produce, a hopeful, and at times even a necessary, measure.

within which our power circulates." So far *any* province whatsoever added within the proper Mediterranean circuit had always a claim upon the republic for some trophy of honour. But, to raise this general claim to a level with triumphal honours, we Romans required[1] that one or other of these two *extra* merits should be pleaded :—either, first, that the province, though not rich, had been won by peculiarly hard fighting ; or, secondly, that, though won with very slight efforts, the province was peculiarly rich. The primary, the indispensable value, as a link in the Roman chain, every province must realise that tended to complete the zone drawn round the Mediterranean. Even a wilderness of rocks would have that value. But, this being presumed, of course, as an advantage given by position without merit in the winner, we required, as the crest of the achievement towards justifying a triumph, either the affirmative value of great capacities for taxation, or the negative value of great difficulties overcome in the conquest. Cilicia, for example, returned little in the shape of revenue to Rome ; for the population was scanty, and, from the condition of society, wealth was impossible. But the Isaurian guerillas, and the Cilician bucaniers, occupying for many centuries caves and mountain fortresses that without gunpowder were almost impregnable, gave a sanguinary interest to the conflict, which compensated the small money value. For eight centuries Cilicia was the scourge of the Levant. Palestine again presented even a bloodier contest, though less durable, in a far narrower compass. But Egypt — poor, effeminate Egypt! always "a servant of servants"—offered, amidst all her civilisation, no shadow of resistance. As a test of military merit, she could not found a claim for any man ; for six hundred miles she sank on her knees at the bidding of the Roman centurion. So far, the triumph was nothing. On the other hand, Egypt was by wealth the first of all provinces. She was the greatest of

[1] "*We Romans required*" :—Originally the test applied to a claim of this nature lay in the number of throats cut—a *minimum* being fixed for a triumph, and a separate *minimum* for the "little go" of an ovation. But this test was applied only in early times whilst the basis of difficulty was more nearly identical. In times of higher civilisation, when this basis became more complex and variously modified, the grounds of claim and the test were modified conformably.

coeval granaries.[1] The province technically called Africa, and the island of Sicily, were bagatelles by comparison; and what, therefore, she wanted as the *negative* criterion of merit, having so much wealth, she possessed redundantly in the *affirmative* criterion. Transalpine Gaul, again, was a fine province under both criteria. She took much beating. In the half-forgotten language of the *fancy*, she was "a glutton"; and, secondly, on the affirmative side she was also rich.—Thus might an ancient Roman have explained and reconciled the apparently conflicting principles upon which triumphs had been awarded. Where a stranger had fancied a want of equitable consistency, because two provinces had been equally bloodless acquisitions, and yet had not equally secured a triumph, he would now be disabused of his error by the sudden explanation that the one promised great wealth, the other little. And, where, again, between two provinces equally worthless as regarded positive returns of use, he had failed to understand why one should bring vast honour to the winner, the other none at all, his embarrassment would be relieved at once by showing him that the unhonoured conquest had fallen at the first summons, possibly as a mere effect of reaction from *adjacent* victories; whilst the other conquest had placed on the record a brilliant success, surmounting a resistance that had baffled a series of commanders, and so far flattering to the Roman pride, but in another sense transcendently important, as getting rid of an ominous exposure which proclaimed to the world a possibility of hopeful opposition to Rome.

Now, exactly the same principle, transferred to the theory of value in exchange, will explain the two poles on which it revolves. Sometimes you pay for an article on the scale of its use—its use with regard to your individual purposes. On this principle, you pay for A suppose twice as much as you would consent to pay for B. The point at which you pause,

[1] Egypt was so capable of feeding vast armies that for that reason only she was viewed as the potential mother of rebellions, as the eternal temptress of the ambitious. Whence grew the Roman rule that no proconsul, no man of senatorian rank, should ever go into Egypt as a lieutenant of the Republic or the Emperor: such a man's powers would have been too ample, and his rank of too much authority.

and would choose to go without B rather than pay more for it, does not rise more than one-half so high on the scale as the corresponding *ne plus ultra* for A. This is affirmative price. On the other hand, sometimes you pay for an article on the scale of its costliness—*i.e.* of its resistance to the act of reproduction. This principle is not a direct natural expression of any intrinsic usefulness; it is an indirect, and properly an exponential, expression of value, by an alien accident perfectly impertinent to any interest of yours: not what good it will do to yourself, but what harm it has done to some other man (viz. what quantity of trouble it has imposed upon him),—that is the *immediate*[1] question which this second principle answers. But, unnatural (that is, artificial) as such a principle seems, still, in all civilised countries this is the principle which takes effect by way of governing force upon price full twenty times for once that the other and natural principle takes effect.

Now, having explained the two principles, I find it my next duty to exemplify them both by appropriate cases. These, if judiciously selected, will both prove and illustrate.

In the reign of Charles II occurred the first sale in England of a RHINOCEROS. The more interesting wild beasts—those distinguished by ferocity, by cruelty, and agility—had long been imported from the Mediterranean; and, as some of them were "good fellows and would strike" (though, generally speaking, both the lion and the tiger are the merest curs in nature), they bore tolerable prices, even in the time of Shakspeare. But a rhinoceros had not been yet imported; and, in fact, that brute is a dangerous connexion to form. As a great lady from Germany replied some seventy years ago to an Englishman who had offered her an elephant—"*Mit nichten*, by no means; him eat too mauch." In spite, however, of a similar infirmity, the rhinoceros fetched, under Charles II, *more* than £2000. But why? on what principle? Was it his computed negative value? Not at all. A granite obelisk from Thebes,

[1] "*Immediate*," because, upon a secondary consideration, you become aware that the trouble imposed on the maker is spared to yourself; yet still the ground of value remains what it was—not a benefit reaped, but an evil evaded.

or a Cleopatra's needle, though as heavy as a pulk of rhinoceroses, would not have cost so much to sling and transport from the Niger to the Thames. But in such a case there are two reasons why the purchaser is not anxious to inquire about the cost. In buying a loaf *that* is an important question, because a loaf will be bought every day, and there is a great use in knowing the cost or negative value, as that which will assuredly govern an article of daily reproduction. But in buying a rhinoceros, which it is to be hoped that no man will be so ill-fated as to do twice in one world, it is scarcely to be hoped that the importer will tell any truth at all, nor is it of much consequence that he should; for the buyer cares little by comparison as to the separate question on the negative price of the brute to his importer. He cares perhaps not very much more as to the *separate* question upon the affirmative return likely to arise for himself in the case of his exhibiting such a monster. Neither value taken singly was the practical reply to his anxieties. That reply was found in both values, taken in combination—the negative balanced against the affirmative. It was less important to hear that the cost had been £1000, so long as the affirmative return was conjecturally assigned at little beyond £2200, than to hear that the immediate cost to the importer had been £2000, but with the important assurance that £5000, at the very least, might be almost guaranteed from the public exhibition of so delicate a brute. The creature had not been brought from the Barbary States, our staple market for monsters, but from some part of Africa round the Cape; so that the cost had been unusually great. But the affirmative value, founded on the public curiosity, was greater; and, when the two terms in the comparison came into collision, then was manifested the excess of the affirmative value, in that one instance, as measured against the negative. An "encore" was hardly to be expected for a rhinoceros in the same generation; but for that once it turned out that a moderate fortune might be raised upon so brutal a basis.

TURKISH HORSES.—Pretty nearly at the same time, viz. about the year 1684, an experiment of the same nature was made in London upon an animal better suited to sale, but almost equally governed in its price by affirmative qualities.

In this instance, however, the qualities lay in excess of beauty and docility, rather than of power and strange conformation. Three horses, of grace and speed at that time without parallel in western Europe, were brought over to England, and paraded before the English court. Amongst others, Evelyn saw them, and thus commemorates the spectacle:—"*December* 17.—Early " in the morning, I went into St. James's Park to see three " Turkish or Asian horses, newly brought over, and now first " showed to his Majesty [Charles II, who died about six " weeks later]. There were [had been] four, but one of " them died at sea, being three weeks coming from Ham- " borow. They were taken from a bashaw at the siege of " Vienna, at the late famous raising that leaguer.[1] I never " beheld so delicate a creature as one of them was; of some- " what a bright bay; in all regards beautifull and propor- " tion'd to admiration; spirited, proud, nimble; making " halt, turning with that swiftnesse, and in so small a com- " pass, as was admirable. With all this, so gentle and tract- " able as call'd to mind what Busbequius speakes to the " reproach of our groomes in Europe, who bring up their " horses so churlishly as makes most of them retain their " ill habits." Busbequius [2] talks nonsense. This, and the notion that our western (above all, our English) horses are made short-lived by luxurious stables, &c., are old "crazes" amongst ourselves. Mr. Edmond Temple, in his Peru,[3] evidently supposes that, with worse grooming, and if otherwise sufficiently ill-treated, our English horses would live generally to the age of forty—possibly, I add, of a thousand, which would be inconvenient. As to the conceit of Busbequius, it is notorious to Englishmen that the worst-tempered

[1] "*Raising that leaguer*":—viz. by John Sobieski in 1683, upon which great event (the *final* disappearance of Mussulmans from central Christendom) is that immortal sonnet of Filicaja's, so nobly translated by Wordsworth: "He [Sobieski] conquering THROUGH God, and God BY him." [This is the closing line of Wordsworth's sonnet entitled "Siege of Vienna raised by John Sobieski," eleven lines of which consist of translation from an ode by Filicaia.—M.]

[2] The French Auger Gisleu Busbec (Latinised "Busbequius"), born 1522, died 1592. He was sent on an embassy into Turkey; and his Travels in that country were once a very popular book.—M.

[3] *Travels in Various Parts of Peru.* London, 1830.—M.

horses in the world (often mere devils in malignity) are many of the native breeds in Hindostan, who happen, unfortunately for the hypothesis, to have oftentimes the very gentlest grooms. The particular horses brought over from the Turkish rout under Vienna, by their exquisite docility, would seem to have been Arabs. The cross of our native breed by the Arab blood, which has since raised the English racer to perfection, was soon after begun (I believe) under the patronage of the Godolphin family. From this era, when Arab velocity for a short burst had been inoculated upon English "bottom," or enduring energy, the Newmarket racer rose to a price previously unheard of in the annals of the horse. So low, however, was the affirmative standard at this period in England, so little had the latent perfections of the animal (the affirmative value) been developed, that of these matchless Arabians, sold on the terms of including the romantically gorgeous appointments for both horse and rider, even the finest was offered for five hundred guineas, and all three together for a thousand. This price had reference (as also in the case of the rhinoceros) exclusively to affirmative value.[1]

PARADISE LOST.—Were you (walking with a foreigner in London) to purchase for eighteenpence a new copy of this poem, suppose your foreign friend to sting your national pride by saying—"Really it pains me to see the English putting so slight a value upon their great poet as to rate his greatest work no higher than eighteenpence"—how would you answer? Perhaps thus:—"My friend, you mistake the matter. The price does not represent the *affirmative* value—the value derived from the *power* of the poem to please or to exalt; *that* would be valued by some as infinite, irrepresentable by money; and yet the *resistance* to its reproduction

[1] "*To affirmative value*":—That is, applied itself to the *direct* service or pleasure anticipated from the animal, calculated on so many years' purchase, not to any *indirect* exponent or measure of this service. In the case of the rhinoceros (and also of the modern race-horse, as compared with the hunter a little further on), the construction of the affirmative value is somewhat different in form, though substantially the same. *There* the animal is viewed productively: both rhinoceros and racer sell upon the ground of affirmative value; they make returns, but returns in money, and not (as the bashaw's horses) in ornament, sense of beauty, luxurious motion, &c.

might be less than the price of a breakfast." Now here, the ordinary law of price exposes itself at once. It is the *power*, the affirmative worth, which creates a fund for any price at all; but it is the *resistance*, the negative worth, or what we call the cost, which determines how much shall be taken from that potential fund. In bibliographic records there are instances of scholars selling a landed estate equal to an annual livelihood for ever in order to obtain a copy of one single book—viz. an Aristotle. At this day there are men whose estimate of Aristotle is not at all less. Having long since reached his lowest point of depression from the influence of sciolism and misconception, for at least fifty years Aristotle has been a rising author. But does any man pay an estate in exchange for Aristotle as now multiplied? Duval's in folio may be had for two guineas; the elder edition of Sylburgius in quarto may be had (according to our own juvenile experience) for ten guineas; and the modern Bipont by Buhle, only that it is unfinished, may be had for less than three. *There* is the reason for the difference between former purchasers and modern purchasers. The *resistance* is lowered; but the affirmative value may, for anything that is known, be still equal in many minds to that which it was in elder days—and in some minds we know that it is. The fair way to put this to the test would be to restore the elder circumstances. Then the book was a manuscript; printing was an undiscovered art; so that merely the *resistance* value was much greater, since it would cost a much larger sum to overcome that resistance where the obstacle was so vast a mass of manual labour than where the corresponding labour in a compositor would multiply, by the pressman's aid, into a thousand copies, and thus divide the cost amongst a thousand purchasers. But this was not all. The owner of a manuscript would not suffer it to be copied. He knew the worth of his prize; it had a monopoly value. And what is that? Monopoly value is affirmative value carried to extremity. It is the case where you press to the ultimate limit upon the desire of a bidder to possess the article. It is no longer a question—for how little might it be afforded? You do not suffer him to put that question. You tell him plainly that, although he might have it copied for forty pounds instead of sinking upon the original manuscript a perpetual estate yielding forty pounds annually, you will not allow it to be copied. Consequently you draw upon that fund which, in our days, so rarely *can* be drawn upon: viz. the ultimate esteem for the object—the last bidding a man will offer under the known alternative of losing it.

This alternative rarely exists in our days. It is rarely in the power of any man to raise such a question. Yet sometimes it is; and we will cite a case, which is curious, in illustration. In 1812 occurred the famous Roxburghe sale, in commemoration of which a distinguished club was subsequently established in London. It was a library which formed the subject of this sale; and in the series of books stood one which was perfectly unique in affirmative value. This value was to be the sole force operating on the purchaser; for, as to the negative value, estimated on the resistance to the multiplication of copies, it was impossible to assign any: no price would overcome that resistance. The book was the VALDARFER[1] BOCCACCIO. It contained, not all the works of that author, but his Decameron—and, strange enough, it was not a manuscript, but a printed copy. The value of the book lay in these two peculiarities: 1st, it was asserted that all subsequent editions had been castrated with regard to those passages which reflected too severely on the Papal Church; 2dly, the edition, as being incorrigible in that respect, had been so largely destroyed that, not without reason, the Roxburghe copy was believed to be unique. In fact, the book had not been seen during the two previous centuries; so that it was at length generally held to be a nonentity. And the biddings went on as they would do for the Wandering Jew, in case he should suddenly turn up as a prize subject for life insurances. The contest soon rose buoyantly above the element of little men. It lay between two "top-sawyers," the late Lord Spencer and Lord Blandford, and finally was knocked down to the latter for two thousand two hundred and forty pounds—at a time when five per cent was obtained everywhere, and readily, for money. It illustrates the doctrine on which we are now engaged that the purchaser some few years later, when Duke of Marlborough, and in personal

[1] Valdarfer was the printer.

embarrassments, towards which he could draw no relief from plate that was an heirloom, or from estates that were entailed, sold the book to his old competitor, Lord Spencer, for one thousand guineas. Nothing is more variable than the affirmative value of objects which ground it chiefly upon rarity. It is exceedingly apt to pall upon possession. In this case there was a secondary value—the book was not only rare, but was here found in its integrity: this one copy was perfect; all others were mutilated. But still such a value, being partly a caprice, and in the extremest sense a *pretium affectionis*, or fancy price, fluctuates with the feelings or opinions of the individual; and, even when it keeps steady, it is likely to fluctuate with the buyer's fortunes.

On the other hand, where a *pretium affectionis* is not without a general countersign from society, we do not find that it fluctuates at all. The great ITALIAN MASTERPIECES OF PAINTING have long borne an affirmative value (*i.e.* a value founded on *their* pre-eminence, not on the cost of producing); and that value pushed to the excess of a monopoly, continually growing more intense. It would be useless now to ask after the resistance price; because, if that could be ascertained, it would be a mere inoperative curiosity. Very possible it is that Leonardo da Vinci may have spent not more than £150 in producing his fresco of the Last Supper. But, were it possible to detach it from the walls of the convent refectory which it emblazons, the picture would command in London a king's ransom; and the Sistine Chapel embellishments of Michael Angelo probably two such ransoms within a week. Such jewels are now absolutely unique—they are secure from repetition; notorious copies would not for a moment enter into competition. It is very doubtful if artists of power so gigantic will reappear for many centuries; and the sole deduction from their increasing value is the ultimate frailty of their materials.

SALMON is another instructive case. At present it is said pretty generally to bear the average price of fifteenpence a pound[1]; and this price is doubtless the resistance value. But, if the price should ever come to represent the affirma-

[1] Since this was written a Dutch competition in the markets of London has reduced the price.

tive or power value, it might easily rise considerably higher. There are many men who would prefer one pound of salmon to four of beef; and up to that level, if the stress should ever lie on a man's intrinsic esteem for salmon, it might ascend easily. But it could not ascend very much higher; because a limit is soon reached at which it would always be pulled up suddenly by some other commodity of the same class in still higher esteem. A majority of palates prefer turbot (*i.e.* true turbot,—not the rubbish which passes for such). And vicarious articles, possibly even superior substitutes, will generally avail to fix a limit on the *maximum* side, beyond which few articles will be pushed even by the severest strain upon their affirmative qualities; that is, by the situation where the question ceases entirely to the seller—What can you afford to take? and is turned against the buyer—What is the utmost that you, rather than lose the article, will consent to give? The simple demand for *variety*, as one amongst the resources of hospitality, might long avail to support a rack price (that is, an affirmative price) for salmon, if it were ever to reach it. People are called upon daily to buy what may allow a reasonable choice to their guests,—that is, what may be agreeable as one luxury *amongst* others, even though to their own estimate it may not avail as one luxury *against* others.

Croton Oil.—This case of salmon represents that vast order of cases where the article is within *limits*. Press as you will upon the desire of a man to obtain the article for its intrinsic qualities, for its *power* to gratify (which, as in itself capable of no exact estimate, might seem susceptible of an *unlimited* appreciation), there is, however, in all such cases, or very nearly all, a practical limit to this tendency. Easily the article may rise to a price double or triple of what would notoriously suffice to overcome the *resistance* or cost. But this very ascent brings it at every step into direct competition with articles of the same class usually reputed to be better. It is of no consequence, in such a competition, whether the superior article is selling on the principle of affirmative value or of negative—selling for its intrinsic qualities or its cost. Turbot, for instance, being at four shillings a pound, whether that four shillings represents a value far beyond the cost, or simply the cost, naturally the candidate for salmon will pause and compare the two fishes with a single reference to the intrinsic *power* of each for the common purpose of gratifying the palate. If, then, he shared in the usual comparative estimate of the two as luxury against luxury, here at once a limit is reached beyond which monopoly of salmon could never extensively force it. Peculiar palates are, for that reason, rare. Limits, therefore, are soon found, and almost universally.

But now we pass to a case where no such limits exist. About nineteen years ago were introduced, almost simultaneously, into the medical practice of this country two most powerful medicines. One of these was the sulphate of quinine; the other was croton oil, amongst drastic medicines of a particular class the most potent that is known. Both were understood to be agents of the first rank against inflammatory action; and, with respect to the last, numerous cases were reported in which it had, beyond a doubt, come in critically to save a patient previously given up by his medical attendants. Naturally these cases would be most numerous during the interval requisite for publishing and diffusing the medicine—an interval which, with our British machinery, is brief. There was time enough, however, to allow of a large number of cases in which it had not been introduced until the eleventh hour. Two of these came under my personal knowledge, and within the same fortnight. Both were cases of that agonising disorder—inflammation affecting the intestines. One was near to London; a mounted messenger rode in for the medicine; returned within a hundred minutes; and the patient was saved. The other case lay near to Nottingham: the person despatched with the precious talisman to the post-office, then in Lombard Street, found the mail just starting; but, by an inflexible rule of office, neither guard nor coachman was at liberty to receive a parcel not entered in the way-bill: the man had not the presence of mind to entrust it with one of the passengers; the patient was already in extremity; and before the medicine reached Nottingham by a coach leaving London the next morning he had expired.

Now, in the case of such a magical charm, to have or to

want which was a warrant for life or for death, it is clear that, amongst rich men, the holder of the subtle elixir, the man who tendered it in time, might effectually demand an oriental reward. "Ask me to the half of my kingdom!" would be the voluntary offer of many a *millionaire.* And, if this undoubted power, occasionally held by individual surgeons, were not neutralised by the honour governing our medical body, cases of excessive prices for critical operations would not be rare. Accordingly, Maréchal Lannes in 1809, who had been accustomed in his original walk of life to a medical body far less liberal or scrupulous than ours, used the words of the dying Cardinal Beaufort—"I'll give a thousand pounds," he exclaimed convulsively, "to the man who saves my life!" Not a very princely offer, it must be owned; and we hope it was not *livres* that he meant. But the case was hopeless; both legs shattered at *his* age were beyond art. Had it even been otherwise, Baron Larrey was a man of honour; and, under any circumstances, would have made the same answer—viz. that, without needing such bribes, the surgeons would do their utmost.

Still the case requires notice. Accidentally in our British system the high standard of professional honour turns aside such mercenary proposals—they have become insults. But it is clear that, *per se*, the value of the aid offered is very frequently in the strictest sense illimitable. Not only might the few monopolists of exquisite skill in operating, or the casual monopolist for an amulet, a charm, like the croton oil, press deeply upon the *affirmative* value of this one resource to a man else sealed for death; but also it is certain that, in applying their screw, medical men would rarely find themselves abreast of those *limits* which eternally are coming into play (as we have illustrated in the case of salmon) with regard to minor objects. A man possessing enormous strength of wrist, with singular freedom from nervous trepidations, is not often found; how very rarely, then, will he be found amongst those possessing an exquisite surgical science! Virtually, in any case where a hair's-breadth swerving of the hand will make the difference of life and death, a surgeon thus jointly favoured by nature and by art holds a *carte blanche* in his hands. This is the *potential* value of his skill; and he knows it; and, generally, we believe that out of the British empire [1] it would be used to some extent. As it is, what value do we find it to be which really takes place in such instances? It is simply the *resistance* value. Disdaining to levy a ransom, as it were, upon the fears and yearnings after life in the patient, or upon the agitations of his family, the honourable British surgeon or physician estimates only the cost to himself; he will take no account of the gain to the other party. He must compute the cost of his journey to and fro; the cost in practice lost during his absence from home; and that dividend upon the total costs of his education to which a case of this magnitude may fairly pretend. These elements compose the resistance to his being in the situation to offer such aid; and upon these he founds his expectation.

By this time, therefore, the reader understands sufficiently our distinctions of *plus* and *minus*—power and resistance—value. He understands them to be the two ruling poles towards which all possible or conceivable prices must tend; and we admit that, generally, the resistance value will take place, because generally, by applying an equal resistance, the object (whatever it be) may be produced. But, by way of showing that it is no romantic idea to suppose a case of continual recurrence where the affirmative value will prevail over the negative,—where an object will draw upon the purchaser not for the amount of cost (including, as we need not say, the ordinary rate of profit), but for an amount calculated according to the intrinsic powers,—we will give the case of

HUNTERS *as against* RACEHORSES.—If a man were to offer you a hunter, master of your weight, and otherwise satisfactory, you would readily give him a fair price. But what *is* a fair price? That which will reproduce such a hunter—his cost; the total resistance to his being offered in this condition. Such is the value, and such the law of value, for a hunter. But it is no longer such for a racer. When a breeder of horses finds one amongst his stud promising

[1] British people are not entitled to judge by their experience in Germany or Italy. Generally, the physician or the surgeon called in is some one founding his practice upon British patronage, and trained to British habits of feeling.

first-rate powers of contending at Newmarket, he is no longer content to receive a cost price for the horse, or anything like it. The man who (as a master of pearl-divers) sells the ordinary seed pearls at the mere cost and fair profit on the day's wages which have earned them, when he reaps a pearl fit to embellish the Shah of Persia's crown, looks to become a petty shah himself. He might sell it with a profit by obtaining even that whole day's wages during one hour of which it was produced; but *will* he? No more than, amongst ourselves, the man who, by a twenty-guinea lottery ticket, drew a prize of £10,000, would have sold his ticket for a profit of cent per cent upon its cost. The breeder of the racehorse would take into his estimate the numerous and splendid stakes which the horse might hereafter win; sometimes at Epsom, on one Derby day, as much as £5000 to £6000; to say nothing of the Leger at Doncaster, or other enormous prizes. It is true that the chances of mortality and failure must also be weighed; and unluckily no insurance has yet been done on racers, except as regards sea-risk. But, after all drawbacks, the owner may succeed finally in obtaining for a first-rate horse (once known for good performances) as much as £4000; whilst the whole value, computed on the resistance, may not have been more than as many hundreds. And this fact, though standing back in the rear as regards *public* knowledge, we may see daily advertised in effect by that common regulation which empowers the loser in many cases to insist on the winning horse being sold for £200, or a similar small sum. Were it not for this rule, which puts a stop to all such attempts without hazard of personal disputes, it would be a capital speculation for any first-rater, though beaten at Newmarket, to sweep all the stakes without effort on a tour through the provincial courses: justice would cease for the owners of inferior horses, and sport for the spectators of the competition.

The last case must have convinced the reader that, however uncommon it may be, the cost—the resistance—does not always take place even in the bosom of high civilisation. And, by the way, amongst many other strange examples which we could state of anomalous values not considered in books of political economy, it would be easy to show that the very affirmative values of things have shifted under shifting circumstances. Pearls were most valued amongst the ancient Romans, diamonds and rubies amongst modern nations. Why ? We are persuaded that, besides other reasons founded on resistance for the varying ratio of prices, this following affirmative reason has prevailed : the Roman festivals were all by daylight, under which sort of light pearls tell most at a distance. The modern are chiefly by lamplight, where the flashing and reverberated lustres of jewels are by far the more effective. The intrinsic *powers* have shifted. As an embellishment of female beauty or distinction, pearls are no longer what they were. Affirmatively they have shifted, as well as in the resistance, or negatively.

SLAVES are valued alternately under both laws. Enter the slave-market at Constantinople,—not in its now ruined state, but as it existed at the opening of this 19th century. The great majority of ordinary slaves were valued simply as effects derived from certain known causes adequate to their continued reproduction. They had been stolen ; and the cost of fitting out a similar *foray*, when divided suppose amongst a thousand captives, quoted the price of each ordinary slave. Even upon this class, however, although the cost (that is, on our previous explanation, the negative value) would form the main basis in the estimate, this basis would be slightly modified by varieties in the affirmative value. The cost had been equal ; but the affirmative value would obviously vary under marked differences as to health, strength, and age. Was the man worth five or eight years' purchase ? —that question must make a slight difference, even where the kind of service itself that *could* be promised happened to rank in the lowest ranges of the scale. A turnip cannot admit of a large range in its appreciation ; because the very best is no luxury. But still a good turnip will fetch more than a bad one. We do not, however, suppose that this difference in turnips will generally go the length of making one sort sell at negative or cost value, the other at affirmative. Why ? Simply because the inferiority in the turnip A is owing to the inferior cost on its culture, and the superiority in turnip B to superior cost. But in the case of the slaves this is otherwise. Upon any practicable mode of finding their cost, it must prove to have been the same. The main costs of the outfit were, of necessity, common to the total products of the expedition. And any casual difference in the individual expenditure, from sickness or a longer chase, &c., must be too vague to furnish a ground of separate appreciation. Consequently the mob, the *plebs*, amongst the slaves, must be valued as the small ordinary pearls are valued—simply so many stone-weight on the basis of so much outlay.

But the natural aristocracy amongst the slaves, like the rarer pearls, will be valued on other principles. Those who were stolen from the terraces and valleys lying along that vast esplanade between the Euxine and the Caspian had many chances in favour of their proving partially beautiful,—by fine features and fine complexions at the least. Amongst the males some would have a Mameluke value, as promising equestrian followers in battle, as capital shots, as veterinary surgeons, as soothsayers, or calculators of horoscopes, &c. All these would be valued affirmatively: not as effects that might be continually reproduced by applying the same machinery of causes to the resistance presented by the difficulties; but, inversely, as themselves causes in relation to certain gratifying effects connected with Mohammedan display or luxury. And, if we could go back to the old slave-markets of the Romans, we should meet a range of prices (corresponding to a range of accomplishments) as much more extensive than that of the Ottoman Porte as the Roman civilisation was itself nobler and ampler than that of Islamism. Generally, no doubt, the learned and the intellectual slaves amongst the Romans, such as Tiro, the private secretary of Cicero, were *vernæ*—slaves not immediately exotic, but home-bred descendants from slaves imported in some past generation, and trained at their master's expense upon any promise of talent. Tutors (in the sense of pedagogues), physicians, poets, actors, brilliant sword-players, architects, and artists of all classes, *savans*, *littérateurs*—nay, sometimes philosophers not to be sneezed at—were to be purchased in the Roman markets. And this, by the way, was undoubtedly the cause of that somewhat barbarian contempt which the Romans, in the midst of a peculiar refinement, never disguised for showy accomplishments. We read this sentiment conspicuously expressed in that memorable passage where Virgil so carelessly resigns to foreigners, — Græculi, or whatever they might be,—the supremacy in all arts but those of conquest and government; and, in one instance,—viz. "*orabunt causas melius*",—with a studied insult to a great compatriot recently departed, not less false as to the fact than base as to the motive. But the contempt was natural in a Roman noble for what he could so easily purchase. Even in menial domestics some pretensions to beauty and to youth were looked for: "tall stripling youths, like Ganymede or Hylas," stood ranged about the dinner-table. The solemn and shadowy banquet offered by way of temptation to our Saviour in the wilderness (see *Paradise Regained*) is from a Roman dinner; and the philosophic Cicero, in the midst of eternal declamations against luxury, &c., thinks it a capital jest against any man that his usual attendants at dinner were but three in number,—old, shambling fellows, that squinted perhaps, two of them bandy-legged, and one with a tendency to mange. Under this condition of the Roman slave-shambles as respected the demand, we must be sure that affirmative price would interfere emphatically to govern the scale. Slaves possessing the greatest natural or acquired advantages would often be thrown, by the chances of battle, into Roman hands at the very same rate as those who had no advantages whatever. The cost might be very little, or it might be none, except for a three months' voyage to Rome; and, at any rate, would be equal. So far, there would be no ground for difference in the price. But, if at all on a level as to the cost, the slaves were surely not on a level when considered as powers. As powers, as possessors of various accomplishments ministering to the luxury, or to the pompous display of some princely household, the slaves would fetch prices perhaps as various as their own numbers, and pointing to a gamut of differences utterly unknown to any West Indian colonies, or the States of Continental America. In that New World slavery has assumed a far coarser and more animal aspect. Men, women, or children have been all alike viewed in relation to mere prædial uses. Household slaves must there also be wanted, no doubt, but in a small ratio by comparison with the Roman demand; and, secondly, they were not bought originally with that view so as materially to influence the market, but were subsequently selected for domestic stations, upon experimental discovery of their qualities. Whereas in Rome—that is, through all Italy and the Roman colonies—the contemplation of higher functions on a very extensive scale, as open almost *exclusively* to slaves, would act upon the *total* market—even upon its inferior articles—were it only by greatly diminishing the final *residuum* available for menial services. The result was, that, according to the growth of Rome, slaves were growing continually in price. Between 650-60 U.C. (the period of Marius, Sylla, &c.) and 700-710 (final stage of the Julian conflict with Pompey) the prices of all slaves must prodigiously have increased. And this object it was—viz. the slave-market, a most substantial speculation—not by any means the pearl market (as rumour stated at the time)—which furnished the great collateral motive (see Mitford's *Greece*) to Cæsar's two British expeditions.

LAND is another illustration, and of the first rank. Ricardo ought not to have overlooked a case so broad as this. You may easily bring it under examination, by contrasting it with the case of a machine for displacing human labour. That machine, if it does the work in one hundred days of one hundred men in the same time, will at first sell for something approaching to the labour which it saves—say, for the value of eighty men's labour: that is, *it will sell for what it can produce, not for what will produce itself*; that is, it will sell for affirmative, not for negative value. But as soon as the construction of such a machine ceases to be a secret, its value will totally alter. It will not sell for the labour produc*ed*, but for the labour produc*ing*. By the supposition, it produces work equal to that of a hundred men for one hundred days; but, if it can itself be produced by twenty men in twenty days, then it will finally drop in value to that price: it will no longer be viewed as a cause equal to certain effects, but as an effect certainly reproducible by a known cause at a known cost. Such is the case eventually with all *artificial* machines; and for the plain reason that, once ceasing to be a secret, they can be reproduced *ad infinitum.* On the other hand, land is a *natural* machine —it is limited—it cannot be reproduced. It will therefore always sell as a power—that is, in relation to the effects which it can produce, not as itself an effect ; because no cause is adequate to the production of land. The rent expresses one year's value of land ; and, if it is bought in perpetuity, then the value is calculated on so many years' purchase—a valuation worthy, on another occasion, of a separate consideration. For the present, it is enough to say that land is not valued on any principle of cost—does not sell at negative value—but entirely on the principle of its powers or intrinsic qualities : in short, it sells for affirmative value—as a power, as a cause, not as an effect.

Popish *reliques* put this distinction in a still clearer light. The mere idea of valuing such articles as producible and reproducible, as effects from a known machinery, would at once have stripped them of all value whatever. Even a saint can have only one cranium ; and, in fact, the too great multiplication of these relics, as derived from one and the same individual saint or martyr, was one of the causes, co-operating with changes in the temper of society, and with changes in the intercourse of nations, which gradually destroyed the market in relics. But we are far from deriding them. For the simple and believing ages, when the eldest son of baptism, the King of France, led by the bridle the mule who bore such relics, and went out on foot, bare-headed, to meet them, these were great spiritual powers ; always powers for exalting or quickening devotion, and sometimes, it was imagined, for the working of benign miracles. This was their affirmative value ; and, when *that* languished, they could not pass over to the other scale of negative value—this was impossible ; for they could not be openly reproduced. Counterfeited, forged, they might be, and too often they were. But this was not a fact to be confessed. They could sell at all only by selling as genuine articles. A value as powers they must have, a value affirmatively, or they could have none at all.

## SECTION V.—ON THE PRINCIPAL FORM OF EXCHANGE VALUE—VIZ. *NEGATIVE VALUE*

Thus far I have been attempting to extricate from the confusion which besets it, and to establish in coherency through all its parts, that idea of value in general, and those subdivisions of exchange value, which come forward as antithetic principles in the earliest stages of the deduction. And thus far it is undeniable that Ricardo's views were as unsound as those of any man, the very weakest among all, who had gone before him. Casual words which he has used, and the practical inference from his neglect to censure, betray this fact. But now the deduction has reached a point at which Ricardo's great reform first comes into action. Henceforward the powerful hand of Ricardo will be felt in every turn and movement of economy.

It may now be assumed as a thing established that there are two great antithetic forms of value, and no more: viz. affirmative value, resting upon the intrinsic powers of the article valued for achieving or for aiding a human purpose; and negative value, which neglects altogether the article in itself, and rests upon an accident outside of the article, viz. the amount of resistance to be overcome in continually reproducing it.

Upon the first form of value there is little opening for any further explanation, because no opening for any error, except that one error which arises from yielding, through *lacheté* of the understanding, to the false impression of the word "use," as though "use" meant use beneficial—a use approved by the moral sense, or the understanding, in contradistinction to a false, factious, and imaginary use. Whereas this is all pure impertinence; and the use contemplated is the simple power of ministering to a purpose, though that purpose were the most absurd, wicked, or destructive to the user that could be imagined. But this misconception is treated in a separate section (viz. in section vi). At present, therefore, and throughout *this* section, we have nothing to distract our attention from the single question which remains :—Value in exchange being founded either on power or on resistance, and the case of power being dismissed to a subsequent section, what is it that constitutes the resistance? This value measured by resistance—once for all, this negative value—being in fact the *sole* value ever heard of in the markets, except for here and there a casual exception, by much the greatest question in political economy is that which now comes on for consideration.

How stood the answer to this question when first Ricardo addressed himself to the subject? According to many writers—according to Ricardo himself and Mr. M'Culloch—the answer was occasionally not amiss; only it was unsteady and vacillating. Is that so? Not at all: the answer *was* amiss—was *always* amiss—was *never* right in a single instance. For what is it to us that a man stumbles by some accident into a form of expression which might be sustained at this day as tolerably correct (simply because ambiguous), if, by five hundred other expressions in that same man's book, we know to a certainty that he did not mean his own equivocal language to be taken in that sole sense—one sense out of two—which could sustain its correctness? You urge as decisive the opinion of some eminent witness, who, being asked—"To whose jurisdiction does such a case belong?" had answered, "To the Pope's"—meaning only that it did *not* belong to that of the civil power; whilst yet the proof was strong against him that he had not been aware of two popes being in the field, pope and anti-pope, and whilst the question of jurisdiction had undeniably concerned not the old competition of temporal and spiritual, but that particular personal schism. A very dubious, because a very latitudinarian, expression is cited abundantly from Adam Smith, and the civil critics in economy praise it with vehemence. "*Oh, si sic omnia!*" they exclaim. "Oh, if he had never forgot himself!" But *that* is language which cannot be tolerated. Adam Smith *appears* to be right in some occasional passages upon this great question, merely because his words, having two senses, dissemble that sense which is now found to be inconsistent with the truth. Yet even this dissembling was not consciously contemplated by Adam Smith: he could not dissemble what he did not perceive; he could not equivocate between two senses which to him were one. It is certain, by a vast redundancy of proof, that he never came to be aware of any double sense lurking in his own words; and it is equally certain that, if the *two* senses now indicated in the expression had been distinctly pointed out to him, he would not have declared for either as exclusive of the other; he would have insisted that the two meanings amounted to the same — that one was substantially a reiteration of the other, under a different set of syllables—and that the whole distinction, out of which follows directly a total revolution of political economy, had been pure scholastic moonshine.

That all this is a correct statement one sentence will prove. What was the foundation, in Adam Smith's view, of that principal exchange value which in all markets predominates, and which usually is known as the cost value? This mode of exchange value it is which I am treating in this 5th section. I have called it negative value; but, call it as you please, what is the eternal ground which sustains it? Adam Smith replied in one word, that it is LABOUR. Well, is it not? Why, at one time it might have been said, with some jealousy, that it was; for this elliptical phrase might have been used by Ricardo himself to denote all which it ought to denote; and, without examination, it could not be known that Adam Smith had not used it in this shorthand way. But proofs would soon arise that in fact he had not. Suppose him questioned thus:—"By the vague general phrase '*labour*' do you mean *quantity of labour*, or do you mean *value of labour*? Price in a market, you affirm, is governed and controlled by labour; and therefore, as double labour will produce double value, as decuple labour will produce decuple value, so, inversely, from double value you feel yourself at liberty to infer double labour, and from decuple value to infer decuple labour. In this we all agree —we moderns that are always right, and our fathers that were always wrong. But, when you say *that*, when you utter that unimpeachable truth, do you mean that from double value could be inferred double *quantity* of labour; as that in Portugal, for instance, because the same cotton stockings will cost thirty shillings which in England may be had for fifteen, therefore two days' labour is required on the bad Portuguese system to equal in effect of production one day's labour on the English system? Is this what you mean? Or, on the contrary, is it this,—that therefore the *value* of labour (that is, wages) may be inferred to be double in Portugal of what it is in England?" Mirrors are undoubtedly cheaper by much amongst us English people in 1843 than they were in the year of Waterloo. I saw in 1832 a small one of eight feet high, the very fellow to one which in 1815 had been used for the very same purpose of filling up a five feet recess, overarched by wooden carvings, between two separate compartments of a library, and thus connecting the two into the unity of one. In every point—of dimensions, of reputed quality, of framing, and of application—the two mirrors were the same, and both had been manufactured on a special order to meet the disposable vacancy; yet the one of 1815 had cost forty-eight guineas, the one of 1832 had cost only thirty pounds. Now, in reporting from Adam Smith labour as the ground of value, and in applying that doctrine to this case of the mirrors, is it *your* construction of the word "labour" that the young mirror had cost so much less than the old mirror in consequence of fewer days' work being spent upon it, or in consequence of the same precise days' work (no more, and no fewer) being paid at a lower rate? I abstract from the quality of money in which the wages happened to be paid. We are all aware that between 1819 and 1832 there was full time to accomplish that augmented value of money which the believers in the war depreciation[1] suppose to

[1] "*War depreciation*":—I do not intend to say one word upon this much-agitated question in so short a work. I will not therefore deny the alleged depreciation of 1811, &c.; for *that* would be arrogant in a place which allows no room for assigning reasons. This, however, I may say without blame, that no proof, good in point of logic, has publicly been ever offered in evidence of the depreciation; consequently, no previous presumption has been created in favour of the supposed counter-movement of the currency, as a possible movement. But the reason why at all I refer to the case is for the sake of negativing the pretended countenance of Ricardo to the war depreciation. True, he maintained this opinion nominally. But, when it is understood that, by Ricardo's definition of depreciation, any separation of the paper currency from the metallic standard (whether growing out of a higher Brazil cost of gold, or out of a real fall in the paper,

have been the natural *antistrophe*, or inverse series of motions, pursued by our English currency under the speculative measures of Sir Robert Peel in his earlier years. For a moment, therefore, the reader might fancy that the cheapness of the one mirror was no more than an expression of a currency re-established in power, and that the dearness of the other had been a mere nominal dearness. But this fancy is destroyed by a comparison with the mass of other commodities, all of which must have been equally affected (if any had) by a fall and rise in the value of money. The dilemma, therefore, resolves itself into these alternative propositions: viz. that the later and cheaper of the mirrors had been produced through some smaller quantity of labour, or else that the same unvarying quantity of labour had been obtained at a very much less rate of wages. Now, which of the two alternative explanations does that man declare for who adopts the vague language of labour being the foundation of price? Does he make his election for quantity of labour, or for value of labour? Either choice will satisfy the mere understanding for the moment, since either will explain the immediate phenomenon of a large and else unaccountable difference in the prices of the two mirrors: but one only will satisfy Political Economy, because one only will stand the trial of those final consequences into which economy will pursue it.

Greatly it has always surprised me that Ricardo should not have introduced in his first chapter that *experimentum crucis* which, about four years later, I found myself obliged to introduce in "The Templars' Dialogues"; because, as the matter now stands, Ricardo's main chapter is not so much a proof of his new theory as an illustration of it. For instance, he begins by saying that, in the earliest period of society, the hunter and the fisherman would exchange their several commodities on the basis laid down: viz. a day's produce of the one against a day's produce of the other.[1] But, if any opponent had gone a step further, so

expressed in a merely apparent rise of gold) equally satisfied *his* conditions of a depreciation, it becomes plain that the whole doctrine vanishes in smoke.

[1] Cavils might be raised against this statement, having no reference

as next to suppose the case of a master fisherman employing twenty journeymen, and the hunter employing a similar body of ministerial agents, the whole question under discussion would have come back in full force upon the disputants. Circumstances would immediately have been imagined under which the quantities of labour had altered for the same produce, or (which is the same thing) where the produce had altered under an unvarying quantity of labour. Opposite circumstances would have been imagined where not the quantities, but the rewards, or prices of labours, had altered; and then, thirdly, circumstances would have been imagined where both alterations had been in motion simultaneously, the one in the fisherman's business, the other in the hunter's. And the resulting prices would have been affirmed to be the same under all these varying circumstances, or to be in any degree capriciously different, according to the views of the writer. Simply as illustration against illustration, one case is as good as another, until it is shown to involve an absurdity. Now, it is true that obscurely, and in a corner, Ricardo *does* indicate an absurdity flowing from the notion of wages governing the prices of the articles produced. But this absurdity should have been put forward pointedly and conspicuously, in the front of the main illustrative case between fishermen and hunters; whereas, at present, it is only said that thus does the hunter, thus does the fisher; and, upon either doing otherwise, that the other will remonstrate. To be sure he will. But the case demanded a proof that neither party *could* do otherwise. Such a proof let me now attempt.

Case the First—where the *quantity* of labour governs the price.

A beaver hat of the finest quality has hitherto cost two guineas. At length, after centuries of beaver-hunting, which have terminated in altering the very habits of the animal,

at all to the real question at issue—viz. quantity of labour against cost of labour—by showing that oftentimes the produce on one side might be none at all. But such cavils would be unsubstantial; they would affect, not the principle, but simply the mode of estimating, or rating, quantities under that principle. The same principle of labour rated by quantity would continue to govern, though the modes of computing that quantity might grow continually more complex.

compelling it to become shy and recluse where once it had been careless and gregarious,[1] naturally the price of a beaver hat will begin to advance. But why ? What is the essential movement that has taken place ? The novice will object that it is not in the quantity of producing labour ; for assuredly the process of manufacturing a beaver skin into a hat will not have been retrograde : if it changes at all, it will be for the better ; instead of the former process will gradually be substituted a shorter. Or, if it should seem not so much a short process that superseded a long one as a cheap process that superseded a dear one, still in any case it would be for the better. And, in fact, though a cheaper process may seem at first sight different from a shorter, eventually they will be found to coincide. For how *can* it be cheaper ? Either, first, by dispensing, through some compendious contrivance, with part of the labour (in which case it is cheaper obviously *because* it is shorter) ; or, secondly, because something (whether implement or material) at a low price is substituted for something formerly used at a higher price. But in that case why *was* the old displaced article at a higher price ? Simply because it required more labour to produce it. This truth is illustrated in the present objection : the novice objects that the hat does not cost more on account of more labour being required to manufacture a hat, but because the raw material is more costly : and this strikes him as being quite a separate element in the cost of an article, and perfectly distinct from the labour spent in producing that article. All this, however, is misplaced ingenuity. The raw material seems to be distinct from the producing labour ; but in fact it is the same thing : it is part of the producing labour contemplated in an earlier stage. The beaver can be valued only as the hat is valued ; on the same principle applied at a different time. How is the manufacturing process more or less costly ? Exactly as it requires more or less labour. How else is the beaver more or less costly ? That also, viz. the raw material, can vary in cost only as it requires more or less labour ; that is, twenty men, fifteen, or ten, within the same number of

[1] For this change in the habits of the beaver, see the reports of hunters, Indians, Canadian half-breeds, &c.

weeks, to secure a given quantity of beaver skins. The manufacturer of rum, of arrack, of ale, of perry, speaks of the labour employed in his own particular process of distillation, brewing, fermentation, as antithetically opposed to the raw material on which his skill is exercised. But this is only because naturally he abstracts his attention from processes belonging to a stage of labour *previous* to his own stage, and with which earliest processes personally he has no connexion. Up to the moment which brings the raw material into his own hands, he *postulates* that article as thus far a product unknown to himself: viz. so far as it is a product from a skill or science not within his own profession. Else he is well aware that the sugar, the rice, the malt, the pears, all alike are valued, and *can* be valued, only upon that same consideration of so much labour applied to their production, which consideration it is that assigns a value and a price to the final product from his own professional series of operations.

## Section VI.—On the Technical Term—*Value in Use*

I. It has been already explained that the capital and influential error of Adam Smith, in his famous distinction between value in use and value in exchange, lies in his cȯ-ordinating these ideas. Yet how? Are they *not* coordinate? Doubtless they are sometimes; doubtless they divide sometimes against each other as collateral *genera* of value; that is, whenever each excludes the other. In the case where a particular value in use has no value at all in exchange, there the two ideas stand in full antithesis to each other, exactly as Adam Smith represents them. But, secondly, value in use is often not *co*-ordinate but *sub*-ordinate to value in exchange. Value in use sometimes *excludes* all value in exchange—that is one mode. But value in use sometimes so entirely *includes* exchange value as to form in fact but one subdivision of that idea; one horn out of the two into which exchange value divaricates.

This has been sufficiently illustrated in the last section,

and it may be repeated once for all in this logical type or diagram:—

*First relation*:

Value, as opposed to non-value,

Subdivides into

| | |
|---|---|
| Value in use. | Value in exchange. |

*Second relation*:

Value in exchange, as opposed to pure teleologic value bearing no price in exchange,

Subdivides into

| | |
|---|---|
| Value in use (as a possible ground of price). | Value in cost (as the ordinary ground of price). |

Any man acquainted with logic will apprehend at once the prodigious confusion likely to ensue when *genera* and *species*, radical ideas and their subdivisions, are all confounded together. A glassful of water, taken out of a brook in England to quench a momentary thirst, has only a use value; it stands opposed as a *collateral* idea (not as a *filial* but as a *sisterly* idea) to value in exchange. And the two hostile ideas jointly compose the general abstract idea of value as opposed to worthlessness; they are its two species as in diagram I. But, on the other hand, a glass of medicinal water, having its value measured by the resistance to its production, is not opposed co-ordinately to exchange value; it ranks *under* exchange value as one of two modes:—1. Teleologic power (= use); 2. Cost. It is only requisite to look back upon the case of the musical toy in Canada, selling, under peculiar circumstances, for a price founded on its teleology,—whilst in London or Paris, at the very same time, in contempt of this teleology (or consideration of serviceableness), it sells on the principle of its cost,—in order to see value in use no longer collateral and opposed to value in exchange; but, on the contrary, to see it coinciding with exchange value, and as one subordinate *mode* of exchange value (incapable, therefore, of opposition to exchange value) to see it dividing against cost as the other mode. In general, it may be said that value in use, as excluding value in exchange, has no place in political economy. From the moment when it begins to interest the economist, it must be because it happens to coincide with the value in exchange: it has itself become the value in exchange.

Here lay the original error, the πρωτον ψευδος, viz. in the false position of use value, as if always and necessarily contra-arranged to exchange value; whereas often enough the use value becomes for a time the sole basis of the exchange value. But this first error is followed by two others.

II. How came Adam Smith to say of water that it bears little or no value in exchange? You might as well say that abstractedly, and without reference to *specific* gravity, pine timber was heavy or not heavy: it is heavy or not in the absolute sense, as you take much of that timber, or little of that timber. Specific gravity, indeed, already presupposes a past collation of weights, because it compares the weights under equal bulks: and then it becomes reasonable to say that lead is heavy, else the proposition is unmeaning. A little water, and in the wrong place, has no value: a great deal of water, and in the right place, even in watery England, has a very great value. Not merely as a fishery, but as a bath for swimmers; as a reservoir, or Roman "castellum," for supplying the domestic purposes of a city; as a torrent, or water-power, for turning machinery; as a dock for shipping, as an anchorage for boats, as a canal for transporting great bulks and weights of commodities—water is often incalculable in its exchange value. The late Duke of Bridgewater derived a larger rental from one of his canals than perhaps he could have done from half the diamonds in the regal treasuries of Europe or Asia.[1] How has a man, in

[1] "*Of Asia*":—The Asiatic princes notoriously put a higher affirmative value on this kind of personal ornament than has in any age been allowed to it in Europe. The queen of Great Britain, so mighty a potentate, has usually (whether queen consort or queen regnant) worn diamonds and rubies on her coronation day worth about one hundred thousand pounds. The king of Oude, a petty Indian prince, raised to that supreme rank by ourselves, has repeatedly, on his own person or his son's, worn such jewels to the value of two millions sterling. In Christendom, Prince Esterhazy's

comparing water with diamonds, the right of staking against any single diamond one ounce of water, rather than ten thousand ounces, or than ten million ounces, or these rather than a grain? Even the ancients, little as they knew of political economy, knew better than this. Before they attempt a comparison between two commodities, they are careful to assign the particular quantities (usually the weights) between which the equations shall be made. Aurelian, for instance, would not allow his wife a silk (or possibly a silk velvet) gown, because he thought it too dear for authorising by so authentic a precedent. But *how* dear? At that time (say 250 years after Christ) it was ἰσοστασιον τῳ χρυσῳ, drew in the scales against gold; a pound weight of the silk tissue exchanged for a pound weight of gold at the ordinary alloy. Thus Plautus, in his Epidicus (Act iii, sc. 3):

> "Næ tu habes servom graphicum, et quantivis pretii!
> Non caru' est auro contra."

> "Indeed you have an accomplished slave, and worth any money!
> He is cheap weighed against gold; *i.e.* against his own weight in gold."

Otherwise, says an old French commentator, he might be sold *au poids de l'or*; and so in many scores of places. To make an intelligible valuation in gold, the *weight* of the article in question is assumed as the basis of the equation. Else it is the old Cambridge problem—*Given the skipper's name, to determine the ship's longitude.*

III. How came Adam Smith (by way of retaliation for stripping water of its exchange value) to say that diamonds have little or no value in use? Diamonds realise the "use" contemplated by political economy quite as much as water. Water has the exchange value of diamonds, diamonds have the use value of water. The use means the capacity of being used,—that is, of being applied to a purpose. It is not meant that by possessing value in use a thing is useful—is valuable—*quoad commodum* or *quoad utilitatem*, but valuable *ad utendum*, *utendi gratia*, with a view to being used; not that it accomplishes some salutary or laudable purpose,

"best coat," overlaid with diamonds, is the most costly single article known or not known to pawnbrokers, but it is not valued at more than half a million sterling.

but that it accomplishes a purpose — however monstrous, pernicious, or even destructive to the user; and that its price, instead of being founded on its cost (or the resistance to its reproduction), is founded on its power to realise this purpose. From the Greek word for a purpose (or final cause), viz. τελος (*telos*), we have the word *teleologic*; to denote that quality in any subject by which it tends towards a purpose, or is referred to a purpose. Thus the beauty of a kitchen-garden, of a machine, of a systematic theory, or of a demonstration, is said to be teleologic; as first of all perceived upon referring it to the purposes which it professes to answer. On the same principle all affirmative value, or value in use, is teleologic value—value derived from the purpose which the article contemplates.[1]

Lastly, upon any other explanation of the word "*use*," as part of the term "value in use," the puerility of the consequences must startle every man whose attention is once directed to the point. It is clear that political economy neither has resources nor any motive for distinguishing between the useful and the noxious; it is clear that political economy has quite as little of either for distinguishing

[1] It would, however, be much more convenient in an amended Political Economy (that is, an Economy in which not only the great doctrines should be formally harmonised and expanded, but in which also a better terminology should be introduced, wearing the simplicity equally with the broad applicability of an algebraic language), that some such term as *teleologic* or *affirmative* should be reserved conventionally, in order to meet the following case:—By teleologic value, unless specially restrained to a more technical service, would naturally be understood the case, a very common one, where the selling price of an article (the exchange value) happened at the moment, or was supposed for any purpose of dispute, to found itself on the use value. But we need also a term expressing this use value—for instance, the value of atmospheric air—in cases where it is not only contemplated apart from any exchange value, but where essentially it repels all exchange value. In such conventional restriction of its acceptation the term teleologic value would become tantamount to the term *riches*, as rightly and sagaciously set up in a separate chapter of Ricardo, by way of a counterpole to all exchange value whatever. Ricardo has been liberally assaulted for this antithesis as *prima facie* absurd and irrelate; verbally it seems so. But the ζευγος, the *dualism* of these polar ideas, riches and value, is a mere necessity of the understanding, and returns upon the severe thinker after all verbal efforts to evade it.

between the truly useful and the spuriously useful. No man has paid for an article less or more because it is fascinating and ruinous; no man has paid for an article, either less or more, because it is dull and useful. On what fiction, therefore, or under what pretence, should political economy insinuate her proboscis into such inquiries? She may "hope that she is not intruding"; but it is certain that she *is*: and, if a value can be tolerated which founds itself on the useful, then with equal reason may be introduced a value founded on the virtuous, or a value peculiar to Birmingham, to Wednesday, to Friday, and to Robinson Crusoe.

But, whilst "the useful" must be deplorably impertinent as a subject of inquiry to political economy, the "use" of any article in the sense of its purposes, functions, or teleological relations, as furnishing the ground for their values or prices, will offer one entire hemisphere in that field of science. And for this reason,—because the purpose which any article answers, and the cost which it imposes, must eternally form the two limits within which the tennis-ball of price flies backward and forward. Five guineas being, upon the particular article x, the *maximum* of teleologic price, the utmost sacrifice to which you would ever submit, under the fullest appreciation of the natural purposes which x can fulfil, and then only under the known alternative of losing it if you refuse the five guineas; this constitutes the one pole, the aphelion or remotest point to which the price for you could ever ascend. But, on the other hand, it is quite consistent with this .potential teleologic price, that, considered as a product (not as itself a power for raising products), measured in its value by the resistance to its own endless reproduction, x might not be worth more than five shillings. The cost of reproducing might be no more. And, so long as that state of things subsisted, you would not listen to any call made upon your ultimate or teleologic appreciation. You would insist on the appreciation by cost—on the five shillings—so long as nothing hindered the reproduction upon those terms. Here you have the other pole, the perihelion, countervailing the higher extreme which comes into play only in that case where circumstances suspend the free reproduction of the article. These, therefore, constitute the two limits between which the price must always be held potentially to oscillate. Consequently, *for itself* this pair of limits—the use and the cost—the use as the positive or virtual measure, the cost as the measure by resistance—must be as all-important as the other pair of limits between the useful and the noxious must be impertinent. But, secondly, the former pair of limits is also the basis or ground of genesis from which the whole science is eventually developed.

Thus, by way of brief illustration, a genuine picture of Da Vinci's or Raphael's sells *always* on the principle of value in use, or teleologic value. An enlightened sensibility to the finest effects of art—this constitutes the purpose or teleologic function to which the appreciation is referred; no regard is paid to the lower limit, founded on the difficulty of reproduction; that being now, and ever since the death of the great artists, a limit in the most absolute sense unapproachable. It is right, therefore, to say that the picture sells for its use, *i.e.* its capacity of being used or enjoyed; and that this price cannot now be intercepted (as so generally the affirmative of prices of articles *are*) by a price founded upon cost of reproducing. So, again, the phial of prussic acid which you buy in a remote Australian colony, accidentally drained of its supplies, at a price exorbitantly beyond its ordinary cost, must be classed as a price founded on value in use, notwithstanding that I will assume it to have been bought with a view to self-destruction. It would argue great levity of heart to view in the light of a useful thing any agency whatever that had terminated in so sorrowful a result as suicide. Usefulness there was not in the prussic acid, as any power sufficient to affect or alter the price; but a purpose there was, however gloomy a purpose, a teleologic use attached to the acid, under the circumstances supposed. Now, if this purpose is considered in the price, then the use of the article, its teleologic function, has operated; and in bar of its more customary ground. But, it is perhaps retorted, "Considered! Why, the purpose, the application, the possible uses of an article, must *always* be considered in the price; for, unless it promised those uses, there would be no price at all" True; and this it is which always causes a confusion: that even in the common case where merely the cost it is which cuts off from a possible line that section of the line representative of the price, still it is the affirmative uses of the article which make it first of all conceivable for any such line to exist. The cost cuts off, suppose from a valuation of twenty (as corresponding to the affirmative use of the article), six as corresponding to itself; but that the twenty should at all exist, without which even the six would be impossible, is due originally, and in all cases, to the affirmative ground, not to the negative, and in those cases even where the negative price actually takes effect. This, however, does not disturb the principle—that, whilst the affirmative value only can cause any fund at all to be available for price, alternately it is either that affirmative value or the negative value of cost which settles how much out of this fund shall be in fact disposable for price. Here, for instance, as to the prussic acid, always it must be the capacity of this acid to meet a purpose which could cause *any* price at all to arise. And this effect of affirmative value must *always* continue to act, even when the ordinary state of things shall have been restored by some English vessel bringing an abundant supply of the acid, and after the cost or negative value shall have been reinstalled as the operative price. This primary and *latent* action of the affirmative value must not be for a moment forgotten. In fact, the confusion arising out of this one oversight has been the real cause why the idea of value has never yet been thoroughly and searchingly investigated. It must be remembered that in every case of price alike, whether *terminating* in a negative or affirmative result, invariably and necessarily it commences on affirmative grounds. Without a purpose contemplated, no article could be entertained in the thoughts for a moment as even potentially susceptible of a price. But, secondly, this being presumed to be realised as a *sine qua non* condition, then always a twofold opening arises: the original, intrinsic, affirmative value has first determined the possible quantity of money, &c., available in the extreme case for price, say twenty. But in the last step it is *either* this affirmative value, *or* the negative, which settles how much of that twenty shall be cut off and rendered effective

—whether the entire twenty, or perhaps only one. And in the very delicate management of forces so contradictory coming *always* into a collision, or into the very closest juxtaposition, it cannot be wondered at that the popular and hurried style of thinking in Economy has led most men into confusion.

Before concluding, it may be well to remark that even the Pagan Greeks, ignorant as they necessarily were on political economy, perceived the main outline of distinction between affirmative and negative price.

A passage exists in the "Characteristics" of Theophrastus which presents us with this distinction in a lively form, and under circumstances which will prove interesting to the reader. By pure accident, this passage came under the separate review of two eminent scholars—Casaubon and Salmasius. Greater names do not adorn the rolls of scholarship. Casaubon was distinguished for his accuracy in the midst of his vast comprehensiveness; and every page of his writing is characterised by an overruling good sense. Salmasius, on the other hand, was too adventurous to be always safe. He was the man for riding steeplechases—for wrestling with extravagant difficulties—or for dancing upon nothing. Yet, with all the benefit from this caution of his intellectual temper, upon the passage in Theophrastus did Casaubon write the most inexcusable nonsense; whilst the youthful Salmasius, at one bound of his agile understanding, cleared the "rasper" in a style that must have satisfied even the doubts of Isaac. The case illustrates powerfully the uselessness of mere erudition in contending with a difficulty seated in the matter—substantially in the thing—and not in the Greek or Latin expression. Here, in Theophrastus, it was not Greek, it was Political Economy, that could put it to rights. I will give the very words, construing, as I go along, for the benefit of non-Grecian readers. Και πωλων τι, *and when selling any article*, μη λεγειν, *not to say* (*i.e.* it is amongst his characteristic traits not to say), τοις ὠνουμενοις, *to the purchasers*, ποσον ἀν ἀποδοιτο, *in exchange for how much he would deliver it*, ἀλλ' ἐρωτᾳν, *but to ask*——Ay, "*but to ask*"—What is it that he asks? Casaubon, we are concerned to report, construes the word thus—*ecquid inveniat damnan-*

*dum*?—*what is it that he* (the purchaser, I suppose) *finds to complain of*? But, besides that such a rendering could not be sustained verbally, it is still worse that this sense, if it *could* be sustained, would be irrelevant. How would it be any substitution for the plain declaration of what price he asked to turn round upon a buyer and insist upon that buyer's saying what blemish could be detected in the article? And then, venerable Isaac, in which of your waistcoat-pockets did you find the word *damnandum*? And again, as the Greek expression had been plural, τοις ὠνουμενοις, to the purchasers, whence comes it that the verb is εὑρισκει, and not *pluraliter* εὑσρικουσι? Ought Casaubon to have been satisfied with that blunder, so apparent, on *his* construction, in the syntax?

Salmasius saw the truth at a glance. *His* version needs no justification: itself justifies itself. Thus it is: "τι εὑρισκει; ad verbum *quid invenit*? hoc est, quid pretium mereat hæc res; quanti valeat?" Instead of saying at a word how much he demands, our knavish friend insists upon asking, τι εὑρισκει;—"*What does it fetch*? What do *we* say, gentlemen, for this glorious sabre from Damascus? What price shall I have the honour of naming for these jewelled stirrups from Antioch?" The antithesis designed is gross and palpable: that it *is* the antithesis, and sharply drawn, between affirmative and negative price—power price (in reference to the power in the article to fulfil human purposes) as opposed to resistance price (or price measured by the amount of resistance to its reproduction)—price, in short, regulated by what x will produce in opposition to price regulated by what will produce x—all this (which is but the same idea under three different formulæ) will appear at once by the following reflection:—What is it that Theophrastus imputes to him as the *form* of his trickery (whatever might be its drift)? It is—that he evaded a question to himself, and turned round upon the company with a question of his own. Now, it is evident that the question of price, when thrown into the negative form as a question about the cost, was a question for *him* to answer, and not for the company. The cost could be known only to himself. But, when our friend has taken his resolution of translating the *onus* to the buyers the only way to accomplish this is by throwing that question about price into a shape which only the company could answer. "Nay, gentlemen, how can I tell the value? Every man knows best what pleasure or what benefit he will draw from an article. Do you mind your own business: the cost is *my* business; but yours is—the worth of the thing for use; for your uses, not for mine." Scamp seems to have the best of it: *their* benefit from the article could not be affected by the terms on which he had acquired it. And thus even Hellas was *up* to this elementary distinction.[1]

## Section VII.—Modes of Capital as affecting Value

Finally, there arises a modification, first indicated by Ricardo, of value, from the different proportions in which capital, fixed or circulating, predominates in the production of the articles. In this case, it can very often no longer be said that the prices of the resulting articles, according to the general rule of Ricardo, vary as the quantities of the producing labour: a disturbance of that law occurs.

The difference between what is called fixed capital and what is called circulating capital has often been represented as shifting and shadowy. However, without entering upon that dispute further at this point, it will be sufficient to say

[1] Salmasius subsequently explained his view of the passage in a short paraphrastic commentary, which agrees exactly with the present in pointing to the double form of exchange value, except as to the temper of the vendor, whom Salmasius (doubtless warped by the title of the particular chapter in Theophrastus, viz. Περι Αὐθαδειας) conceives to be acting in the spirit of insolence. This is part of what Salmasius says, "Superbus et contumax venditor designatur his notis a Theophrasto—qui" [*i.e.* venditor] "merces suas quanti vendat indicare dedignatus, emptorem interroget quanti valeant, et quo pretio emi dignæ sint?" True: this is the nature of the substitution which he makes, but not the spirit in which he makes it. Not as disdaining to declare at what price he sells, but fraudulently, as seeing an interest in evading that question, does Scamp transfer the right of question to himself, and the duty of answer, to the other side. He transfers it from negative value to affirmative.

that they *may* be distinguished essentially. Circulating capital, in its normal idea, means any agent whatever used productively which perishes in the very act of being used. Thus, wages are conveniently said to be for a month, a week, or a day ; but, in fact, a commensurate "moment" of wages perishes upon every instant of time. So of candlelight or gas, so of the porter or drink of any kind allowed by the master of a manufacturing establishment—none of it holds over for a second act of consumption. That part which may accidentally survive is a part wholly distinct, not concerned at all in the first act. But in fixed capital this is otherwise. The workman's tools hold over from one act of production to a thousandth act. The same identical chisel, saw, grindstone, and not successive parts of them, have operated on many hundreds of cases; and, by how much larger has been the range of these iterations, by so much the more intensely is the tool, engine, or machinery entitled to the denomination of fixed. The leading case under circulating capital—what we chiefly think of—is wages ; the leading case under fixed capital is machinery.

Now, in practice, although one kind of capital often preponderates, rarely is it found altogether to exclude the other. Where wages, for instance, form the main element of cost, there will yet be implements required ; and, inversely, the most extensive machines require human vigilance, direction, and sometimes very considerable co-operation. But, though this is always the practical case, for the sake of trying the question it is better to suppose an extreme case, in which alternately the products arise exclusively from a machine, demanding no aid whatever from circulating capital, and again exclusively from human labour, demanding no aid whatever from capital fixed in stationary machines or instruments. On such an assumption, Ricardo undertakes to show that the commodities produced in the first case could sustain a far greater fall in price under the same change in the circumstances, and with the same injury (no more and no less) to the manufacturing capitalists, than those produced in the second.

He bids us suppose a case of circulating capital where, for the production of certain articles, two thousand pounds annually are paid in wages. We are to suppose an opposite case, in which two thousand pounds have been sunk in a very durable machine for producing a particular set of articles. Now, the annual profits will be the same for both parties: say, at ten per cent, two hundred pounds. Consequently we may say of the total products turned out from either establishment — that they will sell for two thousand two hundred pounds in the first case, for two hundred pounds in the second. Some trifle should be added for current repairs on the machine, and also another trifle as a sinking-fund for replacing the machine finally—yet, as this machine is of variable duration, and in one case calculated to last for a century, both provisions are uncertain, and frequently too inconsiderable to affect the results, so that they may be safely neglected.

Now then, such being the circumstances of the two cases, suppose a rise in wages of two per cent to affect the prices of articles issuing from the first establishment. For a time this is peculiar to that establishment; it does not reach the second at first, because *that* by the case pays no wages. But at last it reaches the second set of products also, through the rebound upon profits. The two per cent extra on wages will be forty pounds in the whole. Now, the loss upon wages must be borne by profits. But the forty pounds levied upon two hundred pounds will reduce the prices of the articles by that amount, *i.e.* twenty per cent; whereas the forty pounds levied upon two thousand two hundred pounds is simply transferred to the labourers, and the price continues as it was.

The case here imagined by Ricardo, and which is subsequently varied through lower stages of durability, greatly disturbing the violence of the results as to price, is exceedingly important by its tendency. And he goes on to show, what will naturally have suggested itself to the student, that between different sorts of fixed capital there is the same difference of tendency as between fixed and circulating. And why? Because the durability, which forms the ground of the generic distinction between fixed and circulating, varies also, and therefore becomes a ground for a special distinction, between any different orders of the fixed. When a man sows corn, which is intensely circulating capital, he seems absolutely and violently to throw it away. But this eventually comes back to him in a new shape. But on every year he renews this violent sacrifice of capital. Other modes of capital, in an opposite extreme, as a threshing-machine, last for his life or even longer. Now, the intermediate modes, such as horses, next cows, carts, rakes, as they outlast uses continually less durable, come nearer and nearer to the principle of the circulating capital; and consequently the difference of result upon price, under any changes occurring in productive agencies, tends more and more to become evanescent.

This is the amount of Ricardo's restriction applied to his own general principle of value. An objection, made by Malthus, which to himself appeared fatal, stumbled in the very statement, not conforming to the conditions presupposed by Ricardo. There is, however, some degree of obscurity still overhanging this final section of Ricardo's great chapter on value; and for a large *system* of political economy, which, without regard to names, should endeavour severely to settle the truth as affecting every part, this particular section would require a more searching consideration. But in a little work professing only to state the separate principles (which happen to be fundamental), and the separate *theory* of Ricardo, there seems no reason for extending the inquiry beyond the limits fixed by his own views.

## CHAPTER II

### ON MARKET VALUE

A VERY short chapter, and a very bad one (the worst in the whole series) has been introduced by Ricardo upon *market value*, quite out of its natural place. It stands fourth in succession by the arrangement of the first edition; whereas it ought, upon any principle, to have ranked immediately after the first. I mention this because the dislocation of the chapter from its true place naturally suggests the cause of its unsoundness; it was a hurried after-thought, introduced to provide for inconveniences which, until they had began to crowd upon his experience, the writer had not previously anticipated. What was Ricardo's specific object in this chapter? Was it, as in his great inaugural chapter on value, to amend or reconstitute the old notions current upon this important section of economy? By no means; for that construction of his object there is no opening, since he neither objects to any one point in the old definition and old employment of the idea, nor does he add silently or indirectly any new element to that idea; he neither amplifies the use of this idea, nor regulates by any limitation its logical relations. As he found it he adopts it; as he adopts it he leaves it. Every other chapter formed a distinct precedent against his title to write this. But it was his necessity which threw him upon such an anomaly. He found that a case was gathering upon him which would else call in every page for a distinction and a caution. As often as it should happen that either to the question of rent, of profits, of wages, or of foreign trade, he should apply his own new laws of value, he would be eternally crossed and thwarted by one and the same form of objections: viz. by those which are drawn from market value.

He would be supposed, by the unskilful student, always to overlook *that* from which always and systematically he abstracted. The modifications to value arising out of accidental disturbances in the market, out of casual excesses or casual defects in the supply, are in fact no objections at all. The capital and ruling law determines such an article A to be worth 25. Then supervenes a modification, which, by accident, is equal in virtue to 3; if this modification (from a *defect* in the supply) happen to be + 3, in that case the resulting price will be 28; if it happens (from a corresponding *excess* in the supply) to be − 3, in that case the resulting price will be 22. But alike in either case the original determination of the primary law has had its full effect. To have reached 28, when a casual disturbance arose from an additional 3, argues sufficiently an original or natural price of 25; to have settled at 22, when a disturbance had arisen equal to the effect of subtracting 3, equally argues back to the original price of 25. Consequently all such disturbances are vainly alleged as answers to the capital laws of value, or as in the very least degree objections to those laws. As well might it be said that gravitation is not gravitation because a magnet is so placed as to affect the velocity of descent. The gravitation, you may rely on it, exerts its full power without abatement; and all which is neutralised by the magnet must be fully accounted for. This is what Ricardo contemplates in the 4th chapter. He wishes to check the rash reader by a timely caution—"Do not go on complicating the matter to no purpose, by eternally submitting every assertion upon price to the disturbance of a well-known irregularity. We are all alike aware of that irregularity. It is an irregularity as regards its amount in any particular case; but it is perfectly regular in its mode of action. We cannot tell beforehand what will be the supply of an article in relation to its demand; that is uncertain and irregular; but, once known and certified, we can all anticipate its effects."

The case was the same precisely as when Ricardo announced

beforehand that he should neglect the variations in the value of money. What could be the use of stating every proposition as to price three times over ;—first, in the contingency of money remaining stationary; secondly, in the contingency of its rising ; thirdly, in the contingency of its falling ? Such an eternal *fugue* of iterations, such a Welsh triad of cases, would treble the labour of writer and reader, without doing the slightest service to either. Within ten pages it would become a mere nuisance. Why not, once for all, abstract from such regular irregularities, which affect no principle, but merely tend to make every conclusion needlessly operose and perplexing ? That was the course which Ricardo *did* take in the case of money : he announced his intention of abstracting from all disturbances of that nature : he made it understood, that from this point onwards he would always assume money as ranging at its stationary natural value—that is, at the value predetermined by the cost—without looking aside this way or that to changes in the value from the momentary market supply.

Now, then, exactly that same intention of abstracting from the casual oscillations of a market, which he had announced in regard to money, here in this 4th chapter he desires to announce universally with regard to all other articles whatsoever. He will fatigue neither himself nor his readers by entertaining an eternal set of changes which can be rung upon all cases alike, and which affect no principle in any.

Having thus shown what it *was* that Ricardo designed in this chapter (viz. a general *caveat* through all time coming as to a particular useless practice), and, secondly, what it was *not* that Ricardo designed (viz. a new view of the subsisting doctrine on market value), thirdly, let me have permission to show what it was that he *ought* to have intended. He ought to have disengaged the old doctrine from a foul logical blunder, which (if not the very greatest in political economy) is certainly the greatest upon a point of equal simplicity, and the greatest for practical effect.

What *is* "market value" ? Does it mean value in a market ? Precisely upon that blunder has turned the whole distortion of this doctrine, which else, and separate from its misconstructions, is essential to political economy. Let the reader ask himself this question :—What is the antithesis to "market value?" Upon *that* there is no dispute: all are agreed in calling it "natural value." And what does natural value mean? Confessedly it means the value which is central to the oscillation right and left arising from supply either redundant or defective. Consequently, whilst market value means value as it is disturbed by such oscillations, natural value (being the direct antithesis) means value as it is *not* disturbed by such oscillations. Such being the nature of this famous distinction, how shameful an error it has been in all writers since the idea of market value was first introduced, and much more so in Ricardo, the great *malleus hereticorum*, that they speak of "the actual value,"[1] *i.e.* the present or existing value, as a term interchangeable with that of market value. Ricardo does so in the very first sentence of his 4th chapter. "In making labour the foundation," &c., "we must not," says he, "be supposed to deny the accidental and temporary deviations of the actual or market price of commodities from this their primary and natural price." Actual or market! Why, that would stand if "market price" meant "price in a market"; but it means nothing of the sort. And, if it was designed to do so, then I ask, for what was it ever introduced? Exactly because price in a market is not always the same thing as market price was this latter phrase ever introduced, and guarded as a technical term. Every man will grant that the "actual price" may happen to coincide with the "natural price"; he will grant also (for he must) that actual price may happen at another time to coincide with market price: but, if actual price, or existing price, may at one time coincide with the technical term market price, and at another time with its direct antithesis—that is, may coincide indifferently with A or with non-A—with what colour of decency could a man

[1] "*The actual value*":—"*Actual*," in the sense of *present*, is one of the most frequent (but also of the most disgusting) Gallicisms. *L'état actuel des armées Françaises*, is good French; but to say in English, "the actual condition," &c., is a jargon of foreigners. *Actual* in English can never be opposed to *future*; it is with us the antithesis, 1st and generally, to *possible*; 2d, to *contingent*; 3d, to a representation existing only in words, or by way of pretence.

make actual price and market price to be convertible terms: that is, essentially united, and yet by necessity at times essentially opposed?

Adam Smith it was who first brought up the distinction of market value. What did he mean by it? He meant, value of any article as adfected (purposely I use the algebraic term) by the state of the market, disturbed from its equilibrium. He was not ignorant that no *quantity* of an article, whether in excess or defect, could ever mainly fix the price: the cost it is only that could do *that*; but the quantity in the market would, *if not level to the demand*, be a coefficient in regulating that price. Sometimes this quantity might be a great deal too much for the demand; sometimes it might be a great deal too little; and, accordingly, as either case happened, it would (by raising or by depressing) modify the simple result obtained from the cost. Having thus set up a term, viz. market value, to express cost value as adfected by quantity in excess or in defect, next he looked out for a contradictory term (viz. natural value) in order to express cost value as it is *not* adfected by quantity in excess or in defect.

These two terms, therefore, express the two opposite poles of a *law*. They indicate always an agency of law. But the terms actual value, or value in a market, express only a fact. When you speak of the actual value, meaning in good English the present or existing value, you cannot but be aware that it might coincide equally with the cost price *as* adfected by quantity, or with the cost price as *not* adfected by the quantity; that is, with technical market price, or with technical natural price (which is non-market price). The actual price of a coach-horse, for instance, "sixteen hands high, grand action, six years old," will generally turn out to be a "*market* price" in the true technical sense; for horses never travel entirely out of that circle: they are always somewhat in excess or in defect. And the reason of this is that the breeding of horses cannot adapt itself fast enough to the oscillations in the demand. It is not until an oscillation in one direction has begun to make itself felt steadily in the prices that it is assumed to be certain, and acted upon; and by that time it is too late to countermand the scale of arrangements which has already been in action through four years back. Hence, in horses, or wherever it is impossible to equate the supply abruptly with an altered state of the demand, large elongations occur, this way or that, between the oscillating market price (reflecting the cost adfected by the quantity) and the steady central price, or natural price (reflecting the cost only, without regard to quantity). On the other hand, whilst horses are perhaps always at market value, boots and shoes are never known to bear a market value. Some variation may occur slowly in the price of hides, and therefore of leather. This, however, is not much, where no changes happen in the course of foreign trade, and none in the duties. As to the manufactured article, there is so little reason for supplying it in any variable ratio, and shoemakers are notoriously such philosophic men, and the demand of the public is so equable, that no man buys shoes or boots at any other than the steady natural price. The result of this difference is seen in the two orders of men, shoemakers and horse-dealers. The horse-dealer is always too clever ; whilst it is in no scorn, but in thankful remembrance of such men as Jacob Boehmen, &c., that Mr. Coleridge and many others have declared the shoemakers' craft to be the most practically productive of meditation amongst men. This has partly been ascribed to its sedentary habits ; but much more, I believe, depends upon the shoemaker's selling always at natural, never at unnatural or market, price ; whilst the unhappy horse-dealer, being still up to his lips in adfected price, and absolutely compelled to tamper with this price, naturally gets the habit of tampering with the buyer's ignorance, or any other circumstance that shapes the price to his wishes.

Market price, therefore, is so far from meaning the rude idea of price in a market that such a term would never have been introduced as a technical distinction, except expressly for the purpose of contradicting that rude idea. This, it was felt, might or might not happen to include the double affections of cost and quantity. But what the economist wanted was a term that always should and must include them ; and, observe, no sooner has he got his term, trimmed it, fought for it, than instantly he unsettles it from its foundation. With one Alnaschar kick he destroys the whole edifice upon which he has employed himself so painfully.

But is this confusion of the idea the worst result from the defeated doctrine? By no means. A crazy maxim has got possession of the whole world; viz. that price is, or can be, determined by the relation between supply and demand. The man who uses this maxim does not himself mean it. He cannot say, "I think thus; you think otherwise." He does *not* think thus. Try to extract price for wheat from the simple relation of the supply to the demand. Suppose the supply to be by one-tenth part beyond the demand, what price will *that* indicate for eight imperial bushels of the best red wheat, weighing sixty-four pounds a bushel? Will the price be a shilling, or will it be a thousand pounds? You guess that the first would be too little, and the second too much. Perhaps so; but what makes you "guess" this? Why, simply, your past experience. You fancy yourself ascertaining the price by the relation of supply to demand, and, in fact, you are ascertaining it by privately looking for the cost in past years,—the very thing that you had pledged yourself to dispense with.

Now, mark how a man does really proceed in solving such a problem. He finds upon inquiry that an excess in the supply of wheat by one-tenth will cause a depreciation perhaps by one-sixth: the accident of excess has told to the extent of a sixth. But of what? A sixth of what? Manifestly, a sixth upon the last price of wheat. The pretended result, that could be known by knowing the mere amount of excess, now turns out to be a mere function of the former cost, previous to the depreciation. But that price includes the whole difficulty; for always the price of wheat will express the *cost* in the first place, as the principal (oftentimes the sole) element. This call C. Then, secondly, the other (the movable) element of the price will represent any modification upon this C, by means of too much or too little wheat in the market. This modifying element of quantity call Q; and then any existing price in any particular corn-market will always be $C+Q$ in the case where there is a deficiency; always $C-Q$ in the case where there is an excess; always C (*i.e.* a mononomial) in the case where there is neither deficiency nor excess, consequently where market price does *not* take place, but, on the contrary, the price which contradicts market price, or, in Adam Smith's language, natural price.

Thus it is shown, by pursuing the problem to the last, that every possible case of technical market value (that is, not value in a market, but value in a market whose equilibrium has been disturbed) cannot by possibility rest upon a single law (whether cost on the one hand, or relation of supply to demand on the other), but of necessity upon two laws: briefly, that it must be a *Binomial.* It is scandalous and astonishing that Adam Smith, the introducer of this important distinction, should himself be the first, in very many cases, to confound it with its own formal antithesis. It is still more scandalous that Ricardo—actually making war upon the logic of Adam Smith, and founding his theory upon a much severer logic—should equally have confounded the law of market value with the direct contradiction to that law. Both did so under the misleading of a verbal equivocation [1] in the term "*market*"; and the possibility of this equivocation would be banished henceforth by substituting for "market value" the term binomial value.

[1] "*Verbal equivocation*":—What equivocation? some readers will say. For, though a false result is somehow obtained, it does not instantly appear how the word *market* has, or can have, led to this result by two senses. But it *has.* In one of its uses, and that the commonest by very much, the word *market* indicates a FACT, and nothing more, viz. simply the *ubi* of the sale. But, in another use, this word indicates a LAW, viz. the *conditions* under which the sale was made; which conditions are the three several states of the market as to the balance existing between the quantity of any article and the public demand for it. Every market, and in all times, must offer of every commodity, either first, too much for the demand, or, secondly, too little, or, thirdly, neither too much nor too little; and the term "*market value,*" when pointing to such conditions, points to a coefficient which in part governs the price. But in the popular use, where it expresses only a fact, it points to a mere inert accident having no tendency to affect the price.

## CHAPTER III—WAGES

### SECTION I.

THERE are four elements in the condition of every working body, which (like so many organs of a complex machine) must eternally operate by aiding or by thwarting each other. According to the social circumstances at the time given, these elements must act either in the same direction or in different directions; and conformably to the modes of *combining* the action under four distinct causes, operating by different proportions, and often in conflicting directions, must be the practical result—the tendencies upwards or downwards which will affect wages universally.

The four elements are these—

1. The rate of movement in the POPULATION: Is *that* steadily advancing or slowly receding? Does *that* tend to raise the value of wages, or to depress it?

2. The rate of movement in the national CAPITAL: Is *that* advancing or receding? And does it *pro tanto* therefore tend to raise or to depress the rate of wages?

3. The fluctuations in the price of necessaries, but, above all, of FOOD; Are those fluctuations from one decennium to another tending, upon the whole, to an advance or to a decline? Is the price of food from century to century, when taken with its complementary adjunct in the price of clothes, fire, and lodging, such as, upon the whole, to sustain wages—to stimulate wages—or to depress them?

4. The traditional STANDARD OF LIVING: Is *that* fortunately high and exacting in its requisitions? or is "man's life," to cite a strong word from Shakspeare (whose profound

humanity had fixed his attention upon the vast importance of a high scale in domestic comfort),—"is man's life cheap as brutes'?" Is it in short an old English standard [1] which

[1] "*An old English standard*":—Upon this subject there exists a most inveterate prejudice in Scotland, which ought not to be hard ot overthrow, being absolutely unfounded; only that, to be attacked with success, it must be attacked upon a new principle. It is universally held by the Scotch, or rather postulated as a point confessed and notorious, that the English, as compared with themselves, are a nation luxurious in diet. Now, as to the Scottish gentry, this notion is a mere romance; between them and the English gentry there is no difference whatever in that respect. But, on descending below the gentry, through all the numerous classes of society, you will certainly find a lower diet prevailing in Scotland; and, secondly, a lower regard to diet. As compared with the Scottish, it cannot be denied that the English working classes, and the lower class of shopkeepers, *were* (I wish it could be said *are*) considerably more luxurious as to diet. I know not whether this homely diet of Scotland has, upon the whole, proved an advantage for *her*; very sure I am that a more generous diet has been a blessing of the first order to England. Even as regards health, there is something to be said for a more *genial* diet. That diet which leads people to indifference for eating, may sound more philosophic; but it is not the healthiest: on that point there are conclusive experiments. On the other hand, considered as a political advantage, a high standard of diet is invaluable. Many are the writers who have properly insisted on the vast benefits, in periods of scarcity, which accrue to nations enjoying a large latitude of *descent*; whereas the Swedish or Scottish nation, from habitual poverty of diet (though fortunately a diet improved and improving through the last hundred years), finds itself already on the lowest round of the ladder, whenever the call comes for descending. In a famine what can be *their* resources? This, however, is but one of the great national benefits arising from a high standard of diet. The others lie in the perpetual elevation which such a standard communicates to wages, and to the expectations generally of the labouring classes. Through this higher tone it is, in part, that the English working order has for a century fought up against the degrading tendencies of population irregularly stimulated. Their condition has often locally deteriorated; but, under a lower standard of general domestic comfort, England would, by this time, have approximated to the condition of Ireland.

The fact, therefore, of a less luxurious diet for the working classes of Scotland may be conceded without conceding an unmixed advantage. I have no personal interest in defending a more luxurious standard, being myself a mere anchorite as to such enjoyments; but I cannot overlook the advantage to a nation that under ordinary circumstances its whole level of enjoyment should be raised pretty high. Meantime, the main practical question is still unsettled.

prevails, or a modern Irish standard? Is it that standard which elevated the noble yeomanry of England through six centuries, or that which has depressed to an abject animal existence the Irish serfs, and depressed the houseless lazzaroni of Naples, Peru, and Mexico, to a sensual dependence upon sunshine and sleep? To these four elements some hasty thinkers would add a fifth, viz. the relative quantity of work to be done—and this certainly *is* important; for, undoubtedly, if the population should increase, it will be a balance to that increase if the national work increases by the same proportion, and it will be more than a balance if the national work should increase more than proportionally. But the element of work to be done is already expressed implicitly in the two first elements of population and of capital; for, if the population increase, then the work of raising food must increase commensurately: and, again, if the capital increase, it will force some corresponding em-

Because the English working class is luxurious (or *was* so) by comparison with the same class in Scotland, must it therefore follow that the English working class is luxurious in a positive sense? Relatively to one sole nation it is so: but that one nation is not Europe—is not the world. This has been quite forgotten by the Scotch. And upon a large inquiry it becomes evident beyond all possibility of dispute that Scotland realises a noticeable extreme in that respect; France and Germany the opposite extreme; and that England stands between these two extremes, but much nearer to the Scottish extreme than to the Franco-German. Mere ignorance can shut a man's eyes to this relation of things. Any man having had opportunities of observing the French emigrants in England, or who remembers the testimony of Mr. Cobbett, jun., and other qualified witnesses, to the enormous voracity of the French peasantry, or who reflects on the fact that women universally are untainted in England with the vice of *gourmandise*, and that any women who have made themselves memorable in England by this vice (as, for instance, the Duchess of Portsmouth, with others that I could add) were French women; that the French only have cultivated cookery as a science, and have a large gastronomic literature; or who knows anything of the experience in English inns when French prisoners of war were quartered upon them: will laugh at the idea that the English lower classes in *such* neighbourhood can need any defence. But the Germans are worse than the French. Let a man make himself acquainted with the *universal* duration and excess of the dinner throughout Lower Germany, and he will begin to rectify his opinions upon this subject. Upper Germany is worse still; and Austria, in particular, wallows in sensuality of *all* kinds; but in none so much as that of good eating. Many travellers are

ployment for itself by tentatively exploring every kind of new work that has any chance of proving profitable.

It is more important to notice that all these four modifying causes of wages, though each separately for itself capable of several action, are also fitted to act in pairs, each two as a separate combination, ζευγος, or *yoke* of forces. Thus No. 1, or population, will act on wages at any rate; but it will act differently according as it is supported or thwarted by concurrent changes in capital. Population moving forward too rapidly would, *cæteris paribus*, be unfavourable to the prosperous movement of wages; yet, if No. 2, the national capital —*i.e.* if the funds for employing labour—should advance even faster than the labour, then it might happen that wages would rise, although under a state of the population otherwise unfavourable to wages. This conditional action of one element according to the state of the other is continually exhibited, and often ruinously, in our infant colonies.

beginning to publish the truth on this subject. One in particular, a very clever man, founds upon this one vice (which, too laxly, he calls the *continental* vice) no small share of the continental poverty. They spend their time (says he), which justly he alleges is their money, on good cooking. This charge, observe, applies to seventy millions of men. Even of the Prussian army he remarks that "the *lusty roundabout*, rather than a muscular growth," which strikes the eye in that military body, "is no doubt derived from the good living to which" at home they have been "*accustomed* from infancy." Speaking of all France and all Germany, the same traveller says (p. 368)—"It costs at the least twice as much of human time and labour to dine five millions of French or German people as to dine five millions of English; and time and labour are the basis of all national wealth." Again, "the loss of time in the eating and preparation of food forms a very important drawback on the prosperity of families on the Continent." Again, listen to this: "*Gourmandise* is found to be a vice as troublesome to deal with among *the French soldiery* as tippling with ours." The same vice is the cause of the French depredations in the field. The poor, he says, are infected with this vice, and betray it in their looks and teeth. Finally, he clenches the matter thus:—"In the total, it is fully a fifth of the time and the labour of a continental population that is *daily* wasted in cookery and eating." And what nation is it that he contrasts so favourably for itself with Germans and French? It is the English. And who is the traveller that makes this striking record? An Englishman, you fancy. By no means. It is a Scotchman, Mr. Samuel Laing, in the year 1842. So perish opinions founded on a narrow and partial range of comparison.

Work of some kind, in such colonies, there must be; for there is a population of some class and quality to feed and to furnish with dwelling-houses, firing, and the very coarsest manufactures; as to the finer, these are long supplied by importation. But, with this primary basis for going to work, sometimes there is labour in excess present with little capital for employing it; sometimes there is capital in excess, with no adequate labour of a proper quality for receiving the action of capital. Very lately, and therefore after all the benefit of our long experience on such subjects, the Government commissioners sent down to Paisley (with a view to the relief of that town from her surplus population) shipped off to distant settlements in strange climates mechanics and weavers, who were found more useless for colonial labours than a band of mere gentlemen; having none of the hardy habits which, more even than practised skill, are requisite for rural industry, and, in general, for industry of that elementary class required in young or infant communities. And universally it may be said, as a first consideration in the general theory of colonisation, that not only capital and labour should be harmoniously combined, so that neither agency may languish from defect of the approximate reagency, but also that labour itself, in its several subdivisions, should be more cautiously *assorted* than has generally been the case. Houses form an *instantaneous* class of necessaries in new colonies; those rare cases being excepted in which the season of the year and the climate allow of a long encampment.[1] Yet how can houses advance harmoniously (that is, in such a concurrency of the parts that one part may not be kept waiting for the other) unless the masons or bricklayers are in due proportion to the carpenters—both to the woodcutters and sawyers—and all four classes to the plasterers, slaters (or tilers), and glaziers? Or,

[1] "*Encampment*":—Which mode of life, however, might be extended greatly, if some Asiatic plans of raising a circular, dry terrace for receiving the tent were adopted; and if, secondly, for canvas were substituted hides, tarpaulins, or other substances resisting heavy rains. The Roman expression for a good substantial encampment was "*sub pellibus*"—*under hides*; but this is a point in the science of castrametation which we moderns have too much neglected, and perhaps chiefly from the following cause. To what professional art should we

again, supposing the forest game to be scarce, but that a river, firth, or bay, near to the settlement, offers an unusual abundance of fine fish, how injurious must be that neglect which should defeat this bountiful provision of nature by leaving unsummoned a due proportion of fishermen, boats, nets, and, in some cases, of a curing establishment, completely mounted. Five hundred men thus employed might support the whole colony, and leave its main labour disposable for a wide variety of mixed pursuits ; whilst, otherwise, the whole strength of the colony must be unavoidably sequestered into the one channel of raising subsistence. Mr. Gibbon Wakefield's improvement in colonisation, first suggested about ten years ago, was the earliest step taken upon principle in the philosophic theory of this subject. He saw the fatal schism or divorce which took place continually between capital and labour. Rich men had hitherto bought vast tracts of land at a small cost, not with any view of really enclosing and cultivating their allotments, but in the confidence that a public interest would grow up in the colony, that *other* lands would be improved, and that their own private shares (however neglected), being well situated, and at length *insulated* by thriving farms, would benefit by the *reacting* value from the circumjacent lands ; upon which consummation taking place, it would become *their* policy to sell. Thus was a considerable capital transferred to the colony, but not a capital which had much tendency to attract labour. Mr. Wakefield's system put an end to this abuse, or, at least, to its ruinous operation upon labour. The funds raised by the sale of the colonial land were applied, under regulations of law, and by fixed proportions, to the transportation of proper working families ; as fast as the land sold itself, so fast were the funds raised for the attraction of labour ; consequently, the want, the chief demand, bred commensurately its own relief

naturally look for the encouragement and improvement of tents? Manifestly to the military art. Now, unfortunately for this result, there is a growing indisposition amongst military men to the use of tents. Napoleon, it will be seen, in Las Cases, pronounced them unwholesome, and greatly preferred the practice of *bivouacking—i.e.* of sleeping *sub dio*—as respected salubrity. But this preference could not apply to tropical climates or to others where the dews are very heavy.

—land, as at any rate it is a call for labour, now became a pledge or security for labour. This was a great improvement. But there is still much of the colonising theory in arrear as respects the organisation, in more salutary proportions, of labour according to its great capital varieties. We see that an army is a machine, not merely in the sense of its unity as to purpose through the great artifice of its discipline, but also through the variety of its arms, or organs, for services differing in kind, though yet co-operating to a common result. Social life requires a composition of the same nature in the adjustment of the labour by which it advances towards its purposes; and this composition cannot be neglected without deranging colonies in their infancy, by retarding, if such neglect of assortment does not wholly intercept and strangle, their expansive energies.

From all this, so far as we have yet gone, what is the inference? The inference is that, of the four great elements for determining wages, not one can be relied upon as an insulated or unconditional force; all are dependent upon each, and each upon all. For, if we call the rate of advancing population P, and the rate of advancing capital C, then, because P expresses the *supply* of men, and C expresses the *demand* for men (since men are *supplied* in the ratio denoted by the growth of population, and men are *demanded* in the ratio denoted by the growth of capital for employing them), it follows that in fact $P + C$ makes but one compound force as regards wages; the final effect upon wages being determined by the excess of either element P or C, in its modification of the other. And again, if we denote the average rate of price, upwards or downwards, upon the necessaries of workmen by N, and the traditional standard of living amongst the workmen of that nation by S, then will $S + N$ express practically, through each period of a generation, not two separate forces acting upon wages, but one single force, resulting from the balance or intermodification between the two. In this way the treatment of the question is simplified: we are not called upon, like an Indian juggler, always to play with four balls at once. The four elements, working in pairs, become two; and the problem is this,—to compute *a priori* (that is, by inference from a principle), or to trace *a posteriori* (that is, experimentally), the degree in which wages (known already as an average rate) are modified for the present by the balance resulting from P + C, and, secondly, by the balance resulting from N + S. Population as working against capital; price of necessaries as working against the old traditionary standard of comfort: these, in effect, are the ordinary forces operating in the same direction, or in different directions, upon wages.

In illustration of this principle, we have had of late years a memorable case in our slave colonies. We all know at present, if we did not know at the time, that no legislative experiment was ever conducted with so much sentimental folly, and mischievous disregard of reversionary interests, as the *sudden* emancipation of our West India slaves—that is, the sudden admission to the rank of men of those who, intellectually and in self-restraint, were below the condition of children. Our own levity in granting was dramatically mimicked by *their* levity in using. They were as ready to abuse ungratefully as we to concede absurdly. At present we are suffering the penalties of our folly; and amongst them the mortification of seeing that ancient enemy of ours, always so full of light-minded precipitancy, and once in this very field of slavery manifesting that precipitancy in results so bloody (causing, in fact, a general massacre of her own children by the legislation of fifteen minutes), now, alas! building wisdom upon our irretrievable madness, and putting forth a statesmanlike providence such as used to be characteristic of our English senate, while that English senate has trifled sentimentally in the way once characteristic of Paris. The French scheme now in preparation is as thoughtful and cautious as the English scheme, unhappily irrevocable, was pitiably frantic. More truly and comprehensively than ever that word was applied to such a case, it may be said that the British Parliament ruined the West Indies. For, if Spain by her narrow policy ruined both herself and her magnificent colonies, it cost her three centuries to do so; but we "did the trick" in about as many years—a consummation that could not have been possible except in the case of sugar colonies, which were in reality mere factories. All human follies, however, whether tragic or comic, must have their better and worse scenes.[1] And this was the more to be expected in the West Indies, as circumstances forbade any free circulation of labour between the several islands. Accordingly, in some islands, where the balance upon P + C was particularly favourable to the labourer, as, for instance, in Jamaica and Trinidad, there the derangement of all social interests upon this harlequin experiment was total. The slaves, by relation to the funds for employing them regularly, were in defect, whilst the funds for employing them irregularly, *i.e.* so as to set their natural superiors at defiance, were vast. For, amongst other follies, our senate at home had quite forgotten to make any regulations against their throwing themselves for luxurious indolence (the besetting vice of negroes and lazzaroni) upon the ample waste lands. The same state of things amongst the negroes—the same capital oversights in Parliament—applied also to part of our continental colonies, as British Guiana. But, on the other hand, in islands like Antigua and Barbadoes, where the natural

[1] It struck many as the coolest specimen of audacity on record that not long since a governor of one amongst our English colonies absolutely made it the subject of solemn official congratulation, in writing home, that the emancipated slaves were buying up the estates of their ancient masters. (This language of triumph had been held before, but not before by any official person.) And how? Did *that* proclaim any real advance on the part of the slaves? The purchase money had been accumulated chiefly in their days of slavery, and formed therefore the emphatic measure and expression of the kindness and liberality with which they had been treated. But, after all, the true revolution was in the masters: not the slaves had prospered in the change, but the master had been ruined. The capital being gone which should have cultured the estates, naturally the estates became often nearly worthless; and *under those circumstances* it was that the wretched negro, by uniting himself with his fellows, became the new proprietor. Was *that* any subject of congratulation and self-glorification for a wise man? It is too late now to be wise for the ends of justice. The proprietor has retired, if he was rich—has perished, if he was poor. The social system has been wrecked; property is in ruins; capital has fled. Beginning, as it *has* done, in spoliation, the edifice of society now stands upon an evil footing in the British West Indies. But this will soon become worse (as we may read in the experience of Hayti), unless some redress, such as is yet possible, shall be applied to the anti-social disorders which threaten those colonies. And the nature of this redress cannot be better learned than in the French policy of Duc de Broglie, or (as to this point) in the still more cautious policy of his partisan opponents.

circumstances were different, P in relation to C being much nearer on a level, and no such plentiful resources for idleness to fall back upon, the blow fell more lightly. N + S, as being probably near to the same level in all these islands, might be safely neglected in a question of wages. Now, from this West Indian condition of the labouring class, suddenly summoned to a mighty revolution by a legislature which took no thought *of* this condition, nor *for* this condition, turn to a labouring class ranking in the opposite extreme amongst European nations. The Swiss population are not, *per se* (that is, by any superiority of nature, intellectual or moral), an interesting race. But, by their social economy, they are amongst the most respectable working orders on the Continent. Their population advances, in some places, in the healthiest way—not by excessive births counterworking excessive deaths, but by few deaths (locally not more than one annually upon seventy-five) compensating their few births (sometimes one annually upon forty-five). The rate of increase is therefore generally moderate. On the other hand, capital is nearly stationary. Thus far, therefore, as concerns P + C, the situation of Switzerland is not hopeful; and, but for emigration (which in Switzerland does not act, as it will do generally, to defeat itself by extra stimulation to the rate of population), the distress would be much greater than as yet it appears to be. But why is this? By what privilege in her institutions or usages does Switzerland escape the curse which has so continually besieged the Scottish Highlands, and other regions of a redundant population? There is nothing romantically fine in the present condition of the Swiss. On the contrary, they are a nation of low-toned sensibility; and, from the languor amongst them of all religious principle, they are in danger of great eventual demoralisation. But, in the meantime, they struggle with some success against the downward tendencies of their situation; and they do not yet exhibit a squalid Irish surplus upon their population—one out of four fierce, famishing, and without prospect of regular employment. Still less do the Swiss carry the contagion and causes of pauperism amongst their next neighbours as do the Irish. Their own cup of woe has long been full for the Irish; and through the last score of years, or since the improvement of steam navigation, its overflowings have been settling ruinously upon England[1] and on Scotland. Now, Switzerland at least evades these evils: she neither exhibits misery in her own bosom, as the Scottish

[1] It is perfectly astonishing to hear one mistake current upon this subject. Because the New Poor Law, amongst its many heavy offences against Christian wisdom, sanctions this one measure of natural justice—that, upon becoming chargeable to an English parish the Irish pauper (*if found to be without a settlement*) shall be shipped back to Ireland—it is therefore assumed that the evils of Irish pauperism *quoad* ourselves are now corrected. How so? Was *that* the main evil? It might have become such under the action of a known trick practised locally in Ireland. Subscriptions were at one time raised in certain districts for shipping off mendicants to English ports: at a present cost of one guinea a-head, the town or district in Ireland got rid permanently of those whom it could bribe into emigration. This policy, which is not surprising when played off by a poor country against a rich one, has certainly been crushed in an early stage by the Poor Bill; but, however ruinous that policy was by its menace, actually it had not been realised upon any very large scale. The true ruin of Irish pauperism to England and Scotland is far different, and not of a nature to be checked by any possible Poor Bill. This ruin lies, first and chiefly, in the gradual degradation of wages, English and Scotch, under the fierce growth of Irish competition; secondly, in the chargeableness of Irish pauperism, once settled (or for any reason not liable to removal), upon funds English and Scotch. In Scotland the case is even worse at present than in England; for there the Poor Laws are in so desperate a condition of craziness, by original insufficiency, that the Government will now be violently compelled into an interference with evils too monstrous to be longer tolerated. The Scottish aristocracy have, in this one instance, manifested a bigotry of opposition to the reforms clamorously called for by the exposures of Dr. Pulteney Alison, such as could hardly have been anticipated from a patriotism so sincere as theirs. But the abuses are too crying for any further attempt at disguise. The one great evil of the Scottish Poor Law lies in the mockery of its own professed purposes, in the mere idle simulation of a relief which too often is no relief at all. Cases are before the public in which half-a-crown, or even one shilling, *per annum*, is the amount of each pauper's dividend. But, when the evil of public distress becomes too gigantic to be trifled with in that way, then it is seen, in mighty cities like Glasgow, to what extent the parasitical pauperism of Ireland has strangled and crushed the native vigour of the land. Paisley, with a sudden development of pauperism in 1842, beyond all proportions that had ever been supposed possible, was compelled to draw heavily upon alien funds; and yet, with all this non-local aid, both Scotch and English, the sheer impossibility of feeding adequately the entire body of claimants coerced the humane distributors of the relief into drawing a line between Scotch and Irish. Then it

Highlands often, and Ireland for ever: nor is she the rank cause of misery to neighbouring nations, as is Ireland. But again I ask, through what advantage or privilege of her situation? The answer is undeniable: it is simply through

was that the total affliction became known—viz. the hideous extent in which Irish intruders upon Scotland had taken the bread out of her own children's mouths. As to England, it has long been accepted as a fair statement that fifty thousand Irish interlopers annually swell the great tide of our *native* increase (say two hundred and twenty or two hundred and forty thousand *per annum*), already too rapidly advancing. Yet how has this twofold increase met with any final absorption? In fact, it might be replied that latterly it has *not* been absorbed; and, so far as there was any distress at all through the year 1842 (a distress which, on the faith of many public returns, I greatly doubt—excepting, first, as distress will *always* exist in so vast a working population forced into a variable sympathy with every part of the globe; and excepting, secondly, the *local* distress of Paisley, Glasgow, Stockport, Leicester, &c.), it is to this partial non-absorption of extra labour, falling in with dreadful American derangements of commerce, that the domestic pressure has been owing. A man might, however, demur to the *possibility* of so much alien labour crowding into our great labour markets. Where, he might say, is the opening for so much new labour? And especially since the tendency has been, of late years, not to limit the virtual amount of labour for each person, but (by greatly extending the labouring hours, with the result of at last forcing an interposition from the legislature) materially to augment that individual amount. There has, however, been a change in the channels of labour favourable to the concurrent increase of labour numerically, and of the separate labour for each, and so far favourable to this tide of Irish intrusion. Even where the absolute work to be done has but little increased, the numerical increase of labourers has been great, through the growing substitution of female for male (and above all of childish for adult) labour. Three girls of thirteen, at wages of six shillings to eight shillings a-week, have by myriads displaced the one man of mature age, at wages varying from eighteen shillings to forty-five. This revolution has not *uniformly* been injurious, even to the English working classes; or, at least, its injurious reaction upon the adult working population has not yet had time for reaching its full display. But to the Irish family, starting from so low a *standard* of domestic comfort, the change has acted as a bounty. And in this triple race of the English labour against machinery—against Irish competition—against infant competition—has lain the real opening and possibility for that cruel encroachment upon infant health and happiness which has at length awakened the thunders of public indignation, never again to be laid asleep. At present there is this one sole barrier of *self*-protection for English labour: viz. the high domestic standard of comfort inherited from English ancestors. Left to itself, that barrier, so long assaulted and shaken, would soon

her high patriarchal standard of comfort and respectability. In some countries, merely through the one habit of living too much abroad and in the open air, it has happened that a very low standard of comfort or pleasure is connected with the domestic hearth. *Home* is not there a word of sanctity or endearment. This is the case pretty widely upon Italian ground, and not solely amongst the lazzaroni of Naples. This is the case in Peru, in Mexico, and indeed more or less everywhere in South America. The genial climate has defeated itself as a blessing. Co-operating by its own temptations with the constitutional luxurious languor in the natives, the climate has become a withering curse to the better instincts of the people. But Ireland, but Switzerland, have not been subject to that mode of temptation. Welcome the apparent curses, which (like labour itself) finally become blessings, of stern northern climates! Yet the same temptation in effect has operated upon both, through a different channel. The luxury of excessive indolence had, from the earliest period, fascinated Ireland into a savage life. A scale almost brutal of diet and of lodging had already long reconciled itself to the Irish feelings in the labouring class, when the fatal gift of the potato stepped in to make the improgressive state compatible with a vast expansion of the population. To Switzerland, agitated nobly by the storms of the Reformation, and starting from a much higher point of self-valuation, such a temptation proved none at all. To this day she adheres indomitably to the ancient habits of her fathers. Other nations preserve their economy through their morals; Switzerland preserves her morals through her economy; and even yet her children will not marry without guarantees for the continued prospect, in the coming genera-

give way entirely; and the English labour market would be finally prostrated to a level with any, the very basest, human degradation ever witnessed amongst Oriental slaves. This protection, if it survives at all, will survive through the yet energetic spirit of the English working man. But in the accidents of his situation there is one collateral encouragement to the English native. Machinery, which has so often stranded him for a time, is at length likely to depress the bounty on Irish intrusion; the infant-labour revolution probably has reached its *maximum*; and, in the meantime, Ireland, it may be hoped, by railroads, by good government, and by growing capital, will soon be preparing better days for her own children at home.

tion, of what they witnessed in the last. And thus two nations, not originally standing upon a very different basis of landed wealth, are now seen in the most absolute repulsion to each other, upon the two polar extremities as to comfort and self-respect.

## Section II.

Hitherto we find nothing peculiar to Ricardo in the forces acting upon labour. It was necessary to notice these four elements in that complex machinery which finally moulds the vicissitudes of wages; but, after all, it is only one of the four, viz. the current price of the articles essential to a poor man's household, which can, by any sudden change, produce a correspondingly sudden change upon wages. The rate of increase upon population, the changes incident to capital, the national traditionary standard of domestic life—all these are slow to move, and, when they *have* moved, slow to embody themselves in corresponding effects. Population, for instance, perseveres often through generations in the same prevailing rate; and, if this rate should, from any cause, sustain the most abrupt change, it would take a score of years before that change could begin to tell upon the labour market. But the fourth element, the daily cost of necessaries, alters sometimes largely in one day; and upon this, therefore, must be charged the main solution of those vicissitudes in wages which are likely to occur within one man's life. The other forces vary, by degrees fine and imperceptible, so as to affect the condition of working men deeply and radically from century to century. But such an effect, though sure, and important to the historical grandeur of nations, is not rapid enough to be concurrent with the corresponding changes upon other functions of productive power. We look for an agency upon wages able to keep abreast of these other agencies, fitted by its easy motion for receiving *their* effects, and for returning to *them* a continual modification from itself.

Here, therefore, it is, upon this one force out of four which control the price of labour—viz. upon the poor man's household consumption for the diet of his family, for their clothing, their lodging, for the annual dividend upon the cost and maintenance of his furniture (amongst which only the beds and bedding are expensive), for his fuel (sometimes, from land-carriage, costly), for his candles and his soap, with a small allowance for medicine and medical attendance, and too often (though most naturally) a large one for strong liquors—upon these *items* in a poor man's expenditure it is that the main agency of change settles: schooling for his children he generally obtains *gratis*.

Now the reader is aware that, according to Ricardo's view, an expenditure on this humble scale is chiefly determined by the cost of production upon the land. Yet why? The furniture and the clothes (with the exception of the woollen or iron parts amongst them) do not arise from the domestic soil, though much of the food *does*; yet, even amongst *that*, the tea and the sugar (two very important articles) are wholly foreign; and all the other articles, except fuel, are trivial in price. Certainly it must be granted that the habit of estimating the labourer's expenses by the cost of his diet (nay, exclusively by one item of his diet—bread) is radically false; and of *that* Ricardo is sensible, though apparently he does not allow sufficiently for the true proportion held. The corn-law incendiaries here, as everywhere when they approach the facts or the principles of the question, betray an ignorance which could not be surpassed if the discussion were remitted to Ashantee or Negroland. They calculate a change of ten per cent upon wheat as if it meant a change of ten per cent on wages (though, by the way, often denying elsewhere that wages at all sympathise with the price of food). Now, suppose the total food of a working man's family to cost two-fifths of his total wages, and suppose that of these two-fifths one moiety, *i.e.* one-fifth of the wages, is spent upon flour, and oatmeal, and bread; in that case a change of ten per cent upon wheat will amount to one-tenth upon one-fifth of the total wages. But one-tenth of one-fifth is one-fiftieth, or two per cent upon the total wages; so trivial is the result upon wages from a change in wheat which is very considerable. Suppose the change upon wheat to be even as much as fifteen shillings less upon sixty, *i.e.* twenty-five per cent, then the total change will be one-fourth of one-fifth, which is one-twentieth—that is, five per cent upon the total wages; and everybody is aware that a fall of fifteen shillings upon sixty is greater than we often experience in any single season. Ricardo, indeed, attempts to justify the supposition that, as a natural state of things, an English labourer might spend one-half of his wages upon wheat (p. 106), and the other half upon "other things," by alleging (p. 97) that "in rich countries a labourer, by the sacrifice of a very small quantity only of his food, is able to provide liberally for all his other wants." No; not necessarily. That remark arises only through a neglect (habitual to Ricardo) of the antagonist principle, which is eternally at work to compensate the declensions of land by countervailing improvements of endless kinds: so that at this time, all over western Europe, there cannot be a doubt that, with a far worse soil as the regulating soil for cost, wheat is cheaper than it was a thousand years ago. Yet, if Ricardo were right in supposing a labourer to spend half his wages upon wheat only, then his beer, bacon, cheese, milk, butter, tea, and sugar, must proportionably cost, at the very least, all the rest of his wages; so that for clothes, lodging, fuel, to say nothing of other miscellanies, he would have no provision at all. But these are romantic estimates, and pardonable in Ricardo from his city life, which had denied him, until his latest years, all opportunities of studying the life of labourers.

Meanwhile it will not be denied that flour and bread compose an important item upon the labourer's housekeeping, though not by possibility *so* important as Ricardo chooses to fancy. Now then, so far as this flour and bread are obtained from a soil continually worse (since, 1st, population forces culture for ever upon worse soils, and, 2dly, the very worst always gives the price for the whole), so far the flour and bread would be continually dearer were there no such compensating law as that which I, almost too frequently, have noticed, for the reason that Ricardo too systematically forgets it. Let *us* also forget it for the present, so as to pursue the principle of wages more clearly by pushing it into an extreme which in practice does but rarely take place to that extent. On this basis the following short extract from Ricardo (pp. 105, 106), accompanied by a single word of commentary, will explain the whole of what is peculiar to Ricardo in his theory of wages :—

"When wheat was £4 per quarter, suppose the labourer's wages to be £24 per annum, or the value of six quarters of wheat, and suppose half his wages to be expended on wheat, and the other half (or £12) on other things, he would receive

| | | | | |
|---|---|---|---|---|
| £24 14 0 | when wheat was at | £4 4 8 | or the value of | 5·83 quarters. |
| 25 10 0 | | 4 10 0 | | 5·66 quarters. |
| 26 8 0 | | 4 16 0 | | 5·50 quarters. |
| 27 6 8 | | 5 2 10 | | 5·33 quarters. |

| | £ | s. | d. |
|---|---|---|---|
| He would receive these wages to enable him to live just as well, and no better, than before ; for, when corn was at £4 per quarter, he would expend for three quarters of corn, at £4 per quarter . . . . . . . | £12 | 0 | 0 |
| And on other things . . . . | 12 | 0 | 0 |
| | £24 | 0 | 0 |
| When wheat was at £4 : 10s., three quarters of wheat would cost . . . . . . . . . . | £13 | 10 | 0 |
| And other things . . . . . | 12 | 0 | 0 |
| | £25 | 10 | 0 |
| When at £4 : 16s., three quarters of wheat would cost | £14 | 8 | 0 |
| Other things . . . . . . | 12 | 0 | 0 |
| | £26 | 8 | 0 |

In proportion as corn became dear, he [the labourer] would receive less corn wages, but his money would always increase ; whilst his enjoyments, on the above supposition, would be precisely the same. But, as other commodities would be raised in price, in proportion as raw produce entered into their composition, he would have more to pay for some of them. Although his tea, sugar, soap, candles, and house-rent would probably be no dearer, he would pay more for his bacon, cheese, butter, linen, shoes, and cloth ; and therefore, even with the above increase of wages, his situation would be comparatively worse."

The principle of advance is this :—When wheat was at 80s. per quarter, the labourer had received £24 ; when wheat rose to 90s., it might seem that he should receive

£27; because 80 : 90 : : £24 : £27. But, in fact, he receives only one-half of the difference, viz. 30s. His wages are now £25 : 10s. Why is this? Because only one-half of his original wages had been spent on wheat. But the full development of this principle I refer to the chapter on Rent, that I may not be obliged to repeat myself.

# CHAPTER IV—RENT

## Section I.

The particular situation of this chapter in Ricardo, placed immediately after the chapter on Value, is not without significance. By placing the consideration of Rent where he *does* place it, he is to be understood as viewing Rent under the idea of a disturbance to Value. Under that fiction, or at least under that relation, selected from other relations equally conspicuous, he brings up the question before his own bar. For the ordinary and continual disturbances of value, growing out of the varying proportions between fixed and circulating capital, Ricardo had allowed, in a striking part of his opening chapter. He had shown conclusively that the universal principle of varying quantity in the producing labour as the cause of varying price is subject to two modifications: as, first, that the price will be greater in the case where circulating capital predominates than in the opposite case where fixed capital predominates; secondly, that the tendency will be in the same direction, according to the degrees in which the fixed capital has less and less of durability,—for the plain reason that so far the fixed capital approximates in virtue to the separate nature of circulating capital. These are settled re-agencies of co-causes which sometimes arise jointly with the great general cause of price, sometimes arise singly, and sometimes not at all. They must not be called anomalies or irregularities, any more than the resistance of the air is an irregularity or *exception* to the law governing the motion of projectiles. It is convenient to abstract from this resistance in the first steps of the exposition. But afterwards, when you allow for it, this allowance is not to be considered in the light of any concession, as if originally you had gone too far, and now wished to unmask the whole truth by instalments. Not at all. The original force, as you had laid it down from the first, continues to be the true force: *it exerts its whole agency, and not a part or fraction of its agency*, even under the co-presence of the opposing and limiting cause. If, being left to itself, it ought to have reached an effect of 50, but, under this limiting force, it *has* fallen to 35, then the true logic is not to say that it has yielded to an exception, or suffered an irregularity. On the contrary, all is regular, since, if at first sight it seems simply to have lost 15 (which, *pro tanto*, seems an irregularity), on severer examination it appears to have expended that 15 on neutralising a counter-agency; so that the total force exerted has been equally 50 according to the theory, and according to the true concrete case of experience.

Now, then, is rent a disturbance of value simply in the sense of being a modification (as here explained), or does it suspend and defeat that law? Ricardo has not pushed the question to that formal issue; but, generally, he has endeavoured to bring the question of rent into immediate relation with value, by putting the question upon it in this shape—"Whether the appropriation of land, and the consequent creation of rent, will occasion any variation in the relative value of commodities, independently of the quantity of labour necessary to production?" Whether, in short, the proportions between the two labours producing A and B will continue, in spite of rent, to determine the prices of A and B; or whether this law will be limited by the law of rent; or whether in any case this law will be actually set aside by rent? Upon Adam Smith's principles, rent introduced a new element into price. Is *that* so? It is the question moved at present.

So important a question brings forward the obligation of investigating the new Doctrine of Rent as a duty even for Ricardo, who else could not have any particular interest in discussing a doctrine which had not been discovered by himself. The modern Doctrine of Rent was, in reality, one of those numerous discoveries which have been made many times over before they *are* made ; that is, it had been ideally detected at different eras by some inquisitive and random intellect, prying where it had no business, several times before it was perceived to involve those weighty consequences which give dignity to the truth, by giving practical motives for remembering it. Ricardo had been acquainted with this truth for nearly two years when he wrote his own book. It is not improbable that, *previously* to this knowledge, he had tentatively sketched his theory of value ; but he must have been impeded by the defect of such knowledge in carrying out this theory into a satisfactory harmony with the laws regulating wages and profits ; for both these presuppose the law of rent. Without knowing rent and its principles it is impossible to know the principles which control wages in the first place, and profits in the second.

Natural it is, when a man enters upon a new theme, that he should introduce it by a definition ; and, as regards what logicians call the *nominal* definition, such a course is perfectly right. But, as to the *real* definition, this is so far from taking precedency in the natural process of thought that, on the contrary, it ought to be the last result[1] from the total discussion. However, without insisting upon this, what *is* the definition ? "Rent," says Ricardo, "is that portion of " the produce of the earth which is paid to the landlord for the " use of the original and indestructible powers of the soil."

Can this definition be sustained ? Certainly not. The word "*indestructible*" is liable to challenge ; and, in order that the student may see *why*, first let me explain to him under what prepossession it was that Ricardo introduced that word. He was thinking of the *casual* and the *intermitting* when he suggested the *indestructible*. At pp. 50 and 51 he

[1] "*The last result*" :—A remark very nearly approaching to this is made by Edmund Burke in some part of the little "Essay on Taste," prefixed to his "Essay on the Sublime." Burke, however, a very young man at the date of that work, was not sufficiently cautious. At that time his philosophical reading and meditation could not have been extensive, and he neglected to qualify the resulting definition as the *real* one in contradistinction to the nominal. Naturally, and almost inevitably, the nominal definition goes *before* the discussion ; since, without some περιληψις, or rough circumscribing outline of the subject, a reader cannot be supposed to know the very object or substance of the inquiry.

notices two cases—one being the case of a Norway forest, and the other of a coal-mine or a stone-quarry—where Adam Smith had applied the popular term "rent" as strictly pertinent. But Ricardo thinks otherwise. In any one of these cases he views the payment for the mine or quarry, colloquially called "the rent" as no rent at all in any strict sense. Now, as against Adam Smith, in the *quoad hominem* sense, the censure of Ricardo is not applicable: *he* is but consistent; for he could not be bound to any strictness of distinction growing out of a doctrine which in *his* days was unknown. But understand Ricardo as speaking *of* Adam Smith in an argument spoken *to* more modern writers, and still, even in that case, Ricardo is wrong. He contemplates the Norway forest, the coal-mine, the stone-quarry, as if all alike leased out to the tenant, not with any view to a continued succession of crops, but as simply transferred on the consideration of that crop now ready for removal. He puts the question, in fact, precisely as he would do on the case of a man's leasing out his coal-cellar to another with the privilege of emptying it. Now, this is not the real case of a forest or a coal-mine. In the forest there is a regular process pursued with the purpose of creating a continual succession of "falls," so arranged that, by the fifteenth year, for instance, the section thinned in the first year may be ready again for thinnings, and so on perpetually, according to the nature of the wood. In a coal-mine, again, the known uncertainty of the veins as to direction and density of the different strata gives a reasonable prospect of continuous succession in the annual yield. But suppose all this *not* to be so. Take the case as Ricardo apparently shapes it—viz. that you let off a coal-cellar with liberty to the lessee of emptying it within a year or two. Here the profitable product, the "crop" of the cellar, is known beforehand to a hundredweight, and you are not to suppose any concealment as to this fact, or any deception. Clearly, now, this coal cannot be described as any produce from "the original and indestructible powers" of the cellar. And therefore, says Ricardo,[1] the term "rent"

[1] "*Says Ricardo*," *i.e.* says by the tenor of his argument, says implicitly; else he does *not* say so explicitly; for the case itself of the coal-cellar is not *his* illustration, but mine.

could not be applied in any other than an improper sense to the consideration paid by the lessee of the cellar. But is *that* so ? Not at all. In the modern (and most exclusive) sense of the term, "rent" might be paid by such a lessee. For take the cellar, or take the stone-quarry, and imagine the coal, the stone, or the stercoraceous deposit in the vast crypts cleaned out by Hercules, to have been accurately measured, it would be no impossible bargain that a day's produce from the labour of fifty men in any one of the chambers supposed should be set off against a similar product from known mines, quarries, crypts, in the same neighbourhood, and should be charged with a rent corresponding to the assignable differences in the "put-out." A neighbouring coal-mine, for instance, worked by a hundred colliers, would furnish a standard for the comparison. If our carbonaceous crypt, or our stercoraceous crypt, yielded a produce larger by twenty-five per cent upon the same quantity of labour, then we should have a good ground for rent in the severest sense, although the crypt were notoriously exhaustible in one, two, or three years.

It is not, therefore, the inherent or *indestructible* powers of a subject which will make it capable of rent, but the *differential* powers ; and the true definition of rent is, in the strictest terms, *that portion of the produce from the soil* (or from any agency of production) *which is paid to the landlord for the use of its differential powers, as measured by comparison with those of similar agencies operating on the same market.* Though Aristotle should rise from the dead, that definition (I humbly submit) will stand.

Undoubtedly, there are found cases in England, and cases very numerous, where, at first sight, Ricardo's definition seems almost indispensable for reaching the true distinction between what *is* rent and what is *not.* For instance, he himself supposes the case where "of two adjoining farms," otherwise exactly equal (same size, same quality), "one had all the conveniencies of farming buildings,—was, besides, properly drained and manured, and advantageously divided by hedges, fences, and walls ; while the other had none of these advantages." Now, surely Ricardo has the right to presume that for the improved farm "more remuneration would naturally be paid" than for the unimproved. But would that excess of remuneration be "rent"? "No," says Ricardo himself, "it would not; but, popularly, it would be called rent." And then he goes on to show that the true rent, which probably would be the same in each case, is that part of the total "remuneration" which is "paid for the original and indestructible powers of the soil"; whilst that part of the remuneration which is strictly pseudo-rent must be viewed as "paid for the use of the capital" sunk in the improvements. Is that not sound? Certainly it is; quite sound: and, by the way, it is the more noticeable in Ricardo because it has been accidentally his ordinary oversight to talk of rent as if it were the one great burden on the farmer of land; whereas so much greater is the burden in this island from the capital required that Mr. Jacob[1] (well known in past times to the British Government as an excellent authority) reports the proportion of capital to rent needed in ordinary circumstances as being then little less than four to one. From fifty-two reports made to a Committee of the Lords in the year before Waterloo, the result was that upon one hundred acres, paying in rent no more than £161 : 12 : 7, the total of *other* expenses (that is, of the capital fixed and circulating) was £601 : 15 : 1 *per annum.* And in some other cases, as, for instance, in bringing into tillage the waste lands known technically as "cold clays," the proportion of capital required for some years appeared to be much greater —on an average, three times greater, so that the capital would be ten or eleven times as much as the rent; and in such circumstances, the *total* sacrifice of rent by the landlord would be no serious relief to the improving tenant. Such being the true relation of agricultural capital to rent, which

[1] William Jacob, F.R.S., stood in a position of advantage, on a sort of isthmus, for judging of any question in economy relating to agriculture; for (on the one side) he was well read in the literature of Economy, and (on the other) he was practically familiar with the whole condition and details of rural industry in this island. His "Considerations on the Protection required by British Agriculture, in 1814, is a valuable work. And the talent, together with the moderation and the knowledge displayed in it, recommended him subsequently to the Government as a commissioner for inquiries into Continental agriculture.

generally Ricardo seems to overlook, it would be strange indeed to blame him for this particular passage, in which he does *not* overlook it. The distinction is just and necessary. The payment for the house, barns, stables, fences, drains, &c., is rightly distinguished from the rent; it is interest paid upon capital invested in the farm, and therefore, in fact, lent to the farmer. As reasonably might you call the interest upon twenty thousand pounds which the farmer had brought into his business, either as a loan from the neighbouring bank, or as his own patrimonial inheritance, part of his rent. But still the rent (speaking with that strictness which must always be a duty where we are speaking polemically) is to be calculated from the rating, from the place occupied on the differential scale, howsoever that place has been reached. Now, at this moment, much land is thus or thus rich, in consequence of this or that sum of capital co-operative with its original powers. You are not careful to distinguish between the original power and the acquired power; any more than, with regard to a man of talents, you care to say, "So much is due to nature, so much to education and personal efforts." Often you cannot distinguish. The farmer, indeed, as a private secret, may guess that so much of his nominal rent arises upon the improvements, so much upon the original powers of the land. But the true rent is calculated severely upon these differential powers, however obtained, as found by comparing it with other lands cultivated on the prospect of the same markets; and the only ground for separating the nominal rent into true rent and pseudo-rent is because some improvements do not directly increase the differential powers of a particular estate, but only increase the convenience, the respectability in appearance, the variable divisibility of the estate; or, potentially, they raise a basis upon which, as yet, no additional power perhaps *has* been raised, but on which the tenant (being a man of energy) *can* raise such a power much sooner than otherwise he could. For instance, an excellent road has been made to lime or marl, or new pits of those manures have been opened. Now, it is for the tenant to use those advantages. If he does *not* use them, to him they are as if they did not exist; but, if he does, then he finds a saving of possibly fifty per cent upon all that he fetches, which may be seven or ten per cent on his total costs. So, again, as to better divisions of lands, by which they may be applied to a larger cycle of uses ; or, where the divisions have previously existed, heretofore they may have been rude and fixed. Now, by means of light iron hurdles, they may be much more effectual, and yet susceptible of variable arrangement, according to the wants of the particular season. Or, again, the house upon the estate, the approach to it, and the outhouses universally, may have been improved. Where, indeed, the improvement has tended to the direct conservation of the produce, as by leaded tanks of shallow capacity for receiving cream, or by granaries fenced against vermin, or by reservoirs prepared for receiving manure without waste, they are equivalent to direct augmentations in the soil of natural power.

The logical incidence of the last paragraph, though plain in its parts, may seem obscure in the whole ; and I add this explanation. There is a large distinction into two cases to be made for agricultural improvements. And this was not overlooked by Ricardo. The difference is that one class actually augments the power of your land : it *did* produce ten—it *does* produce twelve. But the other class leaves the power where it was ; having produced ten formerly, it produces ten now. How, then, is it an improvement ? In this way,—that, whereas formerly this ten required a cost of five guineas, now it requires only a cost of three. I do not at all overlook that oftentimes this saving is but an inverse form of announcing an increased power, since the two guineas saved may be used in further corresponding production ; and the blindness to this possible inversion of the case is that which so unaccountably misled Malthus. But sometimes it happens that improvements are not so used, and do not naturally suggest such a use. For instance, on obtaining marl cheaper, you save annually ; but perhaps, even at the old price of marl, you had enough. You feel the difference, therefore, not in a larger amount of marl, for you want no more ; and perhaps you spend the difference *as* income, not productively. So, again, if "Rebecca's Daughters" save you five guineas a summer on tolls, naturally you spend the money in drinking Rebecca's health

—not upon improvements. Now, this distinction of cases is of a nature to fortify Ricardo's distinction between the indestructible advantages of land and its casual advantages in convenience. The first *will*, the second will *not*, operate upon the future rent. So far it seems as if I were justifying Ricardo. But what I *do* say is that the special plausibility, in this instance, of Ricardo's illustration must not lead us away from the fact that even here it is not the indestructibility of the powers, taken singly, which could sustain the difference of the two improvements stated, were not that indestructibility manifested on a differential scale.

## Section II.

Rent having been thus defined as *the series of increments arising upon the differential qualities of land*, no matter in what way that land may happen to be employed, it follows that this series will begin to expand itself concurrently with the earliest advances of the population.

And, because these original differences in quality of soils, keeping pace altogether in their development with the movement of the population, are best understood by a scale of graduations addressed to the eye—at this point, ready for the references and explanations which may be found necessary hereafter, I place such a diagram or ocular construction of the case :—

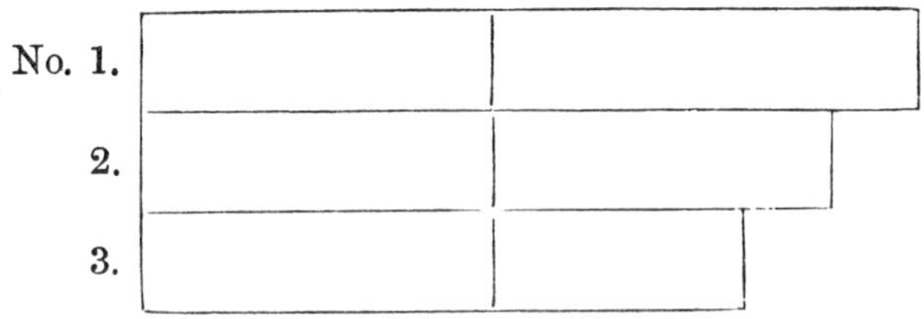


In Tuscany there may be 300, in England many more than 300, qualities of soil expanded ; but three, as amply as 300, will explain the law for the whole.

No. 1 represents the class of soils *first* brought under culture. And why *first ?* For the natural reason that these soils were seen obviously to be the most productive under an equal expenditure of capital: they are first in order of development, which is an act of human choice, because they are first in order of merit, which is a consequence of natural endowment. The precedency allotted by man does but follow and advertise the precedency allotted by nature. And, if a second-rate soil close to a great market like Birmingham, if a third-rate soil close to a great seaport like Newcastle, is sometimes more profitable in the very same year 1770 than a first-rate soil in the wilds of central Cardiganshire—possessing at that time neither a domestic population for consuming its produce, nor roads of any kind for transporting such supplies to the corresponding centres of demand—thus far no doubt the regular expansion of the series will be slightly disturbed: to that extent it cannot be denied that the rigour of the graduation must be interrupted. But it is a sufficient answer to say that, in so large a territory as England, the final effect upon the general balance will be trivial, and, secondly, that lands which are thus accidentally privileged, for which the local position is able to defeat the natural endowment, will be inevitably raised artificially by the compensations of culture and rich manures to the *real* rank of No. 1, which originally they had usurped.

No. 2 represents the second class of soils, called up into the series as soon as the growing population has made No. 1 insufficient.

No. 3 represents the third class of soils called up under the same pressure continually increasing.

Now, in the next step, retaining the very same diagram, let us circumstantiate its *internal* relations by filling in the secondary divisions, which shall be distinguished by a dotted line:—

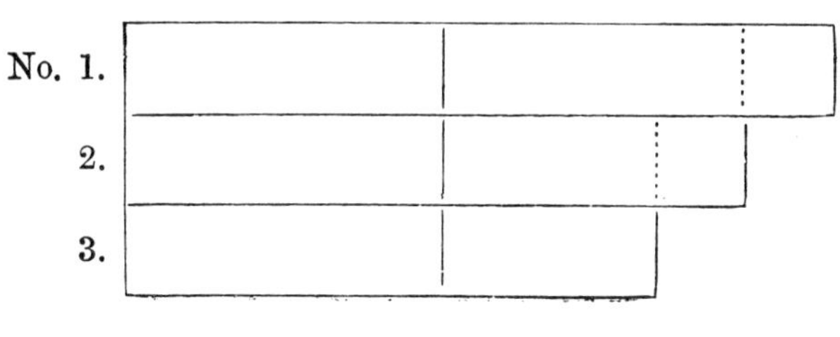

The novice understands that the increments or excesses by which each superior No. runs beyond its next lower No. express and measure the relations of quantity amongst the products. For example, the product upon No. 2 exceeds that upon No. 3, the product upon No. 1 exceeds that upon No. 2; but by how much? By the section which the dotted lines mark off. But this section on each of the upper soils (No. 1 and No. 2),—this absciss marked off by dotted lines—is RENT.

Finally, to complete this preparation of the diagram before any argument or explanation is applied to it, let us mount the whole scaffolding of subdivisions, the tertiary as well as the secondary changes which follow the development of the

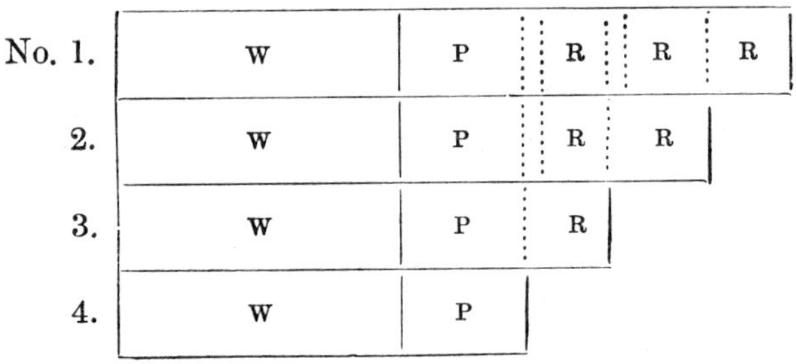


scale, adding the letters denoting the particular function of revenue to which each of these sections corresponds.

To this third and final diagram is added a fourth soil; whereas, in general, it is quite needless to persecute the reader with a scale carried lower than the third round. I suppose it almost superfluous to add that W expresses the function of wages, P of profit, and R the several increments of rent, as they emerge successively under the series of agricultural expansions. When No. 2 was first summoned into use, one single chamber out of the six marked R (viz. that on the extreme east or right hand of the diagram) was struck off *ipso facto* from No. 1 by that movement of No. 2. In the next stage, when No. 3 was summoned, two chambers (ranging north and south on the diagram) were *simultaneously* struck off from No. 2 and No. 1, as equally disposable for rent. And, finally, when No. 4 was summoned, three chambers (all rising perpendicularly on the same meridian, but varying in latitude), were again *simultaneously* struck off, as being each the separate absciss for rent, which became due for the same reason, and therefore at the same moment, on No. 1, No. 2, and No. 3.

## Section III.

"Now," having prepared my tables, and sufficiently armed myself for the decent conjurations of political economy, in the language of Prospero, "Now, I arise," and the reader will suppose me pointing with a long wand, or caduceus, to the hieroglyphics of the diagram; and, if he would further suppose these subdivisions framed of mosaic tablets, ivory and ebony, for instance (as on a chessboard), for symbolising even to the random eye the separate sections of *wages* and *profit*, whilst golden tessellæ at the very least would be proper to express the eternal encroachments of rent[1] (*Acherontis avari*), the logic of what follows would then become more emphatic, and more authoritative, as it always does by many degrees, where it is made to speak *sensuously* to the eye. A *construction* (*i.e.* a geometrical exhibition) of any elaborate truth is not often practicable; but, wherever it is so, prudence will not allow it to be neglected. What is called *evidentia*, that sort of demonstration which "shows out," which is *ostensive* (in the old language of mathematicians), and not merely *discursive*, or founded on dialectic *discursus* of the understanding, is, by a natural necessity, more convincing to the learner. And, had Ricardo relied on this constructive mode of illustrating his chapters upon rent and upon wages, they would not have tried the patience of his students in the way they *have* done; still less would they have baffled the efforts of really able men (when not supported by some obstinate

[1] "*Eternal encroachments of rent*":—Eternal by an argument *ad hominem* which neither Sir Edward West, the original discoverer of the doctrine, nor Ricardo, was in any condition to refuse; as to *them* the encroachments *are* eternal. But I have repeatedly urged elsewhere that this law is checked by an opposite law—this tendency is neutralised from century to century by a counter-tendency.

interest in the study) at deciphering the very outline of their principles. The case is astonishing. Two doctrines in Ricardo's system, viz. Value and Rent (with its *complement* in wages), constitute the well-heads of his economy: these mastered, *all* is mastered; for the rest runs down in a torrent of inferences from these *præcognita.* Yet these two chapters in Ricardo are perhaps his obscurest. Upon Value, though churlishly penurious in illustrations and in guarded distinctions between cases liable to be confounded, the exposition is substantially present; it has a local manifestation. But upon Rent it is not quite certain that all the grounds of decision are present even in cipher. What is clear is general and expansive; what is special, what involves the *differential* portion of the truth, the novel, the esoteric, and the characteristic, all this is thrown upon the overcharged duty of one single page (viz. the last page in the chapter). It is therefore disproportionately brief at any rate; but, by a most unhappy arrangement, even so much as *is* communicated lies dispersed and vagrant through a complex table of numerical proportions; whilst for this table there is wanting some guiding Ariadne's thread to the explorer before he can apprehend even the *principium motus* —that is, in which one of the several columns he must look for the *original* impulse to the series of changes displayed. Action and reaction he perceives to be going on strenuously; but where do they *commence*?

Suppose, now, the wand pointed to diagram the first, and striking the upper part of this diagram. What I wish first to engage the reader's attention is the original starting-point of society as to rent, which (fiercely as many people have disputed it, even in the sense of a possibility) must be assumed even as a postulate of the understanding. It is a mere necessity of logic to assume as the starting-point that primitive condition of the land under which it neither did nor could pay rent. Originally, when the population had called only for No. 1, it is seen by looking back to diagram I. that the land did not trisect itself into rent, profit, and wages. There *was* no rent; there *could* be none; the land bisected itself only into the two capital sections of wages and profit. But exactly on this point it is that many a coarse sceptic comes forward. Let political economy say what it will, he for *his* part will not believe that any proprietor of land would give up his land gratuitously to the public service. All others engaged in the laborious manufacture of corn, of oxen, and of horses, being so notoriously moved to it by considerations reasonably selfish, why should the landowner stand alone in his unappreciated patriotism?

But it is not alleged that he will. And now, since this mode of argument has been adopted as the main thesis of separate books and pamphlets, it is worth noticing it by a severe and formal exposure. For the *first* thing broadly noticeable in such an argument is the puerile style of anachronism which it betrays; assuming (as if it were a matter of course) the modern perfect subdivision of the agricultural class into owners and tenants by lease. On the part of society there is a necessity for an article which, on the part of the owner, it seems by the objection there is no motive for giving up to the public service. But how so? In a period of society so early as that must be when only No. 1 is called for, no separate class of occupants or tenants distinct from the class of owners can have been formed. As yet, no motive towards such a class can have arisen in the secretion of rent, as a separate function of revenue, from profit. There goes to wreck the total objection; for, at this stage of society, profit upon land will be enormous. Now, what reason can there be for supposing that the owner will deny himself an immoderate income because it happens to reach him under the name of profit rather than under the name of rent? Simply by that one exposure, we see how thoroughly the objector has been mastered by his own modern prepossessions.

But, *next*, as the necessity for substitutes and *locumtenentes* on landed properties (*i.e.*, in some sense, for tenants or lessees) must have arisen in *every* period of society, under personal accidents of lunacy, orphan nonage, military absence, &c., long before the case arose as a professional classification, defined and separately guarded by law, it follows that, for such tenants, where at all they existed, necessity would suggest a mode of payment: that payment would naturally be charged on the high rate of profit incident to that early era of society. A division of profits would, in such times, give a higher return to both parties than the whole profits, in other times, to one. But, then, *that* would not be in a technical sense rent? True, it would not: and rent in that scientific sense is exactly what we are denying, as a possibility, at this stage of expansion upon land, viz. when only No. 1 was in cultivation.

*Thirdly*, as the estate could be delegated on the landlord's account to a servant or ministerial agent, even the second arrangement, and also the first, is not indispensable; so that, even in that false sense, rent would not often or necessarily arise.

*Fourthly*, where a nominal quit-rent is received in consideration of kinship or past services, or where feudal incidents of aid might be rendered, both the first, the second, and the third arrangement would often be needless.

*Fifthly*, upon whatever scheme of partition, or of feudal service substituted for partition, a landlord might choose to make his estates profitable, this result is palpable: the land *is* cultivated, or it is *not* cultivated; and in either case what is the event to us? How are we (the maintainers of rent technical in the modern sense) interested in either issue? Say that the land is *not* cultivated: in that case none of us, on either side, is affected. Say that the land *is* cultivated, and on what terms? The landlord receives only some recognition of his feudal superiority: here, then, is confessedly no rent. Again, the landlord, upon some arrangement or other, first, second, or third, enters upon a share, known or unknown, of the profits. Still, what is that to us? Profits are profits, and rent is rent; and the things will not be confounded because an obstinate man attempts to confound the words. It is altogether needless to waste arguments on proving that in the circumstances supposed rent proper *could* not rise. For until No. 2 is called into action how can any difference exist upon the products of soils? Until a difference exists, how can an excess founded on that difference exist? Until such a differential excess exists, how can rent be measured? In any other sense we do not deny rent; in this sense the objector does not affirm it, unless he is of opinion that an excess or difference could arise upon No. 1 by comparison with itself. "Sambo and Quaco are very like each other, but particularly Sambo." On the other hand, if the objector fancies a possibility of refusing this definition, and says—"In my eyes anything shall be rent which is paid to the landlord in consideration of the right conceded to cultivate, and from whatever fund the payment is derived,—equally if deducted by the labourers from their wages, or by the occupying capitalist from his profits;"—in that case where is the dispute between us? Is it we that deny the power of labourers to make such a deduction from wages, and to pay this over to the landlord? On the contrary, this has been practised for generations in Ireland, as respects the conacre. Is it we that deny the power of the farming tenant to deduct a sum for the landlord's demand — 1, from his own profits; 2, from the income of some *other* property belonging to himself; 3, from the bounty of an indulgent aunt or grandmother? On the contrary, this is going on for ever even at this day in England: and to deny it would be to affirm that every man occupied in farming must uniformly succeed: wheresoever he does *not*, the rent (if paid at all) will be paid out of alien funds; in that case it is rent only by a verbal trick. So long as *words* are the only representatives of our ideas, so long there will always be an opening for a trickster to charge upon any verbal distinctions the pretence of verbalism. But the short answer in this case is that rent, considered as an index or exponent to a series of differences upon a scale of soils, *obeys one set of laws—whilst rent*, in the *ordinary lax sense, obeys none.* The ebbs or flowings of rent, taken in the strict sense, are governed by laws as regular as marine tides; but in the vague sense of an acknowledgment to the landlord, made from any fund whatever, rent will be as capricious in its regulating principles as in its original motives.

Next, let me point to that feature in all the three diagrams—that always the *lowest* soil yields no rent. The cause of this, and the effect, are equally apparent. The cause is that *no* soil yields rent until a soil lower than itself has defined and marked off a *difference* of produce. For the same reason why there can be no rent on No. 1 when no other No. is used, there can never be any rent on the No.

which happens to be *lowest* in the scale: equally in both cases there is wanting a *lower* soil, to mark off a difference. Rent is the excess of produce upon any given quality of soil, by comparison with another quality worse than itself. Until this worse quality comes into play, there can be no such comparison, and, by consequence, no such excess. Until there is a point of comparison—that is, until the soil now last in the scale becomes the penultimate—you cannot point to any difference as more than a future possibility. All soils promise a potential difference; but this cannot be realised until a lower base of comparison arises. Such is the cause: the effect is more likely to be contested. It is this:—According to the modern doctrine, the price of the produce on *all* the soils is regulated by this lowest soil; and for this reason—that the price of produce must be such as to cover that which is grown on the *least* advantageous terms. A price sufficient for the upper soils would be quite insufficient to continue the culture upon the lower; since, in a market, no distinction can be allowed in the price for differences of advantage. Of those differences the public has no knowledge; or, if it had, could not allow for them. *Results* are allowed for: qualities of grain, affirmatively better, sell higher; but *grounds* of qualities, as that a man has spent more capital upon his grain, or that he has won an equal grain from a worse soil by superior skill—for these there *can* be no allowance. And, in fact, it is from these disadvantages, as graduated into a regular descending scale, that a regular series of increments becomes disposable for rent. So far an opponent will submit, because he must; but he will dispute the possibility of any such lowest soils existing by a whole class as *rentless* soils. This, however, is the same question recurring which has already been recently canvassed with respect to No. 1. And in a field where it is impossible to find room for *every* discussion it is quite sufficient to make these three replies:—(1st), That a lowest class of soils may always be available as rentless soils, in the case where the owner unites with that character the character of occupying farmer. (2dly), That the *mode* of the non-payment often explains its possibility. A tenant has been able to pay a rent upon land not absolutely the worst, but the penultimate: at this rent he has been warranted in bestowing upon the land so much capital: secondly, he stimulates the land by more capital, and obtains a second though inferior crop: for that secondary crop, equivalent to the crop on a lower soil, he pays no rent. Now, here the rentless capital will be concealed and masked to the general eye by the associated capital which *does* pay rent. This is one of the cases in which virtually the *lowest* land is concerned; for those secondary powers in a higher soil which have been called out by the second application of capital are often exactly on a level with the primary qualities of the lowest. (3dly), A very common case, sometimes a very extensive one, is *where the tenant holds, jointly with superior land, other land of the lowest quality at present susceptible of culture.* The one quality, out of which really is paid all the rent that he *does* pay, shelters and disguises the other quality, out of which, in fact, he pays none. Not the bystanders only, but even himself and his landlord, are possibly deceived. An entire estate, comprehending much good land, but also some too bad for cultivation, has been let on a surveyor's calculation—85 acres of the land No. 4 and No. 5, lying dispersed amongst 1140 of land No. 3, 2, and even 1,—have *virtually* not affected the contract; they have been, in fact, thrown in gratuitously. No. 5 it has been found at that period unprofitable to cultivate. But No. 4 *is* cultivated, and is part of that land which fixes price by paying wages and profits only. It ought, therefore, as the lowest soil actually in use, to pay no rent; how *that* is possible has been shown by the circumstances of the contract; and how such a fact may escape the knowledge even of the parties to that contract is explained by the scattered interfusion of some bad land amongst much that is very good or in various degrees better.

## Section IV.

Now remains the final task. It is seen, it has been proved, that an eternal series of differences is developed upon the land by the unresting advance of population. These differences, these increments, are undeniable: a question arises—How are they disposed of? How do they operate? How do these eternal changes on the land affect the distribution of its produce? We know how a certain phenomenon called rent arises. Its origin, its mode of advancing—these are no longer doubtful. But what we now want to know, what as yet we do not know, is—the *results* of this phenomenon upon all interests connected with the land; its operation upon the amount of their several shares.

Here is, at first sight, a perplexing question. Had the question been confined to this—*What becomes of the increments eternally arising upon land, as each lower quality is developed?* in that case the answer would have been easy. We all know, by this time, that these increments are rent; no rent except from these increments; no increments which can be applied otherwise than to rent. But the real question is larger. There is a singular delusion which takes place here. Because the increment takes place on occasion of the inferior soil being called up, there is a natural *subreptio intellectus*, a hasty impression left on the mind that the inferior soil actually causes the increment—actually *produces* the addition which becomes available for rent. So far from that, so far from adding anything, every descent of this kind upon a lower soil *takes away* something. It *seems* to add—and for the landlord's benefit it *does* add—for it makes *that* a portion of his share which previously had been the share of other people. But, *absolutely* (that is, in relation to the *aggregate* claims of capitalist, farmer, labourer), this increment is manifestly a decrement, and never anything else. Fast as these increments travel *westwards*[1] on the diagram, exactly in that ratio does the residuum—the portion available for the other shares on the land—grow ever narrower and narrower. The evolution of No. 2 (which suppose to have occurred during the Saxon polyarchy) did not add anything to the actual produce on No. 1. The action of No. 2

[1] "*Westwards*":—It would be mere pedantry to refuse this brief terminology, derived from the theory of maps. The diagram is treated as a map, or chart, in which the upper side is by ancient usage the north, &c. The advantage for the diagram is that a single word does the office of a very operose circumlocution.

was simply to measure off on No. 1 a portion equal to its own defect, and to make it otherwise disposable than it had been. But obviously this separation on No. 1 has not enlarged the total shares; *absolutely*, the total produce on No. 1 is left exactly where it was, and the only real change is a different distribution of this produce.

This distribution is the subject of the present section; and it will most merit the attention of the student, first, because (being already *per se* the most difficult part of the subject) it happens to be that part most cursorily explained by Ricardo. And, secondly, it is charged with illusions from the *first*. One of these I have explained—the random impression that the series of increments, which *are* increments only *quoad hoc*, is a series of actual *bona fide* additions. A second illusion is this:—Because all the increments, as fast as they take place, pass into rent, it is a most natural inference that these successive additions do not disturb the distribution of the other shares. Were any part of the increments otherwise applicable than to rent—inversely, were any part of rent otherwise derivable than from the increments—you feel that the work of assigning their several shares to profits, wages, &c., would become perplexed. But you fancy it to be kept exceedingly simple by the known fact that the constant excesses arising through the development of the land scale are not divisible upon any mixed principle—so much to profits, so much to wages; but go in mass, and without one farthing of reservation, to rent. The natural, but false, conclusion from this will be—that rent, being itself quite unaffected by the other shares, will reciprocally not in the least affect those other shares. This, however, is altogether erroneous. From the moment when rent becomes developed upon the land, a perpetual change is going on *derivatively* in the shares allotted to labourers and to farmers. The grounds, the clockwork, of this change lurks in a tabular statement of proportions by Ricardo; this I shall transfer accurately from his pages to my own; and then, because *all* judicious readers complain heavily of the manner in which Ricardo has treated the exposition of this subject, I shall make it my business to fill up the scheme which he, from carelessness (and perhaps more from natural inaptitude [1] for the task of simplifying knowledge), has left so obscure.

TABLE of Proportions drawn up by Ricardo for the purpose of explaining the collateral or parallel changes which take place in the affections of value, through all interests, upon the land, contingently upon each successive development of lower soils.

| Price per Quarter. | Rent in Wheat. | Rent in Money. | Profit in Wheat. | Profit in Money. | Wages in Wheat. | Wages in Money. | Total of Money for Wages, Profit, and Rent. |
|---|---|---|---|---|---|---|---|
| £ s. d. | | £ s. d. | | £ s. d. | | £ s. d. | £ s. d. |
| A. 4 0 0 | None. | None. | 120 qrs. | 480 0 0 | 60 qrs. | 240 0 0 | 720 0 0 |
| B. 4 4 8 | 10 qrs. | 42 7 6 | 111·7 .. | 473 0 0 | 58·3 .. | 247 0 0 | 762 7 6 |
| C. 4 10 0 | 20 .. | 90 0 0 | 103·4 .. | 465 8 0 | 56·6 .. | 255 0 0 | 810 0 0 |
| D. 4 16 0 | 30 .. | 144 0 0 | 95·0 .. | 456 0 0 | 55 .. | 264 0 0 | 864 0 0 |
| E. 5 2 10 | 40 .. | 205 13 4 | 86·7 .. | 445 15 0 | 53·3 .. | 274 5 0 | 925 13 4 |

## COMMENTARY

In this table the case A indicates the original condition of rural husbandry, when as yet no land is under culture but the best (or No. 1 of the Diagrams). Case B indicates, therefore, the secondary condition, when No. 2 is called for. Case C the tertiary condition, when No. 3 is called for, and so onwards. The price of wheat per quarter in the one sole case A must be understood to have been *arbitrarily* assumed by Ricardo ; everywhere else it is *not* arbitrary. It could not signify what price was assumed at the starting-point,—only that Ricardo should have explained how much of his

[1] "*Inaptitude*" :—The facts overlooked in Ricardo's position are two—1st, That, by original conformation of mind, like some other powerful and original minds, he found no genial pleasure in *communicating* knowledge ; 2dly, His mind was in a fermenting state, so that his knowledge was often provisional and tentative. The prodigious events of his era, the vast experiments (even in the relations of commerce and political economy) forced upon nations by the Titan struggle of England with a barbarising despot, taught him often to suspend, to watch, and to listen, as it were, for something yet to come. Hence it happened that certain great principles, few, but sufficient, for a *total* revolution in economy—these he held with the grasp of Talus, the iron man of Crete. In the outlying parts of his own system, meantime, he was sceptical ; and what was not determinate to himself he could not make so to others.

table *was* assumption, and not have left to students a perplexing inquiry about his reasons, where, in fact, no reasons at all existed. It was sufficient at the starting-point to take for a basis any possible price *ad libitum*. But ever afterwards, in the descending scale of cases B, C, D, &c., there is no further room for discretion or arbitrary choice. Each price of wheat in the four which follow is determined by an *a priori* principle: it is derived (as will be shown immediately) by a rule of three proportions from the amount of produce on the land, compared with the same amount when diminished by the growing deductions for rent. These modifications of price, derived from rent, are very important; for through this organ of price it is that rent operates upon the money compensations (however imperfect compensations) to decaying wages, and still more decaying profits. By throwing his eye down the proper columns, the reader will see that wages are always declining in wheat returns, but always rising (though not proportionably rising) in money returns. Profits, on the other hand, suffer in both modes. Their corn returns sell, indeed, with the same advantage from the new price of wheat as that which benefits the wages; but still, as the positive declension of these corn returns is considerably greater for profits than for wages, the money returns will be seen to decline *absolutely* for profits, and not merely (as in the case of wages) proportionately. Lastly, by looking down the two contiguous columns for the changes on rent, the reader will see that rent benefits in both ways—viz. in corn returns, and in money returns. And even *that* is a careless expression of the case; for, in a sense, both wages, and even profits, benefit; that is, if they suffer, they certainly suffer less than they otherwise would do, in consequence of a higher price being obtained for land produce concurrently with *every* expansion of rent. How, then, does the case of rent differ from *their* case? It differs thus: rent benefits *absolutely* in all senses, in wheat not less than in money; wages benefit in money, but lose upon the wheat return; profits lose upon both returns. Originally, for instance (case A), ten labourers had received, collectively, 60 quarters of wheat, or (at £4 per quarter) £240 sterling,—giving to each man six quarters, or, in money, £24. Now, in case B, when rent has commenced, the abstraction of ten quarters for this purpose makes it impossible that the remainder, left for distribution between wages and profits, can allow the same corn return. Accordingly, wages sink in wheat from 60 to 58 quarters, *plus* three-tenths of a quarter. But, on the other hand, as a compensation *pro tanto*, this diminished quantity of wheat sells for £7 more. The ten labourers receive now £247 instead of £240. Does that addition (of 14s. a man) reimburse his loss? Not at all. To do this, the money addition ought to have been double. Each man, if no part of his expenditure were for bread and flour, might rejoice [1] that his money wages were more, even if not commensurately more. But, for every eight bushels of wheat which his family consumes, he must now pay four guineas, *plus* eightpence, instead of four pounds. Say that his household were of four and a half heads, here (under the usual random computation of eight bushels annually per head) we have four and a half times four shillings and eightpence *extra*—that is, precisely one guinea extra on the man's annual outlay; whilst, upon the table of Ricardo, his relief proceeds no further than by 14s., *i.e.* two-thirds of his loss. This, besides, in the case B; but, if such things happen in the green ear, what will happen in the full harvest of development under C, D, E, and quarters of the alphabet still more ominous? By any law that Ricardo impresses on his student, the very wheels of the social *watchwork* must be clogged and motionless long before the land-scale would come in sight of detestable M, or even of gloomy H. Only through that great antagonist force for ever at work in Great Britain—through skill, capital, and the energy of freemen; only by an antagonist law for ever

[1] "*Might rejoice*":—No, he might *not* rejoice. In any case he is bound to mourn, says the man of the superannuated economic systems smashed by Ricardo. But why does he say so? Consistently enough; his doctrine, his creed, is known; wages, for *him*, constitute the basis of price. Do wages happen to rise under a rise of wheat? Prices, he holds, must rise commensurately. *Ergo*, as *all* men use grain or other landed produce, to him it seems that *all* prices must rise, and *pro tanto*. But *we*, Ricardian Protestants, know far otherwise. Even the novice is now aware that a rise in wages would leave prices undisturbed. And now, perhaps, by this practical application of his knowledge, the novice begins to suspect that his studies upon value were not quite so aerial.

operative in throwing back the descents—in raising the soil of case E, in the year 1700, to the level of B as it was in 1500—the soil of O, in the year 1800, to the level of E as it stood in 1600: thus, and only thus, do we escape, have escaped, and shall escape, the action of rent; which action, by the just exposures of Ricardo, tends always to engulf us; which action, by the unjust concealments of Ricardo, ought long ago to have frozen us into a dead lock—anything to the contrary notwithstanding which has ever been insisted on by that great master of economy. The *tendencies* of a natural law like that of rent (which word *rent* I use as a shorthand expression for the case: otherwise it is not rent, but the cause of rent, or degradation of soils, which in very truth is the original principle of movement)—these tendencies it is always right to expose; and Ricardo first *did* expose them. Others had discovered the law; he first applied his sagacious sense to its consequences upon profits, wages, price, and, through them, upon universal economy. That was right; for that we are irredeemably his debtors. But it was *not* right to keep studiously out of sight that eternal counter-movement which tends, by an equivalent agency, to redress the disturbed balance. This concealment has the effect of introducing marvels into a severe science; since, else, what other than a miracle is it that rent has not long ago absorbed the whole landed produce—a result to which so manifestly it tends? Secondly, this concealment withdraws from the notice of young students a truly philosophic instance, or case, of that providential benignity which meets every natural growth of comprehensive evil by a commensurate compensation, or else by a process of positive counteraction. Our own social system seems to harbour within itself the germ of our ruin. Either we must destroy rent, *i.e.* that which causes rent, or rent will destroy *us*, unless in the one sole case where this destroying agency can be headed back uniformly as it touches the point of danger—that point where it would enter into combination with evil co-agencies. Now, this great case of reservation, this saving clause (which, by the intervention of an "*unless*," *i.e.* of an "*if not*," entitled, of course, to the benefits of a Shakspearian "*if*," defeats a dreadful tendency always lying *couchant* in our social mechanism), being almost unnoticed by Ricardo, or not finding a systematic *locus* in his exposition, besides leaving room for a sort of wonderment not creditable to a severe science, has the further bad effect of inviting a malignant political disaffection. Both in France, Germany, and England, a dreadful class is forming itself of systematic enemies to property. As a wild, ferocious instinct, blind as a Cyclops and strong as a Cyclops, this anti-social frenzy has naturally but too deep a root in the predispositions of hopeless poverty. And it happens (though certainly not with any intentional sanction from so upright a man as David Ricardo) that in no instance has the policy of gloomy disorganising Jacobinism, fitfully reviving from age to age, received any essential aid from science, excepting in this one painful corollary from Ricardo's triad of chapters on Rent, Profit, and Wages. A stress lies on this word *triad* ; for it is not from insulated views of rent that the wicked inference arises : it is by combined speculations upon the three. Separate, the doctrine of rent offers little encouragement to the anarchist ; it is in connexion with other views that it ripens into an instrument of mischief the most incendiary. Since Ricardo's time, the anti-social Jacobins—attacking, in France, the whole theory of taxation, of public worship, of national education ; in England, attacking the fabric of civil administration, the liability of one generation to the debts or civil obligations of another, the right to property or to accumulations of any kind ; and, in Germany, going far beyond these insanities of licentiousness—find often a convenient policy in having exoteric and minor degrees of initiation. To the aspirant, during his noviciate, they preach the abolition of entails, of regal courts, of ambassadors, and privileged bodies of soldiery, as appendages of courts ; but on no phasis of the social economy now prevailing do they dwell with more effectual bitterness than on the tendencies of rent as exposed by Ricardo. Here is a man, they argue, not hostile to social institutions, not thinking of them in connexion with any question of elementary justice, who reveals as a mere sequel, as an indirect consequence, as a collateral effect from one ordinary arrangement of landed property, that it does, and must, encroach steadily, by perpetual stages, upon other landed claims, through all varieties of kind and of degree. The evil, they allege, is in the nature of an eclipse; it travels by digits over the face of the planet. A shadow of death steals gradually over the whole disk of what once had offered a luminous field of promise. And that which was meant for the auspicious guarantee of indefinite expansion to human generations—viz. the indefinite expansibility of food and clothing from the land—becomes the main counteraction to these purposes of Providence, and the most injurious monument of social misarrangement. The class of landlords, they urge, is the merest realisation of a scriptural idea—*unjust men reaping where they have not sown.* They prosper, not pending the ruin, not in spite of the ruin, but *by* the ruin of the fraternal classes associated with themselves on the land. Not by accident, but by necessity—not by intermitting effects of position, but by very coercion of their original tenure—it is the organic function of rent-receivers to encroach, to engulf *all* the shares at last, and to approximate this consummation of total absorption by yearly stages of partial absorption; like Schiller's cannon-ball,

> "Shattering *what* it reaches, and shattering that it *may* reach."

And thus, whilst universal society is viewed as the victim of institutions, yet this fatal necessity is received as no plea for those whom it coerces; but the noblest order of men amongst us, our landed aristocracy, is treated as the essential scourge of all orders beside. Now, were all this true, God forbid that it should be charged upon Ricardo as an offence to have exposed it! But it is the little learning here, as elsewhere, which grounds the ignorance and propagates the calumny. No man could know this better than Ricardo. And yet he has suffered these perilous falsehoods (perilous, because fatally "simular" of truth) to accredit themselves upon his authority. These pestilent errors, oftentimes preached by dull men, have borrowed wings and buoyancy from his profound truths unfortunately mutilated. For the whole truth, when not one hemisphere but both hemispheres are exhibited at once, is, that, logically speaking, rents are themselves inevitable consequences, bound up with the necessities of the case; secondly, that, *as* inevitable results, these increments upon land import no blame to landlords, seeing that, under any system of civil interests, and any administration of those interests, such increments eternally arising must be enjoyed by somebody; thirdly, that, having thus reduced the question to a simple case of comparison between country gentlemen (as the most ordinary class of rent-receivers) and any other assignable receivers, Ricardo was too conscientious to pretend that this class was not, amongst us, one of our noblest. If we have led Europe in political counsels since 1642, if we first founded a representative government—by whom else than our country gentlemen, in Parliament assembled, were we ourselves guided?

But, fourthly, Ricardo is chiefly blamable as overlooking that great pursuing counter-agency which travels after the tendency on land, overtakes it continually, and once at least in each century, like an *annus Platonicus*, restores the old relations of our system. Ricardo knew, in that extent which made it a duty to proclaim, that to this indefinite expansion of rent, absolutely unlimited as it is by original tendency, on that very argument, and merely by that proof, some active and commensurate remedy must have always been operating. Too evidently the evil must have found or have generated its own check, else why had it not long ago destroyed us? I have made it a point to dwell a little on this great question, because here chiefly it is that political economy inosculates with politics and the philosophy of social life; and because, from mere inadvertence, Ricardo is here found in a painful collusion with the most hateful of anarchists.

Now remains one sole task. The novice has seen generally that the labourer and the capitalist are affected by changes in rent; it remains to ask, In what exact proportions? Although every fresh projection of rent is carried off "neat" and entire by its own class of owners, and therefore it might be supposed that this class would go off, leaving the two other classes to settle their dividends undisturbed by the action of rent, *that* is not so. Every fresh pulse of rent causes a new arrangement even for that which rent leaves behind, and this new arrangement more and more favours wages at the expense of profits. One short explanation will make this clear, and finish the whole development.

Looking back to Ricardo's table, let us take the case C.[1] And, in order to begin at the beginning, what is the *principium movendi*? Where arises the initial movement? It arises in the fact that, by some descent upon a worse soil, a second separation of rent has taken place. In the first descent, marked B, there had occurred a separation of 10 quarters for rent; in the second descent, marked C, a separation (upon the same soil) of 20 quarters has occurred for the same purpose.

Here pause: for now comes the screw which moves the whole machine. The produce of the soil under discussion is assumed always to be the same total quantity—viz. 180 quarters; for the reader has been told that it is one and the same soil concerned in all the five cases. Consequently, when 10 quarters were made disposable for rent, the remainder was 170; when 20 are taken, the remainder is 160. Now, as

160 : 180 : : £4 : £4 : 10s.

When the original move had been made, wheat was selling at eighty shillings a quarter: it rose under this first move (B) to eighty-four shillings and eightpence. And why? Because 170 is to 180 as £4 is to £4 : 4 : 8. But, when another move (C) has abstracted from the total crop of 180 quarters not less than 20 for rent, by a rule-of-three proportion we see that the price will rise to ninety shillings.

*Step the Second.*—Next, after this case of price, comes the case of wages. How it is that Ricardo would himself have explained the process of adjustment (as sketched on his own table) between wages and the changes caused by rent, per-

[1] "*The case* C":—One, and perhaps the very largest, vice in the science of teaching is that the teacher, chained up by his own subjective pre-occupations, cannot see with the eyes of the novice; cannot dismiss his own difficulties, and enter, as into an inheritance, upon those of his pupil. Not until this moment did it strike me that the reader, having lately heard and read so much of the land-scale (which means the devolution of culture through all gradations of soil, from optimism down to pessimism, in order to meet the expansions of population), will naturally suppose that Ricardo's table rests upon a basis of that kind; that the case C, for instance, means land which is one degree worse than that in case B. Not at all. A, B, C, D, and E, all represent one and the same soil, but continually forced, by *other* soils, into fresh expansions of rent.

haps nobody can say. My explanation is this ; which must (I presume) be sound, as it coincides in the arithmetical result with *his*. Look down the column of prices for wheat, and uniformly the difference between any case, as C and the original case A, must be halved. Thus the half of ten shillings (the difference between C and A) is five. Then, because each labourer's original share had been six quarters, multiply six by five shillings, and the product is thirty shillings. This, for ten labourers, will make, collectively, £15 ; and so much additional money wages—viz. £15—must be paid to the aggregate share of wages under case C, compared with case A. Accordingly, in the column of "wages in money," you see that, having had £240 in case A, the ten labourers will have £255 in case C. Again, for a similar reason,[1] in case D, the price of wheat per quarter is sixteen shillings more than in case A. Half sixteen shillings is eight shillings ; and, multiplying the original quarters of each labourer, viz. six, by eight, you have forty-eight shillings as the additional sum for each labourer,—£24 therefore as the aggregate addition for ten labourers. Accordingly, by the same column of "wages in money," you see that the share of wages on case D, as compared with case A, has risen from £240 to £264.

*Step the Third.*—Remains to ask, What will be the share left for profits ? When abstracting Ricardo's law of profits, I said—by way of condensing the truth in a brief formula—"Profits are the leavings of wages": meaning, that whatever addition is assigned to wages by the law controlling them must be taken from profits ; for, if not, whence can it come ? What other source is available ? Here (as you see) the initial movement, by abstracting 20 quarters from the land produce for rent, has determinately forced on another movement—viz. a change in wages. This has given £15 extra to the ten workmen ; but where was that £15 obtained ? If you say it was obtained from the new price of wheat, now much enhanced, I reply—No : that is quite impossible. First, from the fact—the price of wheat is now 10s. a quarter

[1] "*A similar reason*":—viz. because, 30 quarters out of 180 being now disposable for rent, leaving only 150 for wages and profits, then by the rule of three—150 : 180 : : £4 : £4 : 16s.

more than it was under case A. This extra sum upon 180 quarters makes exactly £90. But £90 is the very sum now paid for rent; the 20 quarters for rent, at £4 : 10s., amount to £90. Consequently, all that is gained in the new money price of wheat goes away upon rent. Secondly, the same thing may be shown *a priori*. For what is it that has raised the price of wheat? The cause of that new price is the inferiority of some new soil not particularly noticed in Ricardo's table, except in its effects. This worse soil, which for that reason regulates the price upon *all* soils, could not furnish the same produce of 180 quarters, except at a higher cost. That higher cost appears to be £90. So far only, and by this process, has the price of wheat been raised; but not through any rise of wages,—which rise, besides, is consequential and posterior to the rise in wheat, and cannot therefore have been causative to the new price of wheat. Not to insist again, at this point, on the doctrine of Ricardo, so fully demonstrated, that no change in price can ever be effected by a change in wages. In the instance now before us, the £15 extra must be paid from some quarter; but it is doubly demonstrated that it cannot have been paid by the new price—*i.e.* by consumers. It remains, therefore, that it must be paid out of profits; for no other fund exists. And, accordingly, by looking into the column of money profits, you see that, in case C, these profits have sunk from £480 to £465. In other words, the 30s. per man, paid extra to the labourer, making £15 for the ten labourers, has been obtained entirely at the cost of profits. The labourers obtain £15 more; but the capitalist is left with £15 less.

Thus, finally, we read off the table of Ricardo into its true interpretation. We are able to *construct* it into a scientific sense for the understanding. The last column to the right hand, I must observe, simply adds to the invariable sum of £720, always disposable for profit and wages, the new sum obtained by a new price of wheat for rent. For example, in case C, where 20 quarters become disposable for rent, and therefore, in money, £90 under the new price of wheat, add this £90 to the old £720, and the total money produce of the land under C is £810. So again, under E, where the price of wheat has risen to £5 : 2 : 10 per quarter, the total money value of rent, now claiming 40 quarters of the 180, will be £205 : 13 : 4 ; and this sum, added to the old £720, makes (as we see) £925 : 13 : 4. But now, if we strike out this final column on the right hand, which is simply an arithmetical register or summation of values travelling along with the expansions of rent, we shall have seven columns remaining—viz. one for the *prices* of wheat, two for *rent*, two for *profits*, and two for *wages*. And the Ariadne's thread for passing along the labyrinth is briefly this : that the second column is a pure assumption, and justly so, where you are entitled to take any quantities you please for a basis. From this second column you take your start ; and, by a comparison derived from this assumption of wheat rent, in a way already explained (viz. by stating the remainder of wheat produce, suppose 150 quarters after paying rent, against the invariable total of wheat produce—viz. 180 quarters), you determine to a fraction the new price per quarter of wheat. This known, next, by a rule which *seems* arbitrary, you learn precisely the new amount (as in column seventh) that will now be required for money wages. But, because the new price of wheat is also known, out of *that* (combined with the money addition to the labourer's wages) you are able to determine the question of column sixth—viz. how much the labourer has lost in corn wages ; and then, as the money gained to the labourer measures the money lost to the capitalist, easily you settle the question of column fifth (money profits) out of column seventh (money wages). Next, through the price of wheat (known *in* column first, and *by* column second), you ascertain readily the question of column fourth ; *i.e.* of wheat profits. There remains only column third (the money value of rent). But this is obviously nothing more than a multiplication of column second, as to any given item, by the corresponding item in column first. As to the objections against the rule for deriving the new rate of money wages—that it *seems* to be arbitrary—I fancy that Ricardo referred to a basis assumed in the chapter on wages, which represents the labourer as *originally* requiring one half of his wages for food or for wheat ; so that the increase in *money* wages acts only on that half. To the latter part of that chapter, in my own account of it, I therefore refer the reader.

## CHAPTER V

### PROFITS

THIS chapter will occupy us for a longer space than the rest; *first*, because (as a dependency upon rent and wages) it furnishes a sort of commentary on those doctrines; *secondly*, because, more than any other doctrine, it is liable, on its own account, to popular fallacies.

Price, rent, and wages, having now been developed, we may say, with respect to the law of profits, not so properly that it is deduced from these three principles by Ricardo as that it deduces itself. Let me not be thought, in saying *that*, to mean any disparagement of Ricardo's services. Greater cannot be imagined. He it was who first made it possible to deduce wages from rent, and therefore to deduce profits from wages. He had so disembarrassed the ground of all perplexities by the time he reached this question of profits that the true theory rather flowed spontaneously from the conditions, as they had been now explained, than called for any effort of inference. But then the very necessity and inevitableness of this inference, the very possibility of dispensing with further discoveries, were due exclusively to Ricardo's previous simplifications. Only by having merited so much in former stages, could he have made it possible, even for himself, to merit so little in this.

In one brief *formula*, it might be said of profits that *they are the leavings of wages*: so much will the profit be upon any act of production, whether agricultural or manufacturing, as the wages upon that act permit to be left behind.

But left behind from what? From the price. The

price, even of landed produce, splits always into wages and profits; and what the price is predetermines the *joint* amount for wages and profits. If the price is ten shillings, then, by this principle, it is asserted—that wages and profits, taken as a whole, cannot exceed ten shillings. (No rise in wages could increase this sum of ten shillings.) But do not the wages and profits as a whole, themselves, on the contrary, predetermine the price? No; that is the old superannuated doctrine. But the new economy has shown that all price is governed by proportional quantity of the producing labour, and by that only. Being itself once settled, then, *ipso facto*, price settles the fund out of which both wages and profits must draw their separate dividends. Call the price x: that sum, that x, makes up the joint values of wages and profits. Taken together, the two functions of wages and profits will always compose x; cannot be less, cannot be more.

But, if *that* is true, then it follows that wages and profits vary inversely: whatever the one loses the other gains; and the gain of either can only be through the loss of the other. Neither of the two can gain *absolutely* or irrespectively of the other: wages being eight shillings, and profits two, then it is possible that profits might rise to three, but only by wages previously falling to seven. Any other rise in profits, such as should leave wages virtually undiminished, could be only an apparent rise through some depreciation in the currency; and that depreciation, changing any one thing nominally, must change all other things: affecting all apparently, really it would affect none.

This being settled, viz. that any motion or change between wages and profits will always be reciprocal, next comes the question—in which of the two will such a change commence? Is it possible, for instance, that an *original* change should take place in profits, and that wages should be affected only in a secondary way? No; this is not possible. Any change that can disturb the existing relations between wages and profits must originate in wages: whatever change may silently take place in profits always we must view as recording and measuring a previous change in wages.

Hence we are brought to the conclusion—that to wages, and to wages only, we must look for an explanation of all principles which govern either themselves or profits. Ricardo's chapter upon profits is substantially no more than a reiteration of his two chapters upon wages and rent. It is known already from those chapters that in all national communities alike there is the same constant tendency (through the increase of population) to descend upon worse soils. There is a counter-tendency which holds this primal tendency in check; viz. the gradual elevation of bad soils to the rank of better, by means of improving science. But this antagonist principle acts very unequally in different communities, and in the same community at different periods. Consequently, the tendency to increased cost of food, by continual descent upon worse wheat land, worse barley land, and worse grazing land, is sometimes for a century together proceeding with activity; whilst the counter-tendency, which depends much upon previous improvements in roads, markets, &c., and upon *general* progress in science, may be altogether torpid. We see, therefore, a natural reason why wages upon the land should, through such a century, continually grow heavier, and the profits, therefore, continually decline. It is only when the antagonist tendency gets into powerful play, or whilst the population happens to be stagnant, that this downward movement is checked. But, says the student, by a most natural objection, what has *that* to do with manufactures? Industry, applied to land, grows dearer, because the declining qualities of the soil oblige the cultivator to employ eleven or twelve men on the worst soil used in the last year of a century; whereas upon the worst soil used in the first year of that century there were employed only ten. It is the *quantity* of labour which has increased (viz., as must always be remembered, or the lowest or *regulating* soil); and that explains why the manufacturer of wheat or oxen must have more wages to pay; he has twelve men to pay instead of ten. But why should the manufacturer of shoes be affected by such a change? Because more men are required upon a score of acres, it will not follow that more will be required upon a score of boots or shoes. Why, therefore, should not the effect upon profits confine itself to capitals employed upon land? The answer is this: even upon shoes there will be a small increase of labour, because the raw material will grow a little dearer as hides grow dearer; and hides will grow dearer as cattle grow dearer, by descending upon worse pasture lands. But this is not the channel through which profits are affected, either upon one sort of industry or another. It is not because the *quantity* of labour increases that corn profits will diminish. That change will merely affect prices. A farmer, indeed, who has to pay an eleventh labourer will certainly have more wages to pay. Where he paid two hundred pounds formerly, now he must pay two hundred and twenty. But the shoemaker will need no eleventh man. True; yet he must pay his ten men at a higher rate. The payment fastened upon the farmer for an extra man, for an extra quantity of labour, is not that payment which will diminish his profits. For that he will be indemnified in the altered price of his produce. Sect. 3 of Chap. I (on Value) has sufficiently established that all changes in the *quantity* of producing labour, whether up or down, settle by corresponding changes upon the price: if the labour required is more, the price of the product is more; if less, less. And the new price indemnifies the employer — whether farmer or shoemaker — for the new quantity of labour. So far, therefore, the cost of the eleventh man is nothing to *him*: yet the eleventh man must be paid for; and that is something to the public, — for, in order to pay him, ten per cent will now be added to the price of their wheat. But thus far the farmer is no further affected by the change than as he also, in the persons of his household, is a *consumer* of wheat. To that extent he must be a sufferer in common with everybody else, but not as a *producer*. Next, however, comes another change. In consequence of this rise in wheat, caused by the necessity of an eleventh man, all the ten men and the eleventh besides will need extra wages. Some addition must be made to their wages; or else, at the new price of wheat, a class of men to whom wheat forms so large an item upon so small a total expenditure would sink suddenly in the scale. Now, *here* it is that the shoemaker will be caught. His shoes, it is true, will not cost more *labour* in making because wheat costs more labour, except indeed by the trifle additional on hides; and that trifle will be repaid in the price of shoes. But how will *that* indemnify the shoemaker for the new *rate* of wages paid to the old quantity of labour? Suppose him to keep ten journeymen, he (you allege) is not in the situation of the farmer: he is under no call to employ an eleventh as a *conditio sine qua non* for obtaining the old amount of produce. Ten men will produce as many shoes now as they did before. True: but will these ten men be contented with the same rate of wages? They cannot: upon them, as much as upon the farmer's men, rests a necessity for reimbursement with respect to the new ten per cent charged upon wheat. Suppose wheat to form one-half of their household expenditure, then five per cent upon their total wages will be requisite to meet the ten per cent upon grain. Suppose (which is more probable) that wheat forms one-third of their total expenditure, then £3 : 6 : 8 upon every hundred pounds paid in wages will be the requisite increase. But, considering the concurrent increase which will affect all articles (such as wool) depending equally with wheat upon the home soil, and considering the increased costs upon advances of capital, it is not too much to say that a ten per cent rise in grain will raise wages universally by five per cent. And in that word "*universally*" we are reminded of the *nexus* between agricultural and manufacturing industry, which effects the translation of changes from the one to the other. The original "move" in the game, viz. the descent upon a soil of lower capacities, is undeniably nothing to the shoemaker. His shoemaking does not therefore descend upon less productive journeymen or more intractable hides: wheat is less in quantity, but shoes are not less in quantity. No; but soon the re-agency of the first change travels back upon the shoemaker by a second. Wheat forms a conspicuous part in the household system of diet for *all* labourers alike. A man does not grow fat because he drives fat oxen; nor does a ploughman's family consume more wheat because the head of it produces wheat. The shoemaker's family consumes as much. And, although the primary change, viz. the increased labour upon growing wheat, is a matter of very great interest to the landowners, and of very little interest to the owners of shoemaking industry, yet, eventually, that primary change which throws new labour on the land has the secondary effect of raising price upon its produce: and then the change becomes quite as interesting to shoemakers as to ploughmen. The shoemaker escapes at first: true; and there is no wonder in *that*; for even the farmer escapes. He hires a new man; but he knows that the new price to be anticipated for grain will pay for the new man. Yet, no sooner is this prospect realised, than the farmer finds *himself* suddenly reached by the new price in his character of consumer; and unfortunately every workman in his service, both ten old ones and an eleventh superadded, is also a consumer. So here comes a sudden call for a *bonus* to twelve families, those of the farmer and his eleven men, notwithstanding the payment of the eleventh man (as to the *old* rate of wages) is undertaken by the public in the new price of wheat. But precisely these secondary changes reach the shoemaker and all *his* workmen through the very same agency at the same time.

Here, therefore, in this complex process, always existing by way of tendency in improving countries, we read the whole law of profits. A change commences upon the land which is nothing at the first to any interest *but* the landed. Originally it is a change which has its beginning and its end upon the land. But unfortunately that inevitable "end" is an augmentation of price upon the produce of land. And then in one hour all the world is overtaken by the change —every man in his consumption; capitalists in wages. In *every* department of industry, unless so far as it is conducted by non-wheat-consuming machines, wages rise so as to indemnify the animal labourer (man, horse, or bullock) for the increased cost of his consumption. And yet this rise of wages, this rise in the *price* of labour (as opposed to a rise in the *quantity* of labour), cannot be fetched back in the price of the products: that has been shown at length in Chapter I: nevertheless it must be paid; and what fund is there available for the payment, except profits? Clearly there is no other, and therefore profits must eternally pay by diminution for these increases in the rate of wages. Consequently, by the natural *nisus* in every country, profits are always descending. But, on the other hand, there is a *nisus*, directly antithetic to this, which is always tending to raise profits, viz. the continual improvement of soils (either $\alpha$ as to the cost of working them, or $\beta$ as to the amount of their produce under the same cost); which in effect, upon any period of two centuries, acts for us precisely as an original endowment of the land with much higher capacities. Land, which ranked as No. 20 at the Crusades may now perhaps stand at the same rating on the scale: it is still No. 20; but the No. 20 land of these days is equal in absolute produce to the No. 4 land of the Crusades. Hence it is, viz. by this counter-*nisus* in the land, that profits have not long ago fallen to nothing. There is a continual tendency towards nothing, which would soon become effectual, through the expansion of population forcing land upon worse soils, were it not continually retarded and fought back through this opposite expansion in the everlasting improvement of science, practical skill, social arrangements, or capital. But, whether profits, under the one tendency, are hurrying downwards for half a century, or, under the antagonist tendency, are abruptly ascending, or, under the two acting in combination, are held stationary—alike in all cases we see that it is the land which gives the original impulse to profits; and, alike in all cases, by and through the same agency of wages. Always there can be no rise or fall for profits which will not presuppose a corresponding fall and rise for wages; always the *initial* movement must take place in the wages.

One sole evasion of this doctrine I can imagine as possible even to a thoughtful man, since I have been acquainted with Mr. Malthus's "Economy."[1] He might argue thus:—"You talk of an eleventh man, as required by the descent of tillage upon a worse soil. And probably you make way for your arguments by that assumption; but there is no such necessity. Tillage descends upon the inferior soil by means of the ten men." Well, be it so; but mark what follows. The produce under these men must be less, or else the very case in discussion is abandoned; the soil would *not* be inferior if ten men (the same number as work the penultimate land) could obtain the same produce. The produce is less by the very terms of the hypothesis. Now, it signifies

[1] "Principles of Political Economy,"—first published in 1820.

not a straw for the principle concerned *how* much less. But say that each man raises, by one-tenth part, less than he did upon the next superior land. Each, in short, raises from the new land nine-tenths of his former product upon superior land: so that, had the total product of the ten been 100 quarters of wheat before the change, it will be 90 after the change. But who does not see that, by mere conversion of the terms, if the whole produce of 100 has been reduced to 90, then each individual quarter of wheat has cost one-ninth of a man, whereas before it cost only one-tenth of a man? Yet this most obvious truth Mr. Malthus failed to see; and he has repeatedly argued, in a case where the produce had sunk whilst the labour employed was the same, as though the return had varied, but not by any variation in the producing labour. It is, indeed, the common paralogism, and too natural to excite much wonder for itself, that, if upon the same farm you have always kept five men, and in 1800 their product was 25 quarters, but in 1840 was 50 quarters, you are apt to view the produce only as variable and the labour as constant: whereas *virtually* both have varied. In 1800, each quarter must have cost one-fifth part of a man. In 1840, each has cost no more than one-tenth part of a man. If the wheat harvest of 1844, by some unprecedented blight or locust attacking the plant in England, should fall suddenly to one-tenth part of what it was in 1843, you could not say with any accuracy that the labour had been the same, but the result different. On the contrary, for the very reason that the number of labourers had been the same, the producing labour must have been by ten times greater. For surely it has cost, by the supposition, ten times as much labour to raise any given portion of produce (one bushel, a thousand bushels, &c.) as it did in 1843. It is, therefore, a matter of no consequence at all whether we assume an eleventh man in order to sustain the *same* produce, or assume a diminished produce from the ten men. This is but an inversion of the same *formula*.[1] Nor would it have deserved

[1] "*An inversion of the same formula*":—Such an inversion, the reader may fancy, might escape a clever man's eye for itself, but hardly when pursued to its consequences. Mr. Malthus, however, has persisted in this blunder, even where it was so pursued, and where it

this notice, were not the blunder so common, and specially so in the "Principles" of Mr. Malthus.

In this instance, therefore, the objector is silenced; because his own case, supposing a less produce with the same labour, does in so many words confess that, with the same number of men to pay (viz. ten, upon his way of stating the case), there will, in the first place, be a diminished fund for paying them. Undoubtedly, in the second place, this diminished corn fund will be compensated in a higher money price. But then, in the third place, this higher price, which merely restores to the farmer the lost powers of labour (that is, makes the ten less effective men equally valuable to him in the money result as the ten men on the old standard), will not also pay the difference between the old and new wages; for the same cause which makes the total produce smaller makes each bushel of that produce dearer: in this it is alleged the farmer finds his indemnification. True, he does so: but that cuts both ways; for precisely in this higher and indemnifying price, when it comes to affect the consumption of himself and his men, he finds also his own damage.

But there is still a final evasion likely to move subconsciously in the thoughts of a student, which it is better to deepen and strengthen until it becomes generally visible than to leave it behind as a rankling perplexity. He has a confused idea that, in the distributions of landed produce, the shares which grow less in quantity sometimes grow larger in value. If a labourer who got 6 quarters last year gets only 5 this year, undeniably his corn wages have fallen, and yet his money wages may have risen: for 5 quarters, when wheat is selling for five guineas, will be worth twenty-five guineas; whereas 6 quarters, when wheat sold for four guineas, would be worth only twenty-four guineas. The labourer is therefore poorer in wheat, but he is a little richer in money.

deeply affected the inference, viz. during his long attempt to overthrow Ricardo's doctrine of Value. He refuses to see, nay he positively denies, that, if two men (never more, never less) produce a variable result of ten and five, then in one case each unit of the result has cost double the labour which it has cost in the other. On the contrary, because there are always two men, Mr. M. obstinately insists that the cost in labour is constant.

Now, the student may fancy that, by an indemnity similar in kind, but perhaps even greater in degree, profits may evade the declension which otherwise accompanies the expansion of agriculture. Where the value of each assignable part may be less, might not a larger quantity fall to the share of profits ; and, where a smaller quantity was allotted to profits, might it not compensate that defect by a much greater value ? No : if the reader pursues the turns of the case through all changes, he will find the following result invariably following :—As worse land is taken into use, the landlord's share rises both in quantity and value : secondly, the labourer's share lessens in quantity but increases in value ; whilst, thirdly, the profitee's (or farmer's) share lessens both in quantity and value. Of two possible advantages, allowed under the circumstances, Rent comes in for both, Wages for one, Profits for neither. And the sole resource for profits against a never-ending declension is that antagonist tendency by which from time to time man defeats the original tendency of the land, raising indifferent land in 1840 to the level of what was very good land in 1340—consequently restoring profits (and often much more than restoring them) to that station which they had lost in the interval.

Except by this eternal counter-agency, profits cannot protect themselves by any special remedy against a continual degradation: that redress, which for rent procures much more than an indemnity, and for wages an imperfect indemnity, will not operate at all in behalf of profits. And this shall be exemplified in a simple case. Eight men, upon a known farm, have hitherto raised eighty quarters of wheat. By a descent upon worse land, under the coercion of rising population, ten men are now required to produce the same eighty quarters. That is, heretofore each man of the eight produced ten: but now, on the lower soil, each man of the ten produces eight. Consequently, *on that land which determines the price of wheat* (see Chapter III on Rent) eight men now produce sixty-four quarters. This produce (since the *least* advantageously grown must rule the price) now becomes the regulating scale for price. Last year, when the produce of 80 quarters from eight men had been the lowest round of the ladder, the price had been £4 the quarter.

Now, when a produce of 64 quarters from eight men is the lowest, the price will rise to £5. For 64 : 80 : : £4 : £5.

But, when the produce was 80 quarters, selling at £4, the total money produce was £320. From which amount deduct the wages of eight men (receiving, suppose each 5 quarters, or £160 in the whole), and there will remain £160 for the profits.

Now, when the produce is 64 quarters, selling at £5, the total money produce will be still £320 ; the higher price having so far compensated the lower produce. From which amount deduct the wages of eight men receiving each the value of 5 quarters (or £200 in the whole), and there will remain only £120 for profits.

It is true that the new rate of wages will not proceed on the old scale of *quantity*: the corn wages will somewhat decline. But this will not help the result: each man may not receive 5 quarters as heretofore, but always he will receive the value of more than 4 quarters at £5 : always the eight men will receive more than £160 ; or else their wages will not have risen under a rise in the price of corn. Always, therefore, from the same fixed sum of £320, the deduction for wages being greater, what remains for profit *must* be less.

This, however, it may be said, is an example drawn from the last round of the ladder—from the very last land under culture: first, from that which *was* last some time back; secondly, from that which at present *is* last. Now, upon such land, it has been shown already (Chapter III on Rent), that the entire return always divides between wages and profits; nothing at all is retained for rent. But you persuade yourself that on superior land, on rent-paying land, possibly the result for profits might turn out otherwise. One sentence will settle that point, and convince you that the logic of the case cannot be disturbed. What is it that determines the amount of rent upon any land whatever? It is simply the *difference* of product between the land assigned and the lowest under cultivation. For instance, in the case just now considered, the difference between the produce of the land now lowest and that of the land lately lowest is the difference between 80 quarters and 64; that is, a difference of 16 quarters. This *whole* difference would become rent upon the penultimate land. And therefore it will serve no purpose to plead the higher money value upon each one of the 64, compared with the old value upon the 80. For it is evident that, when the 16 are deducted for rent, no matter at what price, the remainder of 64 must follow the same exact division between wages and profits as took effect upon the 64 of the lowest land according to the first exemplification. When the rent is deducted, precisely the same quantity remains for the penultimate land as on the very lowest land—disposable for precisely the same two calls of wages and profits—and disposable under the precisely same law of division.

Here, therefore, we see the whole law of profits as it acts upon the largest scale. But at the same time we are made sensible that under this law there must be exceptions. The law is founded ultimately on the decline of land, and consequently of profits on land; to which sort of profits, speaking generally, all others must conform. Yet that sometimes they do *not*, is evident from this, that in that case no rate of profits in any one speculation would or could differ from the ordinary rate. The land is always the same, and subject to the same sort of gradual degradation. If, therefore, the land furnished the *sole* principle of regulation, then in any one country (as England), having the same common land-standard, there could be only one rate of profit. But this we all know to be false. Whence, therefore, come the anomalies? Where lie the other principles which modify and disturb that derived from the land?

It is generally and rightly pleaded, as a sufficient explanation of the irregularities in profits, that originally they ranged themselves upon a scale, differing *apparently* in order that they might *not* differ virtually; in fact, on the same principle as wages. Why do wages differ? Why is it that one workman gets a guinea a-day, and another has some difficulty in obtaining a shilling? Notoriously because, whilst rude labour is open almost to universal competition, some special labour is hazardous, or disgusting, or under a variable demand, or even disreputable from its incidents; but, above all, because it happens to be difficult of execution, and presupposes an elaborate (generally an expensive) education. The labourer is often to be regarded not in the light of a man receiving merely wages, but of a man receiving wages for his daily work, and a considerable interest on the capital which he has been obliged to sink in his education. And often it happens that, as the modern processes of art or trade become more and more scientific, wages are continually rising. The qualifications of a master or of a mate, even in the commercial navy, are now steadily rising. Possibly the wider range of chemical knowledge, in such employments as dyeing, brewing, calico-printing, may devolve in its growing responsibilities chiefly upon a superior rank of workmen. In coining, or striking medals, where the ambition of nations is now driving their governments into substituting for that base mechanic art prevalent in Christendom the noble fine art patronised in Pagan ages, it is probable that a higher class of workmen is slowly coming into request. And in the business of forgery applied to bank-notes, a business which once gave employment to much capital and various talent, simply by rise in one qualification, that whole interest has been suppressed. Besides a peculiar paper, manufactured with difficulty and hazard, the talent of engraving was required in provincial practice. Now, the profits might have paid for skill of that nature; an accomplice might have been elaborately educated for the purpose; but inevitably, as this man obtained the requisite point of excellence, he found that his talent was opening to him a safer channel for employing it: he could now keep a conscience. In the service of one vast public agency, that of travelling, so great has been the rise of qualifications that of late even an academic examination has been talked of for the working engineers, &c., or (as a vicarious measure) a probationary appointment, contingent for its ratification upon the results of a rigorous trial. In medicine, again, the improvement, having kept pace with the expansions of chemistry, botany, and physiology, has spread downwards to the body of druggists: these are the lowest class of medical practitioners; and I believe that now they look for higher attainments in their servants, or for a higher fee as the condition of communicating such advantages.

The writer of the "Critical Dissertation on Value" offended heavily against logic when he represented these varieties of level in wages as inconsistent with Ricardo's doctrine upon the relative quantities of labour. Too readily he allowed himself to suppose that Ricardo had "*overlooked*" facts or consequences which by possibility to have overlooked would have argued a sheer incompetence in one whom elsewhere he does not deny to have been vigilant as well as able. Prices, says Ricardo, are directly as the producing quantities of labour; and the objection is that an article which costs three days' labour at half a crown bears a price, suppose, of ten shillings, whilst another article, costing the very same quantity of labour, but of labour paid at the rate of one guinea a-day, may bear a price possibly of five guineas. How, then, does mere quantity of labour express itself exactly in the price? *Answer*—The gamut, the scale of differences as to the *quality* of labour, is postulated from the first; no man could be so slothful in his intellect as to have overlooked that: it forms the starting-point of the whole calculation. In this objection there is nothing which affects Ricardo. He is not called upon to reply. What *would* be an objection is the case in which it should be shown that, doubling or trebling the quantities of labour, you would not therefore double or treble the prices of the product. Show that, on the rise of labour, in each case, from three days to six days, the price would not rise from ten shillings to twenty, or that it would rise from five guineas to ten (after making the allowance for machinery, &c., which it is superfluous to repeat), and then you have destroyed Ricardo—but not else.

To profits the very same considerations apply. Profits are a mode of wages upon capital; and, naturally, men must be tempted by higher gains, contingent upon success, in order to compensate greater disadvantages arising to themselves from a particular employment. For instance, amongst modern Christian nations, what between a few sincere and many insincere prohibitions, at length the commerce in slaves has been denounced and made punishable. But that which at any period sustained and alimented this extensive trade was the institution of slavery. Now, this, considered as a bribe on the trade in slaves, flourishes more than ever. So long as a vast machinery of servile labour exists diffused through the continent and islands of America, so long there will be a silent bounty always proclaiming itself upon the supplies needed for keeping up that machinery; for African slaves, under whatsoever causes, rarely keep up their own race. Talk, therefore, in what delusive or self-deluding language they may, our home politicians have yet devised no effectual means for suppressing a trade continually more lucrative, or for defeating a commercial interest which thrives by its own ruins. The losses by interception are very great. Doubtless; but these losses furnish a sound plea for extra profits. The higher profit, up to a certain point, is indeed no more than insurance upon the general adventure; but the great advance on the personal share of the risk, which cannot be shifted from the captain, or chief authority on board, entitles him to look separately for an advance on his own individual dividend. This rate of advance, concurrent between the two interests of the captain and the owner, must grow with the growing embarrassments of the trade. At length, indeed, these excesses of risk might reach a point at which they would no longer be supported by a corresponding development in the *affirmative* values of slave labour. A cost or negative value cannot transcend the affirmative value. A slave is but a working machine. So much work may be extracted from him; and the value of this work will mount for a time, as the cost of the slave mounts. But at length the work itself, the product of the slave, will have reached its *maximum* of price. After *that*, if the cost should still go on increasing, the slave passes into a source of loss. This tendency, according to the variety of circumstances, local or personal, ranges through a large scale of degrees: not until it becomes absolute can we look for an extinction of the commerce.

Such and many other causes for variation in profits are always at work. And this variation is real, and proportional to its known causes. But, finally, we are crossed by a new consideration, which sometimes seems to concern the mere *ratio cognoscendi*, and sometimes the *ratio essendi*. Often, to this day, it continues to be difficult, and in ruder times it must have been impossible, to approximate, even by conjecture, towards the true rate of profits in very many employments of capital. The dispute is not on the realities of the case (here the profits are twenty—there, for no adequate cause, fifty), but on the constructions of the case (this man rates the profits at twenty—that man at fifty): or, again, the differences are reversed. Alternately, in short, we are puzzled by the *principium essendi*, and, again, by the *principium cognoscendi*.

Now, then, with respect to both of these principles, the principle which makes profits what they are and the principle which appreciates profits, I will call the reader's attention to four important mistakes.

I. It has been a blunder long current in books, and yet so momentous in its consequences that no epithet of blame can be too strong for it, practically to confound the mere *replacement* of capital with the *profits* upon that capital. When a man distributes the cost of all articles into rent, profit, and wages, or when, upon a sounder economy, he distributes this cost into profits and wages, evidently he commits that mistake: much of the cost is frequently *neither* rent, profit, nor wages. It is simply a restitution of capital, which leaves the whole *positive* returns unaffected.

II. Adam Smith has sharpened our attention to the common case, where that which really is no more than wages for services performed ranks in popular appreciation as profit. A surgeon, for instance, receives as the reward or *honorarium* of his science what is falsely classed as profit on his capital. Under the former case, that which is alike foreign to profit and wages was classed as profit; under this, the confusion takes place internally between the two.

III. When the question arises—How are profits kept down to the average level, or, in other words, suppose that, by any combination amongst capitalists, it were determined arbitrarily to raise profits, where lies the true natural counteraction to such an attempt?—the common answer is, in competition. It is rashly assumed that all such injurious attempts are defeated by the instantaneous introduction of more capital, under rival interests, into the trade or manufacture. But this is not always possible. Capitalists do not so easily enter a trade or withdraw from it. In a country so exquisitely organised as England, it is true that capital moves with velocity where the capitalist cannot move ; and of this we have a luminous explanation in Ricardo.

Ricardo, who, as a stockbroker, stood in the very centre of the vast money machinery accumulated in London, had peculiar advantages for observing and for investigating the play of this machinery. If our human vision were fitted for detecting agencies so impalpable, and if a station of view could be had, we might sometimes behold vast arches of electric matter continually passing and repassing between either pole and the equatorial regions. Accordingly as the equilibrium were disturbed suddenly or redressed, would be the phenomena of tropical hurricanes, or of auroral lights. Somewhat in the same silent arches of continual transition, ebbing and flowing like tides, do the re-agencies of the capital accumulated in London modify, without sound or echo, much commerce in all parts of the kingdom. Faithful to the monetary symptoms, and the fluctuations this way or that eternally perceptible in the condition of every trade, the great monied capitalist, standing at the centre of this enormous web, throws over his arch of capital or withdraws it, with the precision of a fireman directing columns of water from an engine upon the remotest quarter of a conflagration. It is not, as Ricardo almost *professionally* explains to us, by looking out for new men qualified to enter an aspiring trade, or by withdrawing some of the old men from a decaying trade, that the equilibrium is recovered. Such operations are difficult, dilatory, often personally ruinous, and disproportionately noisy to the public ear in the process of execution. But the true operation goes on as silently as the growth of light. The monied man stands equidistantly related to many different staple interests—the silk trade, the cotton trade, the iron trade, the timber and grain trade. Rarely does he act upon any one of them by direct interpolation of new firms, or direct withdrawals of old ones. An effect of this extent is generally as much beyond his power as beyond his interest.

Not a man has been shifted from his station ; possibly not a man has been intruded ; yet power and virtue have been thrown into vast laboratories of trade, like shells into a city. But all has been accomplished in one night by the inaudible agency of the post-office, co-operating with the equally inaudible agencies of capital moving through banks and through national debts, funded or unfunded. Such is the perfection of our civilisation. By the simple pressure of a finger upon the centre of so vast an organisation, a breath of life is hurried along the tubes—a pulse is enlivened or depressed—a circulation is precipitated or checked, without those ponderous processes of change indispensable on the Continent, and which so injuriously disturb the smooth working of general business. Acknowledging, therefore, as a fact first exposed clearly by Ricardo, that enormous changes may be effected, and continually *are* effected, without noise or tumult, through the exquisite resources of artificial action first made possible by the great social development of England; acknowledging by consequence that, for the purposes of competition, capital to any amount may be discharged, with a velocity inappreciable to the Continent, upon a considerable variety of creative industry: there is yet good reason to deny the possibility of that competition which is so generally relied on for the practical limitation of profits seeming to be in excess.

Upon serious reflection, how can any rational man imagine that, as a matter of course, by increasing the manufacture of razors or of scissors, he could increase their sale? That sale is predetermined by the need; and, though undoubtedly a very slight need may come to operate as a great need when the price is suddenly or much lowered, yet *that* is merely a transitional effect; the lower price is probably *binomial* price, and binomial price cannot last; by its very nature it is a force tending to a particular effect, viz. to equilibrate the supply with the demand; and, as soon as that tendency is accomplished, *there* it ceases.

The expression, however, of such a case may be designedly made equivocal. Let us, therefore, force the lurking notions in this sophistry to "show out" and expose themselves; by which means we shall know how to shape the reply.

*Case a.*—The insinuation is sometimes this—That the *rate* of profits will be diminished; that there will be a difference of so much per cent on the manufacture of the given article; and that, by giving to the buyer the benefit of this difference, free competition will reduce profits through an extended sale. But in a large mass of cases no such agency is possible. A man buys an article of instant applicability to his own purposes the more readily and the more largely as it happens to be cheaper: silk handkerchiefs having fallen to half-price, he will buy, perhaps, in threefold quantity; but he does not buy more steam-engines because the price is lowered. His demand for steam-engines is almost always predetermined by the circumstances of his situation. So far as he considers the cost at all, it is much more the cost of working this engine than the cost upon its purchase. But there are many articles for which the market is absolutely and merely limited by a pre-existing *system*, to which those articles are attached as subordinate parts or members. How could we force the dials or faces of timepieces by artificial cheapness to sell more plentifully than the inner works or movements of such timepieces? Could the sale of wine-vaults be increased without increasing the sale of wine? Or the tools of shipwrights find an enlarged market whilst shipbuilding was stationary? The articles and the manufacturing interests are past counting which conform to the case here stated, viz. which are so inter-organised with other articles or other interests that apart from that relation—standing upon their own separate footing—they *cannot* be diminished in price through any means or any motive depending upon the extension of sale. Offer to a town of 3000 inhabitants a stock of hearses, no cheapness will tempt that town into buying more than one. Offer a stock of yachts: the chief cost lies in manning, victualling, repairing; no diminution upon the mere price to a purchaser will tempt into the market any man whose rank, habits, and propensities had not already disposed him to such a purchase. So of professional costume for bishops, lawyers, students at Oxford, or the separate costume for Cantabs.

From cases of the same class, absolutely past counting, we must be sure that the conceit of competition having any unconditional power answerably to contract or expand the market for commodities is fitted only for a childish or inactive understanding. Universally all things which are sold may be thrown into three classes: first, a small class, in which the very least bias given favourably to the price will increase the sale: secondly, a much larger class, in which nothing short of a very strong bias will avail for such an increase; thirdly, a class the largest, in which no bias whatever, from the very strongest impulse communicated to the price, can overcome the obstacles to an extended sale.

*Case β.*—But under this delusive form of words lurks often quite another meaning: not the *rate* of profit is to be diminished by competition, but the separate dividends of each individual. It is not that profits are to fall from 16 to 12 per cent; no, the 16 per cent is to continue; but the ten thousand pounds annually disposable on such a 16 per cent will be otherwise distributed; forty capitalists will have crowded in, to average a gain of £250 for each, where previously twenty had averaged £500. This, however, is a change in many cases quite impracticable; in others, far from beneficial [1] to the public interests; and in any case having no tendency at all to the diminution of price, consequently no possible tendency to an extension of the market. What puzzles the student is this:—From Ricardo he has learned that a change in profits will not produce any change in price. Such a change settles upon wages; in fact, it has settled already upon wages. Any change in profits argues "a foregone conclusion," presupposes a corresponding change *already* made in wages, before the change in profits could arise. And if, therefore, a violent or conventional reduction should take place *originally* in profits, he is at a loss to trace the consequences of what he has been taught to view as impossible. For Ricardo has taught him that a

[1] In reality, the disposition to the engrossment, by large capitalists, of many farms, or of many cotton-mills, which is often complained of injudiciously as a morbid phenomenon in our modern tendencies, is partly to be regarded as an antagonist tendency, meeting and combating that other tendency irregularly manifested towards a subdivision too minute in the ordinary callings of trade. The efforts continually made to intrude upon the *system* of a town, or a quarter, by interpolating an extra baker, grocer, or druggist, naturally reacts, by irritating the counter-tendency to absorb into one hand many separate mills, &c., or to blend into one function many separate trades. In Scotland, for instance, grocers are also wine-dealers, spirit-dealers, cheesemongers, oilmen.

change cannot *commence* in profits ; that function of industry is not liable to any *original* affection of change ; any change must be derivative, must be secondary, which reaches profits. Yet how, if a sudden and violent reduction were made primarily upon individual profits as a desperate resource of competition ? Conventionally and arbitrarily such a change might be made by a little faction of sellers for the sake of underselling others, without any power on their part to meddle with wages. Out of a profit nominally 30 per cent the piratical minority might agree to sacrifice a third ; and sometimes the more easily because on large establishments a considerable *percentage* is often made into a mere fund for replacement of costs that do not exist for petty establishments. For instance, the virtual obligation resting upon a great inn to keep rooms, with fires burning, and other accommodations, baths, servants, &c., *always* in readiness for summary calls, forms one of the titles under which such an inn charges a higher price for a dinner substantially the same in quality than a petty inn exonerated from a similar obligation. As much as 10 per cent, calculated on a mean proportional between the little inn and the great inn, may perhaps be sequestered for such *extra* replacements, before the great inn and the little one could start fairly in competition. So that, undoubtedly, there is room, there is an opening, for such a violent reduction of profits ; and, *a fortiori*, there is room when there happen to be two funds for meeting that reduction : viz. the fund of replacement (falsely called profits), pressing exclusively on the one of two competitors ; the fund of true profits, accidentally high for both. Yet, supposing such a case actually to occur, eventually it will not disturb any reasonings of Ricardo. After all, it is no more than that case of competition so common in England before the era of railways, where two rival coach proprietors ran down the ladder of prices until at length the strife lay on the other side the equation—which of the two competitors should have the honour of giving the more costly dinner *gratuitously* to their passengers. I have myself travelled by coaches who were rapidly nearing the point at which their contest would be—not for payment to be received, but for payment to be given. How did all such struggles end ? By the defeat and retirement of the one party when exhausted of his resources, by the final establishment of the other in a virtual monopoly. Yet, on behalf of our English social condition, it speaks well that this monopoly, out of which the victor naturally paid himself for his sacrifices, was never pushed to any blamable excess. "True," it will be said; "but *that* was because he feared to provoke another competition." Very possibly; and often undoubtedly it was so. Yet that result of itself shows how excellent is the training of a sound and healthy economic state for moderation, equity, reasonable enterprise, and all the moral qualities incident to the position of capitalists in that rank. This is a separate theme hitherto untouched; but, undoubtedly, it will furnish a subject hereafter for special speculation—that as a good police, a good system of national education, a good legislation, a good executive jurisprudence, so also a good basis of political economy recommends itself, *inter alia*, by showing a far greater natural adaptation to the virtues which need encouragement in the productive classes. The case, as a difficulty in political economy, or as any demur to Ricardo, does not merit consideration; nor should I have considered it, except that naturally it arises in the series of phenomena for some notice, and that M. Baptiste Say (who, with as little logical power as Malthus, has even more of ingenuity) chooses, under another form, to consider it weighty. Meantime it is sufficient to reply—as to any conceivable disturbance in price accomplished by a sudden conventional renunciation of profits—that it falls to the ground through one simple explanation. Political Economy undertakes to explain the natural and mechanic effects from the interagencies of certain elements; but, wherever these effects are disturbed by voluntary human interferences, there ceases the duty of economy. As well might you demonstrate the 47th of 1st "Euclid" by sabring a man who should deny it; or insist that the cost of wheat at forty shillings a quarter would not govern its price, because a Turkish pacha, under those circumstances, had fixed the *maximum* at thirty shillings; or that gravitation would not cause a guinea to tend downwards, because you had nailed it to the wall. Once for all, the tendencies or natural effects in political economy, any more than in physics, are not overruled as principles because an external coercion hinders them from operating as facts. *Silent inter arma leges*; and the same thing is true of natural and immanent laws, such as those which silently govern the agencies and re-agencies of the several forces at work in Political Economy. External coercion suspends those laws; and for the time of suspension Political Economy has no existence.

IV. Upon this subject of profits, it becomes plain as we advance that the *esse* is closely connected with the *scire*. To make even a plausible guess at the possibility of diminishing profits, it is esssential to know what regularly they are. Now, when it is considered how often mere wages pass for profits (as noticed at page 272 under No. II)—how often the simple replacement of costs will pass for profits (as explained at page 272 under No. I)—how often an excess of profits will be fancied when there is merely a remuneration for *extra* skill, *extra* risk, *extra* trouble, *extra* uncertainty (as noticed at page 271)—everybody must see that it is a very elaborate problem to ascertain even for one year, still more for a fair average of years, *what* has been the true rate of profits upon the capital employed in any one trade. Nobody but the individual tradesman has the means of ascertaining his own profits; even he very uncertainly; and, as regards the profits of his own occupation generally, he can do no more than guess at them. How, then, is anything at all known to economists on this subject, or even to practical enterprisers? I answer that, as a general case, very little *is* known. In ninety-nine cases out of a hundred, no man knows even the gross nominal profit, far less the true and net profit which remains after all the allowances and distinctions explained. Confidential servants, it is true, and banking-houses, cause the revelation of many secrets; for a manufacturer, eager to obtain aid, will volunteer to his banker that unreserved communication of his affairs which he would scornfully refuse to the demand of curiosity. But no man can reveal more than he knows; and it is certain that, unless in those simple trades which rest on a primary necessity of life (as, for instance, the trade of a miller or of a baker), few managers of an extensive business could safely declare any *rate* of profit upon less than a seven years' average. When an outward-bound vessel from England arrives at Madras or Calcutta, she can declare a daily rate of sailing ; but it would be impossible for her to do so (not being a steamer), in any serviceable sense, after a single fortnight's absence from the Thames. Now, when to this difficulty of approximating towards any representative rate of profit is added the impossibility already explained, in a majority of cases, for any competitor to *act* upon such a declaration of profits, unless he could also, and simultaneously, extend the sale of the article—enough has been said to show the puerility of that little receipt current amongst economists, viz. unlimited competition for keeping down profits to one uniform level. The sole principle under which profits can rudely be known is the principle under which, in any age, profits can at all exist. And what is *that* ? As already explained, it is the rate of profit allowed upon land. For, through one natural link, viz. the equal necessity of landed produce to all workmen alike, this rate becomes the operative rate, in a gross sense, for all productive industry whatsoever. The pasture land and the corn land of every nation constitute, in effect, the *vis regulatrix* for appraising the rate of profit upon all capital, in whatever direction employed. But, because cultivation is always travelling downwards towards land worse and worse, does not this general law of profit authorise us to say that profits must be continually descending as society advances ? No. The student knows,—but he cannot too often be reminded of a truth everywhere forgotten by Ricardo,—that always the land is travelling downwards, but that always the productive management of land is travelling upwards. The two tendencies are eternally moving upon opposite tacks ; and the result is that now, in 1844, under the great Lady of the Isles, profits are undoubtedly higher than in 1344, a period of corresponding splendour under Edward III. Not in an *absolute* sense merely they are higher, as if total England in one age were balanced against total England in another—*that* they are by an excess too enormous to measure—but in the *ratio* they are higher in the returns relatively to the capital employed.

Is there no other mode, simpler and shorter, for ascertaining the rate of profits? Can we no otherwise learn what profits *are* than by reading *a priori* in the agriculture what the possibilities will allow them to be? Yes, notoriously there is an index, far simpler and readier of application, had it always been kept true to itself. This index is INTEREST. Much will be given for money, when much can be made of it. But, unfortunately, in semi-barbarous ages the converse does not hold; the inference is not good that much can be then made of money simply because much is given for it. Until insurance offices, a regular post-office, mercantile law, international intercourse, and other securities to commerce had arisen with rising civilisation, a very large proportion of all usury exhausted itself upon the mere insecurity of capital: the losses were then enormous through social imperfections; and, after ten years' run in such a lottery, the real profits would oftentimes be less than under the very moderate usury now exacted. Trading upon borrowed capital was then undoubtedly a rare case. This is to be lamented; because, else, interest would be a common measure for profits as between all ages alike. We might then say universally that the rate of interest was the *principium cognoscendi* in relation to mean profits, and, reciprocally, that the rate of profits was the *principium essendi* in relation to ordinary interest. Profits would *cause* interest to be thus or thus: interest would *ascertain* profits to be thus or thus. But, between ages in which the proportions allowed on every loan for its mere insurance vary so widely, the ratio of the two is no safe criterion.

Even at present there is a form of speech current amongst public men, silently corrected by the knowledge of all who have any experience, and yet in the last degree misleading to the recluse economist and to the public. It is said daily in every morning paper, it is said in the House of Commons, that money is not at this time worth 2 per cent. Why, surely it is not pretended that as yet there has been any difficulty found in buying into the funds. Now, the funds will give a trifle more than 3 per cent; whilst upon a small part of these funds, for the foolish reason that the dividends upon them are paid at the South Sea house and not at the Bank (which leads people into fancying that they are less solidly engrafted on the national faith), a trifle more can be had. "Ay, but this was money, you are to understand, which I wished to employ during an odd interval between two other employments of it." Yes, now the truth comes out; the brief explanation is that the money could be lent only under the condition of recalling it on a summary notice, or on none at all; and for this condition, which constitutes a special privilege in favour of the lender, naturally (as for any other privilege) he is obliged to pay. A peculiar case has entitled the borrower to a peculiar discount: how does *that* establish any general or prevailing rate of interest? The very case of Exchequer bills may show that it does not. Ricardo, as a man daily witnessing the traffic in such bills, and himself largely partaking in it, reasonably had his attention drawn to the fact that they bore an interest far from corresponding to that on the funded debt. The interest was not so high as it ought to be. Yet why? Could it be denied that the security was equal upon the Exchequer bills? Nay, was it not the very same? For that man deceives himself who fancies that the wicked anti-social enemies of our public prosperity—"Socialists"—"Jacobins"—"Chartists"—would make any distinction between a debt resting upon the assignment of special funds and another debt resting only upon pledges of Parliamentary faith. If that fatal day should ever dawn upon England when villains of this quality will be able "to lay their hands upon the ark of our magnificent and awful cause," of the two debts, they would treat with more consideration this latter, as being rarely more than one to forty when compared with the other. But what *they* might choose to do, in an event abominated by all upright men, luckily has never yet seemed near enough to be worth estimating on the tariff of evil contingencies. No fraction of interest has yet been paid *extra* on the chance of being spared by public robbers; no fraction has been deducted from interest on the notion of standing first in the lists of confiscation. It could not be *here*, it could not be in this remote contingency, that the lower interest yielded by an Exchequer bill found its justification. No, it lay in the *instant* convertibility of this security into money. Had you lodged a thousand pounds with a London banker, doubtless you could draw it out by a cheque within the next ten minutes ; but then for that very reason, by way of balancing so summary a liability, this London banker will allow you no interest, not if you left it in his hands for five years. On the other hand, had you lodged it with an Edinburgh or Glasgow banker, he would have allowed you a fair interest on the sum, whilst the security would be equal; but then for that very reason, by way of balancing that liability to interest, the Scotch banker will not allow you to draw it out unless after a long notice. But throw your thousand pounds into the shape of an Exchequer bill, and without further anxiety you may place it in your writing-desk, certain of realising both advantages, viz. the London advantage of instant availability, the Scotch (or English provincial) advantage of current interest during the interval of non-employment. So far the Exchequer bill has a conspicuous advantage, which, under limitation to the amount of such bills, is very considerable. As compared again with stock in the 3 per cent consols, the Exchequer bill has other advantages, which for a banker become very important. In reality, so great were the advantages when Ricardo wrote (1817) that he estimates the interest per cent on an Exchequer bill at £4$\frac{1}{4}$ ; whilst on a hundred pounds of a stock then existing at 5 per cent (which could be bought at that moment for £95) the interest was about £5$\frac{1}{4}$. The advantage must evidently have been inversely as the interest ; and that advantage lay partly in the instant convertibility, partly in other accidents of convenience valuable to bankers.

But in many other cases of advantage, which upon a gross view seems equalised, there is often an excess upon one side from causes not instantly perceptible. Why should a 3 per cent stock have been more valuable than a 5 per cent stock, both debts having been contracted on the same *virtual* basis of interest? It is not so where circumstances forbid any expectation that either will be paid off. But, when the fall of interest in the general market has made it certain that a prudent government will use the opportunity for reducing their debt, it becomes evident that in England they will commence the operation upon the 5 per cents. If money should *really* sink to 2 per cent it will then answer to pay off the 3 per cents. But we are safe until that happens; and we are safe even after it happens, so long as any higher stock of sufficient magnitude interposes to receive the first assault. A 3½ per cent or a 4 per cent stock becomes an outwork, exhausting for some years the efforts of government, and in the meantime giving security to the inner citadel of the 3 per cents. That sacred fund enjoys the privilege of *Outis* in the den of the Cyclops, viz. of being swallowed last of all. Consequently it must pay for that privilege. And thus, but not until times in which the downward tendency of interest[1] should raise a growing presumption of extensive operations for diminishing the public debt, might a 3 per cent fund bear a higher relative price in the market than a 3½ per cent (both being supposed to stand on our present English footing in their origin).

Ricardo mentions another case, with which I will close this sub-section—as furnishing in fact the direct converse to

[1] "*But not until the downward tendency of interest,*" &c. :—And on the other hand, by parity of reason, if, 1, through draining, 2, guano, 3, bone dust, 4, spade culture, &c., the agriculturists of this country should (as probably they will, if not disturbed by corn traitors), through the known antagonist movement to that of rent, translate the land of England within the next century to a higher key, so that No. 250 were to become equal in power with the present No. 210—and so regressively, No. 40 equal with the present No. 1—in that case all functions of capital (wages, rent, profit) would rise gradually and concurrently, though not equally. Through the known *nexus* between landed capital and all other capital, it would follow that all manufacturing capital (wages and profit) must rise; since, after all, however far removed by its quality or its habits from agricultural industry, not the less the very ultimate refinements of industry in the arts or manufactures must still come back to the land for its main demand, viz. of beef, mutton, butter, cheese, milk, bread, hides, barks, tallow, flax, &c.: even for the haughty artist of cities, the coarse rural industry must be the final *vis regulatrix*. This being so, it follows that under an advance in our agriculture, such as even the next generation will probably secure (through the growing combination of science and enormous capital), profits must rise in their *rate*, and therefore interest. Consequently it will not then answer to the government, under the legal *par* of the English funds, to borrow for the sake of paying off any stock whatever. They will not be able to obtain money on any terms that could offer a temptation for paying off a 3½ per cent stock.

the case so mendaciously paraded, where money yields only 2 per cent, and as furnishing therefore the appropriate answer. "To pay the interest of the national debt, large sums of money are withdrawn from circulation four times in the year for a few days." *Four* times, and not *twice*, because the half-yearly dividends fall at one period for certain stocks, at a different period for other stocks; by which means the disturbance, though reiterated more frequently, is lightened for each operation. Such is the fact—what is the consequence? "These demands for money, being only temporary, seldom affect prices; they are generally surmounted by the payment of a large rate of interest" (p. 415). Now, would it not be monstrous to urge that casual tilt upwards in the rate of interest as a representative change in the current and prevailing rate? Equally dishonest it is, *ex analogo*, to urge, under the notion of being any representative rate, that occasional 2 per cent which is caught at by elaborate artists in the use of money, not as in itself the highest interest, but as the highest compatible with a much higher rate lying in the rear, though suspended for a few weeks.

V. From all these details of the 4th section I argue that, although the τὸ *esse* and the τὸ *percipi*, with respect to profits, stand in some practical relation to each other, especially under the guidance which exists in the mean rate of interest—still even this guidance, as regards any given mode of industry, is doubtful, and not at all certain as the index to the average; whilst to *act* upon it, to apply fresh capital simply because there seems to be an opening advertised for such an application in the reputed rate of profits, would often be found impossible—often ruinous. It would be saying in effect—"Because the Grand Junction Canal is reputed to pay a higher return on its shares than is customary since the depression of canals by railroads, therefore we will make two Grand Junction Canals." The profits perhaps, after all, are not accurately known under all the quinquennial or decennial deductions for repairs, for fluctuations of traffic, for injurious taxes, &c.; but, if they *were*, so far from justifying a second canal, that second canal would probably ruin both. Meantime there is one cause of difference in the very *esse* of profits, as alleged by M. Jean Baptiste Say,[1] which is too momentous if true, and too extravagant if false, to permit me to pass it over in silence. There is a special reason why no English writer should overlook M. Baptiste Say, since he (according to the remark at p. 365, vol. i. of his translator and very able annotator, Mr. Prinsep), beyond other French economists, "has profited so largely by his observation of English affairs, and his acquaintance with English writers." M. Say did not altogether understand Ricardo; but he first, amongst all Frenchmen, read him, adopted him, and at times fancied that he opposed him. In the present question of profits, he had properly and thoughtfully distinguished between profit as "derivable from the employment of capital" on the one hand, and profit on the other hand as "derivable from the industry which turns it to account" (p. 153, vol. ii). So far he is right, if I understand him; and it is difficult to explain the sudden perverseness of his annotator, Mr. Prinsep, who chooses to reject the distinction *in toto* as a "useless refinement."

But, in the course of an attempt (which immediately follows) to illustrate the distinction, he puts forward this case:—"Suppose two houses, in the fur trade for example, to work each upon a capital of 100,000 *francs*, and to make on the average an annual profit—the one of 24,000 *francs*—the other of 6000 *francs* only; a difference of 18,000 *francs*." Very well; what is the inference, what is the "moral" which M. Say deduces from such an astonishing disparity in the profits? Upon a capital of little more than four thousand pounds sterling, the one furrier raises annually for himself a net return of not less than a thousand pounds; whilst his rival pockets only two hundred and forty pounds upon the very same capital, invested at the same time in the very same trade. Now, if this were the result of some single year, it would express no more than one of those casualties (through bad debts, property uninsured, losses by embezzlements, &c.), to which all commercial houses are

[1] This circumstantiality is requisite, because there is another Monsieur Say in the market, of whom (being dead, I believe) it may now be said, without offence, in the words of an ancient Joe Millerism, that, if *he* is a counsellor also, he is not a counsellor *likewise*.

liable in turn. But this, by the supposition, is the *regular* relation between the parties from year to year. How then is it explained by M. Say? How does he wish us to understand it? Why, as "fairly referable to the different degrees of skill and labour":—the thousand pound man is active and intelligent; the two hundred and forty pound man is stupid and lazy. Personal qualities, in short, make the difference.

Yet is that possible? Not, undoubtedly, for the logical purpose to which it is applied by M. Say. Differences there may be, and differences there are, and differences even to that extent, between man and man—between house and house; but not founded on that open and professed negligence. For this, under the action of our social machinery, hardly any opening exists.

> "Nobis non licet esse tam disertis
> Qui musas colimus severiores."

Excesses of negligence, amounting to such a result annually, would, in the case where they are possible, offer no instruction; in the case where they could offer instruction, they would not be possible. For, if M. Say is exposing a mere *lacheté* of youthful luxury, then it is a case rather for a moralist than for an economist. But, if he means it as a representative case, involving some principle as yet undiscussed, then it is insufficiently explained. But it is impossible; and precisely on the following argument:—If, by employing four thousand pounds in his trade, the man could annually clear only two hundred and forty (or very little more than the interest at five per cent), which, without risk or trouble, he could have obtained at the date of M. Say's book, and this at the very time when others were realising four times as much; in that case, the true difference must arise from *his* turning over his capital only once, whilst his rivals turned over *theirs* four and five times. But every prudent tradesman would accept this as a warning to withdraw three-fourths of his capital, when a second year's experience had taught him that he could obtain only one-fourth of the profits reaped by others trading on the same terms as himself; and, *a fortiori*, this policy will be adopted by M. Say's furrier, who is supposed to act in mere laziness. His profits will be the same upon one-fourth of the capital employed unintermittingly as upon the four-fourths employed in succession: his risk will be reduced; and there will be a clear gain by the interest upon the three-fourths of capital now transferred to other hands. Consequently, as cases to be argued in political economy, as *exemplary* cases, these extreme ratios of profit, low and high, stated hypothetically by M. Say, could not exist. As individual accidents, ceasing to operate from the moment when they are ascertained, they fall into that general fund of *known* counter-agencies which, upon all modes of productive industry, compel us to compute by averages and by prevailing tendencies. No man could persist in so perverse a conflict with the manifest current and set of the tide running against him. Or, in the case of actually persisting, his folly would indicate a mere individual anomaly; and such irregularities, having no scientific influence on any general principles of economy, it could be no purpose of M. Say to deal with.

Yet, generally, that many openings exist for a licentious latitude of profits, under circumstances the very same to the public eye, had been long apparent. It was impossible to be otherwise than incredulous as to the current assertions on this subject, which were equally discredited, *a priori*, by the known difficulty of ascertaining *anything*, and *a posteriori*, by the frequent inconsistency of their own particular results. That the current rate of profits, as a thing settled and defined, must be a chimera—this was certain; and for the simple reason—that, in each separate walk of commerce, this rate of profits was a thing imperfectly known to the tradesman concerned. If he—if the men exercising the trade—cannot tell you the general rate of profits even in this one trade, or even his own rate after allowing for all the numerous deductions to be made upon an average of ten years, how much less can a non-commercial economist pretend to draw such a representative estimate for *all* trades? The pretence is monstrous under any machinery which as yet we command for such a purpose.

In harmony with these views, let the reader take the

following case of *judicial* exposure upon this subject, remembering that similar exposures are almost of weekly recurrence:—A bankrupt (described as a mercer) was under examination before a commissioner of bankruptcy, or of insolvency. The commissioner asked him—What, to the best of his belief and knowledge, had been his customary rate of profit? The bankrupt replied firmly, "Six per cent." How, thought every man of consideration, did you indeed face for years this risk, laborious attendance, and (worst of all) this anxiety, for so miserable an addition (two and a half per cent) upon that income which, without either labour, or risk, or anxiety, you might at any rate have obtained from the national funds of your country? In less than a quarter of an hour, by some turn in the examination, it was extracted from him that he turned over his capital every two months. The commodity in which he had chiefly dealt appeared to have been Parisian silks, &c.; and in this trade, upon every thousand pounds the sum gained was not *sixty* pounds annually, as he had led the court previously to suppose, but six times sixty, or three hundred and sixty. It is true on the other hand that not improbably the bankrupt had taken no pains to distinguish the mere *replacements* from the profits, strictly so called. But still it could not be doubted that, in the very strictest sense, his profits were far beyond the low standard understood by the court at first—if not thirty-six per cent, probably twenty-five to twenty-eight per cent; whilst, from the language of the court, as it fell under each impression successively, no inference could be drawn that either had been viewed as startling.[1]

[1] These courts for insolvencies, as well as for bankruptcies, present many openings for discovery to the political economist. In the course of this very examination, another truth came out which may serve to convince the "knowing" men upon town that they are not always so knowing as they think themselves. What notion is more popular amongst the prudential masters of life than the hollow pretensions of cheap shops, and the mere impossibility that they should have any power to offer "bargains"? Now, few people are more disposed to that opinion, as generally sound, than myself. To see "tickets" or "labels" indicating prices below the standard is for every man of sense a caution against that establishment. Yet still the possible exceptions are not few. In this instance, it was proved beyond a doubt, that for many months the bankrupt had gone upon the prin-

Now, what is it that I infer from this case? I infer, 1*st*, that no definite rate of profit can be notorious to the world of commerce, where a court, which may be considered one of its organs, can so quietly adopt by turns a statement so entirely different. I infer, 2*dly*, that M. Baptiste Say has, in a partial sense, grounds for his doctrine; it cannot be denied him, that a possible tradesman may turn over his large capital three, four, or six times, whilst an obscure tradesman in the same line may barely turn over his own small capital once. The very fact of a large capital is by itself a sort of invitation to such a result; for gods and men alike disapprove of the wretch who cannot offer credit. Now, the annual rate upon each hundred pounds must be four times greater to him who four times raises a profit upon that hundred than to him who raises such a profit but once. This is undeniable; and it is therefore undeniable that, upon the two extremes in respect of advantages for selling, the annual profits may be in any degree different. But in answer to M. Say it must be argued—1*st*, that from all such extreme cases the practice is and must be to abstract; and that, probably, such extremes compensate each the other; the average, the prevailing tendency, is what we look at: 2*dly*, that such a case does not prove any different *rate* of profits; for anything that appears to the contrary, the little tradesman has realised the same *rate* of profit upon each hundred pounds as the big tradesman, only his absolute profits have been less, both in the ratio of his less capital, and of his less power to employ it with effect. Power to turn over a hundred pounds four times instead of once is in fact no more than the power to command four hundred pounds instead of one. The same consequences will take place. And, reciprocally, where a man really *has* the four hundred, with a virtual power only of profitably employing one hundred (which case is the very case propounded by M. Say), he will think himself obliged to withdraw three of the hundreds; for he will look upon it

ciple of raising money, for his own instant uses, by selling the Parisian goods below the original cost of the *manufacturer*. Such dishonourable practices certainly soon exhaust their own principle of movement. But, in so vast a community as London, always there must be new cases arising; consequently, always there must be some limited possibility of *real* bargains.

as the locking up of so much useless capital. Or, if M. Say should retort "No: just the contrary; because this man can turn over his hundred pounds only once against the four turns of the big man, *a fortiori*, he must work his four hundred where else he might be content to work one hundred: that is the only resource towards balancing matters—so far, at least, as his power extends"; yet, on the other hand, this is not the case put by M. Say. He supposed a man to make less profit, through industry in that proportion less; but, in this possible answer of M. Say, we have a disadvantage of mere position balancing itself, or tending to do so, by industry in that proportion greater. And in the last result we find the true moral of the case to be simply that one man in the same trade can employ a greater capital than another; sometimes directly, by employing twenty hundreds of pounds where the other can employ only five; sometimes indirectly, by turning over several times (*i.e.* by using for several distinct operations) each separate portion of capital, whilst the other man turns it over only once. But of all such differences between man and man we may say either that they do not affect the *rate* of profits by the least disturbance; or, if in any case they do, in a world of practice where the principle of average must be applied to wages, to rent, and to every mode of return, the inference will simply be, that we must apply that principle also to profits. I have already stated my own incredulity as to the *notoriety* (not as to the existence) of any definite rate upon profits at any period. Such a rate may be approximated conjecturally; it cannot be known. But, if it could, that result must be obtained by abstracting from all extremes, whether one way or the other; and therefore to have proved an extreme would not have disproved a mean rate.

*Finally*, I will answer two important questions likely to rise up in the end before every student:—

Is there, he will ask, any known objection or demur to the law of profits, as stated by Ricardo? That is, any demur to this particular doctrine as distinct from objection to the entire system of Ricardo? I answer that there is none, except the following of Mr. Malthus. He in his Principles, at p. 301 (1st edit.), insists upon it that there is "a main cause which influences profits," quite overlooked by Ricardo. What may that cause be? "The proportion which capital bears to labour." Ricardo had laid it down that the rate of profit upon the land last brought under tillage—upon that land which is presumably the worst in use—must be the regulating rate for all profits whatsoever. No, replies Mr. Malthus; not necessarily. That is one regulating cause, no doubt; but there is another. "When capital is abundant compared with labour, nothing can prevent low profits"; and, inversely, no fertility in the land as yet taken up can separately maintain high profits, "unless capital is scarce compared with labour." But to this, however tortuous the objection becomes by Mr. Malthus's clouded logic, the answer is short. The action is supposed to lie through wages. Mr. Malthus means that the labourers will receive higher wages when capital is redundant, so that the part of the produce left for profits will be smaller; and *versa vice.* But, without entering into the changes incident to the price of labour (for labour does not depend for its value upon any one element as capital, but upon several, which may be all acting in one direction, or all in opposite directions), thus much is evident, that only the binomial (or market) price of the labour could be affected in the circumstances supposed, consequently only the binomial value of profits. A disturbed relation between capital and labour would no otherwise affect labour in its price than as the rate of population would affect it. When population advances too rapidly, the tendency of wages must *pro tanto* be downwards; and so of other elements concurring to the complex value of labour. But none of these potential modifications escaped the eye of Ricardo. Again and again he has pointed them out as fit subjects for allowance when they occur, though he has designedly and avowedly neglected them where they would have interfered with the simplicity of the principal law. What Mr. Malthus brings forward as a second law, such as ought therefore to be capable of defeating and intercepting the first, is nothing more than a tendency to modify the first. In the same spirit of high promise and trivial performance, Mr. Malthus had menaced the whole of Ricardo's doctrine upon Value. The quantity of labour, he would show us, did *not* always constitute the cost of an article ; nor the cost of an article always constitute its price. Why, then, what *did* ? With loud laughter Ricardo heard, as if this were some new and strange proposition, that by possibility the too much or too little of the article might *also* affect the price—a price of twenty might by a scarcity of five be raised to twenty-five, or by a redundancy of five be lowered to fifteen. But who doubted, or had ever doubted, this ? That is *binomial* price. All the points which Malthus exposed as weak and assailable points had always been exposed by Ricardo as points liable to a separate caution. But this is not to answer Ricardo's doctrine of profits : this is simply to exhibit Ricardo's doctrine with those modifications broadly expanded which for good reasons Ricardo had left indicated in a briefer shape.

The other question remains a practical question, and carrying along with it a sting of anxiety to whole generations. It is this :—Amongst all men (even those who pretend to no scientific economy) there is a misgiving that profits, and by consequence interest, must be under a fatal necessity of gradually sinking, until at length they touch the point of extinction. Even Ricardo has too much authorised this false idea. There is no *essential* tendency downwards in profits, more than upwards. True, there is a constant motion downwards upon the land-scale from good to bad, from bad to worse ; and, as that happens to be chiefly concerned in the doctrine of rent,—which again reappears in the doctrines of profits and wages,—Ricardo had a disproportionate necessity for continually dwelling on that particular movement. But to this, which acts from year to year, there is a tendency strictly antagonist, which acts much more slowly at times, and is felt most from century to century. The principle has been repeatedly brought forward and explained, so that there is no reason for dwelling on it here. But, by way of a single illustration from our modern experience in this particular, it may be well to mention these facts. Go back to a period two centuries from 1844, and the current rate of interest will be found nearer to 8 than 7 per cent. Go back to a period only one century from 1844, and interest is found to have fallen so low as 3 per cent. This was the prevailing rate through that part of Sir Robert Walpole's public life which lay in the reign of George II, or, in general terms, from 1727 to about 1739–43. In the course of this latter period interest again began to advance; and in forty or forty-five years more it had risen beyond 5 per cent. During the great Revolutionary War, although limited at that time by law, interest rose in the market much beyond that legal *maximum.* It was more than double what it had been in the reign of George II. In our present era of peace, uninterrupted for twenty-eight years, it has again receded. But this brief abstract of experience through two centuries unites with the *a priori* theory in showing that the rate of interest is under no immutable law of declension. During these two centuries it has not uniformly declined: on the contrary, it has *oscillated* in all directions; and by that one fact, so abundantly established, we are released from all apprehensions of a downward *destiny.* Our fate in that respect is not sealed; it rests very much in our own hands.

# FALSIFICATION OF ENGLISH HISTORY[1]

I AM myself, and always have been, a member of the Church of England, and am grieved to hear the many attacks against the Church (frequently most illiberal attacks) which not so much religion as political rancour gives birth to in every third journal that I take up. This I say to acquit myself of all dishonourable feelings, such as I would abhor to co-operate with, in bringing a very heavy charge against that great body in its literary capacity.

Whosoever has reflected on the history of the English Constitution must be aware that the most important stage of its development lies within the reign of Charles I. It is true that the judicial execution of that prince has been allowed by many persons to vitiate all that was done by the heroic Parliament of November 1640; and the ordinary Histories of England assume as a matter of course that the whole period of parliamentary history through those times is to be regarded as a period of confusion. Our constitution, say they, was formed in 1688-9. Meantime it is evident to any reflecting man that the Revolution simply re-affirmed the principles developed in the strife between the two great parties which had arisen in the reign of James I, and had ripened and come to issue with each other in the reign of his

[1] Appeared first in the *London Magazine* for December 1824, as the last and longest of the series of odds and ends contributed by De Quincey to that periodical under the running title of "Notes from the Pocket-Book of a late Opium-Eater." In 1859 De Quincey detached it from that series and reprinted it, with some slight verbal changes, as an independent article in vol. xii of his Collective Edition of his Writings.—M.

son. Our constitution was not a birth of a single instant, as they would represent it, but a gradual growth and development through a long tract of time. In particular, the doctrine of the king's vicarious responsibility in the person of his ministers, which first gave a sane and salutary meaning to the doctrine of the king's personal irresponsibility ("The king can do no wrong"), arose undeniably between 1640 and 1648. This doctrine is the main pillar of our constitution, and perhaps the finest discovery that was ever made in the theory of government. Hitherto the doctrine *that the King can do no wrong* had been used not to protect the indispensable sanctity of the king's constitutional character, but to protect the wrong. Used in this way it was a maxim of Oriental despotism, and fit only for a nation where law had no empire. Many of the illustrious patriots of the Great Parliament saw this, and felt the necessity of abolishing a maxim so fatal to the just liberties of the people. But some of them fell into the opposite error of supposing that this abolition could be effected only by the direct negation of it. *Their* maxim accordingly was—"The King *can* do wrong," *i.e.* is responsible in his own person. In this great error even the illustrious wife of Colonel Hutchinson participated[1]; and accordingly she taxes those of her own party who scrupled to accede to the new maxim, and still adhered to

[1] This is remarked by her editor and descendant, Julius Hutchinson, who adds some words to this effect:—"That, *if* the patriots of that day were the inventors of the maxim [*the king can do no wrong*], we are much indebted to them." The patriots certainly did not invent the maxim, for they found it already current: but they gave it its new and constitutional sense. I refer to the book, however, as I do to almost all books in these notes, from memory; writing most of them in situations where I have no access to books. By the way, Charles I, who used the maxim in the most odious sense, furnished the most colourable excuse for his own execution. He constantly maintained the irresponsibility of his ministers; but, if that were conceded, it would then follow that the King must be made responsible in his own person: and that construction led of necessity to his trial and death. [Colonel John Hutchinson, who had been a conspicuous officer on the Parliamentarian side in the Civil War, and had sat as one of the King's judges, was exceptionally favoured at the Restoration, and lived to four years beyond it. His wife, Lucy Hutchinson, left memoirs of him and of herself, which were first published by her descendant in 1806, and have since then been a very popular book.—M.]

the old one, with unconscientious dealing. But she misapprehended their meaning, and failed to see where they laid the emphasis: the emphasis was not laid, as it was by the royal party, on the words "can do no *wrong*"—but on "The King": that is, wrong may be done, and in the King's name; but it cannot be the King who did it (the king cannot constitutionally be supposed the person who did it). By this exquisite political refinement the old tyrannical maxim was disarmed of its sting, and the entire redress of all wrong, so indispensable to the popular liberty, was brought into perfect reconciliation with the entire inviolability of the sovereign, which is no less indispensable to the popular liberty. There is, moreover, a double wisdom in the new sense: for not only is one object (the redress of wrong) secured in conjunction with another object (the king's inviolability) hitherto held irreconcilable,—but even with a view to the first object alone a much more effectual means is applied, because one which leads to no schism in the state, than could have been applied by the blank negation of the maxim; *i.e.* by lodging the responsibility exactly where the executive power (*ergo* the power of resisting this responsibility) was lodged.

Here, then, is one example in illustration of my thesis that the English Constitution was in a great measure gradually evolved in the contest between the different parties in the reign of Charles I. Now, if this be so, it follows that for constitutional history no period is so important as that; and, indeed,—though it is true that the Revolution is the great era for the constitutional historian, because he there first finds the constitution fully developed as the "bright consummate *flower*," and, what is equally important, he there first finds the principles of our constitution *ratified* by a competent authority,—yet, to trace the *root* and growth of the constitution, the three reigns immediately preceding are still more properly the objects of his study. Briefly, the *root* of our constitutional settlement was in the three reigns of Charles I, of Charles II, and of James II; but its manifestation by fruits and blossoms was in 1689. In proportion, then, as the reign of Charles I is important to the history of our constitution, in that proportion are those to be taxed with the most dangerous falsifications of our History who have misrepresented either the facts or the principles of those times.

Now, I affirm that the Clergy of the Church of England have been in a perpetual conspiracy since the era of the Restoration to misrepresent both. As an illustration of what I mean, I refer to the common edition of *Hudibras*, by Dr. Grey [1]: for the proof, I might refer to some thousands of books. Dr. Grey's is a disgusting case; for he swallowed with the most anile credulity every story, the most extravagant that the malice of those times could invent, against either the Presbyterians or the Independents: and for this I suppose, amongst other deformities, his notes were deservedly ridiculed by Warburton. But, amongst hundreds of illustrations more respectable than Dr. Grey's, I will refer the reader to a work of our own days,—*Ecclesiastical Biography* (in part a republication of *Walton's Lives*), edited by the present master of Trinity College, Cambridge, who is held in the highest esteem wherever he is known, and is, I am persuaded, perfectly conscientious, and as impartial as in such a case it is possible for a high-churchman to be.[2] Yet so it is that there is scarcely one of the notes having any political reference to the period of 1640-1660 which is not disfigured by unjust prejudices; and the amount of the moral which the learned editor grounds upon the documents before him is this,—that the young student is to cherish the deepest abhorrence and contempt of all who had any share on the Parliamentary side in the "confusions" of the period from 1640 to 1660: that is to say, of men to whose immortal exertions it was owing that the very Revolution of 1688, which Dr. W. will be the first to applaud, found us with any such stock of political principles or feelings as could make a beneficial revolution possible. Where, let me ask, would have been

[1] Dr. Zachary Grey's edition of *Hudibras*, "with large annotations and a preface," was first published in 1744, and later copies of it are very common.—M.

[2] Dr. Christopher Wordsworth's six volumes of *Ecclesiastical Biography: Or Lives of Eminent Men connected with the History of Religion in England from the commencement of the Reformation to the Revolution* appeared in 1810, and were in their second edition at the date of this reference to them by De Quincey.—M.

the willingness of some Tories to construe the flight of James II into a virtual act of abdication, or to consider even the most formal act of abdication binding against the king, had not the great struggle of Charles's days gradually substituted in the minds of all parties a rational veneration of the king's *office* for the old superstition in behalf of the king's *person*,—which would have protected him from the effects of any acts, however solemnly performed, which affected injuriously either his own interests or the liberties of his people? *Tempora mutantur: nos et mutamur in illis.* Those whom we find in fierce opposition to the popular party about 1640 we find still in the same personal opposition fifty years after, but an opposition resting on far different principles: insensibly the principles of their antagonists had reached even them; and a courtier of 1689 was willing to concede more than a patriot of 1630 would have ventured to ask. Let me not be understood to mean that true patriotism is at all more shown in supporting the rights of the people than those of the king. As soon as both are defined and limited, the last are as indispensable to the integrity of the constitution as the first; and popular freedom itself would suffer as much, though indirectly, from an invasion of Cæsar's rights as by a more direct attack on itself. But in the 17th century the rights of the people were as yet *not* defined; throughout that century they were gradually defining themselves,—and, as happens to all great practical interests, defining themselves through a course of fierce and bloody contests. For the kingly rights are almost inevitably carried too high in ages of imperfect civilisation; and the well-known laws of Henry VII, by which he either broke or gradually sapped the power of the aristocracy, had still more extravagantly exalted them. On this account it is just to look upon democratic or popular politics as identical in the 17th century with patriotic politics. In later periods the democrat and the patriot have sometimes been in direct opposition to each other; at that period they were inevitably in conjunction.

All this, however, is in general overlooked by those who either write English History or comment upon it. Most writers *of* or *upon* English History proceed either upon servile principles, or upon no principles; and a good *Spirit of English History,*—that is, a history which should abstract the tendencies and main results (as to laws, manners, and constitution) from every age of English History,—is a work which I hardly hope to see executed. For it would require the concurrence of some philosophy with a great deal of impartiality. How idly do we say, in speaking of the events of our own time which affect our party feelings,—"We stand too near to these events for an impartial estimate; we must leave them to the judgment of posterity"! For it is a fact that of the many books of memoirs written by persons who were not merely contemporary with the great civil war, but actors and even leaders in its principal scenes, there is hardly one which does not exhibit a more impartial picture of that great drama than the histories written at this day. The historian of Popery does not display half so much zealotry and passionate prejudice in speaking of the many events which have affected the power and splendour of the Papal See for the last thirty years, and under his own eyes, as he does when speaking of a Reformer who lived three centuries ago, of a Bible Translator into a vernacular tongue who lived five centuries ago, of an Anti-pope, of a Charlemagne or a Gregory the Great, still further removed from himself. The recent events he looks upon as accidental and unessential; but in the great enemies or great founders of the Romish temporal power, and in the history of their actions and their motives, he feels that the whole principle of the Romish cause and its pretensions are at stake. Pretty much under the same feeling have modern writers written with a rancorous party spirit of the political struggles in the 17th century. Here they fancy that they can detect the *incunabula* of the revolutionary spirit: here some have been so sharp-sighted as to read the features of pure Jacobinism; and others [1] have gone so far as to assert that all the atrocities of

[1] Amongst these Mr. D'Israeli (the father of the Right Honourable Benjamin Disraeli) in one of the latter volumes of his *Curiosities of Literature* has dedicated a chapter or so to formal proof of this proposition. A reader who is familiar with the history of that age comes to the chapter with a previous indignation, knowing what sort of proof he has to expect. This indignation is not likely to be mitigated by what he will there find. Because some one madman, fool, or scoundrel makes a monstrous proposal—which dies of itself unsupported, and is

the French Revolution had their direct parallelisms in acts done or countenanced by the virtuous and august Senate of England in 1640! Strange distortion of the understanding, which can thus find a brotherly resemblance between two great historical events which of all that ever were put on record stand off from each other in most irreconcilable enmity: the one originating, as Coleridge has observed, in excess of principle; the other in the utter defect of all moral principle whatever: and the progress of each being answerable to its origin! Yet so it is. And not a memoir-writer of that age is reprinted in this but we have a preface from some red-hot Anti-jacobin warning us with much vapid commonplace from the mischiefs and eventual anarchy of too rash a spirit of reform as displayed in the French Revolution,—*not* by the example of that French Revolution, but by that of our own in the age of Charles I. The following passage from the Introduction to Sir William Waller's *Vindication*, published in 1793, may serve as a fair instance: "He [Sir W. Waller] was indeed at length sensible of the "misery which he had contributed to bring on his country" [By the way, it is a suspicious circumstance that Sir William [1]

in violent contrast to all the acts and the temper of those times—this is to sully the character of the Parliament and three-fourths of the People of England. If this proposal had grown out of the spirit of the age, that spirit would have produced many more proposals of the same character and acts corresponding to them. Yet upon this one infamous proposal, and two or three scandalous anecdotes from the libels of the day, does the whole *onus* of Mr. D'Israeli's parallel depend. *Tantamne rem tam negligenter?*—In the general character of an Englishman I have a right to complain that so heavy an attack upon the honour of England and her most virtuous patriots in her most virtuous age should be made with so much levity: a charge so solemn in its matter should have been prosecuted with a proportionate solemnity of manner. Mr. D'Israeli refers with just applause to the opinions of Mr. Coleridge: I wish that he would have allowed a little more weight to the striking passage in which that gentleman contrasts the French Revolution with the English Revolution of 1640-48. However, the general tone of honour and upright principle which marks Mr. D'Israeli's work encourages me and others to hope that he will cancel the chapter, and not persist in wounding the honour of a great people for the sake of a parallelism which—even if it were true—is a thousand times too slight and feebly supported to satisfy the most accommodating reader.

[1] Sir William and his cousin Sir Hardress Waller were both re-

first became sensible that his country was miserable when he became sensible that he himself was not likely to be again employed, and became fully convinced of it when his party lost their ascendency]: "he was convinced, by fatal experi-"ence, that anarchy was a bad step towards a perfect govern-"ment, that the subversion of every establishment was no "safe foundation for a permanent and regular constitution; "he found that pretences of reform were held up by the "designing to dazzle the eyes of the unwary, &c.; he found, "in short, that reformation by popular insurrection must "end in the destruction, and cannot tend to the formation, "of a regular government." After a good deal more of this well-meaning cant, the Introduction concludes with the following sentence—the writer is addressing the Reformers of 1793, amongst whom "both leaders and followers," he says, "may together reflect that upon speculative and "visionary reformers" [*i.e.* those of 1640] "the severest "punishment which God in his vengeance ever yet inflicted "was to curse them with the complete gratification of their "own inordinate desires." I quote this passage not as containing anything singular, but for the very reason that it is *not* singular: it expresses, in fact, the universal opinion: notwithstanding which, I am happy to say that it is false. What "complete gratification of their own desires" was ever granted to the "reformers" in question? On the contrary, it is well known (and no book illustrates that particular fact so well as Sir William Waller's) that as early as 1647 the Army had too effectually subverted the just relations between itself and Parliament not to have suggested fearful anticipations to all discerning patriots of that unhappy issue which did in reality blight their prospects. And, when I speak of

markable men. Sir Hardress had no conscience at all; Sir William a very scrupulous one; which, however, he was for ever tampering with, and generally succeeded in reducing into compliance with his immediate interest. He was, however, an accomplished gentleman, and, as a man of talents, worthy of the highest admiration. [The book from which De Quincey quotes is *Vindication of the character and conduct of Sir William Waller, Knight, Commander-in-Chief of the Parliamentary Forces in the West: explanatory of his conduct in taking up arms against King Charles the First: written by himself, and now first published from the original manuscript, with an Introduction by the Editor: London*, 1793.—M.]

an "unhappy issue," I would be understood only of the immediate issue: for the remote issue was the Revolution of 1688, as I have already asserted. Neither is it true that even the immediate issue was "unhappy" to any extent which can justify the ordinary language in which it is described. Here, again, is a world of delusions. We hear of "anarchy," of "confusions," of "proscriptions," of "bloody and ferocious tyranny." All is romance: there was no anarchy, no confusions, no proscriptions, no tyranny, in the sense designed. The sequestrations, forfeitures, and punishments of all sorts which were inflicted by the conquering party on their antagonists went on by due course of law; and the summary justice of courts-martial was not resorted to in England. Except for the short term of the two wars, and the brief intermediate campaign of 1648, the country was in a very tranquil state. Nobody was punished without an open trial; and all trials proceeded in the regular course according, in the ancient forms, and in the regular courts of justice. And, as to "tyranny,"—which is meant chiefly of the acts of Cromwell's government,—it should be remembered that the Protectorate lasted only a quarter of the period in question (1640-1660): a fact which is constantly forgotten even by very eminent writers, who speak as though Cromwell had drawn his sword in January 1640, cut off the king's head, instantly mounted his throne, and continued to play the tyrant for the whole remaining period of his life. Secondly, as to the *kind* of tyranny which Cromwell exercised, the misconception is ludicrous. Continental writers have a notion, well justified by the language of English writers, that Cromwell was a ferocious savage, who built his palace of human skulls and desolated his country. Meantime, he was simply a strong-minded, rough-built Englishman, with a character thoroughly English, and exceedingly good-natured. Gray valued himself upon his critical knowledge of English History; yet how thoughtlessly does he express the abstract of Cromwell's life in the line on the village Cromwell,—"*some Cromwell, guiltless of his country's blood*"! How was Cromwell guilty of his country's blood? What blood did he cause to be shed? A great deal was shed, no doubt, in the wars (though less, by the way, than is imagined): but in those Cromwell was but a servant of the Parliament; and no one will allege that he had any hand in causing a single war. After he attained the sovereign power no more domestic wars arose: and, as to a few persons who were executed for plots and conspiracies against his person, they were condemned upon evidence openly given and by due course of law. With respect to the general character of his government, it is evident that, in the unsettled and revolutionary state of things which follows a civil war, some critical cases will arise to demand an occasional "vigour beyond the law"—such as the Roman government allowed in allowing the dictatorial power. But in general Cromwell's government was limited by law: and no reign in that century prior to the Revolution furnishes fewer instances of attempts to tamper with the laws, to overrule them, to twist them to private interpretations, or to dispense with them. As to his major-generals of counties, who figure in most histories of England as so many *Ali Pachas* that impaled a few prisoners every morning before breakfast,—or rather as so many ogres that ate up good Christian men, women, and children alive,—they were disagreeable people, who were disliked much in the same way as our commissioners of the income-tax were disliked in the memory of us all; and heartily they would have laughed at the romantic and bloody masquerade in which they are made to figure in the English histories. What, then, was the "tyranny" of Cromwell's government which was confessedly complained of even in those days? The word "tyranny" was then applied not so much to the mode in which his power was administered (except by the prejudiced) as to its origin. However mercifully a man may reign, yet, if he have no right to reign at all, we may in one sense call him a tyrant: his power not being justly derived, and resting upon an unlawful (*i.e.* a military) basis. As a usurper, and one who had diverted the current of a grand national movement to selfish and personal objects, Cromwell was and will be called a tyrant; but not in the more obvious sense of the word.

Such are the misleading statements which disfigure the History of England in its most important chapter. They mislead by more than a simple error of fact. Those which

I have noticed last involve a moral anachronism; for they convey images of cruelty and barbarism such as could not co-exist with the national civilisation at that time; and whosoever has not corrected this false picture by an acquaintance with the English literature of that age must necessarily image to himself a state of society as rude and uncultured as that which prevailed during the wars of York and Lancaster —*i.e.* about two centuries earlier. But those with which I introduced this article are still worse, because they involve an erroneous view of constitutional history, and a most comprehensive act of ingratitude. The great men of the Long Parliament paid a heavy price for their efforts to purchase for their descendants a barrier to irresponsible power and security from the anarchy of undefined regal prerogative. In these efforts most of them made shipwreck of their own tranquillity and peace; that such sacrifices were made unavailingly (as it must have seemed to themselves), and that few of them lived to see the "good old cause" finally triumphant, does not cancel their claims upon our gratitude, but rather strengthens them by the degree in which it aggravated the difficulty of bearing such sacrifices with patience. But whence come these falsifications of history? I believe from two causes:— first (as I have already said), from the erroneous tone impressed upon the National History by the irritated spirit of the Clergy of the Established Church. To the religious zealotry of those times the Church was the object of especial attack; and its members were naturally exposed to heavy sufferings; hence their successors are indisposed to find any good in a cause which could lead to such a result. It is their manifest right to sympathise with their own order in that day; and in such a case it is almost their duty to be incapable of an entire impartiality. Meantime they have carried this much too far. The Literature of England must always be in a considerable proportion lodged in their hands; and the extensive means thus placed at their disposal for injuriously colouring that important part of history they have used with no modesty or forbearance. There is not a page of the National History, even in its local subdivisions, which they have not stained with the atrabilious hue of their wounded remembrances: hardly a town in England which stood a siege for the King or the Parliament but has some printed memorial of its constancy and its sufferings; and in nine cases out of ten the editor is a clergyman of the Established Church who has contrived to deepen "the sorrow of the time" by the harshness of his commentary. Surely it is high time that the wounds of the seventeenth century should close in the nineteenth, that History should take a more commanding and philosophic station, and that brotherly charity should now lead us to a saner view of constitutional politics, or a saner view of politics to a more comprehensive charity. The other cause of this falsification springs out of a selfishness which has less claim to any indulgence—viz. the timidity with which the English Whigs of former days and the party to whom they [1] succeeded constantly shrank from acknowledging any alliance with the great men of the Long Parliament under the nervous horror of being confounded with the regicides of 1649. It was of such urgent importance to them, for any command over the public support, that they should acquit themselves of any sentiment of lurking toleration for regicide, with which their enemies never failed to load them, that no mode of abjuring it seemed sufficiently emphatic to them. Hence it was that Addison, with a view to the interest of his party, thought fit when in Switzerland to offer a puny insult to the memory of General Ludlow; hence it is that even in our own days no writers have insulted Milton with so much bitterness and shameless irreverence as the Whigs,—though it is true that some few Whigs, more however in their literary than in their political character, have stepped forward in his vindication. At this moment I recollect a passage in the writings of a modern Whig bishop [2]—in which, for the sake of creating a charge of falsehood against Milton, the author has grossly mistranslated a passage in the *Defensio pro Populo Anglicano*: and, if that bishop were not dead, I would here

[1] Until after the year 1688 I do not remember ever to have found the term Whig applied except to the religious characteristics of that party; whatever reference it might have to their political distinctions was only secondary and by implication.

[2] Watson, Bishop of Llandaff. [For De Quincey's full account of him see *ante*, Vol. II, pp. 194-203.—M.]

take the liberty of rapping his knuckles,—were it only for breaking Priscian's head.

To return to the clerical feud against the Long Parliament:—It was a passage in a very pleasing work of this day (*Ecclesiastical Biography*) which suggested to me the whole of what I have now written. Its learned editor (Doctor Wordsworth, brother of the great poet), who is incapable of uncandid feelings except in what concerns the interests of his order, has adopted the usual tone in regard to the men of 1640 throughout his otherwise valuable annotations; and somewhere or other (in the life of Hammond, according to my remembrance) he has made a statement to this effect,—that the custom prevalent among children in that age of asking their parents' blessing was probably first brought into disuse by the Puritans. Is it possible to imagine a perversity of prejudice more unreasonable? The unamiable side of the patriotic character in the seventeenth century was unquestionably its religious bigotry; which, however, had its ground in a real fervour of religious feeling and a real strength of religious principle somewhat exceeding the ordinary standard of the nineteenth century. But, however palliated, their bigotry is not to be denied; it was often offensive from its excess, and ludicrous in its direction. Many harmless customs, many ceremonies and rituals that had a high positive value, their frantic intolerance quarrelled with; and, for my part, I heartily join in the sentiment of Charles II—applying it as *he* did, but a good deal more extensively—that *their* religion "was not a religion for a gentleman." Indeed, all sectarianism, but especially that which has a modern origin—arising and growing up within our own memories, unsupported by a grand traditional history of persecutions, conflicts, and martyrdoms,—lurking, moreover, in blind alleys, holes, corners, and tabernacles,—must appear spurious and mean in the eyes of him who has been bred up in the grand classic forms of the Church of England or the Church of Rome. But, because the bigotry of the Puritans was excessive and revolting, is *that* a reason for fastening upon them all the stray evils of omission or commission for which no distinct fathers can be found? The learned editor does not pretend that there is any positive evidence, or presumption even, for imputing to the Puritans a dislike to the custom in question ; but, because he thinks it a good custom, his inference is that nobody could have abolished it but the Puritans. Now, who does not see that, if this had been amongst the usages discountenanced by the Puritans, it would on that account have been the more pertinaciously maintained by their enemies in Church and State? Or, even if this usage were of a nature to be prohibited by authority, —as the public use of the liturgy, organs, surplices, &c.,— who does not see that with regard to *that*, as well as to other Puritanical innovations, there would have been a reflux of zeal at the restoration of the King which would have established them in more strength than ever? But it is evident to the unprejudiced that the usage in question gradually went out in submission to the altered spirit of the times. It was one feature of a general system of manners fitted by its piety and simplicity for a pious and simple age, and which therefore even the seventeenth century had already outgrown. It is not to be inferred that filial affection and reverence have decayed amongst us because they no longer express themselves in the same way. In an age of imperfect culture all passions and emotions are in a more elementary state—speak a plainer language—and express themselves *externally*: in such an age the frame and constitution of society is more picturesque ; the modes of life rest more undisguisedly upon the basis of the absolute and original relations of things. The son is considered in his sonship, the father in his fatherhood; and the manners take an appropriate colouring. Up to the middle of the seventeenth century there were many families in which the children never presumed to sit down in their parents' presence. But with us, in an age of more complete intellectual culture, a thick disguise is spread over the naked foundations of human life; and the instincts of good taste banish from good company the expression of all the profounder emotions. A son, therefore, who should kneel down in this age to ask his papa's blessing on leaving town for Brighton or Bath would be felt by himself to be making a theatrical display of filial duty, such as would be painful to him in proportion as his feelings were sincere. All this would have been evident to the learned editor in any case but one which regarded the Puritans. *They* were, at any rate, to be molested ; in default of any graver matter, a mere fanciful grievance is searched out. Still, however, nothing was effected ; fanciful or real, the grievance must be connected with the Puritans : here lies the offence, there lie the Puritans : it would be very agreeable to find some means of connecting the one with the other ; but how shall this be done ? Why, in default of all other means, the learned editor *assumes* the connexion. He leaves the reader with an impression that the Puritans are chargeable with a serious wound to the manners of the nation in a point affecting the most awful of the household charities ; and he fails to perceive that for this whole charge his sole ground is that it would be very agreeable to him if he *had* a ground. Such is the power of the *esprit de corps* to palliate and recommend as colourable the very weakest logic to a man of acknowledged learning and talent !

In conclusion, I must again disclaim any want of veneration and entire affection for the Established Church. The very prejudices and injustice with which I tax the English Clergy have a generous origin ; but it is right to point the attention of historical students to their strength and the effect which they have had. They have been indulged to excess ; they have disfigured the grandest page in English History ; they have hid the true descent and tradition of our constitutional history ; and, by impressing upon the literature of the country a false conception of the patriotic party in and out of Parliament, they have stood in the way of a great work,—a work which, according to my ideal of it, would be the most useful that could just now be dedicated to the English public,—viz. *a Philosophic Record of the Revolutions of English History.* The English Constitution, as proclaimed and ratified (but not created) in 1688-9, is in its kind the noblest work of the human mind working in conjunction with Time, and what in such a case we may allowably call Providence. Of this *chef d'œuvre* of human wisdom it were desirable that we should have a proportionable history. For such a history the great positive qualification would be a philosophic mind : the great negative qualification would be this (which to the Established Clergy may now be recommended as a fit subject for their magnanimity),—viz. complete conquest over those prejudices which have hitherto discoloured the greatest era of patriotic virtue by contemplating the great men of that era under their least happy aspect,—namely, in relation to the Established Church.

Now that I am on the subject of English History, I will notice one of the thousand misstatements of Hume, which becomes a memorable one from the stress which he has laid upon it, and from the manner and situation in which he has introduced it. Standing in the current of a narrative, it would have merited a silent correction in an unpretending note. But it occupies a much more assuming station ; for it is introduced in a philosophical essay ; and, being relied on for a particular purpose with the most unqualified confidence, and being alleged in opposition to the very highest authority (viz. the authority of an eminent person contemporary with the fact), it must be looked on as involving a peremptory defiance to all succeeding critics who might hesitate between the authority of Mr. Hume, at the distance of a century from the facts, and Sir William Temple, speaking to them on a matter within his personal recollections.

Sir William Temple had represented himself as urging, in a conversation with Charles II, the hopelessness of any attempt on the part of an English king to make himself a despotic and absolute monarch, except, indeed, through the affections of his people.[1] This general thesis he had supported by a variety of arguments ; and, amongst others, he had described himself as urging this, that even Cromwell had been unable to establish himself in unlimited power, though supported by a military force of *eighty thousand men.* Upon this Hume calls the reader's attention to the extreme improbability which there must beforehand appear to be in supposing that Sir W. Temple,—speaking of so recent a case, with so much official knowledge of that case at his command, uncontradicted moreover by the king, whose side in the argument gave him

[1] Sir William had quoted to Charles a saying from Gourville (a Frenchman whom the King esteemed, and whom Sir William himself considered the only foreigner he had ever known that understood England) to this effect : "That a king of England who will be the man of his people is the greatest king in the world ; but, if he will be something more, by G— he is nothing at all."

an interest in contradicting Sir William's statement, and whose means of information were paramount to those of all others,—could under these circumstances be mistaken. Doubtless, the reader will reply to Mr. Hume, the improbability *is* extreme, and scarcely to be invalidated by any possible counter-authority; which, at best, must terminate in leaving an equilibrium of opposing evidence. And yet, says Mr. Hume, Sir William was unquestionably wrong, and grossly wrong. Cromwell never had an army at all approaching to the number of eighty thousand. Now, here is a sufficient proof that Hume had never read Lord Clarendon's account of his own life. This book is not so common as his *History of the Rebellion*; and Hume had either not met with it, or had neglected it. For, in the early part of this work, Lord Clarendon, speaking of the army which was assembled on Blackheath to welcome the return of Charles II, says that it amounted to fifty thousand men; and, when it is remembered that this army was exclusive of the troops in all garrisons—of the forces (six thousand at least) left by Monk in Scotland, and, above all, of the entire army in Ireland—it cannot be doubted that the whole would amount to the number stated by Sir William Temple. Indeed, Charles II himself, in the year 1678 (*i.e.* about four years after this conversation), as Sir W. Temple elsewhere tells us, "in six weeks' time raised an army of twenty thousand men, "the completest, and in all appearance the bravest, troops "that could be anywhere seen, and might have raised many "more; and it was confessed by all the Foreign Ministers "that no king in Christendom could have made and com- "pleted such a levy as this appeared in such a time." William III, again, about eleven years afterwards, raised twenty-three regiments with the same ease and in the same space of six weeks.

It may be objected indeed to such cases, as in fact it *was* objected to the case of William III by Howlett in his sensible *Examination of Dr. Price's Essay on the Population of England*, that, in an age when manufactures were so little extended, it could never have been difficult to make such a levy of men, provided there were funds for paying and equipping them. But, considering the extraordinary funds which were disposable for this purpose in Ireland, &c., during the period of Cromwell's Protectorate, we may very safely allow the combined authority of Sir William Temple, of the King, and of that very prime minister (Clarendon) who disbanded Cromwell's army, to outweigh the single authority of Hume at the distance of a century from the facts. Upon any question of fact, indeed, Hume's authority is none at all; for he never pretended to any research.[1]

[1] The words "for he never pretended to any research" are an addition in the reprint of the paper in 1859.—M.

# A TORY'S ACCOUNT

OF

# TORYISM, WHIGGISM, AND RADICALISM

## IN A LETTER TO A FRIEND IN BENGAL [1]

NEVER yet did a great country more plainly stand in the circumstances of a crisis—vast, rapid, and decisive—than the England of 1835. So much is evident to you in India, as to us on the spot.

"England," you say, in one of your last letters, "stands, or seems to stand, on the threshold of great changes; nay—were it not that such a word is full of sorrow, and is, in a Roman sense, *abominable*—of great revolutions." And you ask, "Are the people of England aware of this?" Imperfectly, I believe, they are. In a spirit of hope, or of fear, according to their several positions, all men are now looking with intense interest upon the great political forces which are gathering and getting into motion amongst us; and with a certain anticipation of some portentous births in which they are to issue. There is no slackness of interest amongst us; but to some of us it seems that this interest is not of the right quality,—that it is too much an interest of curiosity, and as if attached to mere scenical changes. You remember the case of that Frenchman who, at an early stage of the French

[1] Published originally in *Tait's Edinburgh Magazine* for December 1835 and January 1836 in the manner described in the Preface: first reprinted in 1863 in vol. xv of Messrs. Black's revised issue of De Quincey's Collective Edition.—M.

Revolution, wished earnestly for a prolongation of his life, on no higher interest than that of a novel-reader,—in order, viz., to know "*how it would end.*" The novel had then advanced no farther than the second or third chapter : even the hero was doubtful ; or, perhaps, he had not yet been introduced. We who live now are aware that, in fact, he had *not.* We have read the novel to its *dénouement* ; and we know that the true hero of the French Revolution did not, in a proper sense, come forward until the year 1796. We have seen his rising, his culmination, and his setting ; and the singular effect to us, from the utter abolition of the whole system which he created, and the perfect obliteration of its whole *personal* memorials, is—a sense of unreality, of phantom life, as if all had been no more than a gay pageantry in the clouds. This by the way.

But, returning to the Frenchman, *his* feeling was a natural one—yet surely unworthy of a patriotic heart, and below the dignity of the occasion. Ours is somewhat more mixed. We do not all look upon our prospects from this station of neutral curiosity: some of us have an interest of fear the profoundest ; but it is the fear of fascination. The rattlesnake has his eye upon us, and has mastered our volitions. The times to us seem already pregnant with great events, which must, by a natural necessity, travel onward to the birth, whether the throes of labour be severe or light, and spite of all that *we* can offer of hindrances from without. Hence it is that we are all passive and acquiescent,—not in a spirit of sympathy or toleration, but of utter despondency and of hopeless abhorrence. There is but one powerful will amongst us, one indomitable will: Mr. O'Connell, only, represents the absolute and the unconditional ;—all others are temporisers, waiters upon occasion and opportunity, compromisers, oscillators. And, according to all human appearances, this one quality of demoniac energy, and a Titan strength of purpose, imperturbable and remorseless, will prevail,—will triumph finally over all opposition from mere talents, though they should be a thousand times superior, and over all interests, the plainest and the largest, that are not equally cemented into unity. In saying this, I judge upon a large basis of observation ; and, more especially, I think myself entitled to draw an indication of the future from the sort of support lately given to Sir Robert Peel. Do I subscribe, then, to the partisan statements, — that the addresses to that minister were *hole-and-corner* addresses? Far from it. Seven or eight hundred addresses, bearing on an average twelve hundred signatures (which I have reason to think a moderate assumption), will represent the feelings of nearly a million male adults, or perhaps of eight hundred thousand families; deducting, therefore, four millions of the British population from the opponents of Sir Robert Peel's policy,—whilst, on the scale of respectability, whether tried by property or education, these four millions may stand over against all the rest of the nation, as an adequate and countervailing balance. But, be that as it may,—whether less or more numerically, whether less or more in significance and value,—the support was not what it should have been. The earthly is ill-matched against the demoniac; neither can the blows of fanaticism be parried by weapons tempered in the armouries of fear or of prudential caution. Therefore—if the past were at all to be relied upon as representative of the future—therefore, I should say, Despair! to all who partake my views. Hope there is none under such tactics, opposed to such an enemy.

But I come now to the business of my letter. You demand of me that I should give an account of my creed and profession as a Tory; that I should explain, as fully as possible, what *is* Toryism; what it has been generally understood to mean in past times, and what it means now; what are its relations to Whiggism; what are their joint relations to the new creed of Radicalism; and what are the several powers, pretensions, and prospects of all three, as governing principles of action amongst the people of England, and in the national councils.

The questions you have here proposed teem with confusions; many more have been artificially nursed or propagated by the press. On that subject, one word beforehand.

The newspapers, and other political journals of this country, are conducted with extraordinary talent, — with more, in fact, than was ever before applied in any nation to the same function of public teaching. Indeed, without talent of a high order, and without a variety of talent, it would be a mere impossibility that an English journal should sustain its existence. Perhaps it would be impossible to show any exception to the rule; unless in the rare case where a provincial newspaper has inherited from a past generation a sort of monopoly, or privilege of precedency, as a depository of advertisements. Advertisers go where they have been used to go, on a certain knowledge that readers interested in advertisements will, by a reciprocal necessity, go where advertisements are most sure to be found; and, therefore, a monopoly of this nature is most secure where it is most intense. But, allowing for this single exception, the political press of England has so much more than its fair proportion of natural talent that, for thirty years and upwards, it has even acted injuriously upon the literature of the country, by impressing too exclusive direction upon the marketable talent of the young and the aspiring. Other modes of intellectual exercise have been starved or impoverished, that this might flourish exorbitantly; and the result is that never amongst men has there been an exhibition of so much energy, vigilance, sagacity, perseverance, as we of this day behold in our political press. This is our Briareus,—this is our sole Briareus. But their qualities of honour and good feeling do not keep pace with their ability. An American spirit of violence and brutality is gaining ground in our public press; and that is a spirit which soon diffuses itself. Even in private disputes, where one party is violent, personal, overbearing, rapid, and visibly on the fret to interrupt at every moment, the wisest and the coolest feel it difficult to resist the contagion of the case. My party, therefore, if it does not already, very soon *will* adopt the tone of its antagonists. At present, it seems to me that the violence which I complain of, the rancorous hatred, and the utter abolition of candour, are chiefly conspicuous amongst our opponents; and not without adequate motives. The Tories are exposed to the combined attacks of Whigs and Radicals; whereas either of these parties has but a single enemy to face. Moreover, the Tories are the sole obstacle in the path of the Radicals. The Whigs are the objects of their contempt; the Whigs are in their grasp; that party cannot move a step, neither win nor retain office, nor carry any one great public measure, without the support of the Radicals,—or, in many cases, without the forbearance of the Tories. This is known on both sides: the tone of mortification and internal despondency is visible in every act of the Whigs,—the drooping tone of men trading confessedly upon other people's funds and other people's credit: whilst the Radicals wear the erect and cheerful air of men confident in their own resources; borrowing nothing, owing nothing; having no exposures to fear, no ultimate defeats to face; the sole question for them being as to the particular point at which their victories will stop. Meantime, the Whigs wreak their embittered feelings upon *us*. For it cannot be denied that the Tories were they who, by excluding the Whigs from office for half a century, drove them into the necessity of an alliance with the Radicals. The price paid down was the Reform Bill; and there the Whigs hoped to have stopped. But the Radicals have made them sensible that this is no more than a means, and, as a means, even not yet effectual without further amendments and collateral aids. These, and the whole train of ends to which the improved means will be applied, now open upon the gaze of the Whig party like the never-ending line of Banquo. Their co-operation will be exacted in the warfare at hand upon these great questions down to the final battle. The Radicals know their allies: suspect them they do not; for the treachery which is in their hearts has been put on record by many overt acts in and out of Parliament, and is, besides, involved in their very circumstances as a part of the aristocracy. But, if they venture to act upon their secret wishes, to falter, or hang back,—then the Radicals know their power, and the instantaneousness of that absolute redress which they can apply. This existence for a party so properly *precarious*, hanging upon entreaty and sufferance, is humiliating. It is natural that this humiliation should revenge itself upon those who were indirectly the authors of it. As against the Whigs, therefore, I see no reason that the Tories should much complain of the scurrilities pointed at their name and party. But in the Radicals this tone has surprised me. Take, for instance, "The Examiner" newspaper. Two things I used to admire in that journal,—its extraordinary talent, and its integrity.[1] This latter quality I am now compelled to doubt, —or, at least, I see that it is capable of descending to political tricks, and to what is commonly felt to be a mode of intriguing,—when I find him affecting a confidence in Whigs, and an exultation in their restoration to power, which his whole public existence proves that he cannot really entertain. It is convenient to dissemble at this moment; and he does so. But, formerly, I gave himself and his party credit for as little choosing as, in fact, they needed, to dissemble. To him I know that the difference between Whigs and Tories is as the difference between aristocratic anti-reformers who disguise their principles and who do not disguise them. And, besides this general charge against "The Examiner," as irreconcilable with that high-minded candour and frankness which conscious strength enables his party to maintain, I complain of two other offences against that spirit of honour which he *might* profess:—1*st*, The adoption of that practice so common and excusable in lower journals, of ascribing to the Tory party, as principles, many rules of action which they would themselves universally disavow; 2*dly*, The habit of stating great public questions as lying between a party and the nation, when it is notorious that they lie between the nation and itself, as divided upon different principles, and in proportions which no man of sense would undertake to compute.

Now, addressing myself to this large question you have proposed, of Toryism, its nature and grounds, its several aspects, and its future fortunes, according to all present and apparent probabilities, — I shall begin by affirming that Toryism, in its widest sense, stands in three capital relations, perfectly distinct and independent: one permanent, which dates from its origin, and is co-essential with itself; one accidental, dating from the French Revolution; and one of recent birth, not accidental, but derivative, and arising in the way of inference from its own distinguishing principles. The first relation is that which Toryism bears to the British

[1] During the palmy days of this celebrated London weekly newspaper, *The Examiner*, it was edited by Mr. Albany Fonblanque (1793-1872). A selection of his political articles in it was published in 1837 in three volumes, with the title *England under Seven Administrations*.—M.

Constitution, and which is otherwise expressed by its relation to Whiggism considered as a body of political principles. The second is that which Toryism bears to Whiggism, as a mode of partisanship or party policy, the modern aspects of which point chiefly to the French Revolution, and to the great foreign questions arising out of that event. The third relation of Toryism is that which it bears to the new doctrines of Radical Reformers, or of that section amongst political men denominated the *Movement* party; and this relation is in no respect capricious, or matter of accident, inasmuch as it grows inevitably, and by way of logical deduction, from the differential principles of its own peculiar creed.

Great confusion, the very greatest, has arisen from neglecting to draw the line sharply between these several aspects of Toryism; and, were it only for the sake of accurate thinking, I might be excused for dwelling a little on these primary distinctions, and pointing your attention to the consequences which attend them in our practical judgments, whether upon things or persons. But, for the particular task which I have undertaken,—the task of unfolding, and also of valuing, the true meaning and tendencies of Toryism,—this preliminary attempt to clear the ground is a *conditio sine qua non* towards any possible success. Many things are true of Toryism, or have a meaning, at least, when said of Toryism in one phasis, which are false or inconsistent, or without a plausible sense, when said of it in another. Political rancour, indeed, and the blindness of partisanship in moments of strong excitement, are daily betraying men into a use of the term *Tory* which defeats itself by the very enormity of its latitude. Nothing in human thought or action that happens to be odious to the writer of the moment but is described as being traditionally "Tory,"—"Tory" by its essence, "Tory" by tendency or by prescription. And this licence of use, which at length leaves the word without any distinct meaning at all, is carried into such ludicrous extremities that I have lately read in a London newspaper some alleged pre-occupation of horses and carriages by the party opposed to Lord John Russell in South Devon (baseless in all probability even as a fact) described as "an old Tory trick." The ingenious writer, it is very possible, looks upon ale and brandy, together with the suspicious art of drinking, as originally among the devices of Tory corruption. But graver abuses are practised upon this party term, and by more thoughtful writers. And the same sort of abuses, though not perhaps to the same extent, is practised upon the correlatives, *Whig* and *Radical*: all which abuses are chiefly facilitated by the shifting relations in which they stand, and best evaded by a chronological deduction of the words Whig and Tory from their earliest origin. It has been remarked by a profound scholar that the investigation of religious controversies is best pursued through a regular study of ecclesiastical history; and the same thing holds good of this political investigation. Its clearest historical deduction is the best logical account of its true genesis and its philosophic interpretation.

The British Constitution, which had been unfolding and maturing itself for centuries, obtained its final expansion and its settlement in the seventeenth century. People are apt to forget that a *constitution*—by which I mean the equilibrium of forces in a political system, as recognised and fixed by distinct public acts—cannot advance faster than civilization: each is bound to the motions of the other; for the political forces cannot be adjusted to each other until those forces are finally developed. Now, what great change was silently going on in this country throughout the Tudor reigns? What civil forces were then gradually evolving? These in particular: a new distribution of landed wealth, and a gentry. Upon the basis of two great changes—1*st*, the breaking down of the feudal aristocracy by Henry VII, 2*d*, the breaking down of the church aristocracy by his son—that mighty revolution was effected for England in particular which Harrington has propounded in his "Oceana"[1] as universally the determining ground of power.[2] Civil power

[1] James Harrington (1611-1677), author of *Oceana*, a famous treatise of speculative politics, published in 1656, and dedicated to Cromwell, then Lord Protector.—M.

[2] And, by the way, *another* revolution was then silently prepared, upon the cause of which there has been much disputing without result; simply because one cause only was assigned, when in fact there were two. Mr. Bulwer, of late ("England and the English"), Lord Auckland many years ago, and numbers beside, have ridiculed those who deduce English pauperism from the suppression of the

and its equilibrium, says Harrington, is determined solely by the distribution of the landed balance ; where *that* is placed, there is placed the power. Gradually, therefore, the power, because gradually the land, had been slipping down from the

monasteries. *Early* in the reign of Henry VIII, says Mr. Bulwer, and therefore *before* the dissolution of these religious houses, there are, in express laws and elsewhere, indications of pauperism. Certainly, pauperism, as a national disease, *began* in the previous reign. Latimer alone, writing in Edward VI's time,—an author upon whom elsewhere Mr. Bulwer relies,—complains heavily of the extensive depopulations in progress for some time back. There, where formerly flourished a populous village, we find now-a-days a single shepherd boy or two, tending large flocks of sheep ! I quote his meaning, though not his exact words, not having his sermons at hand. Now, it is clear to any reflecting reader that, on the one hand, these changes must have been going on through one or two generations previous to the date of Latimer's sermons,—which suppose 1550 ; otherwise they could not have been so extensively accomplished as the very nature of his complaint implies. Yet, on the other hand, it is equally clear that Latimer points in these complaints to a state of things still within the memory of his elder auditors ; he is making his comparison between a vicious present (as *he* views it) and a happier past. But the transition he denounces as even then going on, and the two states then equally under the cognisance of the existing generation. For it could not have answered any purpose to fix the eyes of man upon some Arcadian condition of remote ages, or of merely possible prosperity. Latimer is manifestly bemoaning a revolution yet raw and unreconciled, —one which had passed within the knowledge of those to whom he appealed,—which was in fact still going onwards. In one place he dates the change expressly from his grandfather's time. The case, therefore, tells its own history. Henry VII had operated upon the feudal habits of the aristocracy by two separate acts : 1*st*, By abolishing the long trains of martial retainers ; 2*dly*, By removing the bars to the alienation and subdivision of landed estates. These two acts aided each other. The nobility, finding no benefits of feudal pomp in a large body of dependants,—these being now by law rendered utterly useless for show or for defence,—began necessarily to seek some countervailing benefits from the territorial domains hitherto applied to the support of a vast retinue now suddenly made unavailable by law. Lands were now applied to the purposes prescribed by rural economy. Many were consequently turned into sheep walks ; and those which were otherwise applied, as for instance to agriculture, were still able to disencumber themselves of a large surplus population. The economic use of land had now superseded the feudal use. The *maximum* of produce from the *minimum* of labour had now become the problem for all land whatsoever. And, as the produce, thus continually increasing, with a continually decreasing amount of labour, could no longer be consumed in kind, hence arose a con-

hands of the high nobility and the church, where originally it was concentrated, into those of a new order, having new political relations,—viz. a gentry. This class was chiefly a growth of the Tudor days; indeed, for three parts in four, of Queen Elizabeth's days. Strange it is to contemplate the gentry of her reign as represented by its *élite* in the House of Commons. The honest burgesses of that House—still entitled to wages, and timid, even to servility, in the presence of the Upper House—before the throne crouched with almost Oriental prostration. The Queen rated them as she would have done her menial servants. Every attempt at dealing with the foreign policy of the Government was harshly stifled as an intrusion into privileged mysteries; and, strangely enough, the House was repelled from such liberties,—not as beyond their jurisdiction merely, but as beyond their intellectual faculties. Barely, indeed,

tinually greater opening for exotic luxuries. These tastes, with other consequences, formed so many increasing temptations to the alienation of estates, the facilities for which had been prepared concurrently. Upon this breaking up of the great feudal and ecclesiastical estates arose a new order of secondary aristocracy; a gentry, formed in part from the younger brothers of the upper aristocracy, in part from the magnates of towns. That was one effect; but another—that other with which we are now concerned—was that an immense surplus of population was thrown off upon the nation. This formed a stream continually increasing; and, in the following reign, this stream became confluent with another stream from the monasteries. And these two bodies of surplus population, making, perhaps, not less than 350,000 souls in a total population of nearly 5,000,000, composed the original *fundus* of the pauperism for which Elizabeth provided: first, by a crude law in the beginning of her reign; secondly, by an improved law towards the close of it—which last law has ever since formed the basis of our pauper code, Those who have read the book of Lord Selkirk, published about thirty years ago [*Observations on the Present State of the Highlands of Scotland by Thomas Douglas, Earl of Selkirk*, 1805.—M.], are aware that the very same process was repeated in the Scottish Highlands after the rebellion of 1745-6, and the abolition of the heritable jurisdictions. Martial retainers, and the very purpose to which only they could be applied,—viz. feudal quarrels,—were then severely and resolutely put down by Government; forts were built, military roads opened, permanent garrisons established, to enforce the new policy of a Government at once strong and enlightened, provident and vindictive. The chieftains, like the English nobles, were obliged to seek a new use in their retainers; which use, it was soon found, could be better attained from the tenth

did the House, in its collective capacity, venture to raise its eyes beyond the latchet of the Queen's slipper, except only in the two cases of religion or of money. These were transcendent cases; for the direct service of God, or the immediate money interests of the whole nation, seemed to raise a case of duty on a level with that which they owed to the crown. But no *indirect* interest, either of the altar or the hearth, was held to constitute a privileged or even excusable case for remonstrance. Such was the abject condition of the Commons' House through the long reign of the last Tudor. The gentry were then in the process of growth; but, as yet, their strength was neither matured nor consciously made known. Now, leap over the entire reign of her successor, the first Stuart, during which things were in struggle; and pass, by a rapid transition, to the Parliaments convoked about the middle of the first

than from the whole. Πλεον ἡμισυ παντος. The nine-tenths were therefore turned adrift. In Scotland, as previously in England, it took about two generations to bring the principle into full play; for the lords, as also the chieftains, were variously situated, and were of various tempers; some catching eagerly, and from the first, at the utmost gain; others hankering to the last after their ancient usages and their hereditary pomp. So far the cases were the same in England and in Scotland. But one capital difference arose from the general circumstances of the country. After 1745 there was an outlet for all the surplus Scotch Highlanders in the British colonies; and, accordingly, Lord Selkirk himself turned a strong current of emigration into Prince Edward Island in the Gulf of St. Lawrence, and afterwards, when that island was sufficiently colonised, into the Canadas. But for England, during the sixty years of Henry VII and Henry VIII (1485-1545), there was no outlet whatever. The whole surplus was thrown back upon the domestic resources of the land. And, doubtless, many a fierce retainer, as also many a big-boned monk, was to be found amongst those "masterful beggars," "stout thieves," and "Abraham men," who plagued our ancestors so much during the sixteenth century, and were so plentifully and so frivolously hanged. This deduction of pauperism, though collateral to my main purpose, I have thought it right to give; because the subject is so much of a *quæstio vexata*; because no party has hit upon the whole truth; because that solution to which Mr. Bulwer and others object is half the truth; and because the previous and the confluent cause, which I now allege, makes the complement, or other half of the truth. The paupers of England arose out of two acts emanating from Henry VII, as well as from that single act of his son which, doubtless, taken by itself, is insufficient to meet the case.

Charles's reign. The effect is like that of a pantomime. From a House of Commons as homely and as humble as a *Storthing* of Norway, composed of farmers, village leaders of vestries, and illiterate attorneys, or procurators for the narrowest local interests, time and political growth have brought us to a brilliant and enlightened assembly, renewing the image of a Roman Senate, and claiming a jurisdiction co-extensive with the affairs of Christendom. What was it that had worked the change? The growth of a new order. A gentry had been gradually reared. Taking advantage of the opportunities which had first arisen in the jealousy directed to the great baronial landholders by Henry VII, which had since been favoured by the spirit of the law courts, and by the legal fictions in subversion of entails, and which had subsequently been greatly promoted by the distribution of the church lands—a new class had silently developed itself in the course of about one century; and the great political value of that revolution lay in this, that the new class was essentially a middle class, having relations downwards as well as upwards, and common interests connecting them with the order below them as well as that above them. Hitherto the only phantom of a middle class had been confined to towns; and it was a class most imperfectly adapted to the functions of a middle order, being in violent repulsion to the landed interest, and narrow in its powers. But this new order of landed gentry was diffused over the face of the country, and, for the first time, effected a real cohesion between all the forces of the state, by filling up the gulf which had divided hitherto the aristocracy from the commonalty, and the interests of real from those of movable property.

Such was the great, though silent, revolution which had been travelling forwards through the sixteenth century, and which in the early part of the seventeenth (from 1625 to 1640) might be said to have reached its consummation. And this revolution it was which produced (as I will for ever affirm) the great civil war, properly called the *Parliamentary War*. A new and most powerful order in the land instinctively called for new powers, and for a new position amongst the ruling forces of the State. The House of

Commons was then ripe for assuming that place as a legislative body, and also as a controlling body over the acts of the executive, which it possesses at this day. But Charles and his counsellors—imperfectly aware of the great revolution effected in the equilibrium of the political forces, simply because it had been effected gradually and not violently, and reading History in a superstitious spirit—insisted upon adhering to the old usages of his predecessors, when many capital resemblances of the cases had vanished, except for the external forms. Charles was conscientious in his obstinacy, for he did no more than tread in the very footsteps of the most popular and glorious amongst his immediate predecessors, and, where all the names continued the same, it was hard to perceive that the things had essentially altered. It is also to be added that, even if Charles had been persuaded into conceding to the House of Commons those extended powers which they claimed, this concession would not have reached the necessity of the case; for his policy was to adjourn the Parliament after the shortest possible session, so that no improved powers would have been available without a violent invasion of the royal prerogative. And, in fact, we know that this violence was one of the earliest acts of the great Parliament which met in November 1640. They were obliged to exact of the king a promise that he would not dissolve them. A twofold defect oppressed the House—defect of power, and defect of duration.

From this review of the political changes between Henry VII and the Parliamentary War, a theory arises with respect to that great event different from any which has been adopted hitherto. Hume, and all other writers, have argued the case as though one of the two parties were necessarily in the wrong, and in the wrong upon the whole question at issue. They say, therefore, continually "This is unlawful" and "That was unconstitutional." But, in fact, neither party was in the wrong, essentially. The forms of the constitution, so far as any constitution had then been developed, were generally with the King; and, as to the spirit of the constitution,—a difficult point to ascertain at any time,—it would be too much to expect that it should be philosophically abstracted, and valued, and applied, between two interested and impassioned disputants. But I affirm that, in fact, the constitution did not as yet exist as a whole. It existed by parts, and in tendencies then bursting into life; it was, and had been for a century back, in progress—in a progress continually accelerated; but it was not until the latter half of the seventeenth century that it was matured.

In reality, it is manifest that, until all the parts of a machine exist, the law or principle of that machine cannot be stated. And, whilst as yet the different orders of English society were not perfectly developed, it must be impossible to talk of a constitution which expresses their mutual relations. Now, I have been insisting that the English gentry, the order which furnishes its *materiel* to the House of Commons, did not complete its development until the beginning of the seventeenth century, and that, even after this event might be viewed as accomplished, it had yet to get itself recognised for what it was in the State. The House of Commons, which was its sole organ, was a most inadequate organ,—suited to the old functions of that body which filled it, but not to the new functions of a regenerated order, which had gradually moulded itself out of the ruins projected from the explosion of two great territorial bodies. The new creation could not incarnate itself (so to speak) in the old and imperfect organization. This seemed to be rebellion and wilful revolution; whilst, in fact, it was the mere instinct of growth. No provision had been made (how should it, unless prophetically?) for the due action of the new order by the existing constitution,—because the constitution itself was a growing thing and waiting for its expansion, whereas Charles viewed it as a perfect whole long since matured. Hence arose a war, and almost, for wise men, we might say, a necessity for a war.

Out of that war arose two great results. And it is the more necessary to direct the attention to them because a common notion has prevailed that the whole acts of the Long Parliament, and all that was gained by the Parliamentary War, were cancelled and annulled by certain illegal acts into which some part of the Parliament was afterwards betrayed, and also by the defect of some constitutional forms. This defect could not *but* exist in a struggle between the different powers in the state ; and it has been too pedantically urged by Hume,—and short-sightedly, for it existed on both sides. I say, then, that two great results were obtained by that war, and never again lost. The House of Commons assumed, in Charles the Second's reign, that place for which it fought : even in that reign, and under the reaction of a senseless enthusiasm for the King's person, the House assumed, and steadily maintained, that place of authority and influence which had been refused by Charles I. Nor has it ever lost the ground then won. It has continued to have regular sessions, and to be the great court for transacting the national business,—a function which Charles I. would have sequestered almost entirely into the hands of a Privy Council, or other parts of the executive government. This is one great result. The place and functions of the Commons' House have been ascertained, and according to their own claim ; and not the constitution, as a previous existence, was suffered to prescribe its place and functions to the Commons' House, but, on the contrary, the struggle of the Commons has prescribed its outline to the constitution. The other great result was that the King's place in the constitution has been equally ascertained. Charles the First, it is well known, would not hear of a responsibility attached to the executive, no matter where it might be lodged. He peremptorily forbade his ministers to render any account of their actions, except privately to himself—least of all, to Parliament. And, of course, he did not mean by that act to acknowledge any personal responsibility. *That* he viewed as the last consummation of insolent treason. Neither must you say that this was the idea of a despot ; for even the patriots of those days had very unsteady notions on the extent and true *locus* of the executive responsibility. In particular, the excellent and truly noble-minded wife of Colonel Hutchinson complains of it as a mere courtly adulation that people said "the King could do no wrong." But her descendant and editor reproves her for this,—justly observing that we are deeply indebted to those who first raised up that refined doctrine ; which is, in fact, but another form for saying that we cannot accept of a responsibility lodged in a quarter where delicacy and reverence might often seduce us from enforcing it, but that we must have a real, obvious, available responsibility, liable to no scruples in its exercises, and therefore lodged in a subject. Hence it followed also that the king cannot act by himself—that he must act by ministerial agents,—a doctrine which, by itself alone, has since that day saved the nation, at many a crisis, from civil tumults the most ruinous.

Here, then, are two great features of the British Constitution which could not have pronounced themselves before the seventeenth century. A Commons' House, in adequation to a landed body (not noble, *i.e.* not having an organ in the Upper House), could not be constitutionally defined until the landed body itself had arisen. Neither could the sanctity and inviolability of the sovereign be safely recognised until other principles of ministerial responsibility had been established, which never would have been established unless through these struggles of the Commons. In fact, the King, in our constitution, is a great idea — and a somewhat mysterious idea ; and, universally, it is true that, where two ideas are correlates and antagonist forces, they explain themselves and define themselves at the same time ; for the one is a rebound from the other.

Hence I arrive at one object of this historical deduction, —viz. that the distinction of Whig and Tory, or any distinction which could be fitted for us of this day, in our advanced state of political refinement, could not have arisen sooner than the seventeenth century. It was in reference to the great movements which I have been tracing—movements which smouldered through the sixteenth century, but did not break into flame until the seventeenth — that these party distinctions first arose. They refer to everything most essential in the changes and the settlements that I have been unfolding. There was a prodigious ferment in the first half of the seventeenth century ; in the earlier bisection of the second half there was a general settling or deposition from this ferment. And, as we see now, with respect to the Bonaparte system, that *things* remain whilst *persons* have vanished,—the destruction of the German Empire is ratified, the Legion of Honour still survives, whilst the fleeting agents are almost forgotten,—so of the English political settlements we may affirm that, generally, they are to be traced up to struggles which the generations who have benefited by them would willingly disown. It is true, nevertheless—and in despite of all disowners and protesters—that the English Revolution of 1688-9 did little more than re-affirm, with greater precision, the principles latent in the Parliamentary War. And to those principles it is that the distinctions of Whig and Tory have reference. Indeed, here again is a proof that the Revolution of 1688-9 was only a re-affirmation of principles previously put into action,—that the terms *Whig* and *Tory* arose before that Revolution, and yet were found so sufficient that they continued to be the sole terms in use after the Revolution.

What, then, was the original application of these terms? Let us first inquire into the mere verbal meaning. You are aware that very often indeed denominations are not derived from essential differences, but from accidents. Thus, the *Roundheads* were so named, not from their distinguishing principles, but from the external accident of wearing the hair cut close: that fashion distinguished them at first sight from the Cavaliers, who wore the hair long. The *Jacobins*, again, of our days, derived their name from their place of rendezvous. Now, with respect to *Whig* and *Tory*, it might be expected that two hostile names, pointing to each other, should have arisen at the same moment, and also under the same common aspect; that is, that some common idea should have been chosen from which each name should have been struck off under an opposite relation. But the true history of the case was different: each name arose separately for itself, and possibly in a different place. The word *Tory* had, from the first, a political application. Originally, it designated a particular class of Irish freebooters, and was probably first used in Ireland to express, in a calumnious form, that class of politicians who attributed to the king a right of levying taxes without consent of the subject appearing by his proxy in Parliament. *Whig*, on the other hand, was doubtless first used in Scotland, and applied to the supposed sourness and ascetic temper of the religious dissenters. To *whig*, in the northern counties of England as well as in Scotland, means to turn a thing acid; thus, if you pour milk upon rum, and do it so slowly or so unskilfully as to coagulate the mixture, you are said "to *whig* it." And, by the way, I must here observe, that a derivation given by Sir Walter Scott ("Military Memoirs of the Great Civil War," p. 90, published in 1822) from the word, "*Whig*, to make haste," is mere nonsense. Nonconformists and Puritans of every class were taxed with scowling on the common social enjoyments of the world: that was expressed by calling them the *sours* or *Whigs*, as it were, in the cup of life. It is well known that most of our civil rights were contended for in the seventeenth century under the mask or under the advantage of religious claims: the Dissenters of every class were connected uniformly with the opponents of the existing Government; and by this name, expressive of a churlish unsocial temperament, it seems that they were disparaged. The Duke of Lauderdale, it is probable, transferred the word from Scotland about 1670-5. It there met with the word *Tory*, previously transferred from Ireland; and both were gradually extended and amplified into larger applications, and now, having once come into collision, began reciprocally to receive determinations from each other.[1]

This is my account of the early history of the words, before they had been moulded, by repeated use and reverberation from each other, into direct antagonist terms. Such at length they became; and so much modified they were by long usage that at last they settled into a direct philosophic contra-position, agreeably to their constant acceptation ever since.

This acceptation it is that I am now to explain; and I

[1] The word *Tory*, according to Skeat, is from the Irish *toiridhe*, meaning searcher, plunderer, and is found in that sense in an Irish State Paper of 1656,—"*tories* and other lawless persons." Although De Quincey's derivation of *Whig* is generally accepted and not unplausible, a more exact derivation seems to be that which traces it to *Whiggam*, an old Ayrshire or West of Scotland word or ejaculation of carters to their horses, meaning *Gee-up!* Skeat favours this derivation. "Whig," he says, "is a shortened form of *whiggamor*, applied to certain Scotchmen who came from the west to buy corn at Leith,—from the word *whiggam* employed by these men in driving their horses. A march to Edinburgh made by Argyle [in 1648, in the interest of strict Scottish Presbyterianism] was called the 'Whiggamors' Inroad' ['*Whiggamores' Raid*']; and afterwards those who were opposed to the Court came to be called *Whigs*. The glossary to Sir Walter Scott's novels has: '*whiggamore*, a great Whig; *whigging*, jogging rudely, urging forward.' To *whig awa'* is to jog on briskly."—M.

request your attention to it, as a matter curious in itself, and as one doubly curious from the perpetual blunder which has been made in all attempts at unfolding its latent meaning and relations. Let me sharpen your attention by saying that even Edmund Burke, subtle politician as he is, fell into the common error on this point. A word will explain the case, and rectify all its positions. If I say of two parties that they were Trinitarians and Anti-Trinitarians, you understand at once that both could not be right: one party must be in the wrong. But with respect to *Whig* and *Tory* this does not hold. There is no necessity that either should be in error. On the contrary, there is a high necessity that both should be in the right. For it is not as in a dispute between two contradictory views, where both cannot co-exist, and where either, taken singly, presents a complete and adequate theory of the subject: here the two ideas are so far from excluding each other that both are co-essential to the entire construction of the principle. The meaning of Whig and Tory was finally settled, practically, in the long debates at the Revolution of 1688-9; and, abstracting from the use then and there made of the terms, I am entitled to say that a Whig is he who, in the practical administration of affairs, takes charge of the popular influence, guides it, and supports it; a Tory, on the contrary, is he who takes charge of the antagonist or non-popular influence, guides it, and supports it. There are two great forces at work in the British Constitution; and the Constitution is sustained in its integrity by their equilibrium—just as the compound power which maintains a planet in its orbit is made up of the centripetal force balancing the centrifugal; and as reasonable would it be to insist on the superior efficacy of the centripetal force to the centrifugal, or *vice versa*, as to ascribe any superiority to the Whig or the Tory, considered in their abstract relation to the constitution, or to charge any demerit upon either. Essentially, they represent the total sphere of the constitution, each representing one hemisphere. And, in this view, neither is wrong, nor can be wrong: both are right. And so far from being hostile to each other, each is right only by means of and through his antagonist: for, if the Tory were not, then the Whig would be in the wrong, and so of the Tory in the absence of the Whig. Taken jointly, they make up the total truth. In this relation, therefore, which is the only *permanent* relation of Whig and Tory, it is evident that mere misunderstanding of the case has ever countenanced the attacks on either side ; and Sir F. Burdett's declaration that a Tory would soon be as scarce as a phœnix is answered at once by saying that, change the name as much as you please, both Tories and Whigs must coexist with the British Constitution. Whilst *that* lasts, these parties must last,—because they are the mere abstractions, or representative names, of the two antagonist forces, balanced against each other in that political *scheme*.

Let us next say a word or two upon the *second* relation of Tories,—that relation which they have occupied, and do now occupy, to the Whigs, as a political body of partisans : not as they are concerned with the British constitution, or as representing any interest of that constitution, but as they are concerned with the conduct of public affairs,—with peace, with war, with alliances, with commerce, with taxes, with public debts, with police, and the other great chapters of national economy.

To this point—the relation of Whigs and Tories, *not* to the constitution, or to any principles bearing on the constitution or arising out of it, but simply to the current business of the nation—I must exact a severe attention ; for there is really no end of argument, no purpose to be answered higher than that of two brawling housewives, if the monstrous confusion is to be tolerated of urging, as against the creed of Whig and Tory, objections which apply only to their partisan policy, their tactics of defence or offence, and their conduct in reference to Continental wars. Many a man means by a Tory him who supported Mr. Pitt in his anti-Gallican wars. Those wars it *happened* that the Tories supported, and the Whigs opposed. What then ? The Tories did not support them *as* Tories, nor the Whigs oppose them *as* Whigs. In neither instance did the party policy flow out of their distinguishing creeds, nor had that policy any relation to those creeds. It is of no importance, therefore, towards the valuation of Tory and Whig principles that the wars of the Revolution should be justified, as we Tories justify them, or should be denounced, as the Whigs have always denounced them. It is no reflection upon a Tory, *as* a Tory, whether he were wrong for twenty-five years in this anti-Gallican policy—utterly and ruinously wrong—or, in the most exemplary sense, right. Wrong or right, that foreign policy leaves the question still entire and untouched which respects the appraisement of Tory principles; for those principles were not concerned—no, not by the finest constructive casuistry, nor by the subtlest implication—in any one chapter or article of that policy. The severest Whig purist might, for anything to the contrary in his Whig creed, have coalesced, to this extent, with the Tory. That he did *not* coalesce, but placed himself in an attitude of fierce hostility, did not arise out of Whiggism—not at all; but out of his party position in the first place (the fact that his party were out of office, and thus under the usual obligation of partisanship to say *No* when the King's minister said *Yes*); out of this, in the first place, and, secondly, out of a weaker sensibility to the dangers of an alliance with Jacobinism, to the contagion of its passions, or to the efficacy of its example. The facts I believe to have stood thus:—Mr. Pitt, it is now known, upon many arguments and indications,—some derived from private testimony, but many of a public nature, and recorded in our annals, both diplomatic and parliamentary,—was pacifically disposed towards France, and upon very strong considerations, during the period from 1788 to the summer of 1792. Whatever may have been his unfriendliness to the first aspects of the Revolution and to its democratic tendencies, it is certain that this feeling would not have been allowed any practical weight in his plans, as being more than compensated, and the balance, as respected the question of war, more than restored, by his general reasons for maintaining a friendly intercourse with France. His reasons, I say, were general; but amongst them were some of a special nature, financial as well as commercial, which, at all times, perhaps, had more than their due weight in his mind. I do not admit, as a notion in any degree true with regard to him, still less with regard to the Tories in general, that any displeasure, or reserve even, had arisen towards the French Revolution in its earlier stage, either as arguing for its cause, or as promising for its effect, a large infusion of democracy into the future government of France. I deny that this great event was frowned upon, or could have been frowned upon, by any English Tory, in so far as it taught the French nation to look for a new birth of their civil polity, and for happier days; in so far as it bade the people, the untitled and unprivileged people, to assume their true place in the State,—the place assigned to them in ancient days, and even yet recorded in many old traditional forms (see Hottomann, Boulainvilliers,[1] and scores beside), and in various institutions not yet antiquated in 1788. I deny that the Revolution was unpopular with the Tories in so far as it claimed for the people a strong hand in making their own laws, and in so far as it opened the path for a purification of the executive government, with its old prescriptive abuses,—for a better and more open administration of judicial justice, and, above all, for the instant abolition of the French fiscal system, with its vast train of ruinous frauds on the one hand, and of odious immunities on the other. In so far as the French Revolution did, or promised to do, any of these things, it neither was, nor to a consistent Tory could have been, other than a favoured object, and welcomed as a birth of our own example. Not for these things, any or all, were the worst among the French democrats, or the most violent explosions of democracy, objects to us of jealousy or fear. And therefore it was that, even up to the summer of 1792, Mr. Pitt continued to think of war with France as utterly impolitic, —as an event that ought to be averted, and that yet could be averted. In that summer even,—nay, I believe, even after the fatal 10th of August, when the re-gathering of old constitutional elements was finally abandoned, as it were by national proclamation,—Mr. Pitt still continued to answer most gloomily and doubtfully to all warlike overtures from the Continent, and, in particular, to a private question from the Court of Versailles, Whether it were his purpose to abandon the French monarchy, and to look on as a passive or acquiescing spectator whilst the ruin was consummated

[1] Francis Hottoman, French lawyer, 1524-1590; Henry de Boulainvilliers, French historian, 1658-1722.—M.

which had already travelled so far? This question was renewed, and even more privately and earnestly, from the Queen of France, as a person more alive, by the activity of her understanding, to the perils which surrounded the throne and the royal family. Mr. Pitt's answer was again vague and indecisive; and so much so that the Queen, who had never heard of any policy not bottomed in principles of selfishness or of vainglorious rivalship, went to her death under the firm persuasion that Pitt had sacrificed the royal cause in France to a sentiment of national jealousy; that his wishes went, perhaps, no further than the humbling of France, and (as she fully believed) to the exacting a personal vengeance from the unhappy Louis for his aid (secret before it was avowed) to the cause of American independence; but that, unhappily, he had found it impossible to arrest, at the point which would have satisfied his own narrow purpose, that frenzy which she presumed the English minister to have originally encouraged. The Queen's impression did Mr. Pitt great injustice; but I mention it because it is one proof, amongst many, how strong must have been those pacific dispositions towards France which led that acute princess to interpret them as proofs of a secret and selfish friendship to all the enemies of the Crown, and to the worst of the Jacobin incendiaries. Pitt, the original Pitt, as self-determined and formed upon his own favourite views of policy, was so far from being hostile to the French Revolution in its first movements,—nay, in any of its movements up to the judicial murder of the King,—that, in order to become hostile, as a first step towards placing himself in opposition, he was obliged to sacrifice his own early and favourite scheme of continental policy. He could no otherwise become an enemy to revolutionary France than by abjuring his own peculiar plans. His case in relation to the French Revolution was that of all Tories. Not, therefore, I say, for what there was of hope in the French Revolution did we Tories scowl upon that event, but for what we saw even then of ill omen in the rear; not for what it promised, but for what we feared too probably of defeated promise in the national weakness of character; for what we witnessed of blight in the very moment of birth; and for what we anticipated of treachery in the character of those who were then rising into power. Things good and things bad,—good (though oftentimes aërial) in hypothesis, bad and ruinous in the practical realization,—were too inextricably interwoven in the first stages of the French Revolution; and one reason for this mixed growth of poisonous weeds and medicinal herbs was a fact first pointed out by Burke,—that, whereas with us every man is trained in some sphere or other, narrow or wide, to public business, and to the necessity of those forms which practice suggests for its own guidance and restraint, in France the army of regular official agents in every department of the national service had completely disqualified the body of the people for public affairs, by denying them the preparatory discipline. Good and evil arose in their births, until that time came when the evil arose without the good. And the vicious interpretation of our Tory conduct is that we hated the blossom because we hated the blighted fruit; that we scowled upon the early glories of the dawn because we could not smile upon the heavens when lowering with storms and surcharged with thunder-clouds. But in what did we differ from the Whigs? For what it promised, for what resemblances it offered to our own Revolution of 1688, we, no less than the Whigs, hailed the French Revolution of 1788. And how could we do otherwise? Were we not *equal* contributors to the British Revolution? Did we not *equally* participate in expelling irresponsible tyranny from the throne? Did we not *equally* co-operate in the Act of Settlement, by which the succession to the throne was for ever limited? The difference between us in 1788-1790 was simply this,—that one party gave a confiding love to the promises of the new-born liberty, whilst the other gave an equal love, but coupled with a large reserve of doubt and suspicion. This was a difference which did not concern or implicate the quality of our love for what was genuine, but the mere prudential validity of our doubts in regard to what might be spurious. Time, and the succession of tumultuous years, have left the saddest of testimonies to our accuracy. But, had it been otherwise, the result would not have impeached our love for what was good in the French Revolution, but only our sagacity in deciphering the future, and the needless alarm with which we had troubled the serene prospects in reversion.

Some people who have been accustomed to regard the Tories as identified with the enemies of the French Revolution, and generally of every manifestation of popular feeling, will be apt to feel as though mystified by this representation; and, groping about in the dark for some argument, they will say, perhaps, "But, after all, you Tories, by your very name and classification, are understood to be unfriendly to popular or democratic influences: so much is notorious; for this is the very ground of distinction between yourselves and the Whigs." Here comes in availably and triumphantly the logic of my statement under the first head. The Tories and the Whigs equally concur to the two influences,—the democratic and the antagonist influence in the English Constitution. The Tories, it is true, are charged with the keeping or administration of the anti-democratic forces; the Whigs with the keeping or administration of the pure democratic forces. But this regards only the *practical* management of the service: it has no relation to the theory of the forces; since each party must have equally concurred to each several function of the Constitution. As well might it be said that, because a man attends exclusively to one wheel in a system of forces, he is justified in attributing to this wheel an exclusive importance. He knows *his* wheel produces its ultimate action only through the manifold aids, and, perhaps, resistances of other forces. The Tory is able or willing to tend the anti-democratic powers of our Constitution, only because he knows that another and sufficient party is charged with the exclusive management of the opposing powers. Hence I infer that, though professionally, as it were, attached to the superintendence of one set of influences by preference to another,—and though, in times of trouble, he may have seen occasion to signalize his attachment to one set pre-eminently,—the true and philosophic Tory cannot be supposed to wish for any preponderance to either, or to regard the one principle as being at all more indispensable than its antagonist. Either in the political system, therefore, of England, or under analogous circumstances in the system of any foreign land, a Tory must ill understand his own creed who does not wish well to the democratic influences as much as to those which are peculiarly consigned to his own guardianship. His duty, in a practical sense, is confined to the aristocratic force; as the Whig's, in the same practical sense, to the democratic force. But, in a philosophic sense, the affection of each should settle upon both: for the total Constitution, *which they have both co-operated to frame*, is not democracy, is not aristocracy, but is made up of a wise temperament from each.

Mr. Pitt, therefore, and the Tories, welcomed what was good or of fair promise in the French Revolution, but distrusted the men of the Revolution, and distrusted the growing necessities of their position. Mr. Fox and the Whigs, not loving the good more, distrusted the men and their position less. With equal love, except where they differed as to the interpretation of the signs, the two parties had a very unequal measure of hope and confidence. Power and office happened to be lodged with those who saw reason to distrust, and thus the war arose. Upon that war, or its management, I am not going to say one word. But, having made the above explanation on the Tory way of viewing the French Revolution, I shall now go on to say that—wrong or right in its origin, well or ill conducted, successful or not successful in its termination—the war of the Revolution had no reference whatsoever to either Whig principles or Tory principles. The war had no relation to the cause or interests of royalty. It was not a war for restoring a particular family to the throne, or for asserting the general rights of thrones. Had it been so, we should have set up the Bourbons on an eminence of wealth and splendour, and surrounded them with a court; all which we forbore to do. A *locus penitentiæ* was wisely provided for from the first, and a retreat left open to either belligerent according to the circumstances. For, if Mr. Pitt had fettered himself by an improvident resolution that he would not treat with Napoleon Bonaparte, that was merely a personal act,—the English Government was no party to it. No object, therefore, was pursued in that war which can be connected with Tory principles. We assumed arms as men who would else have been compelled to assume them under circumstances of heavy disadvantage,—that is to say, after some allies had been weakened or destroyed, and much of the mischief accomplished which we sought to avert. Our main object was security for our own interests, and a timely repulsion from our own shores of those disorganizing principles which had already produced so much bloodshed and tyranny in France. Now, these are objects of an universal nature, having no relation whatsoever to any party, or to any set of political principles. All nations defend themselves, whether they have Tories amongst them or not. And, if the Tories happened to lead in this resistance to France, that was because the Tory party was at that time in office. But a vast majority of the nation, neither Whigs nor Tories, followed and supported their leading. What was the behaviour of the Whigs? History will call it traitorous; for the word *unpatriotic* is too feeble for the case. To have disapproved the war was open to them; but not to exult in the difficulties of their countrymen, to sympathize with the enemy, or to proclaim all resistance to him hopeless and irrational. This the Whigs did. But do I charge their conduct upon Whig principles? Far from it! To many cases which arose in that war Whig principles had little or no application. With respect to others, as the Spanish resistance to a foreign tyrant, Whig principles were so far from being chargeable with the Whig discountenance of that struggle that, on the contrary, those very principles furnish the very strongest reproach to the Whig policy on that occasion. Just a century before, the Tories, I am sorry to say, were playing the same traitorous part. During the last years of Queen Anne, Lords Oxford and Bolingbroke were applying themselves to the task of obliterating the brilliant services of the Whigs from 1704 to 1710. And (monstrous as such a statement may appear) there is too much reason to believe that they tolerated a treaty which else they would not have tolerated, because it was fitted to furnish a sort of presumption that the war had not been so glorious or decisive which could admit of such a termination. The Treaty of Utrecht was to be used, they hoped, as an exponent of the true value attached to the services of Marlborough. In this the Tories (that is, the leaders of the Tories) acted perfidiously. In other instances during those years we know that they were perfidious according to a legal sense, and had incurred the penalties of high treason. But *then* they acted as Jacobites, and in effect renounced their Toryism; nor in the other and more public cases did they at all rely upon Tory principles, or make any appeal to them. They had been in desperate opposition to the Whigs, not upon any question of principles, but for power and office. Gaining both unexpectedly, they were tied by their previous opposition to a certain line of conduct; that conduct arose, not out of any principles whatever, but out of partisanship, intrigue, and accidents of position. In the same causes originated the Whig conduct with reference to the wars of the French Revolution. The case of Queen Anne in 1710 was exactly reversed from 1807 to 1815. Each party in succession had carried the frenzy of opposition to their rivals up to the very brink of public treachery,—in neither case, however, with any view to their distinguishing principles, but solely on grounds of party violence, of party interest, and of mortified ambition.

Let the logic of this important distinction be no longer lost sight of; and, if we are to hear continually of "Tory misrule," &c., let it be remembered that for innumerable public measures applied to questions of taxation, of funding, of Irish administration, of war, and many others, no charge lies or can lie against Tory principles,—as being, by their very essence, inapplicable to most questions of this nature. When the Tory party are made responsible for political acts, let it be remembered that this party, considered as a body of Parliamentary leaders, stand in two relations: to their immediate opponents for the time, a body of rivals who may or may not happen to be Whigs, fiercely contesting with them the enjoyment of power and place; and, secondly, to a permanent body, the depositories and conservators of a particular influence in the constitutional system. Acts done by some Tory minister or *clique* in the first relation, supposing them bad, are utterly impertinent as charges against a national party who stand in the second relation. The very men have vanished, or are continually vanishing, from the public scene who are concerned in the first relation; nor had they, at any time, a national existence. But the other relation is immortal, national, and coeval with the Constitution.

This distinction settled, which has been the parent (whilst

neglected, or not sharply pressed) of infinite misapprehensions, let us now come to a more urgent question,—a question, or rather *the* question, of this day,—the relation of Tories to the revolutionary party, the party known by the name of Radicals.

In a question of relation between any two objects, it is necessary that something should be known of both. Toryism I understand, and Whiggism I understand; but what is Radicalism? I am now going to value the pretensions of Toryism in relation to the new faith of Radical Reform. To do so with effect, I ought, first of all, to know the main articles of that faith. But *is* there such a faith? Has the new church any peculiar or novel creed? Or is it only a new mode of administering old principles, better adapted to the times, and resting, perhaps, upon new political influences? These questions ought not to have been left for my answering, or rather for my investigation: as to an answer which would be valid for all who are interested in the case, *that* is impossible. You, in Bengal, who have had Mr. Buckingham amongst you,[1] may fancy it easy enough to give the analysis of Radicalism. For the very thing which made the politics of Mr. Buckingham perilous,—the very thing which excused (nothing else could have excused) the harshness and the summary despotism applied to himself and to his newspaper establishment,—was, as we all know, the too palpable existence of political evil and reformable matter in a country situated as our Indian empire is, and, under the wisest management, must be for generations to come. Reform principles were dangerous, precisely because they were but too intelligible. I do not mean to say that such principles were therefore of easy application: it did not facilitate the administration of reform that the objects were evident which allowed of reform. In a state of society affected by so many remarkable circumstances of position, of conquest imperfectly cemented, of religion, of caste, of military tenure, of language, it may be a matter of infinite delicacy, and also of time, to apply a reform either safe or effectual, though all the world should be agreed upon the actual, and palpable, and omnipresent existence of the abuse; and therefore there is no

[1] I suppose, James Silk Buckingham (1786–1855) traveller and miscellaneous writer.—M.

inconsistency in my speaking of Mr. Buckingham's system of agitation as perilous, whilst, at the same time, I describe it as full of practical meaning and applicability. It was so; it spoke a language but too readily interpreted by the passions, and the situation of those whom it addressed. But, if you judge of reform or of agitation, as applied to English affairs, by what you saw of either in Bengal, you err grievously. The reforming principle with you stood upon a vast and a solid basis; with us it stands upon one so narrow that it will never justify the agitation which must be kept up in order to keep itself alive; for an artificial agitation becomes necessary in exact proportion to the *non*-reality of the evils which it parades. Here I make my stand; and it would give me pleasure to hear any philosophic reformer meeting my view of the case, which may be expressed in two propositions:—1*st*, That, large as is the whole body of Reformers, it is *not* large, but shrinks into sectarian limits, *any one object of reform being given.* Given the general necessity of reform as a universal thesis, Reformers seem to compose the mass of society. Given any particular case of reform, the affirmative party come forward as a narrow sect. 2*dly*, I say that, if all the known objects for which any section of Reformers has ever contended were thrown into a common fund, and credit allowed to the Reform party collectively upon these disjointed *symbola* or separate contingents, as upon a joint-stock property,—even thus, there will not be realized a sufficient interest to justify, or so much as to explain, the impassioned vehemence of the Reformers. What would I infer from *that*? I would infer that the real objects which govern the leaders of the *movement* are not those which they avow, but such as for the present they find it prudent to dissemble. Let me speak to each point separately.

First, with respect to the schisms amongst the Reformers, I affirm peremptorily that the term *Radical* is used with as large a licence, and as little care for precision, or for any one practical use of language, as the term "*middle class*"; which, in the fraudulent acceptation of modern incendiaries, confounds all the unnumbered gradations of English society which lie between the very highest and the very lowest. The common term *Radical* would entitle us to presume some unity of purpose. Will the present Reformers arrogate such a unity to their party, and tell us in what capital object it is seated? For my part, I know of only one point in which they all agree, and that is negative,—they all dissent, or believe that they dissent, from the Tories. But that tells us, at the most, what it is which they do *not* profess. Yet not even that; for the *Tory* supposed in their opposition is a Tory of their own fiction. As to the *positive* articles in their creed, the following statement exhibits the case according to my view; and I do not think that any temperate Reformers will call it in question:—Suppose the alphabet to represent the total number of subdivisions already existing amongst the Reformers. A is a patron of some one proposed change in our institutions,—of this one and of none beside; B is a patron of this and of one other; C of this and two others; and so on, until we come to the formidable Z, who patronises two round dozens of such changes; all of which changes, so long as they are yet untried, enjoy, by anticipation, the flattering name of *reforms*. And hence, by a parity of right, the whole twenty-four orders of these Reformers are all equally relied on, in argument, for drawing together as in a common cause. But try it in action, propose the practical test of some special object, and the nominal union of the Reformers instantly breaks up into schisms and internal feuds,—some professing even downright hostility to the object in question, and the major part indifference. Z, for example,—the zealot Z, who declares himself beforehand for everything wearing the aspect of change,—Z counts backwards as far as A for a cheerful support on some single question. Upon a second question equally dear to himself, he is aware that he can count back only to B; upon a third, only to C; and so on. The sections represented by A, by B, by C, &c., will forsake him in succession; until at length he will be reduced to the feeble support of X, Y, Z; and, finally, for his twenty-fourth object, in *his* eyes perhaps ranking not at all below any of the others, he will have to depend upon himself alone,—to speak by a scholastic abstraction, upon his own *Zedeity*. For what purpose, you will ask, do I insist upon this artifice, which may seem a common party stratagem? I do so because it is used not only to throw dust in the eyes of us, their opponents, but because it dupes themselves. Here and there a question is found which does really engage the active affections of so large a majority among us,—suppose the question of the Reform Bill,—that, without much violence to the truth, it may be called a *national* object. Hereupon the Reformers, who, as to this one question, count back from omnivorous Z to fastidious A, assume the title of the national party,—or, perhaps, *tout court*, of "the nation"; and with some show of reason as regards this one great popular question. It is true that we Tories have still the old right of appeal from the nation ill-informed to the nation well-informed, and from the nation guessing at results to the nation dealing with absolute experience; but still, for the mere matter of fact, the Reformers were in that instance a national party. Once having established that title, these same Reformers are determined to plead it beneficially upon all other questions whatsoever,—and very often it makes the strongest nerve of their argument,—as though the title of national, which inhered in the particular *question*, inhered in the *persons* of the Reformers, and could henceforwards be urged indefinitely on behalf of any object patronised by the same party. On the memorable question of the Reform Bill the Reformers were certainly identified for the time, and for that particular service, with a very large majority of the British people. They proved their identification by practical tests; they arrayed "Unions," technically so called, upon a scale of immensity that resounded throughout Europe, and must have appalled even you in Bengal. Those Unions counted themselves by tens of thousands; one in the centre of England mustered above a hundred thousand; and their relations to the existing government were far more those of jealousy and mutual suspicion, as between a body overawing and one overawed than of confidence and reciprocal gratitude. The terror of these Unions, I can assure you, sat more heavily upon the hearts of their nominal friends, Lord Grey's administration, than upon any of us, their formal antagonists. Now, these terrific federations were evoked by the Reformers. The same Reformers evoked through every city of this great empire vast triumphal arrays of the population in celebration of their victory. Whether for achieving the victory, or for commemorating it, they were able to put forth a power greater than that of kings the most despotic. And thus far they were entitled to style themselves "*national*," or even, in a popular sense, "*the nation*." But their power ceased with that question. Nay, for that very question they would not again be able to receive the same support. It is a fact that the people have been deeply disappointed in the vague expectations which too generally they built upon the Reform Bill. For, what has it accomplished? The main change, as respects the electors, is that what was once valued as a distinction has ceased to be such. To have an eight-thousandth or a ten-thousandth share in the manufacturing one or two legislators is too trivial an honour to be valued; and, in reality, is so little valued that, except where angry passions have been roused, there is a general torpor in qualifying for the exercise of this franchise. *Registration*, the test of political zeal, languishes. But, after all, the value of the Reform Bill must lie in the result. Not how, or by what sort of means, the end is attained, but what *is* the end attained,—there lies the question. Not the changes in the electors, but in the quality of the elected,—*that* is the point for us. Now, what sort of a House of Commons have we had since the great Reform? Of course, I say nothing of the House now sitting,—*that* is notoriously a heaven-descended senate, perfect and immaculate. But, limiting my remarks to the previous Houses under the Reform Bill, the changes perceptible to the public eye have been chiefly two:—First, The absolute disqualification of the House for carrying on the King's government. Without any one advantage as yet gained to the public service, such is now the restiveness and the self-contradictiveness, the pertinacity in one direction, and yet the unsteadiness in another, of the Commons' House, that the indispensable machinery of an executive administration will not work smoothly for any continuance, no matter who is minister. The French Government is annually advancing upon the same path of perplexity. The public business in each country is destined apparently to endless stagnations for the future,—endless ruptures of administrations, and endless dissolutions of Parliament. And the final tendencies of these changes are such that I will not lower their importance by treating them incidentally. The other change,—and it is a change already perceptible to the public eye,—lies in the altered tone of manners prevalent through the whole course of debate for the last two years. Formerly the House of Commons was a school of gentlemanly manners, the most dignified in the annals of man,—more so than that "assembly of kings," the Roman Senate, in this important feature, that personalities (not only oblique personalities and such as were said *of* a member, but direct apostrophes *to* a member) were tolerated by the Roman manners, and treated as mere figures of rhetoric, whereas by the English Parliament they were checked and stifled in the birth. Since the Reform Bill,—partly from the effects of that Bill and the invitation which it holds out to the spirit of popular licence, and partly, it may be, from the uncontrolled temper of particular members,—a mixed tone has prevailed, of puerile levity, of histrionic buffoonery, and of street ruffianism. This latter feature has been sometimes explained out of the Irish infusion into our national councils, which, since the Emancipation Bill, has been, for two reasons, of a more democratic quality: first, because the Irish representation, having been more Popish, has really settled into lower grades of rank and property; and, secondly, because the Irish representation has fallen too generally under one insolent domination, which adopts the policy of personal abuse as one of the weapons most effective in party warfare. But no matter how explained,—for the reasons alleged, or for whatever reasons, —Parliament, in its general temper and tone of manners, has been in some degree ruffianised; and what remains of good breeding, or decorum, or gentlemanly restraint, may be set down to the account of those regulations inherited from an unreformed House which a reformed one will perhaps be ashamed to abrogate, but which it never would have spontaneously enacted. It will be odd, indeed, as a spectacle, yet apparently it is one not very improbable, if our senate should invert the natural relations to the nation which it represents, and should gradually ripen amongst us a model of Kentucky violence, whilst the people, in its lowest classes, have been, for many years back, outgrowing their insular roughness. Yet such things have been. The Athenian people, at that same era when they had attained their utmost expansion in general civility and in the arts of refinement, and reputed themselves not so much the patrons as the sole depositaries of *παρρησια*, or the right of free speaking, yet carried their illiberal hostilities to such excess in their debating assemblies that, amongst all the political harangues still surviving, and those delivered by the boldest of their orators, not one but teems with earnest passages deprecating interruption or personal violence so often as the conscientious speaker approached a topic which he knew to be unpopular. Whether we are tending to a state of Athenian licence and scurrility I will not presume to say. But, if some further changes were made in the same direction,—were a five-pound qualification substituted for the present,—I cannot doubt that we should reach that consummation *per saltum*. Meantime, the whole upshot of the Bill, according to its working hitherto, has been what I say: no valuable change as respects the electoral body; as respects the body elected, a change of temper and manners altogether for the worse; and, in the same body, as a machinery for co-operating with the executive, precisely that change and no more which, whilst hanging a drag on the smoothness and velocity of its motion, has done nothing to improve its purity. The movement and play of public business is *sufflaminated*,[1] and not in a way which looks like accident; and all this with no tittle of countervailing benefit to any one national interest.

Now, if these are the weightiest results from the Reform of Parliament, it is with some reason that the people are disappointed. With reason, or without reason, it is certain that they *are* so. And vainly indeed would the Reformers appeal again to those tremendous agencies, now sleeping, which once they invoked with so much effect. The poor mechanics and day-labourers who walked in those triumphs, and sacrificed their daily bread to one day's joyous parade, did so because they looked for some golden age which was thence to date its bright unfolding of happier years. What

[1] "*Sufflaminated*":—*i.e.* clogged, from the Latin *sufflamen*, a break, or drag-chain, to break the motion of a wheel. *Aliquando sufflaminandus erat* is Ben Jonson's famous description of Shakespeare's conversation: *i.e.* "You had sometimes to put on the drag to stop him; such was his fluency."—M.

a mockery, how hollow a pageantry of political juggling, would they have held it, could they have believed that all this drama was to terminate in securing office and retiring salaries to some score and a half of Whig lords and gentlemen! As yet, the people have seen no other result from this all-celebrated Reform; nor is it likely they will. And the issue as respects them—*i.e.* the people of the lower orders—is that henceforth they will err by defect rather than by excess, in estimating the value of any promises connected with changes in the constitution of Parliament.

Yet, because it is undeniable that, three years ago, in behalf of a scheme yet untried, the Reformers *did* possess power in a terrific extent, they have ever since continued to assume that, in opposing *them*, we oppose the nation. That is their main reliance. As a party opposed to a party, they would lie under the common presumptions of error; but, as the nation opposed to a party, they have a dispensation from argument, and an immunity from error. If they can prevail by logic, it is well; but, if not, *that* also is well; for a nation is entitled to be made happy on its own terms, even if those terms should happen to involve a multitude of errors. It is the case, in *their* representation, of a party interested, and absolute master in the last resort, arguing against a mere speculative dialectician, who has no stake in the question litigated. Such is the use which they make of a single victory on a single chapter of their creed. But I, in answer to these pretensions, maintain that, from a single coincidence with the people, they unwarrantably infer a general identification with the popular wishes or interest. I affirm that, on many points, the Reformers are not only a party, a section, but also a very narrow party, a very slender section; and that this is hidden from their own, as it is from general, observation by the accident that the same men who compose this narrow party, this slender section, are those who once were conspicuous in leading a really national movement, and leading it by pretty nearly the same organs of the press as they now employ. So much in explanation of my first proposition,—that the Reformers, if large as a collective body, are *not* large when thrown into those subdivisions which would arise instantly upon putting to the vote any one separately of those several objects which they patronise.

But I rest more upon the second proposition,—that, if all these several objects, each resting on the support of an insulated section amongst the Reformers, were, by a monstrous concession, assumed to be common objects, objects pursued with the common forces of the whole party, even thus there would not result a cumulative interest sufficient to sustain a national movement, or even a national sympathy. The Reformers, if they are not national, are nothing. As a party, we Tories, we Whigs, are older than they: we have the rights of primogeniture; and, moreover, we grew out of the constitution itself, whereas they have grown out of the wantonness of peace and the defect of excitement succeeding to a season of adventurous war, and out of the political agitation which attempted to supply that defect. Besides that, we Tories and we Whigs,—though, doubtless, one of us *was* a rascally party as respects the mere conduct of affairs since the French Revolution,—yet, as respects the constitution, as respects political principles, we cannot *but* be right, since we exhaust the whole possibilities of political principle. The ground, the whole *arena*, is preoccupied; there is no standing-room for a new party, under any conceivable description or designation, except upon the allegation that we—the Tories and Whigs—have neglected our constitutional functions; that, being speculatively right, we have, in practice, suffered our own principles to lie dormant. The Reformers, therefore, are bound, in strict logic, to follow the precedent of Edmund Burke, in relation to the Whigs. He had professed himself a Whig in all parts of his life. But, suddenly, the Whigs, or some of them, announced such opinions with regard to the French Jacobinism as were shocking to his views of the English Constitution. In this dilemma how did he proceed? Did he abjure Whiggism? Did he set up a new party, a new creed, a new doctrine of Radical Burkeism? By no means. He contended that Whiggism, as interpreted by Mr. Fox and the Duke of Norfolk, was not the Whiggism of their common constitutional ancestors,—not the Whiggism which they had inherited from 1688-9. And upon that logic he composed his famous appeal from the new (or spurious) to the old (or genuine) Whigs; and many persons of great intellectual power and experience—such as Mr. Wyndham, the Duke of Portland, etc.—saw reason to accompany his secession in that instance. Why the Reformers should not have followed this example I can only explain by supposing that the accidental part supported by Whigs and Tories in relation to office and current affairs, all transitory and fugitive aspects of Toryism or Whiggism, had blinded them to the permanent and fixed relations which the two parties occupy in regard to the constitution; which relations if any new men usurp, they, in effect, become Whigs and Tories under a mere change of name. Either the Reformers have committed the error here indicated, or else they mean to say this: "We assume no permanent functions of control in regard to the constitution,—ours is an occasional office: we see or fancy certain great abuses,—we confederate for the purpose of abating them,—and, whenever that service shall be accomplished, our confederation is, *ipso facto*, dissolved: we are an occasional *Fehm-Gericht*,—an occasional array against an occasional mass of evil." This way of representing their position as a party, and this way only, clears them of the impertinence (to use the word in its proper Latin sense) which belongs to all intrusions upon other men's provinces. They have interfered only for a specific service,—for the abatement of abuses to which, it seems, the Whigs and Tories were pretty equally blind.

Let us now, therefore, inquire closely what *are* the abuses which the Reformers have denounced; what *are* the reforms which they propose to introduce? By *that* we shall learn how far the Reformers stand, as a party, upon any sufficient basis, and shall have an answer to the question I have raised: Whether the whole amount of objects for which they contend (that is, *openly* contend) can be held sufficient—even treated as a common fund, and not as a series of separate interests belonging to separate sections of the reforming body—to warrant the name of a national interest, or to warrant the wish, as well as the expectation, of promoting them by a national movement.

Now, then, counting over the different objects for which,

at any time, the Reformers have openly contended, we shall be astonished to find them so few. 1. *Household Suffrage*,—or the substitution of a five-pound for a ten-pound qualification, or, generally, any means whatever for enlarging the electoral basis,—some Reformers treat as a *sine qua non* ; but others speak of it with doubt, or with indifference, or with positive disapprobation. 2. A measure which at present wins more general favour is the *Disfranchisement of the Spiritual Peers* in the Upper House. 3. *The Ballot*, a favourite scheme amongst very earnest and energetic Reformers, is still discountenanced by numbers of those who, at one time or other, have been looked up to as leaders of the movement,—by Lord Brougham in particular, and, so recently as the 19th of May 1835, by Lord John Russell, even while yet smarting from the uncicatrized mortification of his Devonshire campaign, and openly ascribing his defeat to intimidation. Now, where a personal interest so keen as this will not overrule a man's objections, the case, as in relation to him, may be thought hopeless ; and yet I question myself whether some who have hitherto opposed the ballot are not covertly preparing a case of alleged extremity to justify its adoption, which case would, of course, derive the strength of a rebound from the fact and the notoriety of their previous opposition. The talk is more and more of "intimidation" ; every species and variety of influence, however laudable and salutary, by which the upper ranks are connected with the lower, being denounced under that name. Rejected candidates have a natural licence for complaining : we all construe *their* complaints indulgently. But another class, the class of timid voters, have reasons still more urgent for pleading intimidation where nothing of the kind exists. Shopkeepers of a petty order, who cannot afford to make enemies either amongst Reformers or anti-Reformers, especially where their natural temper concurs with their position in producing a timid love of quietness,—men hating strife constitutionally, perhaps, as much as they fear it in policy, and very often having no decided views on the party questions at issue,—are apt enough to plead a vague necessity of complying with some overruling influence in some imaginary background, where no such influence has been, in fact, put forward or insinuated, and where the alleged necessity of their situation has existed only in pretence, or, at most, in suspicion. These cases of merely presumptive intimidation will multiply exceedingly, as the cases multiply of electioneering contests. Intimidation, and obscure insinuations of intimidation, will be offered as the best general way of shaping an evasion from the persecutions of canvassers, until it will be said that a case of necessity has arisen for the Ballot. That measure will therefore triumph ; but at present the Reformers are greatly divided upon its merits.

These three measures—one for enlarging the constituency, —one for giving effect to that enlarged constituency by liberating them from alien influence,—and a third for altering the present constitution of the Upper House,—are so evidently parts of the same system, all having the same obvious purpose to throw a vast infusion of democracy into the legislative forces of the land, that he who objects to any one of them stands declared, in that act, an enemy, or at the least a hollow friend, of the reform principle. Sir William Molesworth, during the late struggle in South Devon, talked with zealotry for the Ballot: why?—because he is a sincere Reformer, and knows that the whole purposes of his party can be obtained but slowly and imperfectly without the Ballot. Lord John Russell opposes the Ballot: why? because he, by interest and by connexions, is, and must be, an aristocrat; and, if he avails himself of aid from the reform party, it is because the path of the Reformers coincides, for a certain part of the way (or may, by skilful management, be made to coincide), with the path of his own political *clique*. But, though he has gone into this dangerous alliance for momentary considerations of benefit to his party (in reality it is evident that Lord John's private party must have gone to wreck in 1830 but for this alliance, and equally evident that, on many subsequent occasions, that party has been violently held above water by this artificial connexion), yet it is impossible to suppose that any relations merely personal can absorb those permanent relations to the aristocratic interest in which he is placed by his rank, his numerous and illustrious connexions, and the vast possessions of his family. It happens, also, that Lord John, before he came into a situation that required him to practise any arts of dissimulation, had written for many years as a regular author,—had written very respectably, and upon themes connected with political and constitutional questions: by a rare misfortune for himself, he, more than any other of his party, was *committed* in the diplomatic sense; and thus it happens that we have a key to his native opinions, and can appreciate the basis of his views before they had received any disturbing impulse from the difficult circumstances of his position. Lord John, therefore, in common with other aristocratic Reformers, keeps his eye for ever fixed upon that parting point at which *his* road is to diverge from that of the Reformers. He has a quarrel in reversion whenever it shall seem that the hour has struck for this parting; and not impossibly this very question of *Ballot* is destined to furnish the matter of quarrel. Far am I from supposing it at all shocking to our historical experience that Lord John Russell, like the too famous father to the reigning King of the French, might go on, to the very catastrophe of the great drama, with the avowed enemies and destined destroyers of his order. The case is common enough. But, in this instance, drawing my auguries from the known respectability of the man, I believe that Lord John will effectually co-operate with those who meditate ruin to the aristocracy of England,—and too probably will accomplish it,—not by going along with them to the end, and glorying in his own shame,—I believe him too good a man, and too discerning a man, for *that*,—but by lending them a hesitating sanction, and, with many misgivings, yielding to their demands an unsteady assistance, until, at last, growing alarmed, and halting with an air of defiance, he finds out that his sanction and his assistance are become alike indifferent to the Reformers. He will first see cause to resist when all the powers have been surrendered by which resistance can be made effectual.

# ON THE POLITICAL PARTIES OF MODERN ENGLAND[1]

After an interval of a year and something more, I resume my letter on the political parties of modern England. An interruption of that duration was likely to have acted disadvantageously on the interest. For upon what was that interest founded ? It was an interest founded upon the danger

[1] Written in 1837, but not published till 1863, four years after De Quincey's death. The circumstances, already explained generally in the Preface, were, more in detail, as follows:—The Editor of *Tait's Magazine*, in printing De Quincey's preceding "Account of Toryism, Whiggism, and Radicalism" in the pages of the magazine for December 1835 and January 1836, had done so under this general preliminary caveat:—"The Tories are continually complaining that " their principles are misrepresented in the Liberal magazines and " newspapers. So little has that great national party into which the " Whigs and Radicals are gradually melting down to fear from the " freest and most sifting discussion, that we rejoice in affording an " opportunity to one of the most able and eloquent of the Tory " adherents of defining the political tenets, and unfolding the " principles of action, by which the Tories have been guided since they " first arose as a distinct party in the state." Not content with this general intimation, the editor had *footnoted* De Quincey's paper pretty liberally throughout with comments of which the following are specimens:—To the words "countervailing balance" *ante*, p. 315, this: " Against this adjustment of the national balance it is scarcely worth " while to protest. Mr. De Quincey is too candid for a Tory " advocate."—To De Quincey's words "the tone of its antagonists," *ante*, p. 316, this: "We dissent and protest here. Are the *John* " *Bull* and the *Blackwood* things of yesterday ? Whether was Cobbett " less or more scurrilous when a Tory party writer than when he " became a Reformer ? The Tory abuse, vulgarity, and gross per-" sonality of the *Times* fairly eclipse the same qualities displayed by

which threatened an ancient state in the very heart of her civil polity; upon the grandeur of that state, and upon the eminence of that danger. Now, in the course of this interval, such has been the quality of our experience that no one of the dangers apprehended at its commencement has taken a less louring aspect, and new ones have arisen. In fact, great advances have been made by the Radical party: not, indeed, in things won and accomplished, but in the pretensions put forward; in the haughtiness and gross plainness of their

"that print while Liberal,—with the addition of the most brazen-faced "impudence."—To De Quincey's words "as humble as a Storthing of Norway," applied to the English House of Commons in Elizabeth's reign, *ante*, p. 324, this: "Mr. De Quincey greatly underrates the real "power of Parliament even in this fortunate reign. There was power "of the purse,—existing and exhibited,—and, with the outward show of "humility to a female sovereign, considerable sturdiness of purpose." —To De Quincey's words "nor had that policy any relation to those creeds," *ante*, p. 332, this: "We deny this *in toto* and maintain exactly "the reverse."—To De Quincey's words "is made up of a wise temperament from each," *ante*, p. 338, this: "We can only sincerely "regret that Mr. De Quincey, and the Tories who, with him, under-"stand what he concludes their 'creed,' form so very small a "minority at the present time that there cannot be a half-dozen such "Tories in Great Britain."—To De Quincey's words "stand in the second relation," *ante*, p. 340, this: "It is useless to demur at this "time to the wire-drawn distinctions of this ingenious but sophistical "statement. We are arguing with the Tories of deeds and things, and "not of creeds and words."—To De Quincey's words "*Registration*, the test of political zeal, languishes," *ante*, p. 345, this: "This alleged "indifference to the exercise of the franchise is a gratuitous slight to "the intelligence of the people which does not require to be contro-"verted."—To De Quincey's words "some score and a half of Whig lords and gentlemen," *ante*, p. 348, this: "It will be the fault of the "people themselves if Reform bear no better fruits; and we deny the "indifference and deadness of the mass. It is not much above three "months since their tens and hundreds of thousands were abroad to hail "O'Connell with unabated heart and hope."—These and other similar censures by the editor roused De Quincey's pugnacity; and, though he had then on hand for *Tait* the continuation of his Autobiographic Sketches, of which two or three instalments did appear in *Tait* in 1836 and 1837, he had set himself to work on another experiment in "cutting blocks with a razor" by preparing another elaborate article on the History of British Party Politics, which should include an answer to the more important of the footnotes thus sampled. After the article had been completed, however, Mr. Tait declined to have any more of that kind of matter, even from De Quincey; and hence, though written in 1837, it was not till 1863 that it saw the light. It

language, no less than the audacious character of extremity which marks their tendency. At present it may be truly said that, with the wind setting strong upon the most perilous shore, we ride at single anchor. That anchor is the House of Lords; and, if that gives way, all is lost. Thenceforwards, for people like you or me, England will be no habitable land.

There cannot, in fact, be a better illustration of the treasonable audacity which has begun to characterise the schemes and the language of the Radicals than this very assault, according to its variety of plans, upon the House

was then published from the original manuscript, with the title *Political Parties of Modern England*, in the same volume of Messrs. Black's reissue of the Collective Edition of De Quincey which contained the reprint of the paper *Toryism, Whiggism, and Radicalism*. Messrs. Black printed with it the following note from De Quincey to Mr. Tait, which they had found among Mr. Tait's business papers:—

"Tuesday, about ½ past 3 p.m.

"MY DEAR SIR,—After more labour than ever I had upon any "article whatever, I have completed my paper on *Whig, Tory, and* "*Radical*. There are, however, 2 notes which I wish to add on "historical points; and perhaps it may be ½ past 6 before I have "finished these. The total article is just half-way between 1¼ and "1½ sheets of Blackwood; that is, from 5 quarters to 6 quarters. "The money, therefore, ranges between 12½ and 15 guineas. Now, "taking the lower sum, may I depend upon having it—if I call with "the note at 7 to ½ past 7 this evening? I assure you that the time "I have spent over this article—writing, cancelling, rewriting—has "been more, and the labour greater than upon any 4 equal articles I "ever wrote; and I have brought myself into serious embarrassment "by this long doing and undoing. In fact, from a delay of the "E. Ind. Co. to pay up some arrears until a set of papers about "'*Off-reckonings*' come from India, and unfortunately a simul-"taneous delay from a Remitter in Cumberland (in consequence of a "stoppage at a Carlisle Bank and subsequent refusals of all local "Banks to discount upon the usual agricultural security)—I had "fallen into such arrears when I last saw you, that I *then* wanted the "money and a great deal more: a portion now.—Yours ever,

"T. DE Q."

This note may possibly refer to the rejected article; but it seems rather to refer to the prior *Tait* article to which the rejected one was intended to be the sequel. At all events, it is a touching record of the hard straits through which, in those old Edinburgh years, De Quincey had to navigate his literary industry.—M.

of Lords. Were things called by their right names, it is as much and as decidedly treason, by all its bearings and instant tendencies, as any direct act against the king's crown, and in its consequences a thousand times worse than to have compassed the death of any the best prince that ever lived. So little does any reverence dwell in Radical minds for the existing restraints of law and the constitution that in most of the schemes which have come under my notice not one word is said on that point which is the most perplexing of all,—viz. by what power known to the laws of this land any revolution in the Upper House is to be undertaken. Perfectly overlooking the fact that this legislative body owes no obedience to any other power in the state, but is on a footing of absolute equality with all, and as much entitled to abolish or to remodel the Lower House as that House to attempt either one or the other process upon the Upper, — the Radicals confine their whole discussions to the particular mode and the extent of change which will meet their ulterior purposes. Not who, and by what arms, is to be the reformer, but how large and destructive is to be the reformation,—*that* is the Radical point of mooting. Here, however, at least, Radicalism will find itself at fault. *The House of Lords will not be reformed* on this side of a civil war,—which war, on the part of the reforming faction, will be a rebellion, and liable to the pains of a rebellion. The nation, in its better and more powerful sections, is well aware of these two capital facts: 1*st*, That, even if the Lords' House were not (as it is) the sole bulwark of our liberties, yet to tamper with its present constitution, as known to the laws and usages of the land, would not merely *infer* a revolution as its immediate consequence, but would in itself, formally as well as virtually, *be* a revolution, and as complete a one as ever was effected in modern days; 2*dly*, That, were this otherwise, and supposing that, without any gross violation of the constitution, some remodelling of the House might be devised—supposing, even, that good results might be anticipated from such a measure (always, however, allowing for the uncertainty of political anticipations)—supposing, in short, all the circumstances exactly what they are *not*,—even in that case the change could not be encouraged, no, nor so much as entertained for one moment's speculation, by any good patriot, because there are no known forces, reconcilable with elementary law, which are competent to the task of working the least change in a body which is itself a fountain of all lawful change. There are no known functions of any public body or corporation recognised by the law of England which point to any such task, or are applicable to such a task, as that of reforming either House of Parliament. And changes, even good and salutary in themselves, which cannot be accomplished without a preliminary breach of law or contempt of sacred rights, are not the changes which the people of Great Britain are accustomed to countenance. Therefore, I undertake to predict, for the private rumination of Radicalism, that no such reform of the Lords' House as has been so freely denounced since the Parliamentary session of 1836 will or can be undertaken; and *that*, not only because the nation would be roused to a sense of the impending ruin, and to a sense of the real principles at work, by a revolutionary proposal so definite in its character, but also because no public body durst so far overstep its powers, or commit so palpable an absurdity, as to take the first step towards any such object. Let any man figure to himself the outrage upon common sense which would be involved in a member of the Commons' House seriously making a motion and a speech, and the House itself dividing upon a question of changes to be wrought in the tenure of power, or in the administration of power belonging to a body, or in the very composition of a body, which stands on the most perfect equality of title and legislative authority with the pretended house of reformers, over and above the advantage of being the highest court of jurisprudence in the kingdom, and the court of final appeal, whilst the other House is no court at all. The House of Commons has no more power to take one step towards such a pretended reformation than it has to debate upon the partition of Persia; and, arrogant as that House has sometimes shown itself (and needlessly arrogant, as in the arrest of Sir F. Burdett—amenable to the common course of law—by the Speaker's warrant), I am well persuaded that it will never seriously lend itself to a malice so entirely impotent. For into what shape could the House throw the expression of its will? A law, or anything resembling a law, it could not pass in the supposed case of hostility to the other House. A *resolution*, then, at the uttermost, would be the highest shape in which they could give expression to their revolutionary frenzy. To this *brutum fulmen* the Lords would not need to pay any the least attention; nor is there, indeed, any known channel, or any rational form of business, by which either House could communicate with the other on such a subject. However, as new cases introduce new forms and new resources, suppose Mr. Roebuck to march up to the bar of the Lords, armed with a message conveying the fact of such a motion and resolution, and declaratory of a wish on the part of certain Commons that their Lordships would forthwith surrender their power and privileges to a reform committee of the Lower House. What follows? First, a committal to Newgate of the individual messenger, and a message to the Commons notifying that fact. And the winding-up of the affair would be the bringing of the offender to the bar a little before the session closed, a reprimand severely expressed from the Chancellor, and finally, his liberation upon payment of his fees. Or, imagine the House of Commons sufficiently extravagant to pursue the matter, with what colour of right could they support their absurd message? They would find it impossible to deny the fact of their own original aggression; with whatever intention, they must concede that they had been in error as regarded known and settled rights; useful or not useful, they must concede that they had entertained a question, a debate, and a vote, upon the rights of others equally sacred with any of their own. And the charge against the House of Lords would then reduce itself to this, that they had "disobeyed a resolution of a House of Commons,"—a new species of crime, and as much known to our jurisprudence as it would be to charge a bishop, dean, and chapter, with disobeying the orders of the Admiralty. The House of Lords laughs at schemes for reforming it,—unless, indeed, such as arise within its own body. It is doubtful whether the Lords themselves possess any considerable powers in that direction; most certainly they have none which go to the extent of a complete alteration in the composition of their body, or in the title (viz. hereditary succession and immediate summons of the Crown) by which they hold their seats. These titles to their legislative office it is as little in the power of the Lords to alter as in that of the Commons. For any alteration here, as it affects the Lords immediately, finally affects the Crown and the rights of the Crown. Banish the peers by inheritance, and the aristocracy is destroyed (politically speaking); banish the new peers summoned by the Crown, and the King is destroyed *pro tanto*; banish the spiritual peers, and the Church is destroyed; make the House elective, and the whole government and polity of these kingdoms are destroyed, and will be instantly converted into a new thing, an anomalous monster, having no relation to the ancient constitution, and (upon many considerations peculiar to this country and to the arrangement of its property) so utterly unlike any known precedent that it must leave the deepest anxiety and uncertainty for the practical working of such a system, and no one certainty but this—that not a relic would survive of the old British Constitution.

Now, resuming the business of my letter, I have first to complain of some oversights committed by my censor. The first is an unwise one: unwise, for it is not wholly without choice, a choice influenced by his daily reading. The very ablest men (and my censor I have reason to think one who is certainly of that number) are and must be emasculated by the constant quality of what they read, whenever that reading lies amongst the unpremeditated polemics of daily newspapers. Newspapers, it is true, have their points of preeminence; and it is even an advantage—nay, a very great one—for the eloquent expression of what a man feels, that he should be driven to express himself rapidly. There is the same advantage as in conversation. And what is that? Simply this: that, when thoughts chase each other as rapidly as words can overtake them, each several thought comes to modify that which succeeds so intensely as to carry amongst the whole series a far more burning logic, a perfect life of cohesion, which is liable to be lost or frozen in the slow progress of careful composition. The case approaches that of personal passion, whether of rage, grief, or revenge. When was it ever found that a man in passionate anger did or could wander from his theme? Incoherence there might be *apparently* in his words, or his transitions might be too rapid to be intelligible to an unsympathising hearer; but the essential thoughts could not be otherwise than closely knit together. Rapid and extempore composition, therefore, has its own special advantages; but they are advantages which appeal to the sensibilities. But, to balance this potent advantage as regards the instant sensibilities, there are evils more than compensatory as regards the understanding. There can in such rapidity be no looking back, so as to adjust the latter sweep of the curve to the former; there can be no looking forward, so as to lay a slow foundation for remote superstructures. There can be no painful evolution of principles; there can be no elaborate analysis; there can be no subtle pursuit of distinction. Passion, indeed (and I have been saying so), has a logic of its own, and a logic as intense as a process of crystallization: but it is a crystallization among the separate parts *ab intra*: for between the parts *ab extra* the transitions are naturally more than lyrically abrupt.

In politics, of necessity, persons mix with things: cases of the moment mix with principles. And the temptations of personality, concurring with the unavoidable application to the topic of the hour, all combine to force a man into capricious and desultory transitions, however intensely fused may be each separate fragment of his disquisitions. Hence, for all readers, or at least for all students of the daily press, there arises a sad necessity of weaning their minds from the severities of logic. And a man who descends from long habits of philosophic speculation to a casual intercourse with fugitive and personal politics, finds even in the very ablest minds [an infirmity of step which retards his pace, . . . at first surprises him].[1]

Precisely from this habituation to the hasty thinking of the daily press, and not otherwise, can I explain the first oversight of my censor; which must have grown out of hurry and inattention. I will point out this error by referring to a letter from another person, practised in

[1] The words in brackets are erased in the MS., where the sentence is incomplete.

politics, which errs in the very-same way :—After taxing my paper with other faults, the writer goes on to say—"You "have neglected to pursue the history of the Whigs and "Tories; you have given us no running commentary on "their conduct at different eras; you have not illustrated "their principles as applied to the main critical cases which "have arisen since the Revolution of 1688-9." Now, on my part, in answer to this objection, I demand to know, What concern have I with the "*conduct*" of the Whigs and Tories? My object from the first was not to give a history of our political parties, but an account of their principles, of their creed, of their doctrinal code. And this, I contend, with my purposes, was the only useful way of treating the subject. I will explain.—The capital object of my paper was to facilitate a valuation of the Whig and Tory principles, as contrasted with the Radical, and therefore to bring them into a close comparison. Now, principles and creeds may be compared; but, as to the course of action pursued by the old constitutional parties as compared with the modern reforming parties, there are as yet no materials: the Muse of History, as regards the Radicals, sits yet in silence "waiting for a theme." The Radicals have not yet come forward on the stage as actors. For a few years they have prompted and suggested to the Whigs; but no Radical administration has yet existed: and until then there is no field of comparison. Secondly, as respects the Whigs and Tories, not one in five hundred cases of political experience has had any relation to Whig or Tory principles; which fact shows the uselessness of pursuing their conduct through the details of our history. The two parties have acted as any other confederations of men in ancient history, or in modern continental history; that is, they have opposed each other as *Ins* and *Outs*, as men having power against men in quest of power,—parties which would have existed no less had Whig and Tory never been heard of. This or that war, for instance, bearing no possible relation to Whiggism or Toryism, has been supported on the one side as useful to some interest of commerce, or of a supposed balance amongst the states of Christendom; it has been opposed on the other side as too rashly undertaken, as too carelessly planned, or as too feebly conducted: all of which arguments furnished colourable views of policy, true or not true for that occasion, but in any case perfectly remote from considerations of Whig or Tory doctrine. Such a tax, again, was bad on general grounds of economy, or it violated some pledge which had been given, or it was ill graduated, or it was collected at a disproportionate expense. But still, right or wrong, these grounds of opposition involve no appeal to the characteristic principles of Whig and Tory. Even the Regency question—one of those most entitled to be held a constitutional question of all which occurred throughout the last century—was debated on arguments aloof from Whiggism or Toryism. And Mr. Fox was influenced to the course he took, of maintaining a right in the heir-apparent, upon any incompetence in the sovereign, to assume the regency as a trust which had devolved to him by legal succession, not assuredly by any reliance on Whig principles (on the contrary, Mr. Pitt's doctrine that any regency, and the personal shares in any regency, must be a mere creation of Parliament, wore a much more popular air, and so far would have had the better right to be called the Whig doctrine). Not, therefore, on Whig principles was Mr. Fox moved to take this unpopular course, but entirely upon personal motives of friendship for the Prince of Wales. The American War is another of the rare cases for which Whig and Tory principles have been thought available; but upon no reasons which argue any clear acquaintance with Whig and Tory distinctions. The case of Colonies had not been specially reserved at the great era of settling our Constitution, and was therefore not specially provided for. And, as to the general case of taxation imposed upon bodies not directly represented,—*that* was surely virtually discountenanced as much by the Tories as by the Whigs,—the settlement of the Revolution having been the joint work of both. Hence I argue that to have pursued the Whigs and Tories through a course of historical cases which rarely belonged to their creed *as* Whig or Tory, but almost universally to their position as ministerial or anti-ministerial, could have answered no useful purpose. Finally, over and above the two arguments already stated against the reasonableness of such an historical deduction (the first against its possibility, the second against its use and relevance), I contend that, even were it possible, and were it relevant, still the public interest and the particular question I had undertaken, of appraising the three chief denominations of party amongst us, must be far more deeply affected by an account of their separate principles than of their separate conduct. "*We*," says my censor, "*care comparatively nothing for your dormant creed.*" A more unwise saying it would be difficult to devise. Creeds are eternal: if dormant, they may be recalled to life: if betrayed, they are open to revindication. Men are transient—as transient as their passions; past conduct is no pledge for future conduct, even in the same men coming into new positions and contradictory interests; but in a profession of faith you have at least an appeal to the conscience of the individual, and you have the authority which belongs to the standards of ancient wisdom, owned for such through many generations. If at this present moment it were desirable for any purpose to bring under the eyes of a Spaniard (standing, suppose, in the circumstances of doubt and inquiry which Mr. Blanco White has described as belonging to his own case) a comparison of the Church of England with that of Papal Rome, in which direction would you turn your appeal?—to *the pretensions* and character of the English Clergy, or to the Thirty-nine Articles as interpreted and explained by the learning of three centuries? to the variable *fact* of the clerical conduct at different eras, and to an estimate of their social value and consideration at these eras; or to the eternal monuments of the creed professed by the Church of England, and the secondary but still important settlements of her discipline and ecclesiastical government? Most assuredly to these last. For the Spaniard would himself say, "I am occupied with an interest transcending personal regards, towards an attempt to estimate the truth and value of the English Confession. Possibly, if all other means of judging were denied me, some very imperfect aid might be drawn from the prevailing character (or reputed character) of the English priesthood: conjecturally, the Church might be measured by her ministerial agents; but surely this indirect appraisement would be preposterous for one who enjoys the most absolute access to all the *direct* means of making up his judgment on the Anglican Church, and can apply his mind to the very words and professions of the Anglican Church, by way of ascertaining for himself what is her title to be held a depositary of divine truth." Besides, any well-informed Englishman would in such a case be disposed to tell the Spaniard that a judgment of the Anglican Church built upon the very fairest appreciation of her clergy must be conflicting or contradictory in its final result. The clergy have varied with the circumstances. In the age of martyrdom,—viz. the middle of the sixteenth century, when the reformed churches were everywhere in the agony of conflict with the established corruptions of Christianity,—no church had been so zealous or so memorably lavish of her blood as the English. During a second stage of her history, when she was placed so far in a station of security as to find herself militant no longer by secular forces, but those of intellèct and erudition, she had become the most learned and the most intellectual of all churches; and indeed she might be called not so much the *most* learned, as the *only* learned church,—since even the Papal Church, which ranks nearest to her, has attained to distinction as a body [1] only through one or two of her many orders,—viz. the Jesuits and the Benedictines. At length, in a third stage, unfortunately for her own dignity and usefulness, the Anglican Church reached a position of absolute repose ; the unsettled relations between herself and the Papists were now terminated by the final exclusion of Popish families from the throne ; and even the Protestant Dissenters were placed by various acts of toleration in a condition which left them thenceforwards liable to no irritation, active or passive : they could neither

[1] After all, the distinction of the Church of England is even more splendid in right of her potent intellects than of her great scholars. Bellarmine, Baronius, Huet, &c., may possibly confront our Ushers, Sandersons, Lightfoots, and Stillingfleets ; though even here, in a numerical sense, the English Church is far the richer. But what antagonists, many or few, can the Church of Rome produce to our Jeremy Taylors and Barrows ? The French Bossuets, Fenelons, Bourdaloues, &c., whatever may be thought of their meagre and attenuated rhetoric, are one and all the most commonplace of thinkers : not one of them makes any effort after forcible thinking.

irritate effectually, nor be irritated. Under the torpor of this situation, concurring with the taint to our national morals sustained in various ways at the era of the Restoration (which did not purge itself off in less than a century), the English clergy sank to the lowest point of depression in the interval between the English and the French revolutions. They were still the most learned and accomplished clergy by far in the world ; in fact, the Popish clergy were, generally speaking, illiterate, all *their* learning being confined to the monastic orders. They were also a body of gentlemen, and useful for their moral examples, their attainments, and their beneficence, as so many centres of civilization dispersed over all the parishes of England. But, at the same time, it must be granted that gradually, from the absolute annihilation of their *militant* condition in a political sense, and the general tone of ease and comfort in their finances, they had become the least of a spiritual-minded clergy known perhaps in Christendom. The pastoral duties to their flocks were all crowded and depressed into a few periodical formalities and freezing ceremonies: even these were sustained only by custom, by the necessities of canonical obedience, and by official jealousy of intrusion upon their privileged ground by unqualified persons. And this state of things arose, unfortunately, not so much from conscious negligence, as from systematic depression of the pastoral office, and alienation from all vigilant religious sensibility, under the general name of enthusiasm. The delineations, accordingly, which we find of the clerical character in the novels of the first half of the eighteenth century are such as could not (with every allowance for exaggeration) have been offered as representative pictures at any other period of the Church's history. At length, however, the evil had reached its height, and a reaction commenced. The Methodists had been originally projected from the Church herself. For one generation, probably, they produced little impression that was externally visible upon the Church. But at length men of family and social consideration, as well as scholars in the two universities, began to join them : the soil was prepared ; a vast machinery of religious societies began to get into motion ; and a fourth stage was entered of Church History, as applied to the character of the clergy. Within the last forty or fifty years, the English clergy in every rank (perhaps even more in the highest than lowest) have passed through a process of silent reformation. A very large infusion of what is called technically "evangelical" principles has been poured into the Church, —into the highest ranks, I repeat, at least as much as into the lower ; and the complexion of the whole body is now so altered, judged by its sermons, tracts, public speeches, support given to religious societies of every denomination, that, by comparison with its own state seventy years ago, it may be called an Apostolic Church. This is a point which can be determined only by those who have connexions which enable them to speak with knowledge ; for the mass of public writers know nothing of the real existing Church, but merely echo an invidious clamour now superannuated, and perhaps always grounded in the main upon tithes. However, the immediate purpose I had in this reference to the varying history of the Church was to show that, if the appeal were made to the history or character of the clergy, then the report must be as variable, and speak as variable a language, as belongs to the whole range between the self-sacrificing spirit of a primitive martyr and the most absolute dedication to the world. But the creed is a monument that cannot change.

Upon these arguments, and the spirit of these arguments, I pronounce my censor wrong in supposing it any part of my duty to have traced the *conduct* of the Whigs and Tories. My business was with their creed. And to that I now return. My censor has made it necessary that I should do so, having apparently never opened his eyes to the main principle on which my whole theory of our two English constitutional parties is built. I judge this because he has made no objection or demur of any sort to my full and open statement of that theory, and first opposes it by a point-blank contradiction when I am simply making an application of this theory to a particular case. The case is that of Mr. Pitt, of whom I affirm, that up to a certain stage of the French Revolution he might have smiled approvingly upon its promises (and probably *did* so), not less cordially than any Whig the most ardent — *as* a Whig, and speaking in that character. That restriction must always be borne in mind, because there is nothing to hinder any pure Republican, the most alien to the British Constitution, from calling himself a Whig; and many a fierce Republican has done so. Upon this case of illustration,—Mr. Pitt's case in relation to the French Revolution,—the censor denies it roundly as a case within the verge of possibility. Mr. Pitt smile approvingly upon the French Revolution! impossible! "*He could not*," says the censor; and that is the amount of his reply. Now, a blank negation is at any time met sufficiently by a blank re-affirmation. And, with respect to this particular negation, as regards the mere question of fact apart from the question of principle, it is notorious that Mr. Pitt not only might consistently, but *did* in very deed sympathize with the French Revolution in a degree which made it necessary for Edmund Burke to couch his political vision from the cataract which obscured the sanity of his views. Even in a recent Radical journal (by way of an argument *ad hominem*) the censor will find it noticed that in the matter of the French Revolution Burke (though as yet still connected with a *soi-disant* Whig party) "betrayed principles *less popular* than those of the minister; and that afterwards, when Burke (as it was termed) went over to him, the junction took place, not by the former being converted by the latter to anti-popular principles, but by Burke converting the minister to his own anti-jacobinism." —(Lond. and West. Rev., No. 8; and 51, p. 496, *Art.* Wraxall's Memoirs.) The Radical writer of this paper goes on to say (ibid. p. 497) that "for some time after that event" (viz. the French Revolution) "Pitt *coincided with Fox* in regarding it as auspicious to the friendly relations between France and England,"—words which could not have been more apposite to the present question if they had been expressly written with a view to it, and (which is more important) words in harmony with the entire tenor of the debates in those days, and in equal harmony with all the attested glimpses of Mr. Pitt's private sentiments, as expressed either in conversation or in confidential letters.

Here, therefore, at least, the censor will find himself in error as to the question of fact. But, even had it been otherwise, this could not have affected the question of principle there concerned,—viz. that a true Tory, understanding his own principles, let Mr. Pitt have done as he would, was bound to rejoice in the first promises of the French Revolution — though, perhaps, to "rejoice with trembling." Was it, or was it not, a resemblance of his own Revolution, to which he by his ancestors had set his seal? If it was, if there were the same great principles acknowledged, of representative government, of limits set to the regal power, of accountability lodged in quarters where it could be enforced, of universal contribution to the national burdens without immunities for any rank or order, of personal security from summary acts of oppression, open or secret,—if these and other grand cardinal grounds of social liberty were laid down solemnly, and hallowed in the earlier acts of that mighty Revolution, then I affirm that both Whigs and Tories, supposing them masters of their own original creeds, must in consistency have concurred fervently to an act which was but a republication of their own immortal precedent—that precedent by which they had inaugurated their own political birth as parties. The disturbing lights of present circumstances too often withdraw the attention of all parties, whether political or religious, from their own original principles,—those principles which first confederated them into parties; too often also it happens that, from mere disuse of exercise in first principles, from the total defect of occasions which might adequately call them out (a case which eminently belongs to the prosperous and secure condition of England throughout the latter half of the eighteenth century), men, otherwise the most intelligent, fall into a dim or lukewarm recognition of their own distinguishing creeds; and, above all, it has been found continually that the possession of power indisposes a man to admit any principles whatsoever in their perfect authority which are likely to prove personal obstacles. Cromwell was originally a lover of freedom, and perhaps would never have been other than a lover had freedom not clashed with his personal views. All these reasons might have concurred to make Mr. Pitt scowl upon the French Revolution, *had* he scowled; which it is clear that he did not. But no matter for individual examples; it will remain true after all that the ideal Tory was pledged by his faith to an approbation of the French Revolution in its early stages. And the censor, in contradicting me, has failed to observe that his contradiction is planted in the wrong place: the general inference that a Tory was bound to sympathise with the earliest stages of the French Revolution is already involved in my theory of the relations between Whigs and Tories,—which theory, therefore, and not a casual illustration of it, the censor ought to have impeached.

That he has not done this I ascribe to his having been thrown off any distinct apprehension of it by the hurried style of reading which is become a mere necessity for a political writer, or even a large political observer, in these days. In this I mean no reproach, for there is a sheer incompatibility between seeing largely of all aspects and accurately of each. So that I have no cause to complain, and do not complain; but the fact is still so, that he has failed to observe my peculiar view of our original constitutional parties, without which he could not do justice to anything I have said,—that theory being the ground of the whole.

This view, therefore, this theory, I shall re-state with amendments,—not merely by way of a *résumé* or recapitulation introductory to what I have to say of Radicalism, but also because in and for itself I contend that my views on this subject are the first which give meaning or coherency to the history of these kingdoms. Let it be understood that I offer my present theory as in defiance of all former theories. I contend that no previous account of Whigs and Tories, of their origin, or of their relations, is self-consistent, or even intelligible; and I contend also that all are historically false. The history of England, and still more that of Scotland, is grossly falsified in all the main circumstances connected with the narrative chapters of Whig and Tory progress, and is thrown into absolute contradiction in its philosophic chapters. Bear with me whilst I reassert my own scheme: it will contain but little of repetition,—it will not be long. And, at the same time, remember that, if just, it will have a further value than according to its present position,—a value not in relation to fugitive politics, or their more fugitive aspects, but in relation to philosophic and self-consistent history.

I have already made you acquainted with my leading thesis in this speculation,—a thesis which at once changes the whole field and area of the question. It is this: that the kind of opposition between Whig and Tory is not, as the current notions make it, logical,—that is, contradictory each of the other, in the way, for instance, that a Christian and an anti-Christian are opposed, an Episcopalian and a Presbyterian, a theist and an atheist. All these denominations and counter-denominations are of such a nature that they obviously exclude each other. Theism, for instance, being true, Atheism (as a mere rebound of that proposition) must be false. Not only cannot both consist in the same subject, but even in different subjects both cannot be simultaneously true: one must be false (speaking of speculative truth); one must be wrong (speaking of practical). Either of such alternatives being assumed for a substance, the other instantly becomes a shadow. But the opposition between Whig and Tory is not of this kind, as has been universally assumed and argued upon: it is not logical as between *A* and *non-A*, between *is* and *is not*, between true and false, between wrong and right. The opposition is of the same nature as that which takes place in algebra when quantities equally real, but in opposite direction, are treated as positive and negative. A ship sailing eastwards is carried by currents certain distances to the west: the motions in one direction you put down as affirmative, those in the other (equally real, observe) as negative, and it matters not which you call affirmative, which negative: so far is there from being any true logical negation in the matter which would imply one of the two to be necessarily a nonentity; and the opposition between the two is of that nature which can allow them actually to exist in the same subject, though not simultaneously. A still better illustration, because including this circumstance of simultaneity, may be drawn from the case of action and reaction in mechanics, or from that of attraction and repulsion in dynamics; for these forces, though in perfect opposition, are so far from therefore excluding each other that they cannot exist apart,—each, in fact, exists by and through its antagonist.

In perfect analogy to these cases is the relation between

Whig and Tory. But how little this can have been perceived is evident from the universal language of our political literature, in which the case is treated as one of standing and irreconcilable dissension with regard to the separate pretensions of the Crown and the People. The notion is not merely that the Whigs carry the popular claims, for example, to a higher point (which might still be a *fixed* point) than the Tories, and that, in the same proportion, these Whigs depress the claims of the Sovereign ; but this notion is carried even to the preposterous extremity of supposing each party to seek an *unlimited* extension of privilege for that one among the triple forces of our constitution whose interest it espouses. If this were really so, if it had been the prevailing policy and the rationale of that policy among the Tories to seek the unconditional depression of the popular interest, and reciprocally of the Whigs to seek the unconditional depression of the Crown, then, indeed, we must acknowledge a blank opposition between the two parties in the main articles of their separate creeds. That an interpretation so idle of the refined differences between two parties arising in the very bosom of civilization, and at the most intellectual era of the most intellectual of nations,—interpretations so gross of differences so spiritual,—ever could have been entertained by reflective men, is marvellous. Mere orators, and public men with public merits of the popular order, are little qualified to meet any question which lies below the surface,—the opinion of such men is of no authority in the second or third generation from their own day ; but that Burke should have so far yielded to the vulgar error as to speak of it in common conversation as a problem still pending and *sub judice* whether Whigs or Tories were "*in the right*" would be humiliating if it were clearly established. But I doubt the fact : to the philosophic understanding of Burke such an error was impossible. There is an explanation which, whilst it palliates or even cancels the peccant part of his meaning,—that part which seems to countenance the vulgar error,—is equally useful in accounting for the rise of that vulgar error amongst men in general. I will state it immediately.

Meantime, you understand that I deny broadly and universally, and place amongst the vast catalogue of vulgar errors, that notion which attributes any logical opposition to the relations between Whigs and Tories—any such opposition as would make it necessary, if one were pronounced right, that the other should be pronounced wrong. Both are right; and not only so,—not only can these party differences co-exist without violence to truth,—but, as in the mechanical law, formerly referred to, of action and reaction, they are *able to exist only by means of their co-existence.* The true view of their relations is this, that each party forms one hemisphere; jointly they make up the total sphere. They divide, it is true, the functions of the constitution,—one party administering the popular or democratic, the other administering the anti-popular or timocratic functions. But, in dividing the functions, they still distribute their care over the whole. In so exquisite a system of balances as is at work in the British constitution, there is a constant reason for fear that in one function or other the equilibrium should be disturbed. Consequently, it is fit that to every organ through which the constitution acts or is acted upon a vigilant jealousy should be directed. This jealousy cannot, by any possibility, be rendered so keen and effective if lodged comprehensively and indiscriminately, for all parts of the constitution, in the same general hands, charged alternately with the duty of repressing the Crown and the People, as it would be if assigned dramatically, by separate parts or castings, to separate agents. Human nature itself would make it a self-defeating jealousy if it were necessary for the same man to vary his own passions to suit the varying circumstances; and the task of training his feelings this day in one direction, and to-morrow in another, would be a mere impossibility for any man of steady feelings,—such feelings as it could be otherwise right to rely on. Habits are the great pledge for the due performance of duties; and habits, *to be* habits, cannot be supposed applying themselves to variable or contradictory impulses. Hence it is that the Whigs have charged themselves with one class of duties to the British Constitution, and the Tories with another. Not that I would wish to represent this wise division of labour as having been originally prescribed by human foresight, but that, under the wise leading of human nature, and under the natural tendencies of human passions or interests, things having once settled into this arrangement or into this tendency, the result was seen and approved by the deliberate judgment of parties. An advocate would not feel himself entitled (or, if entitled, not reconciled) to the practice of urging the presumptions strongly against an accused person simply by the balancing *right* of that person to take off the effect of evidence, and in the utmost degree that he could to throw dust in the eyes of the court; but perhaps he *may* feel reconciled to this by the consciousness that the very extremity of this rigour on his own part, and the anticipation of it, like the intensity of a mechanic force, will be the very best pledge in the long run for a corresponding extremity of effort in the reaction. And thus the guardians of the Crown prerogative are warranted in pressing this prerogative to the very uttermost tension by the certainty that thus, more effectually than by all the bribes in this world, they will ensure the permanent reaction of the Democratic party in defence of popular privilege. But that, in the very midst of this bisection of the public spirit into two polar forces of reciprocal antagonism for the sake of a steadier, stronger, and more continuous action, there does, in fact, preside latently and in the rear a transcendent regard to the total interest in the most comprehensive sense; that neither party wishes the weight of the other party to be diminished, much less annihilated, as is often imagined, by an excess of blundering in respect of principles (for as to personal influence, and the question of Ministerial power, *that* is quite another thing);—all these truths flow like so many corollaries from that great consummating act by which, at the same moment, our constitution was finally established, and our two great constitutional parties originally inaugurated. You understand, of course, that I mean the Revolution of 1688-9. For let me ask any man who clings to the old notion that the Whigs and Tories are hostile parties (hostile, I mean, as depositaries of principle, not in the very different sense of parties seeking against parties possessing power), and that they wish (or have reason to wish) each other's destruction,—such a man let me ask how he will reconcile this notion of essential hostility with the unanimity and absolute harmony which they manifested in the most critical and important measure, the measure most fitted to divide men otherwise hostile of all which ever have agitated this nation. Did the Whigs and the Tories adjust the measure of the Revolution in the way of a capitulation—that is, by mutual concessions, by reciprocal sacrifices of interests which had confessedly held a high party value? Was the Revolution, in the sense of Roman law, a *transactio*,—that is, was it a compromise in which both parties, under a sense of their situation and doubtful power, yielded up some capital principles? Nothing of the sort. Never was there a measure to which both parties more cordially or unreservedly concurred in all that touched upon principles: for the articles on which they much differed were articles of a personal pressure: as, for instance, should the nephew of the exiled king stand first and single in the substitution; or, 2*dly*, be associated with that king's eldest daughter (in which case, undoubtedly, there was a personal wrong to the younger daughter and to her children); or, 3*dly*, be coldly remanded to his original place in the line of succession? These questions were certainly personal questions, and merely personal; for the least unscrupulous of the deliberators never meant to raise a precedent, in the case of calling William to the throne, that should be construed in favour of nephews generally by preference to daughters. On every question of principle, all questions which concerned the rights of kings, of people, of the church, the mode of administration, the exercise of the prerogative, and the tenure of property, both parties coalesced, and both were equally forward. No capital opposition was raised but from a third party, connected by no ties of principle whatever, but purely by private considerations, either of fidelity, gratitude, or disinterested attachment to the king's person—viz. Jacobites. And it must also be remembered that in other instances of opposition, *not* capital, the parties were often neither Whigs, Tories, nor Jacobites; for there were many in both Houses who professed neither the great principles of the two former parties nor the personal bias of the latter.

Here then I take my stand. The Revolution, taken with its commentary in the trial of Sacheverell, was the great record of our constitution; an act declaratory and enactory;

for at the same time it proclaimed and republished former principles of freedom, defined and limited all which were of dubious construction, and solemnly enacted those integrations of our social system which had been hitherto entrusted respectfully (but, as recent experience had shown, dangerously) to the royal forbearance or the ministerial responsibility. By this great act was ascertained for ever the true *locus* of each function belonging to a state: the power of the sword (so agitating a topic of dispute forty odd years before); the power of the purse; the power of legislation (which the last years of Charles II, his avowed intentions, and the insinuations of James in his very first speech from the throne, had threatened to centre in the king and his privy council); the power of the press and of confederate petition; the municipal powers all over the kingdom, and, by consequence, the unfettered power of choosing juries (both of which had, by implication, been assailed in the *Quo warranto* writs of Charles II); the powers of the Church and of freehold property as against the Crown; and, finally (to omit many other great stipulations of present or future consequence), the executive power in its pretensions to a right of dispensation, and indirectly to the maintenance of a standing force. To this great charter of our rights, as collected from the written documents and the acts of the Convention and subsequent Parliament, who were the parties? who the main movers and authors of the measure itself which led to these senatorial acts,—viz. of the great secession from the reigning king and the adhesion to the Prince of Orange? Simply the Whigs and Tories; and, had either party proved recusant, instead of a bloodless revolution, without even a civil commotion worth notice, or the disturbance of individual rights, we must have had a civil war. The inference as to the unity of Whigs and Tories in every matter of principle I need not repeat. But one thing I must add,—that this unity is the more evident because (as I shall immediately show) the Whig and Tory parties were first ascertained by the Revolution; or, rather, it would be more accurate to say that these parties, in their full maturity, were a twin-birth with that great event. And I hold it a mistake to suppose that Whigs and Tories were formally opposed to each other as antagonist forces previously to that era. The word *Whig* was often used, but the word *Tory* hardly ever; and the first field in which they were brought into direct antithesis was in the north or Protestant part of Ireland; whence they passed to Dublin; and from Dublin, about the year of the Revolution, to London.

Now, upon this theory of the absolute unity between Whigs and Tories as to principle, and their bisection into parties of mutual repulsion only for practical effects, it will be demanded, Whence then comes the universal belief that the Whig is every way opposed to the Tory? I answer, from these three causes:—

1. From the original separation for the purpose already explained,—viz. the more entire dedication of one agency to one class of constitutional objects.

2. Still more from this cause: that, once separated into distinct bodies on this principle of the division of labour, each body acting separately, as was natural, in a distinct province, they became marked out to the sovereign as two parties having distinct personal connexions, and by means of these connexions having varying forces of property and borough interest, and national influence, amongst them. Hence arose a reason to the king for choosing his ministers now amongst one party, now amongst the other,—with no view to any sort of principles, good or bad, but simply to the party connexions. Thus it was that the Whigs and Tories came to be viewed under new and shifting relations as Ministerial or in Opposition, *Ins* or *Outs*, men having power and men seeking power.

3. Even apart from this relation to the momentary possession of power and place, the simple circumstance of uniform confederation for the same line of policy (however unconnected that policy might be with principles of any quality, and however disconnected within itself),—nay, the mere force of names as rallying points for men in public acts,—would again tend to disturb and confuse the original distinctions on which Whig and Tory parties proceeded, viz. the distinctions of function: that is to say, the attention of men would be far more frequently called to the *nominal* distinctions of party connexion, from acting in concert with Nottingham,

Bolingbroke, Oxford, or on the other side with Marlborough, Somers, Godolphin, than with any profounder characteristics. And these *nominal* party unities are quite sufficient to explain the whole habit of attributing to Whig and Tory that kind of hostility which never can attach to them *as* such, but do and will always attach to them in other superadded characters: first, of partisans confederated under two different sections of the aristocracy; and, secondly, of men in the king's service or out of that service and therefore, by the necessities of parliamentary tactics, in opposition. Seeing that Whigs and Tories were always in fact opposed to each other, it was natural enough to suppose them opposed *as* Whigs and Tories; for, though in that character they were really united (except as to the separate mode of applying their principles), yet, as this one difference of practical functions had availed naturally to keep them distinct and aloof, it led by consequence to the other differences of personal connexion and taking or not taking office.

These distinctions justify[1] Burke. When he spoke of it as a thing not decided whether his own party or the Tories were in the right, he meant doubtless to speak of neither with any reference to principles, but simply in their character of parties abetting a different line of public policy,—one, suppose, a warlike, the other a pacific, policy, but neither having any the least connexion with popular or anti-popular creeds. In reality, if a foreigner were to enter as a student upon a course of English History for the two last centuries, he would find himself continually at a loss to understand the *rationale* of our party distinctions. He would find that the vast majority of public acts ascribed to the Tories, and

[1] And also I submit to my censor that the same distinctions justify me in a passage where he supposes a contradiction. I speak of the Whigs as immortal and co-eternal with the constitution; elsewhere I speak of them as a decaying party. Certainly. In the first sense, I speak of them as the assertors *speculatively* (in conjunction with Tories) of certain great principles embodied in the British Constitution, and as the assertors *practically* (in reaction to the Tories) of one moiety of these principles,—the democratic moiety. In the second sense I speak of them as a body of partisans, in or out of power, opposed to another body out or in. In this latter sense, I find many orthodox Radical authorities for holding the Whigs to be a party almost defunct.

said by the historian to have been opposed by the Whigs, had no discoverable connexion with any principles at all that bear upon either popular or aristocratic pretensions. Many other cases he would find in which the Tories had taken the popular side, the Whigs the aristocratic. For instance, Mr. Fox's India Bill, by denying all control over Indian affairs to the proprietors of India stock, certainly treaded upon an aristocratic path. Again, his theory in the Regency question was better suited to the atmosphere of old France than of old England; whilst Mr. Pitt's proceeded upon a due regard to the democratic influences in our mixed constitution. Mr. Fox would have had us believe that the mere fact of an incapacity in the sovereign, when solemnly put on record, at once devolved the regency upon the heir-apparent, as an estate that had lapsed. Mr. Pitt, with a noble contempt of self-interest, which obviously pointed all men's ambition towards the rising sun, insisted that a regency, and every place in a regency, must be the mere creation of Parliament. In this instance there is but too much reason to suspect Mr. Fox of having complied with his private bias in favour of the existing Prince of Wales. But there are other cases in which the Whig party, without even Mr. Fox's apology, promoted measures violently opposed to their traditional principles (as guardians more peculiarly of democratic rights), by clamorously coming forward to abet the most conspicuous tyrant in history. They fought against the Peninsular warfare, or any other mode for showing our sympathy with outraged Spain, even to a point of *acharnement.* But this they did, it will be pleaded, not in their character of Whigs, but as opponents, by hook or by crook, to the Ministerial policy of those days. Exactly so: that is the very thing I am saying; and the foreign student here supposed would very soon discover that in a vast majority of cases neither Whig nor Tory did or could model his conduct upon any system of Whig or Tory principles that ever was conceived, and precisely because the questions are rare indeed which bear any relation whatever either to popular pretensions or to anti-popular. And from all this I deduce the following inference,—that the common notion (that notion which Mr. Burke was assuming in the case referred to) of an original and essential hostility between Whig and Tory first took its rise, and has since sustained itself, by observing them in constant opposition as an *acting* party: which circumstance has availed naturally to obscure the primary truth, as I shall always maintain it to be, that as a *speculative* party, as a party appealing to political principles, they are the very same party under two different phases,—one looking to one interest of the constitution, the other to the other; but phases, surely, not arguing any essential differences or hostility, since hostility there can be none between different parts of the same constitution.

At this point, therefore, you will observe that, if the censor persists in rejecting all appeal to creeds as of no importance, if he persists in urging the appeal to the acts of the two parties, in that case, although I deny utterly the pretence that the Tory acts, taken comprehensively, have been less friendly to civil liberty than those of their antagonists, and although I have shown in some cases (and might show in many others) that upon the whole the Whigs have manifested a much greater insensibility to such interests in any case where they happened to clash with personal party objects,—yet, if it had been otherwise, as any such hostility to freedom must have arisen from the particular position of the Tories as the king's ministers at the moment, and not from their peculiar principles, the censor has precisely the same evil to apprehend from the Whigs, now that their time has come for occupying power and place. For instance, Mr. Pitt, in a period of war upon a fearful scale, and afterwards with much less reason his successors in a period of profound peace, suspended the *Habeas Corpus* Act. Well, no man can imagine that either one or the other ministry did this as Tories; they did it as the persons then carrying on the government, and responsible to the nation for the security of towns, districts, arsenals, and generally of the public peace. Any danger which menaces interests so vast and so feverishly susceptible of derangement is likely to be exaggerated, and to prove a trying temptation to him upon whose shoulders the total responsibility has settled. And, on the other hand, it is a homage to public freedom which costs a man absolutely nothing to depreciate the danger and the necessities of the crisis when he happens to be himself released from all pressure of the responsibility, and when the utmost realisation of the dangers apprehended would but serve his own nearest interest by loading his antagonist with blame. Take an illustration from rioting. Innumerable have been the local riots in this free country, and almost as innumerable the shades of conduct and the varieties of forbearance amongst the magistrates. Some, from native timidity and want of nerve, have proceeded at once to the very harshest extremities. Others scarcely would find any circumstances sufficient to warrant the application of military force. And wherefore these differences? Would any man attempt to explain them out of Whig and Tory principles,—as though the generous, forbearing, and confiding magistrate must naturally be a Whig, and the timid one a Tory? Obviously, they are due to differences of bodily temperament and of moral disposition. But in the case which called for the suspension of the *Habeas Corpus* Act the responsibility was on a scale far transcending that which can have ever attached to a local magistrate; and, perhaps, under the same circumstances, the boldest of men and the most fervent Whig would have adopted the same course,— supposing, always, that he was under the same *onus* of responsibility.

Making these distinctions, and clearing themselves from the confusion, so often used to darken these questions, between the acts which are done in the superinduced character of king's minister and those which are done in the original character of Tory,—every honest Radical must feel that there is not one atom of difference between the two parties, except what arises from being *in* or *out*, which difference is now altogether in favour of the Tories. Can it be pretended for one instant that the Whig aristocracy are less an aristocracy? Are they less decorated with titles, stars, and garters? Did they, before the Reform Bill, traffic less habitually in boroughs? At this very moment, do the Whig nobility and landed proprietors less regularly avail themselves of their natural influence over the voters on their estates? Do they, or ever did they, less firmly support the practice of entails, or any other connected with primogeniture? Do they less disdainfully recoil from unequal alliances in their families? Many more such questions might be asked; and, considering the sort of answer which must be given to them, an honest Radical must blush scarlet.

Having stated with rigour my theory of the relations between the two great constitutional parties of England, it may be useful to say a word or two on the case treated historically; by which means I shall be able at the same time to support what I have said, and to apply myself with better effect to Radicalism. The history of this subject must naturally be confused when the theory is false. You must be well aware that the first Earl of Strafford and the first Earl of Clarendon, Lord Treasurer Southampton, and the first Duke of Ormond, are not unfrequently called *Tories.* Mr. Fox, with all the benefit of modern research, does not scruple to allow himself in that mode of expression, with what propriety we shall see; and indeed no writer whom I have yet seen, whether historical or directly political, escapes the same leading errors. The fact of so very general a consent in this direction might have weighed with me to suspect my own grounds, were it not that the palpable error, which I have so repeatedly had occasion to press upon your notice, of neglecting (but rather, I should say, of overlooking) the capital distinction between a party considered as a depository of certain principles, and the same party as a depository of ministerial power, entitles me to slight all my predecessors for so much of their opinions as arises out of this oversight. The justice of criticism cannot refuse me this concession,—that the thousand reviews of any question whatsoever, conducted in perfect ignorance of some capital distinction, are of meaner authority than any single review written under the benefit of this guiding light. It will be evident, indeed, to any thoughtful interpreter of English History, that he who can deliberately call Lord Clarendon a Tory uses that word in a sense so vague and unlimited that Cicero, Atticus, or even Marcus Brutus, might be termed Tories with equal propriety; as, on the other hand, with a view to the democratic agencies which he employed for his own elevation, Cæsar might be termed a Whig. But such a latitudinarian use of these designations would end in conveying a mere loose analogy, in a case where he must be supposed in quest of a close and special determination. Amongst the decorations of rhetoric such an application of party distinctions may have its value ; but severer purposes demand a corresponding severity in the terminology : low thinking only can allow of a lax use of language.

The rise of parties in England may be traced back to the reign of Charles the First. It is true that before that era the rudiments were forming, and large materials were gathering, for the future construction of organized parties. But as yet they were slenderly combined, and too exclusively *personal* in their objects. I have elsewhere ascribed the growth of Parliamentary power and dignity, which advanced chiefly in the reign of the first James, but manifested itself as a *conscious* strength not very emphatically before the reign of the first Charles, to the large expansion of a *gentry*, or junior nobility, throughout the sixteenth century, in consequence of the inroads made upon the great feudal aristocracy by the sagacious measures of Henry VII,[1] supported as

[1] It must be evident that from the beginning of the twelfth century the English aristocracy had possessed a latent strength which was constantly and instantly called into powerful vitality upon the least encouragement from any symptom of weakness in the Crown. And this strength was apparently a growing strength up to the latter end of the fifteenth century. Looking back through a period of less than one hundred years from the battle of Bosworth to the minority of Richard II, Henry VII could not fail to observe that four kings (and in effect five) had been obliged to fight for their crowns with rebellious subjects, and that in reality some of the more potent amongst these subjects, as the Percys and the Nevilles, must have felt that the crown had been held as a mere donation from themselves. The evil was imminent and deadly. His own crown was held by the same tenure ; and already perhaps the Stanleys and Mowbrays might be revolving new revolutions and more profitable treasons. The evil was to be cured by attacking its causes. What were they ? Precisely the same as were employed in the latter days of the Republic by the colossal nobility of Rome : viz. enormous estates, landed and in money ; secondly, schools of gladiators. It has, perhaps, been too little noticed that all the potentates amongst the Roman nobility kept what was in fact a body-guard, sometimes a considerable army, in the *scholæ gladiatoriæ*,—ostensibly kept for civic purposes (the public shows were held such), but in reality as a "strong back" to purposes of personal ambition. Cæsar, besides his gladiators, possessed one entire legion composed of his own hired servants. Exactly corresponding to these foundations of power were those of the English

they were by measures having the same tendency on the part of his son. The most direct of these measures, a prohibitory measure, attacked the mercenary supporters of aristocracy,—the standing *nucleus* of armies; the other, a permissive measure, withdrew the props from the main basis on which the aristocratic power was built,—viz. territorial wealth locked up into masses by the spirit of ancient usage and of legislation. The same measures, applied in other directions, were pursued through the reigns of the succeeding century, until their operation had been universally diffused and made effective. Out of the partial ruins which followed was recomposed a new order,—an order which was first known in England,—viz. an inferior nobility connected upwards and downwards, dignified enough, by descent in a large proportion, and by property, to maintain a concurrent political authority with the *haute noblesse*, and yet popular enough in its sympathies, by means of the continual interfusion kept up between itself and the working order, to stand forward as a general trustee for protecting the interests and for uttering the voice of the Commons of the land. That order had certainly existed before the revolution of Henry VII, but in too narrow and uncombined a form to support an independent authority and settled influence upon the legislation of the land or the administration of the government. Two circumstances gave at intervals to the House of Commons a premature character of grandeur and independence, but an unsteady character, because as yet insufficiently supported by the intrinsic power of property and the sanction of public opinion; and these were: 1*st*, the occasional necessity in which the Crown found itself of breaking the odium attached to unpopular measures by sharing it with a popular body; 2*dly*, the interest of particular sovereigns to obtain a guarantee for arrangements

nobility. The *retainers* were the *gladiators*; and the estates, though for different reasons, were equally inalienable, and frozen, as it were, into abiding masses. The power could never be dissolved where the estate could not. With one hand, therefore, and by a direct blow, Henry attacked the *gladiatorial schools* of England; with the other, and by a side blow, he sapped the territorial power. And his son followed up these blows by similar attacks directed against the same power lodged in spiritual hands.

on behalf of their children which were not of a nature to be fulfilled in their own lifetimes. The testamentary settlements of kings were then of a more aspiring and comprehensive character, so as to require a corresponding superiority of character in the witnesses and the trustees charged with the executory duties. The pride of prerogative, doubtless, must have struggled against this humiliating appeal (as it would then be felt); but such feelings naturally yielded to parental affection, to paramount interest, and in some instances to the necessities of the situation. But, in spite of these casual and momentary exaltations given to the character of Parliament, by which it seemed at times to anticipate its present station of authority, the instances are far more numerous, and of a picturesque liveliness, which recall us to the general tone of depression and conscious inferiority of function marking the demeanour of the Lower House to the Crown, and even to its fellow-labourers of the Upper House. The censor thinks I have exaggerated the features of this inferiority, and he notices particularly the two cases of religion and taxation as those in which the Commons exhibited a jealous and haughty reserve in their intercourse with the other members of the Legislature. True; and, as those were exactly the cases which I had myself excepted, I do not see why the censor should imply that I had overlooked them. We might add the case of their own privileges, in which the Commons manifested a punctilious rigour at all times. But upon questions of foreign policy they ventured with the timid step of an aggressor; and from all such intrusions, as well as from those of still more delicate character, into the privileged recesses of the court or the royal household, the House of Commons was harshly, insolently, and sometimes ferociously repelled. There are cases even in the sixteenth century of members suffering capital punishment for pushing their inquiries too curiously or too presumptuously into the conduct, past or to come, of royal personages. Not until the era of James I. did the Parliament assume the masculine tone of a national senate; not until that of his son was this tone so systematically sustained and mutually understood that on either side menacing eyes began to be visible—louring fronts, and the gathering elements arranging themselves for hostility. During this whole period,—the period from the accession of the Scottish family to the imperial throne up to the termination of the Civil War, and for the eight years which intervened between that termination and the supremacy of Oliver Cromwell,—that is, during a period of fifty-one years,—the minds of men were in the most intense fermentation; crude and extreme notions were cherished upon each side, as was inevitable from that sort of hostility which *could* make its appeal to the brutal decision of the sword. Between extremes so determinate as these there could not be any compromise, nor (according to the language of that day) any "*temperament*,"—that is, neither that sort of compromise which arises from reciprocal sacrifices, where so many principles are adopted from A, and an equal number (or equal weight) from anti-A; for this would be a treaty of equality which cannot be supposed to take place amongst parties standing on such unequal grounds,—one the conqueror, the other conquered: nor, again, that sort of compromise which arises from a *tertium quod*,—ideas which partake equally of the two hostile ideas, what logicians style a *medium participationis*; for this sort of treaty presupposes an adjustment and harmonious equilibrium of principles such as cannot so well be the cause as the effect of a peace between the parties. The Civil War raged for nearly three years,—beginning in the autumn of 1642, ending virtually with the battle of Naseby about the middle of June 1645.[1] Then came an interval of peace for three years, interrupted by the short Scottish inroad of 1648, defeated at Preston; which was, in fact, but one day's fighting (with a little episode on the Thames and in Essex). Then came another peace of two years, followed by the entrance of Charles II on the stage of

[1] After this battle nothing beyond a few skirmishes took place in the open field, or what, in modern phrase, are called *affairs*. That of Sir Jacob Astley's cavalry on the last day of the year, according to the existing calendar (viz. March 24, 1646), was absolutely the last movement,—no arrears even of the war surviving, except the formal submission of such garrisons as had not been previously reduced. In fact, therefore, Naseby terminated the war; and that occurred about thirty-two months after the first shot was fired at Edgehill. I mention this because I have found universally such incorrect notions to prevail about the duration of the war, and still more so of Cromwell's ascendancy.

Scotland, his coronation, the short campaign of 1650, terminated, in effect, by the battle of Dunbar, and next year the summary campaign of Worcester. This makes up the whole of the war ; which would not, all put together, make more than three years' actual state of war, apart from Ireland, as far as England or English armies were concerned. And yet most people suppose the whole period of twenty years, from the convening of the Long Parliament in November 1640 to the restoration of Charles II, to have been a belligerent period. And Cromwell, who did not ascend to the formal supremacy until thirteen years after the opening of this period, and died twenty months before its close, the same people generally imagine to have governed throughout the whole or nearly the whole of it. However, though absolute oppression of the public voice did not take effect for anything approaching to the duration commonly supposed, and though the war itself was unexpectedly short, and therefore the plea for anything like martial law could not be long, still it is certain that partly the expectation of war (which, in fact, but for the heavy amercements by fine and sequestration, would have been a reasonable expectation), and partly the simulated expectation of war as a plea for keeping up a standing army, had the effect of stifling that free exercise of thought which might have resulted in the organisation of regular constitutional parties at an earlier period. After the establishment of the Protectorate there was an end of all hopes in that direction, until peace and non-military government were restored with Charles II.

This reign has been described most justly by Sir J. Dalrymple as the least easy to interpret of all which compose our History. It is the reign, *par eminence*, of plots, conspiracies, cabals, and intrigues. And yet it will be evident, on a little consideration, that it is not a reign dignified by constitutional parties fully organised. And yet it is true that some regular tendencies began now to shape themselves towards that consummation. Many great principles of the Constitution had now been ascertained, particularly the leading one of the king's vicarious responsibility in the persons of his ministers. This principle had not been even understood by Charles I. He considered it an insult to himself that his ministers should be called to account, exactly of that kind which any master of a family conceives offered in the attempt to scrutinize his household arrangements. That, in a subject, was seditious insolence. Did he then mean that the accountability lay in himself? That was treason. And thus there was absolutely no hope left amongst those who adhered to Charles's doctrine, nor any use in laws, however good, which after all were left to an irresponsible administration. For so little had been gained with that order of men by all the terrific experience of the last twenty years that the act which they continued to deplore most was the judicial execution of Strafford,—not for the individual wrong, which *was* a wrong (considering the law on the one hand, and his acts on the other), but for the wrong done to the character with which he was clothed, of king's minister. However, that most men had been weaned from this way of thinking appears from the case of Charles's sons. Even James in his Memoirs frequently quotes, and sometimes in its constitutional meaning, the new formula which embodies this doctrine of ministerial responsibility (viz. that the king can do no wrong); and, as to Charles II, he not only acknowledged it in outward show, but practically gave way to it on several occasions. Other advances had been of the last importance. Especially, at the very moment of the Restoration, the last wrecks of the king's feudal revenue and feudal influence had been given up, so that under any ordinary circumstances the power of the sword (now at length justly settled in the king) became an empty name without the concurrence of the people; that is, in effect, the power was finely balanced and divided. These advances led to a further advance,—viz. not to the mere doctrinal concession of a use in Parliaments, but to the practical necessity of holding them. And, again, the special rights of one branch of Parliament, particularly that of impeachment, were ascertained. All these were constitutional advances; and, as to individual laws, more were passed in this despotic reign of importance to some capital interest of the subject than in any which had preceded. So much so that the year 1679 has been fixed on by one eminent writer, with the sanction of Mr. Fox, as "the period at which our constitution had reached its greatest theoretical perfection," notwithstanding the accompanying acknowledgment, which also Mr. Fox quotes, "that the times immediately following were times of great practical oppression."[1]

It may be that this notion of the year 1679 being the culminating epoch of our constitution may have been Mr. Fox's reason for adopting the year 1680, with Rapin, as the era at which the party distinction of Whig and Tory first came into use. He can hardly be supposed to have felt much respect for Rapin's reason, which is so truly absurd as to remind one of the old Joe Miller story which represents a traveller as saying, "What do you call this place—Lincoln? Ay; you may well call it lincoln; for I never was so pestered with fleas in my life." Pretty much as Lincoln is thus supposed to arise out of the word *fleas*, so (according to Rapin) do the words Whig and Tory arise out of *addresser* and *abhorrer*; for he gives no better reason for referring Whig and Tory to the year 1680 than that in this year arose the momentary distinction between those who, upon principle, chose to address the king on a certain occasion, and those who chose to express their abhorrence of that principle. Mr. Fox will appear to have somewhat more reasonable grounds for this preference of 1680 as the true era of our great party distinctions, if he were accurate in representing the previous era as that which had ripened our constitution. But a slight glance at the condition of public affairs at that moment, and the relations between the several organs of the state, as well as between the existing parties, will convince you that, so far from all confusions in theory having then settled down into place and order, the very chaos of all political elements was actually brooding over the various parties which dis-

[1] In Charles James Fox's *History of the Early Part of the Reign of James the Second* (published in 1808) there is this passage:—"The abolition of the Court of Wards, the repeal of the Writ De Heretico Comburendo, the Triennial Parliament Bill, the establishment of the rights of the House of Commons in regard to impeachment, the expiration of the Licence Act, and above all the glorious Statute of Habeas Corpus, have therefore induced a modern writer of great eminence to fix the year 1679 as the period at which our Constitution had arrived at its greatest theoretical perfection."—M.

tracted the state,—all parties in positions so anomalous, and the rationale of the complex movements so difficult to be deciphered even by us at this day who overlook all the game, that it would have puzzled both Œdipus and the Sphinx combined to guess at the result. We had then a king who hung loose upon the world, unpledged to posterity by any care for his successor; for he had no legitimate child, and all other pretensions falling short of that did not so much interest as distract him. We had, besides females, four male pretenders to the throne, all liable to exclusion according to any claim that had yet been created; except that one who, upon prudential grounds, was most liable to exclusion, and against whom a formal Parliamentary exclusion had been actually urged. These pretenders were—two natural sons of the king, his nephew, and his brother. Neither were these pretensions mere verbal demonstrations; for all of them, as we learn from Barillon, the French ambassador, had parties in and out of Parliament actively supporting their claims. We had a public, in all that part of it which concerned itself with politics, not only corruptible, not only corrupted, but even the object of fierce rivalry amongst the several corrupters. The King of France bribed [1] the King of England, his brother, his ministers, &c., and at the same time bribed all those who were, had been, or might be, conspirators against this King of England. He bribes even the great patriots, and amongst them Algernon Sidney. He bribes the existing Parliament against the King, and the King against all future Parliaments. He bribes especially against Spain and Holland; Spain, again, offers to bid against the bribes of France; and Holland, through the Prince of Orange, at one time also bribes the King of England. The King of France, moreover, bribes a great English minister; but, hearing of another man who will undertake to ruin him, he gives this man a bill for about £8000, made

[1] In estimating the amount of these bribes, as in all other references to French money at that time, there is a gross mistake made by taking the *livre* at its modern value of tenpence. Thus, in various books, now lying open before me, upon the reign of Louis XIV, in English translations, the constant version of *a million of livres* is £40,000, whereas it should be £80,000, or very little less.

payable so many months after the ruin of the other man; but, when the bill falls due, he pays it with a discount of 50 per cent, on the allegation to the indorsee that the man had been only half ruined. Even in this scene of confusion, it will be difficult to descry any place or possibility for fixed constitutional parties to stand and act with systematic purpose. But, to look a little further, we find the King of England himself planning a scheme for driving one part of his subjects into rebellion, and upon this methodical calculation,—that he might thus have a plausible pretext for raising an army which, once levied, he would not need to disband until it should suit his own pleasure. We find the same king, to evade the new doctrine of ministerial responsibility, drawing up a treaty with his own hands, and sealing it with a pocket seal. We find the brother of this king, when exasperated at his banishment from court, protesting, not in one, but in a score of letters, that he saw no hope for himself but in a civil war,—which, accordingly, he determines to raise in Scotland and Ireland. Whereupon, by the very next post, the King of France begs that his Highness will not forget, in such a case, the old connexion of Louis and Co.,—that he has a large assortment of arms upon his hands, and provisions in abundance, which he will immediately ship off to his order. But, happening, in a few posts after, to hear that a republican army is likely to do a little business in the same article of civil war, and precisely against his Highness, he desires his ambassador at London to wait upon the gentlemen at the head of the concern, and declare how much pleasure it will give him to be favoured with their commands; both offers being, as is evident from the confidential communications now exposed to public view, perfectly sincere. However, you will say, in the midst of this general political depravity, though most of the party connexions were at best merely personal, still there might be some small body of men, obscured from separate notice by acting at different times with different men, and acting indiscriminately with all at intervals, according to any views they had of what was best for the moment and under the circumstances, who might keep alive within their little circle some recognition of what was due to the constitution. And here might lurk the salt of regeneration—the nucleus of true believers—the original Whigs and Tories. But I believe you will find that the very enormity of evil in our political system of those days expresses itself peculiarly in this,—that all parties almost of necessity took the form of personal parties. This arose out of the fact that our greatest political danger, that of Popery, in the prevailing circumstances of Europe, was then actually incarnated; for it took a personal shape and substance in the Duke of York. Had the nation been Popish, or inclined to Popery, the case would have been very different. But, as things were, and with the certainty that the nation would pull one way and its future king another,—about which king, moreover, there was no one fact so absolutely made out as his sublime obstinacy, and his desperate determination to sacrifice the whole world to his absurd conscience,—the danger was assuredly no trifle or chimera. Hence you see that all parties, cabals, factions, in this reign had been pointed to personal objects. The great events of the reign —the Popish Plot and the Exclusion Bill—were both personal and hurled at the same person. And, coming, lastly, to the two great parties, what were they denominated? Not surely Whig and Tory?—that is not the designation which you hear of them: no; but the *Country Party* and the *Court Party.* Now, then, I ask, What was the Country Party? It was so called upon a sort of double meaning; for it was the party composed chiefly of country gentlemen, men living upon rural estates, and it was the party which professed country, *i.e.* patriotic, views. And of what elements did this party consist? Chiefly and originally of High-Church men,—men who leaned too much to the kingly prerogative, and strenuous haters of what were called Commonwealth men. Now, under this Country Party were gathered (see Dalrymple and K. James's Memoirs) all those who were then styled Republicans, as well as those who maintained the divine right of kings in the utmost extremity. I might pursue this subject farther, but I have said enough; the fact may be shown from the records of those days. Whatever may be said by more recent writers, the two great parties had no public existence until that great event out of which they grew; and *by* that they must be measured. For, though the names were adopted from other quarters, they were adjusted, on their introduction into a *public* use in England, to a meaning which designated fixed relations to the constitution; and, detached from those relations, they have no import at this day; and those relations they fill up and exhaust.

Now, if this be so, then the Radicals must bear a relation to some other constitution; and, indeed, they now avow that the form of government to which they give their affections is a pure Democracy. If this is generally avowed by the Radicals, why spend any words in deducing it by any detail of argument or of historical deduction? But it is *not* avowed generally as yet; though doubtless the tendency is in that direction, and upon any national encouragement it would be avowed universally. Meantime this doctrine, however kept in the rear, and in military language *refused* to the gross public,—viz. the doctrine that all they are doing has for its object some other and different Constitution, some other and different mode of administering the government, and not at all any possible improvement of our existing Constitution or Government,—this doctrine is the esoteric one of the Radicals who are in the secret. And it is useless, as with regard to *them*, to discuss any mode or degree of improvements applied to the old forms. They must all be discussed on another footing,—viz. as with reference to a pure democracy.

Even in that shape, even *as* a pure democracy, Radicalism will not be able to exist upon a very extended scale. There are strong reasons for believing that, upon that one principle of Universal Suffrage, Radicalism would and must dissolve any extensive community. England would break up into small confederations,—some Radical, some half Radical, and even then, as a primary condition, demanding the expulsion (as so often occurred in the little Greek republics) of the aristocratic orders. Riches could not co-exist with Radical forms; for the possession of wealth infers anti-radical feelings. The union of several rich men would give local triumph to aristocratic notions,—aided, I mean, by the indirect influence which cannot but accompany wealth under any arrangements of law, property, or usage. Even apart from the case of wealth, the democracy of universal suffrage would be too intense for those but one or two steps raised in the social condition. A state of civic privilege which consists in the denial of all privilege would forfeit the main springs of hope, fear, and ambition, by which even the purest patriotism is nursed ; and the result would be that Radicalism, even to maintain itself, must relax the sternness of its principles, and thus soon make way for the gradual restoration of all which it had destroyed. This would be its *euthanasy* ; but other and more fearful agonies would too probably step in for hastening the catastrophe. These it would be unpleasant to dwell upon. But the catastrophe itself, by some agency or other, it seems impossible to evade, unless upon one of two assumptions : either upon the assumption of a coercion from without, which Radicalism disclaims ; or on the assumption that all men were philosophers, which we all of us disclaim.

# CALIFORNIA AND THE GOLD-DIGGING MANIA[1]

WHEN a new comet is descried, we set ourselves to trace the path on which it is moving; so that, if it seems likely to trespass on our own orbit, prudent men may have warning to make all snug aloft, and ready for action; authors, in particular, seeking to correct the proofs of any book they may be publishing before the comet has had time with its tail to sweep all the types into "pye." It is now becoming a duty to treat California as a comet; for she is going ahead at a rate that beats Sinbad and Gulliver, threatening (if we believe the star-gazers of our day) to throw universal commerce into "pye"; and other Californias are looming in her wake, such as Australia and the South Sea island now called Hawaii[2]: they are crowding all sail towards the same object of private gain and public confusion; anxieties are arising in various quarters; and it is daily becoming more a matter of public interest to assign the course upon which they are really advancing, and to measure the dangers (if any at all) with which they are practically charged.

In the case of California, the most painful feature at the outset of the *termashaw* was the torpor manifested by all the governments of Christendom as to a phenomenon that was leading their countrymen by wholesale into ruin. Helpless

[1] Contributed to *Hogg's Weekly Instructor* in 1852: reprinted in 1871 in the second of the two volumes published by Messrs. Black as supplementary to De Quincey's own edition of his Collective Writings. The original title was "California" simply.—M.

[2] *i.e.* by missionaries in their dictionaries of the Sandwich language: but formerly better known to sailors as that *Owhyhee* where Captain Cook was massacred.

and ignorant as that army of children which in an early stage of the Crusades set forward by land for Palestine,—knowing as little as those children of the horrors that besieged the road, or of the disappointments that would seal its terminus, supposing it ever to be reached,—from every quarter of Europe rushed the excited ploughman and artizan, as vultures on the day of battle to the supper of carrion; and not a word of warning or advice from their government! On the Continent this neglect had its palliation. Most governments were then too occupied by anxieties and agitations derived from the approaching future, or even by desperate convulsions derived from the present. But whither shall we look for the excuse of our own government? Some years ago it was, by inconsiderate Radicals, made the duty of government to find work for the people. *That* was no part of their duty; nor *could* be; for it can be no duty to attempt impossibilities. But it *was* a part of their duty officially to publish remonstrances and cautions against general misapprehension of apparent openings, that too often were no real openings, for labour, and against a national delusion that for ninety-nine out of a hundred was sure to end in ruin. Two things government were bound to have done: viz. 1st, To have circulated a circumstantial account of the different routes to San Francisco, each with its separate distances assigned, and its separate varieties of inconceivable hardship; 2d, To have sent out a party of surveyors and mineralogists, with instructions to report from time to time, at short intervals, upon the real condition of the prospects before the gold-diggers, upon the comparative advantages of the several districts in California as yet explored with these mineral views, and upon the kind of labours, and the kind of tools or other apparatus, that had any reasonable chance of success. Had this been done, some myriads of energetic and enterprising men, that have long since perished miserably, would have been still available for the public service. California, be its real wealth what it may, was a "job," a colossal job; and was worked as a job by a regular conspiracy of jobbers. The root of this conspiracy lay and lies (in all senses *lies*) up and down the United States. It is no affront, nor intended as such, to the American Union, or to

Mr. Barnum, if I say that this gigantic republic (which, by the seventh census, just now in the course of publication, has actually extended its territorial compass in a space of ten years from about two millions of square miles, which it had in 1840, to three and a quarter millions of square miles,[1] which it had reached last midsummer) produces a race of Barnums on a pre-Adamite scale, corresponding in activity to its own enormous proportions. The idea of a Barnum does not at all presuppose an element of fraud. There are many honourable Barnums; but also there is a minority of fraudulent Barnums. All alike, good Barnums and bad Barnums, are characterised by Titanic energy, such as would tear into ribbons a little island like ours, but is able to pull fearlessly against a great hulk of a continent, that the very moon finds it fatiguing to cross. Now, it happened that the bad Barnums took charge of the California swindle. They stationed a first-rate liar in San Francisco, under whom, and accountable to whom, were several accomplished liars distributed all the way down to Panama, and thence to Chagres. All along the Atlantic seaboard, this gathering volley of lies and Californian "notions" raced with the speed of gunpowder trains up to New York; in which vast metropolis (confounded amongst its seven hundred thousand citizens) burrowed the central bureau of the swindle. Thence in ten days these poetic hoaxes crossed over to a line of repeating liars posted in Liverpool and London; from which cities, of course, the lies ran by telegraph in a few hours over the European continent, and thence by Tartar expresses overland to Indus and the Ganges. When the swindle got into regular working order, it was as good as a comedy to watch its mode of playing. The policy of the liars was to quarrel with each other, and cavil about straws, for the purpose of masking the subterraneous wires of their fraudulent concert. Liar No. 5, for instance, would observe carelessly in a Panama journal that things were looking up at Sacramento, for (by the latest returns that could be

[1] I quote from an abstract of the census in the *New York Journal of Commerce* for December 5, 1851, transmitted by an American friend before it had been published even in the Washington journals. This estimate does not include a vast extent of *watery* domains.

depended on) the daily product of gold had now reached a million of dollars. Upon which No. 8 at Chagres would quote the paragraph into a local paper, and comment upon it thus with virtuous indignation: "Who or what this writer may be, with his daily million of dollars, we know not, and do not desire to know. But we warn the editor of that paper that it is infamous to sport with the credulity of European emigrants. A million, indeed, daily! We, on the contrary, assert that the produce for the last three months, though steadily increasing, has never exceeded an average of half a million—and even *that* not to be depended on for more than nine days out of ten." To him succeeds No. 10, who, after quoting No. 8, goes on thus: "Some people are never content. To *our* thinking, half a million of dollars daily, divided amongst about fourteen hundred labourers, working only seven hours a day, is a fair enough remuneration, considering that no education is required, no training, and no capital. Two ounces of tobacco and a spade, with rather a large sack for bagging the gold, having a chain and padlock—such is the stock required for a beginner. In a week he will require more sacks and more padlocks; and in two months a roomy warehouse, with suitable cellars, for storing the gold until the fall, when the stoutest steamers sail. But, as we observed, some people are never content. A friend of ours, not twelve miles from San Francisco, in digging for potatoes, stumbled upon a hamper of gold that netted forty thousand dollars. And, behold! the next comer to that locality went off in dudgeon because, after two days' digging, he got nothing but excellent potatoes; whereas he ought to have reflected that our friend's golden discovery was a lucky chance, such as does not happen to the most hard-working man above once in three weeks."

Then came furious controversies about blocks of gold embedded in quartz, and left at "our office" for twenty-four hours, with liberty for the whole town to weigh and measure them. One editor affirms that the blocks weighed six quintals, and the quartz, if pulverised, would hardly fill three snuff-boxes. "But," says a second editor, "the bore of our friend's nostrils is preternaturally large; his pinch, being proportionable, averages three ounces; and three of his snuff-boxes make one horse-bucket. Six tons, does he say? I don't believe, at the outside, it reaches seven hundredweight." Thereupon rejoins editor No. 1: "The blockhead has mistaken a quintal for a ton; and thus makes us talk nonsense. Of course we shall always talk nonsense when we talk in *his* words and not in our own. His wish was to undermine us; but so far from doing *that*, the knowing reader will perceive that he confirms our report, and a little enlarges it."

Even in Scotland, as far north as Perth and Aberdeen, the incorporation of liars thought it might answer to suborn a youth, to all appearance an ingenuous youth, as repeating signalist in the guise of one writing home to his Scottish relations, with flourishing accounts of his success at the "diggins." Apparently he might have saved his postage, since the body of his letter represented him as having returned to Scotland, so that he might have reported his adventures by word of mouth. This letter was doctored so as to leave intentionally a very slight impression that even in California the course of life was chequered with good and evil. It had been found, perhaps, that other letters in more romantic keys had overleaped their own swindling purpose. The vivacious youth therefore admitted frankly that on some days he got nothing, except, perhaps, a touch of catarrh, even in California. Finally, however, with all his candour, the repeating signalist left one great mystery unsolved. He had been getting nothing on some days; but still, after all these cloudy seasons had been allowed for, his gains had *averaged* from three to four guineas a day during the period of his stay. That being the case, one could not well understand what demon had led him ever to quit this garden of the Hesperides for Perth or Aberdeen, where no such golden apples grow either on the high-roads, or even in gentlemen's "policies,"—both of which regions are beset with mastiff-dogs and policemen.

But why, or for what ultimate purpose, do I direct these satiric glances at the infant records of California, and the frauds by which she prospered? No doubt the period of her childhood, and of the battle which she had to fight at starting with an insufficient population, was shortened exceedingly and alleviated by unlimited lying. An altar she ought to raise to the goddess of insolent mendacity, as the tutelary power under which she herself emerged into importance; this altar should be emblazoned upon the shield of her heraldic honours; this altar should stand amongst the quarterings on her coins. And it cannot be denied that a preliminary or heralding generation has perished in the process of clearing the way for that which is now in possession. What by perils of the sea and the greater perils of the land route, what by "plague, pestilence, and famine, by battle and murder and sudden death" (to quote our English Litany), within the precincts of the gold districts, probably not far from a quarter of a million are now sleeping in obscure graves that might have been saved by the interference of surveyors, guides, monitors—such as a benign and Christian government in Europe would assuredly have authorised officially. But these things are not disputed; or only as a question of extent. The evil is confessed. But, small or great, it is now over. War, it is true, and war of that ferocious character which usually takes place with the vindictive Indians, apparently is now imminent; but this will be transitory, possibly favourable to peace and settlement, by absorbing the ruffianism of the state. And, in the meantime, the iniquity[1] of the Lynch law is giving way and

[1] Naturally one might suppose that Lynch law would not be liable to much of downright injustice, unless through disproportionate severity in its punishments, considering how gross and palpable are the offences which fall within its jurisdiction. But the fact is otherwise. If with us in Europe the law that superintends *civil* rights works continually injustice by its cruel delays, so often announcing a triumph over oppression to an ear that has long been asleep in the grave, on the other hand, the Lynch code is always trembling by the brink of bloody wrong through the very opposite cause of its rapturous precipitance. A remarkable case of this nature is reported in the Washington and New York journals of Christmas last. A man had been arrested on a charge of robbery in some obscure place two hundred miles from San Francisco. Reasons for doubt had arisen amongst the intelligent, and amongst consciences peculiarly tender, but not such reasons as would have much weight amongst an infuriated mob. Two gentlemen, a physician and a young lawyer, whose names should be glorified by history, made a sublime though fruitless effort, at great personal risk, to rescue the prisoner from the bigots who had prejudged him. Finally, however, he *was* rescued; but, as may be supposed, in a place

thawing, as a higher civilisation is mounting above the horizon. After a preliminary night of bloodshed and darkness, California will begin to take her place amongst the prosperous states of the American Union. And the early stage of outrage and violence will, upon retrospect, rapidly sink into a mere accident of surprise, due to the embarrassments of vast distance, combined with the suddenness and special temptations of so strange a discovery.

But, all these extraordinary accidents allowed for, it cannot surely be my intention (the reader will say) to raise doubts upon the main inference from all that we have heard—viz. the prospect of a new influx into our supplies of gold, setting in with a force and a promise of permanence that, five years ago, would have read to the exchanges of Europe like a page from the *Arabian Nights.*

The first principle of change in our prospects—first in importance, and likely to be the first chronologically in tempering our delusions, and taking the shine out of our various El Dorados — is one which never seems to have occurred in the way of a remote scruple to the blockheads who report the different local discoveries as they explode in California, one after another, like the raps from a schoolboy's cracker. One and all, they are anxious only about one solitary element of success—viz. the *abundance* of the gold. They seem never to have heard that diamonds and emeralds

so slenderly peopled, with no result beyond that of gaining a little additional time—*i.e.* so long as the hiding-place of the prisoner should remain undiscovered. Fortunately this time proved sufficient for the discovery of the real offender. He was taken at San Francisco, two hundred miles off. Luckily he confessed: and that took away all pretence for raising demurs. But so satisfied were some of the witnesses against the innocent prisoner with their own identification of the criminal—through his features, build of person, size, apparent age, and dress—that they resisted even the circumstantialities of the regular judicial confession. Some of these incredulous gentlemen mounted their horses, and rode off to San Francisco; where, upon visiting the prison, to their extreme astonishment, they found a man who presented a mere duplicate and *facsimile* of the prisoner whom they had left behind. It is true that precipitancy would not often be misled into injustice by this specific error; but neither is this specific error the only one, by many a hundred, that might give a fatal turn to the sentence of a jury deciding by momentary and random gleams of probability.

are not scarce as they are for want of known diamond and emerald mines, nor pearls for want of vast unworked pearl-fisheries. Some of these have scarcely been opened, for want of even a delusive encouragement; others, having been worked for ages, are now closed without hope of returning to them. Emeralds and sapphires are lying at this moment in a place which I could indicate; and no policeman is on duty in the whole neighbourhood to hinder me or the reader from pocketing as many as we please. We are also at perfect liberty to pocket the anchors of Her Majesty's ship the Victoria (120 guns), and to sell them for old iron. Pocket them by all means, and I engage that the magistrate sitting at the Thames police-office will have too much respect for your powers to think of detaining you. If he does, your course is to pocket the police-office and all which it inherits. The man that pockets an anchor may be a dangerous customer, but not a customer to be sneezed at. What need of laws to intercept acts which are physically unapproachable? Many a mine and quarry have been abandoned under ordinances of nature *defying* you to work them; many other under changes making it (though possible) useless to work them. Both these little sets of objection *have* occurred (yes, have already occurred) in California, and *will* occur more and more.

I never heard of any ancient prince, wilful as he might be, insisting upon hanging his chief baker unless he baked him an apple-pie furnished from the Garden of the Hesperides: not but the apples might have been "good bakers"; but then the dragon was to be taken into consideration! And over many a mine in this world there is, in effect, a dragon of one kind or other watching to preserve them from human violation. And, suppose the prohibition not to be absolute, but that, with proper machinery for pumping out water, &c., and with improved arts of working, you could raise the precious metal, still, if every pound weight of gold, which, at modern prices, may be valued roundly at £50 sterling, cost you in raising it £70 sterling, it is presumable that you would not long pursue that sort of game. Both in England and Ireland, we have fallen upon silver and gold many scores of times. We have had boxes and trinkets and very large vases wrought out of this native metal; but invariably we have been obliged to say adieu to these tantalising game preserves. To work them was too costly. "One or two more such victories," said Pyrrhus the Epirot, "and I am a gone 'coon." And five discoveries of gold-mines in Ireland are supposed to be as ruinous as two potato-famines. In California there have been evidences not to be misunderstood that, let the gold be as plentiful as the periodical romances state it to be, nevertheless the exhaustibility of that gold which could be *worked profitably* was indicated not only as certain but as very near. This term, when approached too nearly, has again been thrown to a distance in several cases by fortunate and critical discoveries of other gold more accessible (as recently at Mariposa). But, whenever I read of men digging down to depths of sixty or seventy feet, I know by that one fact that the general reports, describing gold as a thing to be picked up for stooping, must be fraudulent fables circulated on behalf of men and on the instigation of men who have houses to let, building-ground to sell, and "water-privileges" to mortgage. No man would patiently be digging to vast depths who knew that others generally won their gold as easily as a man digs up potatoes, unless he also knew that such enviable prizes were sown as thinly as twenty-thousand pound prizes in our English lotteries of the last generation.

Here, then, is the first thing to pause upon—viz. that, however "handy" this gold may lie in California or in Australia, however "sweetly" it may work off for those meritorious vagabonds who first break ground in the virgin fields, one thing is undeniable,—that the course of further advance will not be upwards from good to better, but downwards from good, or very good, or charming, to decent, to rather bad, and lastly to disgusting. This is a very ugly fact; and the cunning amongst the workers, or rather amongst those who have something to sell amongst workers, attempt to break the force of this fact, by urging that as yet the aids of science and machinery have not been applied to the case,—so that any advantage which is now possessed by the vagabonds must soon be greater. That is true: past denying it is that concert, and combination, and the resources of capital, will tell upon the gold-fields, and reduce the labour, which already is reduced by comparison with other gold-fields. Certainly, in the first stage of all, the progress will, by means of machinery, lie from good to better. But that momentary period of success will not avail to alter or to hide the ugly truth that in all future stages—that is, in every stage *subsequent* to that in which the gold is found upon the surface—the inverse course must take place: that is, not from good to better, but from good to something continually worse. What is it that ultimately and irresistibly determines the value of gold? Why is it, for instance, that in modern times gold has generally ranged at about fifteen times the value, weight for weight, of silver? Is it, as ignorant people fancy, because there is fifteen times as much silver in the market of the world as there is of gold? Not at all, my poor benighted friend: it is because any given quantity of gold, say a hundredweight, requires fifteen times as much labour (or, more comprehensively, fifteen times as much capital) to bring it to market as an equal quantity of silver; and nothing will permanently alter that ratio but what alters the quantity of labour involved in one or the other; and nothing can permanently reduce the value of gold but what reduces the cost of bringing it to market. Now, I defy any vagabond whatever, whether old vagabond of California, or young vagabond of Australia, or younger vagabond of Owhyhee, or most young vagabond of South America, to deny that his labour is at the best (*i.e.* is most productive) when it is starting. His first crop of gold is taken off the surface, as with us poor old women and children are hired at sixpence a-day to pick stones off the land. Next comes the ploughman: it begins to be hard work, my friend, that ploughing for gold! And, finally, comes the sinking of shafts, and going down for hours into mephitic regions of carbonic acid gas, and after-damp, etc. Neither is there any dispensation from this necessity of going downwards from bad to worse, except in the single case of crushing quartz. Machinery must prodigiously facilitate that labour; and, so long as the quartz holds out, that advantage will apparently last. But this quartz must, I suspect, be one of the rare prizes in the lottery; and amongst quartz itself, as amongst vagabonds, there will be a better and a worse. And the signs of these differences will soon become familiar, and the best will be taken first; and thus here again the motion forward will be from bad to worse.

But now, as I can afford to be liberal, and leave myself ample means, in Yankee phrase, to "whip" the vagabonds after all, let me practise the graceful figure of concession. I will concede, therefore, what most vehemently I doubt, that for a few years these new gold-fields should work so kindly as seriously to diminish the cost of producing marketable gold. In that case, mark what will follow. You know the modern doctrine of Rent, reader. Of course you do, and it would be presumption in me to doubt your knowing it. But still, for the sake of a foolish caprice that haunts me, suffer me to talk to you as if you did *not* know the doctrine of Rent.[1] I will state it in as brief a compass as perhaps is possible. In a new colony, having a slender population, the natural order in which the arable land is taken up must be this: in the first stage of the process, none but the best land will be cultured; which land let us class as No. 1. In the second stage, when population will have expanded,—more wheat, and therefore more land, being wanted,—the *second* best will be brought into culture; and this we will call No. 2. In the third stage, No. 3 will be used. And so onwards; nor can there reasonably be any deviation from this order, unless through casual error, or else because occasionally an inferior soil may compensate its intrinsic inferiority by the extrinsic advantage of lying nearer to a town, or nearer to a good road, or to a navigable river, etc. By way of expressing the graduations of quality upon this scale, suppose we interpret them by corresponding graduations of price. No. 1 for the production of a given quantity (no matter what) requires an outlay of twenty shillings; No. 2, for the same quantity, requires twenty-five shillings; and No. 3, which is very perverse land indeed, requires thirty shillings. Now, because

[1] Very grievously, I suspect myself here of plagiarism from Molière. In one of his plays, Mons. Y. says to Mons. X., "You understand Greek, I believe?" To which Mons. X. replies, "Oh yes, I understand Greek perfectly. But have the goodness, my dear friend, to talk to me as if by chance I did *not* understand Greek."

twenty shillings paid the full cost of No. 1, then, as soon as the twenty-five shillings land is called for by the growing population,—since in the same market all wheat of equal quality must bear the same price, which price is here twenty-five shillings,—it follows that a surplus of five shillings arises on No. 1 beyond what the cost of culture required. For the same reason, when No. 3 is called for, the price (regulated of necessity by the *most* costly among the several wheats) rises to thirty shillings. This is now the price for the whole, and therefore for No. 1. Consequently, upon this wheat there is now a surplus of ten shillings beyond what the culture required; and upon No. 2, for the same reason, there is a surplus of five shillings. What becomes of this surplus? It constitutes RENT. And, amongst other corollaries, these two follow: first, that the lowest quality of land under culture, the last in the descending scale, pays no rent; and secondly, that this lowest quality determines the price for the whole, and the successive development of advantages for the upper qualities, as the series continues to expand, always expresses itself in successive increments of rent. As here, if No. 4 were taken up at thirty-five shillings, then rent would immediately commence on No. 3, which would pay as rent the difference between thirty and thirty-five shillings—viz. five shillings. No. 2 would now pay ten shillings, and No. 1 (I am happy, on its owner's account, to announce) would pay fifteen shillings.

Well, this is that famous doctrine of RENT which drew after it other changes, so as, in fact, to unsettle nearly all the old foundations in Political Economy. And that science had in a manner to pass through the Insolvent Court, and begin the world again upon a very small remainder of its old capital. What I wish to observe upon it in this place is—that this doctrine takes effect, not merely upon arable land, but also upon all mines, quarries, fisheries, etc. All these several organs of wealth involve within themselves a graduation of advantages, some yielding more, some less, some still less, on the same basis of cost. Now, before California entered the gold market, to what quarter did Europe look for her chief supply of gold? Ancient gold, melted down—some of it, no doubt, gold that had furnished toilet equipages to Semiramis, and chains of decoration to Nimrod or the Pharaohs,—entered largely into the market. But for new gold, innocent gold, that had never degraded itself by ministering to acts of bribery and corruption, we looked chiefly to Russia. I remember an excellent paper, some four years back, on these Russian gold-mines in the chains of the Ural Mountains. It was in a French journal of great merit, viz. the *Revue des Deux Mondes*; and, to the best of my remembrance, it reported the product of these mines as being annually somewhere about four millions sterling. But it would be a great mistake to suppose that the whole of this product rested on the same basis of costs. There can be no doubt that the case which I have just imagined as to wheat had its exemplification in these gold-mines. No doubt there are many numbers in the scale which are not worked at all, nor could be profitably worked unless science should discover less costly modes of working them. But, even as things now are, with many parts of the scale as yet undeveloped, it is certain that a considerable range of numbers, in respect of costliness, is already under culture. Suppose these (as in the wheat case) to be Nos. 1, 2, 3. Then, if California or Australia should succeed in seriously diminishing the cost of producing gold, the first evidence of such a revolution would show itself in knocking off No. 3 in the Ural mines. Should the change continue, and in the same direction, it would next knock off No. 2. And, of the whole Ural machinery, only No. 1 would at length survive, or, in other words, only that particular mine, or particular chamber of a mine, which worked under the highest natural advantages, producing a given weight of gold at a cost lower than any other section of the works producing,—suppose, an ounce of gold at the cost of thirteen ounces of silver, when elsewhere the same quantity cost fourteen ounces, fourteen and a half, etc. Always, therefore, any *bona fide* action of California upon the cost of gold would show itself, first of all, in a diminishing supply from Russia.[1] But, then, for a con-

[1] The supply furnished by Borneo, upon what data I know not, is often rated at one million sterling. So that the two great annual influxes of gold do not apparently exceed five millions sterling. But all

siderable time, this increased supply from California, having Russia to pull against, would so far neutralise and counteract any sensible impression that otherwise it might produce in Christendom. This would happen even if the product of California had really been ten millions sterling for the first three years, and fifteen millions for 1850—that is, forty-five millions in all. According to my own view, as already explained, it is not likely that California could reduce the cost of gold, except for the first year or two; after which the cost would travel the other way, not by decrements, but by increments, sure if slow. No greatly increased quantity of gold could continue to flood the gold market, unless the cost were seriously reduced. The market of Europe would repel it; and this discouragement would react upon the motives of the productive body in California. But, were it otherwise, and supposing the cost reduced by eight per cent, or, in round terms, from its present mint price in London to seventy shillings an ounce, a stimulus would be thus applied to the consumption of gold for various purposes, which, in defiance of the lowered natural price, would quicken and inflame its market price. It is clear, from what has already happened in the United States and in France, that gold would enter more largely into the currencies of nations. It is probable, also, that a very large quantity, in the troubled condition of the political atmosphere throughout Europe for many years to come, will be absorbed by the hoarders of Christendom. Certainly I do not deny that unexpected discoveries of gold-fields, apparently inexhaustible, have been made, and almost simultaneously made, in regions as remote from each other as some of them are from ourselves. In several quarters of the American continent, both north and south, in the Sandwich Islands, in Africa, in New Zealand, and, more notoriously (as regards impressions on Europe), in Australia (viz. in the island of Van Diemen, but on a still larger scale, in the continental regions of Victoria and Port Phillip), gold is now presenting itself to the unarmed and uninstructed eye upon a scale that confounds the computations of avarice. "There is some trick

this must give way, or must be greatly lowered in cost, before any great impression could be produced by California.

in all this," is the natural thought of every man when first hearing the news. He wonders how it was that many people did not read such broadcast indications twenty years ago. That thought raises a shade of suspicion upon the very *facts in limine.* And next, as to the *construction* of the facts, a misgiving comes over him, that possibly there may be too much of a good thing. Many people remember the anecdote connected with the first importation of Brazilian emeralds into Europe. This happened at an Italian port, viz. Leghorn; and the jeweller, in whose trade none but Oriental emeralds were as yet known, struck with admiration at the superior size of one offered to him by a stranger, bought it for a very high price,—upon which the stranger, exulting in his good fortune, displayed a large trunk full of the same jewels. But, on this evidence of their abundance in certain regions of Brazil, the jeweller's price sank in the ratio of seven shillings to twenty-five guineas. At present, however, the public mania travels in an opposite direction. The multiplication of gold is to go on at a rate accelerated beyond the dreams of romance; and yet, concurrently with this enormous diffusion of the article, its exchangeable value is in some incomprehensible way to be steadily maintained. This delusion is doubtless but partially diffused. But another, equally irreflective, seems to prevail generally: viz. that, under any circumstances whatever, and travelling towards whatever result, the discovery must prove a glorious one in respect to the interests of the human race. And the rumour of other and other similar discoveries, in far distant regions, equally sudden, and equally promising to be inexhaustible, is hailed as if it laid open to us some return of a Saturnian age. *Jam redit et Virgo, redeunt Saturnia regna.* I, on the contrary, view this discovery as in any event almost neutral with respect to human prosperity, but in some possible events as likely to be detrimental. Fighting, with Mr. Cobden's permission, will go on for millions of years yet to come; and, in pure sympathy with the grander interests of human nature, every person who reads what lies written a little below the surface, will say (as *I* say), God forbid that it should not. In that day when war should be prohibited, or made nearly impossible, man will commence his degeneration. But, if we change not (as change we never shall) in respect to our fighting instincts, we shall change, if the gold fable prospers, a good deal as to the fashion of our arms. Like Ashantees, not a corporal nor a private sentinel but will have a golden hilt to his sword, and a golden scabbard. Still, as people to be plundered by marauders in the nights succeeding to a great battle, we shall not rate much higher. A pound of gold more or less will make but a little difference. "I consider it no object," will be said by the plunderer. And, even if buried in a golden coffin, we shall not be more worth looking after by the resurrection-man; but on a morning parade, under a bright sun, we shall be far prettier to look at. Such would be the upshot if the gold fable were realised.

Seriously, let us calculate the probable and the possible in the series of changes. What I infer from the whole review taken in combination is, that the anticipations in respect to the revolutions at hand are vague and indeterminate, and, in half, contradictory. One may gather from the arguments and the exultations, taken together, that some dim idea is entertained of the California supplies uniting with the previous supplies (from Russia and Borneo especially), and jointly terminating in the result of making gold in the first plentiful, and then (as an imaginary consequence) cheap in relation to all other commodities. In this one reads the usual gross superstition as to the interaction of supply and demand. The dilemma which arises is this:—California does, or does not, produce her gold at a diminished cost. If she does *not*, no abundance or redundance could be more than transitory in its effect of cheapness; since, the more she sold on the terms of selling cheaper and producing no cheaper at all,—which is the supposition,—the more she would be working for her own ruin. But, on the other hand, if she *does* produce at a diminished cost, which is the only ground of cheapness that can last, then she drives Russia effectually out of the market—Nos. 3, 2, 1, in the inverse order illustrated above; and the effect of her extra supplies is simply to fill up a *vacuum* which she herself has created. At least that will be the final effect to the extent of five millions sterling per annum. But, if she and Australia jointly should *really* supply more than this sum, it does not follow that, because produced at a lower cost, this *extra supply* will command an *extra* market. The demand for gold is limited by the fixed and traditional uses to which it is applied. Mr. Joe Smith, the prophet of the Mormons, delivered it to his flock, as his own private and prophetic crotchet, that the true use of gold, its ultimate and providential function on this planet, would turn out to be the paving of streets and high-roads. But we poor non-Mormonites are not so far advanced in philosophy as all that; and, unless we could simultaneously pave our roads with good intentions, which (it is well known) are all ordered for another place, we have reason to fear that the trustees of every road, the contractors and the paviors upon it, would abscond nightly with so much high-road as they laid down in the day. There are at this moment three openings, and perhaps no more, for an enlarged use of gold, in the event of its becoming materially cheaper. Many nations would extend the use of gold in their currencies. Secondly, the practice of hoarding—once so common, and in Oriental lands almost universal, but in Europe greatly narrowed by the use of paper currencies, and by the growing security of property—will for many years revive extensively under the action of two causes: first, under the general political agitation of Europe; and, secondly, under the special doctrines of communism, so avowedly friendly to spoliation and public robbery. *La propriété—c'est le vol*, is a signal held aloft for all Christendom to take care of their pockets. The fine old miser, therefore, of ancient days, brooding night and day over his buried gold, will again revolve upon us, should gold really become cheap. Finally, the embellishment of human persons by gold trinkets, ornaments, and the more lavish use of gilding in the decoration of houses, furniture, etc., would further enlarge the new demand. But all this only in the case of a real cheapness. And, even if *that* were realised (whereas hitherto there are no signs of it), this unfortunate check to the extended use of gold would inevitably arise intermittingly: the diminished cost of production, by the supposition, reduces the price of gold—that is, reduces the *natural* price. But, in the meantime, every *extra* call for gold, on the large scales supposed, would instantly inflame the *market* price of gold, and virtually cancel much of the new advantage. This counteraction would again narrow the use of gold. That narrowing would again lower the market price of gold. Under that lowering, again, the extra use of gold would go ahead. Again the extra cheapness would disappear, and consequently the motive to an enlarged use. And we should live in the endless alternations, hot fits and cold fits, of an intermitting fever.

But, on *my* view, there will arise that preliminary bar to such a state which I have already explained. In the earliest stage of these new gold workings, one and all, the result will be this—a tendency to *lower* the producing cost of gold; and this tendency will, in the second stage, be stimulated by the aids of science: and thus, finally, if the tendency could act long enough, the price *would* be lowered in the gold markets of the world. But this is an impossibility, because, before such an effect could be accomplished, the third stage of the new diggings would reverse the steps, tending continually to *increase* the cost of gold, as the easy surface gathering was exhausted. The fourth stage would recede still further from the early cheapness, as the mining descended, and had to fight with the ordinary difficulties of mines; and the fifth stage would find the reader and myself giving up all thoughts of sporting gold tables and chairs, and contentedly leaving such visions to those people who (according to the old saying) are "born with a gold spoon in their mouths."

## On the Final Catastrophe of the Gold-digging Mania

So long as California, and California exclusively, was concerned in this portentous craze, there were two drawbacks upon any eventual ruin to be anticipated (come when it would), in so far as it could affect ourselves. First, there was this drawback—that the bubble was not by two-thirds[1]

[1] "*Not by two-thirds upon so large a scale*":—It is in the last degree difficult to obtain any reports that can be relied on. In the absence

upon so large a scale as it has been since Australia became a party to the mania; consequently, in that proportion the ruin from the final explosion of the bubble promised to be less. Secondly, the people concerned in the Californian affair were not chiefly from Great Britain. By a large majority, they were people from the United States: some being Yankees,—that is to say, Northern Americans from the New England States (viz. Massachusetts, Rhode Island, Connecticut, &c.); but more being from the central states of Virginia, Maryland, Kentucky, Ohio, &c. Generally speaking, however, the Californian population represents adequately the activities of the earth: it is a *cosmical* population, drafted from every climate and region, that, having within itself the stirring impulses of progress and adventurous industry, happens also to have the advantage of easy access to maritime districts, and the means of nautical emigration. The final crash will, therefore, to us English, be far ampler *now* than it could have been under the original restriction to the stage of California; not merely through the far larger development of the evil, but also through the more immediate connexion of the chief sufferers with ourselves. What shape then will the crash assume? Or, how am I entitled to talk of *any* crash? Or so fluently to characterise this popular rush to the gold diggings as a "craze," a "bubble," and a "mania"?

The reasons are not far to seek: they are plain and

of official returns, there is naturally an invitation held out to the double spirit of romance, moving its wings in an atmosphere of unlimited credulity, and also of furious self-interest having an equal motive (though not the same motive) to exaggeration. I speak, therefore, as everybody *must* speak, under correction from better authorities, if any such shall come forward; although it must be still borne in mind that even official returns, supposing them fully organised, could do little more than apply a conjectural correction to those irregular transmissions of gold which, under various motives (sometimes of politic concealment, sometimes of ignorant distrust), are going on largely amongst a population so mixed and disorderly as that of Australia. Taking, however, such authorities as could be found, and collating them together, I had reason to estimate the Californian produce *annually* at about twenty-seven millions sterling when California stood alone, and to estimate the *present* Australian produce at three times that amount, or very nearly one million sterling per week.

obvious. I will state them ; and, if any reader can reply to them without practising evasions, and without forging facts, let him do so. I confess that, if mere authority of position and audacity of assertion in the public journals ought to have any weight against blank force of logic and inexorable facts of experience, I myself should have consented to be silenced oftentimes when I had not been convinced. But in every one of these journals I read such monstrous oversights as to the permanent conditions of the question that I am not summoned to any deferential treatment of the adverse views. If, in arguing the merits of a particular course through a difficult navigation, my antagonist begins by ignoring a visible rock lying right ahead, it is for *him* to explain such an oversight ; and, until he does explain it, my right it is to spend very little ceremony upon the circumstantialities of his arguments.

The public journals of this island, whether literary or political, have almost monotonously welcomed the large discoveries of gold—as if necessarily, *prima facie*, and without further discussion, subjects of universal congratulation to the human race. And it is evident, from the language used in many instances, that excess or superfluity is, in the judgment of these journals, not an affection incident in the case ; not an element that can ever enter into the logic of the estimate. Whereas, on the contrary, I assert that no product whatsoever of this earth, be it animal, mineral, or vegetable, but is liable to most pernicious excess : excess embarrassing, or by possibility ruinous, to the prosperity of human industry ; excess confounding to human foresight. Everything, without exception, is liable to this ruinous reaction from excess ; and beyond almost anything else gold is in that predicament.

There are many things which, though otherwise susceptible of such an excess, are able for a long time to evade its inconveniences, by virtue of their own variable flexibility in applying themselves to human purposes. The scale of their application is often so elastic, narrowing or expanding according to circumstances, that the danger of excess is for *them* permanently thrown to a distance. Iron, for example, is interchangeable at this day for so many purposes with wood that, long after the margin for a large *extra* use had been exhausted within the field of its own regular applications, it would find another *extra* margin by trespassing within the field ordinarily occupied by wood, or by brick, or by marble. A wooden house was sent out to St. Helena for Napoleon; but at this day, the ready-made houses sent out from New York and London to California are chiefly of iron. So again of ships, of light bridges, of gates, of fences, of balconies, &c. Wood and iron will probably for generations relieve their own superfluities by alternate encroachments on each other, according to the alternate advantages which each material, under shifting circumstances, may happen to obtain in the market. Wheat, again, in seasons of extra cheapness, when oats have happened to be unusually dear, has usurped to a considerable extent upon the ordinary oatmeal diet of a whole peasantry. It is not common, but it does sometimes happen, that wheaten flour is substituted for oatmeal; similar substitutions are without end; so that excess of production is a point not very easily reached in the case of many articles. A very large majority benefit, in the event of over-production, not merely by their own independent capacities of expansion, but also by the corresponding capacities of contraction in some other article which ordinarily has been employed as a substitute.[1]

But now, without further delay, let us come to the possible expansions in the use of gold; for, substantially, that is the sole question at issue. Gold is so enormously more costly, bulk for bulk, than all other articles of luxury and ornament, excepting only jewels and pearls, that it cannot possibly benefit by the second mode of expansion here noticed, viz. by some other article contracting or retiring in order to make room for it, but solely by the alternate mode, viz. by the extension of its own separate use, according to the

[1] And this in cases where the use or office of the article must be strictly vicarious and substitutional. But in large classes of things—as, for instance, children's toys, gifts of affection, parting memorials, ornaments for mantelpieces, or brackets, &c.—a large range of substitution is possible when the function of the article may be totally different. A watch, for instance, may be presented by substitution for a fan; or a porcelain vase for a brace of pistols; or a crucifix for a pearl necklace.

ordinary mode of using it. The plain, flagrant, and undeniable fact meets us upon every road that connects human calculations with the subject, that the whole frenzy of gold-digging will be suddenly pulled up—in one month will be frozen into abrupt extinction—by mere failure, blank failure, of demand. So far as its own proper use can be enlarged, so far there is an opening for an extension of the demand; but, as to any substitutional use, *that* is inconceivable.

This mortal wound to the whole bestial scene of sensuality and robbery (robbery, for such it is, consequent upon the helplessness of the Government) has hidden itself, naturally enough, from the poor, illiterate vagabonds that compose the plundering army of diggers. And it is possible to excuse some blindness upon such a prospect, even in educated people, under the misleading influence of such a case as this. A river, suppose at a mile distance, has been swelling for many days, and at length is overflowing its banks. The flood, continually increasing, travels hourly in the direction of your own house. But, before it can touch that house in the slightest degree, it must fill up to the very brim a deep valley which is interposed between that river and the house. So long, now, as this intervening valley wants one hair's-breadth of being full, there is not a vestige of any warning given to you that an awful calamity is at hand. At noon, suppose exactly as the clock strikes twelve, the overwhelming deluge is pouring in at every window and door within its level. Sixty seconds before the clock struck, you could have sworn that every window-sill was dry as dust. Not otherwise (what by accident, and what by uncalculating ignorance) the whole phenomena of the gold case have darkened themselves to the unreflecting observers. There were *many* valleys to be filled up before the overflowing river could reach our own unalarmed house. There were, first of all, the *hoarders*, a class most numerous under Oriental despotisms, but even in Christian Europe not at all an insignificant class; since, when the sovereign does *not* plunder, the lord paramount over vassals often *does*. The year 1848 armed, as against the menaces of communism, many millions of hoarders —say thirty millions at ten pounds sterling a-man. That would account for the burial of three hundred millions sterling. Then make a corresponding allowance for Asiatic hoarders. But, as all Asiatic populations (reserving only Japan, China, and Hindostan) are miserably slender, and also, man for man, are poorer, allow, perhaps, one hundred millions sterling for this class. Thirdly, allow for the sovereign hoarders—viz. the several governments in Europe, who, under some strange misconception of the case, have taken occasion to build up a gold currency at the very moment when ordinary foresight should have proclaimed to every nation the necessity of converting any gold articles in their possession into glass, stone, marble, copper—anything, in short, that was not under absolute judicial sentence of depreciation. All these allowances may amount to five hundred and fifty or six hundred millions. These millions constitute the valley that had to be filled to the brim before the surplus could enter ruinously into your own house. How far off may be that consummation I do not pretend to say. Certainly not very far. The Russian, the Californian, and the Australian, added to some other more trivial contributions from parts of Africa, from the island of Borneo, &c., cannot now yield much under seventy-five millions sterling per annum. About one hundred and fifty millions, therefore, are added biennially; and four such biennial contributions would produce the entire sum wanted as the vacuum to be filled up. But already, some years ago, this filling up had commenced; and, previously to *that*, the stock of gold locked up in ornamental articles was already very large. Upon *any* calculation, near indeed we must stand, fatally near, to the epoch at which, pretty suddenly, all further demand for gold must cease.

Upon you it is—you, the opposers of this view—that the *onus* rests of howing into what shape the demand for gold will transmigrate, when once it shall have been thoroughly satisfied and gorged in all shapes which hitherto it has assumed. How romantically impossible any new shape must be will appear from this one consideration:—At the time when the Californian mines were discovered, how was it that the world got on as respected its gold wants? Tell me, you that dispose so lightly of the whole threatening catastrophe, was or was not the produce of the Russian Ural Mountains, added to other more trivial sources, sufficient (when combined with the vast *accumulated* stock long ago in the universal gold markets) for the total purposes of this terraqueous globe ? Was it, or was it not ? No evasions, if you please. If it was,—hearken to the dilemma which besieges you !—then how are you simple enough to suppose that the same planet which found six or seven millions as much as its annual necessities could absorb should suddenly become able to digest seventy-five millions ? If, on the other hand, it was *not* sufficient—if you endeavour to explain some small fraction of the marvel by alleging that, in fact, the Ural product of gold was not measured by the capacity of the earth to absorb, but by the limited power of Russia to produce—then I demand why it was that the Ural price of gold did not steadily increase ? Had more gold been wanted by the earth, more could readily have been furnished by Russia, upon a very small advance in the price. Precisely because this advance of price was not forthcoming—that is to say, precisely because the supply was fully up to the demand—we obtain the clearest evidence that all the Californian and Australian gold has spent itself upon no necessity of ordinary annual recurrence, upon no demand that can last, but upon filling up extraordinary chasms that cannot repeat themselves—such, for instance, as replacing silver or paper currencies with gold ; and therefore that, when that service is fulfilled—which is the only service of a large national nature that can still be in any degree unsatisfied—thenceforward, of mere necessity, we descend again into that condition of limited demand which, for years, had been met sufficiently by the Russian supply of five or six millions sterling per annum.

For, now, if you question this, and fancy that the Australian supply of gold is, by some unspeakable process, to create a demand for itself, tell us how, and illustrate the shape which this new demand will take. Do not fence with the clouds, but come down to earth. You cannot deny that, two years ago, when we had no Australian gold, the goldsmiths of this earth did very well without it. Say not a word, therefore, of the Californian gold ; every ounce of Australian gold, were there no other addition, should logically be so much more than is wanted. How, then, do you suppose that it is eventually to be disposed of? Because, until we know this, we cannot pretend to know whether it is a laughing matter or a crying matter. As to fancying that Australian gold will continue to force a market for itself, you cannot seriously suppose that a man who never thought of buying a gold watch or other trinket when such articles were made of Uralian gold will suddenly conceive a fancy for such an article simply because the gold is raised in an English colony, and, though no cheaper, has, by its redundant production, ceased to impress the imagination. If it were really true that gold, because it was dug up in extra quantities, could therefore command an extra market, why not apply the same theory to iron, to coals, or to calico? A comfortable doctrine it would be for the English manufacturer, that, in proportion as he increased his production, he could extend his market,—*i.e.* could extend his market precisely as he overstocked it. And yet, of all things, gold could least benefit by such a forced increase. Calico might be substituted for linen cloth, iron in many applications for wood, coals for turf; but gold can be substituted for nothing. If a man resolves to substitute a gold watch for a silver one, surely his motive for doing so is not because gold is produced in one latitude or one longitude, having previously been produced in another. It is very clear that, long before California or Australia had been heard of, no man who wished for a gold watch had any difficulty in obtaining it, if only he could *pay* for it; and that little part of the ceremony, I presume, he must submit to even now.

Why, yes—certainly he must pay for it; but here dawns upon us the real and sincere fancy of the advantage worked by the new gold diggings: some confused notion arises that he will pay less. But then, exactly in that proportion falls away the motive for undergoing the preternatural labour of the diggings. Even this, however, will not avail; for so costly is gold, under any conceivable advantages for cheapening it, that, even at one-half or one-quarter of the price, gold trinkets would not come within the reach of any class so much more extended than the class now purchasing such articles as to meet within a thousand degrees the increased produce of gold. In articles of absolute homely use, it is clear that gold never can be substituted for less costly metals. Ornamental gold articles, on the other hand, are in their total possible range (considering that they do not perish from year to year) ludicrously below the scale which could do anything for the relief of our Australian gold. It is not, therefore, only that the monstrous and hyperbolical excess of gold, as measured against any conceivable use or application of gold, would terminate in forcing down the price of gold to a point at which it would no longer furnish any encouragement whatever to the gold-digger; but, even at this abject price (or at any price whatever), gold would cease to command a market. It is natural enough that the poor simpletons who are at the diggings, or are hurrying thither like kites to carrion, should be the dupes of the old fantastic superstition which invests the precious metals with some essential and indefeasible divinity. But the conductors of great national journals should have known better; and, if they do really entertain the conceit that gold must always be gold (that is, must have some mysterious value apart and separate from any use which it can realise), in that case they ought to have traced the progress of a gold nugget, weighing, suppose, a pound, through the markets of the world, under the condition that all their markets are plethorically overstocked.

Some such case has been pressed, apparently, on the attention of men lately; and the answer—the desperate answer which I understand to have been extorted—was this: —It was contended that the mere market for female ornaments throughout Hindostan would suffice to provide a vent for the Australian surplus through many years to come. Now, this allegation might easily be disposed of in one sentence—viz. thus: If the Hindoo women are able and willing to pay the existing price for gold—viz. from seventy to seventy-five shillings per oz.—why did they *not* pay it long before Californian digging arose? Russia would *always* have furnished them gold at that price. How is it, then, that they are in any want of gold ornaments? Russia would gladly have received an order for an annual excess of two million ounces. The dilemma is apparently not to be evaded: either these Hindoo women cannot afford the price of gold ornaments; or, on the other hand, they *have* afforded it, and are already possessed of such ornaments. However, that I may not be said to have evaded any possible argument, let us review the statistics of the case. First of all, it is *Hindoo* women of whom we are speaking; and properly, therefore, twenty millions of Mahometans—*i.e.* ten millions of females—should be subtracted from the population of India. But waive this, and call the total population one hundred millions. I distrust these random computations altogether; but let that pass. The families, therefore, may count for fifty millions. Now, more than one-half of the human race are under the age of fifteen. It is true that, in a country where many a woman marries at twelve, the age for ornaments must be dated from a much earlier period. Yet, again, as decay commences at an age correspondingly even more premature, possibly it would not be unfair to deduct one-half as the sum of those who fall below or rise above the age for personal ornaments. However, on this and other distinct grounds, deduct only ten millions; and suppose fifteen millions of the remaining forty to be already in possession of such ornaments. There remain, therefore, twenty-five millions as the supposed available market for gold. Now, according to what I remember of Dr. Buchanan's very elaborate statistics applied to the Mysore territory,[1] and taking this as the standard, I should hold one ounce of gold to be a large allowance for each individual female; for, when alloyed into jeweller's gold, this would be equal to four ounces weight. On that basis, the market of India would take off twenty-five million ounces of gold. But, if we are to believe the current reports, within the last twelve months the Australian diggings produced about fifteen million ounces of gold, reckoned locally at nearly seventy shillings an ounce. Next year, naturally, the product will be much larger; and in one year, therefore, on the most liberal allowance, all India would be adequately supplied with gold by Australia alone; and, as gold does not perish, this would not be a *recurrent* demand. Once satisfied, that call would be made no more;

1 "*Journey from Madras through the Countries of Mysore, Canara, and Malabar.* By Francis Buchanan, M.D., 1807."—M.

once filled, that chasm would not again be empty. And what is to become of the Australian gold in the year succeeding? Are we to have spades and ploughshares manufactured of gold, or how? But away with such trifling! One might draw amusement from human folly in cases that were less urgent; but, under circumstances as they really stand, and hurrying, as we actually find ourselves, down a precipitous descent that allows no time for looking forward nor escape in looking back, which of us could be childish enough to dwell upon the comic aspects of the calamity? And these two results will very soon unfold themselves. First this, viz. that, without reference to the depreciation of gold—not stopping to ask upon what scale *that* would move, suppose it little, or suppose it much—alike in any result the possibility of finding new extension of market for gold, under the exhaustion of all conceivable extensions applied to its uses in the arts, must, by such flying steps approach its final limit that in that way separately a headlong depreciation must overtake us without warning.[1]

Secondly, another depreciation, from another quarter, will arise to complicate and to intensify this primary depreciation. The sudden cessation of the *demand*, from mere defect of further uses and purposes, will of itself establish a sudden lock in the clockwork of the commercial movement. But of a nature altogether different, and more gigantic in its scale, will be the depreciation from inhuman and maniacal excesses.

I add a few paragraphs as my closing remarks; and, in

[1] "*Without warning*":—The mistake is to imagine that the retrogression must travel through stages corresponding to the movement in advance; but it is forgotten that, even if so—even upon that very assumption—the movement would *not* be leisurely, but, on the contrary, fearfully and frantically fast. What a storm-flight has been the forward motion of the gold development! People forget *that*. But they also forget altogether the other consideration, which I have suggested under the image of an interposing valley needing to be filled up; which necessity of course retarded for two or three years, and so long therefore masked and concealed, the true velocity of the impending evil. If an enemy is obliged to move underground in order to approach one's assailable points, during all this hidden advance it is inevitable to forget the steps that are at once out of sight and inaudible.

order to mark their disconnexion with each other, I number them with figures. They all grow out of the subject, but do not arise consecutively out of each other.

1. On this day (Thursday, Dec. 16, 1852), being the day when I put a close to these remarks, I have just received the *Times* newspaper for Monday, December 13, 1852, and in that paper I observe two things: 1st (on col. 1 of p. 5), that the *San Francisco Herald* reports the exportation of gold as amounting probably to five and a half millions of dollars for the month then current (November); and that this is given as likely to be the representative export is plain from what precedes; for, says the *Herald*, "The production, instead of falling off (as croakers long ago predicted), seems to be steadily on the increase." Here we find a yearly export of more than fourteen millions sterling announced joyfully as something that may be depended upon. And, in the midst of such insane exultation, of course we need not be surprised that "a *croaker*" means, not the man that looks forward with horror to the ruin contingent upon such a prophecy being realised, but upon him who doubts it. Secondly, I observe (col. 2 of p. 3) that, in a brief notice of the translation published by Mr. Hankey jun. from M. Leon Faucher's *Remarks on the Production of the Precious Metals*, there is extracted one paragraph, the first which has ever met my eye taking the same view as myself of the dangers ahead, though in a tone far below the urgency of the case. "I can hardly agree," says Mr. Hankey, "that there is so little ground for alarm as to a depreciation in the value of gold in consequence of the late discoveries." He then goes on to assign reasons for his own fears. But, as he actually allows a considerable weight amongst the grounds of his fears to the few hundred thousands of sovereigns sent out to Australia with the view of meeting the momentary deficiency in coin, and which (as he rightly observes) will soon be returning upon us and aggravating the domestic glut, anybody taking *my* view will naturally infer the exceeding inadequacy of his fears to the real danger. The sovereign will prove a mere drop in the ocean.[1] On this same day, I have read letters

[1] Mr. Hankey, meantime, happens to be Governor of the Bank; and, that being so, his opinion will have weight. That is all I ask. In the

from Australia announcing further vast discoveries of gold, viz. at a distance of about twenty miles from Adelaide. The same accounts confirm what I cited earlier in this paper as the probable annual amount from Australia *previous to this last discovery* as reaching fifty-one or fifty-two millions sterling *per annum*, by showing that in eleven months—viz. from October 1851 to September 1852—the export shipped from *Victoria alone* had been ten millions sterling. Between California and Australia, supposing the present rates of production to continue, within three years the earth would be deluged with gold. It is true that a sudden crash will intercept the consummation, but in a way that will work ruin to more nations than one.

2. Why is it that we speak with mixed astonishment and disgust, horror and laughter struggling for the mastery, of the mania which possessed the two leaders of civilisation (so by all the world they are entitled), England and France, London and Paris, about one hundred and thirty years back? The South Sea Bubble amongst the English in 1718-19, the Mississippi Bubble amongst the French in 1720—wherefore is it that we marvel at them? that we write books about them? that we expose them in colours of pity and scorn to our children of this generation? In simple truth, we are as gross fools as our ancestors; and indeed grosser. For, after all, the loss was local and partial at that time. Not one family in ten thousand suffered materially; but, as things are now proceeding, none will escape, for the ruin will steal upon us in a form not at first perceived. *It is already stealing upon us.* But why, I ask, would any prudent man—any reflecting man—have seen through the bubbles of our ancestors? My answer is this: Such a man would have scented the fraud in the very names. The Mississippi!—the South Sea! Why the lies of Falstaff were not more gross, or more overflowing with self-refutation. The Mississippi was at this time a desert, requiring a century at least, and a vast impulse of colonisation, to make it capable of any produce at all. The South Sea was a solitary wilderness, from which (unless in blubber and spermaceti) not a hundred

tendencies we coincide: the only difference is as to the degree. And for *that* the Australian exports of gold will soon speak loudly enough.

pounds' worth of any valuable commodity could have been exported. Both were mines of pure emptiness—not mines exhausted; there never had been anything to exhaust. And, in fact, I remember nothing in all comedy, or universal farce, that can match these two hoaxes upon London and Paris, unless it were a scene which I remember in one of Foote's after-pieces. He introduces a political *quidnunc*, possessed by the Athenian mania of hunting eternally after some new thing. His name, if I recollect, is Gregory Gazette. And, in one scene, where some pecuniary fraud is to be executed, Sir Gregory is persuaded into believing that the Pope has, by treaty, consented to turn Protestant, upon being put into possession of Nova Zembla and selected sections of Greenland. Was there anything less monstrous than this in the French or the English craze of 1718-20? Or is there anything less monstrous in our present reliance on the Hindoo women for keeping up the price of gold?

3. I need not say, to any man who reflects, that fifty such populations as that of Hindostan, or even of Europe (which means a very different thing), would not interrupt the depreciation of gold, or retard it for two years, under the assumption of an influx on its present scale. M. Chevalier, a great authority in France on all questions of this nature, has supposed it possible that the depreciation might go down as far as fifty per cent on its present price; though why it should stop *there* no man can guess. Even, however, at that price, or, in round expressions, costing forty shillings an ounce, it will yet be eight times the price of silver; and one moment's consideration will suggest to us the hopelessness of any material retardation to this fall by any extended use of gold for decorations in dress, houses, &c., through the simple recollection that all the enormous advantages of a price eight times lower have not availed to secure any further extension to the ornamental use of silver. Silver is much more beautiful than gold in combination with the other accompaniments of a table, such as purple and golden and amber-coloured wines, light of candles, glass, &c. Silver is susceptible of higher workmanship; silver is worked much more cheaply; and yet, with five shillings an ounce to start from, instead of forty, services of silver plate are, even yet, in the most

luxurious of cities, the rarest of domestic ornaments. One cause of this may be that silver, as a service for the dinner-table, finds a severe rival in the exquisite beauty of porcelain; but that rival it will continue to find; and, in such a rivalship, gold would be beaten hollow by any one of the competitors, even if it had the advantage of starting on the same original level as to price.

4. But, finally, there occur to you as a last resource, when dinner-services and Hindoo women are all out of the field, the *currencies* of the earth. Yes: there it is, you think, that the diggings will find their asylum of steady support. Unhappily, my reader, instead of support, through that channel it is that we shall receive our ruin. Were it not for currencies, nobody would be ruined but the diggers, and their immediate agents. But, as most of these were ruined at starting, they would at worst end as they began. The misery is that most nations, misconceiving the result altogether, have already furnished themselves with gold currencies. These, on the mistake being discovered, will hurry back into the market. Then the glut will be prodigiously aggravated; but in that way only can the evil be in part evaded. If gold continued with ourselves to be a compulsory and statutable payment, and our funded proprietors were still paid in gold, every family would be ruined. For, if nominally these proprietors are but about three hundred thousand, we must remember that many a single proprietor, appearing only as one name, virtually represents tens of thousands—bankers, for instance, charitable institutions, insurance offices, &c. So wide a desolation could not by any device of man reach so vast a body of helpless interests. The first step to be taken would be to repeal the statute which makes gold a legal tender for sums above forty shillings, and at the same time to rescind the mint regulations. The depreciation will not express itself openly, so long as these laws are in force. At this moment, in Staffordshire and Warwickshire, within the last six weeks, iron and coal have risen cent per cent. Part of the cause lies beyond a doubt in the depreciation of gold; and this would declare itself were gold no longer current under legal coercion.

*P.S., written on January* 27, 1853.—More than a calendar month has elapsed since the proof of this article was sent to me. Two facts have transpired in the interval. The return of the steamer called the "Australian" confirms the romantic estimates previously received,—the single colony of Victoria yielding, according to the careful interpretation of the London *Standard*, at the present rate, twenty-five millions sterling per annum. The other noticeable fact is the general survey, on New-year's-day, by the *Times City* reporter, of the prospects for the current year, 1853. He pronounces that there is "no cloud" to darken our anticipations; or, if any, only through political convulsions, contingent, by possibility, on the crazy moneyed speculations afloat in Paris. The superfluous gold he supposes to be got rid of by various *investments*; though he himself notices the nugatoriness of any investment that simply shifts the gold from one holder to another. No possible investment can answer any purpose of even *mitigating* the evils in arrear, unless in so far as it does really and substantially *absorb* the gold, *i.e. withdraw it from circulation* by locking it up in some article of actual service in that identical form of gold. To invest, for instance, in the funds, is simply to transfer the gold from the buyer of the stock to the seller; and so of all other pretended "*investments*," unless really and truly they withdraw the gold from circulation and from commercial exchange. Meantime, the solitary hope is that the gold quarries may soon be exhausted.

# IDEA OF A UNIVERSAL HISTORY ON A COSMOPOLITICAL PLAN

### A TRANSLATION FROM KANT [1]

WHATSOEVER difference there may be in our notions of the *freedom of the will* metaphysically considered, it is evident that the manifestations of this will, viz. human actions, are as much under the control of universal laws of nature as any other physical phenomena. It is the province of History to narrate these manifestations; and, let their causes be ever so secret, we know that History, simply by taking its station at a distance and contemplating the agency of the human will upon a large scale, aims at unfolding to our view a regular stream of tendency in the great succession of events,—so that the very same course of incidents which, taken separately and individually, would have seemed perplexed, incoherent, and lawless, yet viewed in their connexion and as the actions of the human *species* and not of independent beings, never fail to discover a steady and continuous, though slow, development of certain great predispositions in our nature. Thus, for instance, deaths, births, and marriages, considering how much they are separately dependent on the freedom of the human will, should seem to be subject to no law according to which any calculation could be made beforehand of their amount: and yet the yearly registers of these events in great countries prove that they go on with as much conformity to

[1] Appeared originally in the *London Magazine* for October 1824: reprinted by De Quincey in 1859 in vol. xiii of his Collective Edition of his writings.—M.

the laws of nature as the oscillations of the weather. These, again, are events which in detail are so far irregular that we cannot predict them individually; and yet, taken as a whole series, we find that they never fail to support the growth of plants, the currents of rivers, and other arrangements of nature, in a uniform and uninterrupted course. Individual men, and even nations, are little aware that, whilst they are severally pursuing their own peculiar and often contradictory purposes, they are unconsciously following the guidance of a great natural purpose which is wholly unnoticed by themselves, and are thus promoting and making efforts for a great process which, even if they perceived it, they would little regard.

Considering that men, taken collectively as a body, do not proceed, like brute animals, under the law of an instinct, nor yet again, like rational cosmopolites, under the law of a preconcerted plan, one might imagine that no systematic history of their actions (such, for instance, as the history of bees or beavers) could be possible. At the sight of the actions of man displayed on the great stage of the world, it is impossible to escape a certain degree of disgust: with all the occasional indications of wisdom scattered here and there, we cannot but perceive the whole sum of these actions to be a web of folly, childish vanity, and often even of the idlest wickedness and spirit of destruction. Hence, at last, one is puzzled to know what judgment to form of our species, so conceited of its high advantages. In such a perplexity there is no resource for the philosopher but this,—that, finding it impossible to presume in the human race any *rational* purpose of its own, he must endeavour to detect some *natural* purpose in such a senseless current of human actions; by means of which a history of creatures that pursue no plan of their own may yet admit a systematic form as the history of creatures that are blindly pursuing a plan of nature. Let us now see whether we can succeed in finding out a clue to such a history, leaving it to nature to produce a man capable of executing it,—just as she produced a Kepler who unexpectedly brought the eccentric courses of the planets under determinate laws, and afterwards a Newton who explained these laws out of a universal ground in Nature:—

### PROPOSITION THE FIRST

*All tendencies of any creature to which it is predisposed by Nature are destined in the end to develop themselves perfectly and agreeably to their final purpose.*

External as well as internal (or anatomical) examination confirms this remark in all animals. An organ which is not to be used, a natural arrangement that misses its purpose, would be a contradiction in physics. Once departing from this fundamental proposition, we have a Nature no longer tied to laws, but objectless and working at random; and a cheerless reign of Chance steps into the place of Reason.

### PROPOSITION THE SECOND

*In Man, as the sole rational creature upon earth, those tendencies which have the use of his reason for their object are destined to obtain their perfect development in the species only, and not in the individual.*

Reason in a creature is a faculty for extending the rules and purposes of the exercise of all its powers far beyond natural instinct; and it is illimitable in its plans. It works, however, not instinctively, but tentatively, by means of practice, through progress and regress, in order to ascend gradually from one degree of illumination to another. On this account, either it would be necessary for each man to live an inordinate length of time in order to learn how to make a perfect use of his natural tendencies; or else, supposing the actual case that Nature has limited his term of life, she must then require an incalculable series of generations (each delivering its quota of knowledge to its immediate successor) in order to ripen the germs which she has laid in our species to that degree of development which corresponds with her final purpose. And the period of this mature development must exist at least in idea to Man as the object of his efforts: because otherwise his own natural predispositions must of necessity be regarded as objectless; and this would at once take away all *practical* principles, and would expose Nature, the wisdom of whose arrangements must in all other cases be assumed as a fundamental postulate, to the suspicion of capricious dealing in the case of Man only.

PROPOSITION THE THIRD

*It is the will of Nature that Man should owe to himself alone everything which transcends the mere mechanic constitution of his animal existence, and that he should be susceptible of no other happiness or perfection than what he has created for himself, instinct apart, through his own reason.*

Nature does nothing superfluously, and in the use of means to her ends does not play the prodigal. Having given to Man reason, and freedom of the will grounded upon reason, she had hereby sufficiently made known the purpose which governed her in the choice of the furniture and appointments, intellectual and physical, with which she has accoutred him. Thus provided, he had no need for the guidance of instinct, or for knowledge and forethought created to his hand ; for these he was to be indebted to himself. The means of providing for his own shelter from the elements, for his own security, and the whole superstructure of delights which add comfort and embellishment to life, were to be the work of his own hands. So far indeed has she pushed this principle that she seems to have been frugal even to niggardliness in the dispensation of her animal endowments to Man, and to have calculated her allowance to the nicest rigour of the demand in the very earliest stage of his existence : as if it had been her intention hereby to proclaim that the highest degree of power, of intellectual perfection, and of happiness to which he should ever toil upwards from a condition utterly savage, must all be wrung and extorted from the difficulties and thwartings of his situation, and the merit therefore be exclusively his own ; thus implying that she had at heart his own rational self-estimation rather than his convenience or comfort. She has indeed beset Man with difficulties ; and in no way could she have so clearly made known that her purpose with Man was not that he might live in pleasure, but that by a strenuous wrestling with those difficulties he might make himself worthy of living in pleasure. Undoubtedly it seems surprising on this view of the case that the earlier generations appear to exist only for the sake of the latter, viz. for the sake of forwarding that edifice of man's grandeur in which only the latest generations are to dwell, though all have undesignedly taken part in raising it. Mysterious as this appears, it is, however, at the same time necessary, if we once assume a race of rational animals as destined by means of this characteristic reason to a perfect development of their tendencies, and subject to mortality in the individual, but immortal in the species.

### PROPOSITION THE FOURTH

*The means which Nature employs to bring about the development of all the tendencies she has laid in Man is the antagonism of these tendencies in the social state—no farther, however, than to that point at which this antagonism becomes the cause of social arrangements founded in law.*

By antagonism of this kind I mean the *unsocial sociality* of man,—that is, a tendency to enter the social state, combined with a perpetual resistance to that tendency which is continually threatening to dissolve it. Man has gregarious inclinations, feeling himself in the social state more than Man, by means of the development thus given to his natural tendencies. But he has also strong anti-gregarious inclinations, prompting him to insulate himself, which arise out of the unsocial desire (existing concurrently with his social propensities) to force all things into compliance with his own humour,—a propensity to which he naturally anticipates resistance from his consciousness of a similar spirit of resistance to others existing in himself. Now, this resistance it is which awakens all the powers of Man, drives him to master his propensity to indolence, and, in the shape of ambition, love of honour, or avarice, impels him to procure distinction for himself amongst his fellows. In this way arise the first steps from the savage state to the state of culture, which consists peculiarly in the social worth of Man. Talents of every kind are now unfolded, taste formed, and by gradual increase of light a preparation is made for such a mode of thinking as is capable of converting the rude natural tendency to moral distinctions into determinate practical principles, and finally of exalting a social concert that had been *pathologically* extorted from the mere necessities of situation into a *moral* union founded on the reasonable choice. But for these anti-social propensities, so unamiable in themselves, which give birth to that resistance which every man meets with in his own self-interested pretensions, an Arcadian life would arise, of perfect harmony and mutual love, such as must suffocate and stifle all talents in their very germs. Men, as gentle as the sheep they fed, would communicate to their existence no higher value than belongs to mere animal life, and would leave the vacuum of creation, which exists in reference to the final purpose of man's nature as a rational nature, unfilled. Thanks, therefore, to Nature for the enmity, for the jealous spirit of envious competition, for the insatiable thirst after wealth and power! These wanting, all the admirable tendencies in man's nature would remain for ever undeveloped. Man, for his own sake as an individual, wishes for concord; but Nature knows better what is good for Man as a species; and she ordains discord. He would live in ease and passive content: but Nature wills that he shall precipitate himself out of this luxury of indolence into labours and hardships, in order that he may devise remedies against them, and thus raise himself above them by an intellectual conquest, not sink below them by an unambitious evasion. The impulses which she has with this view laid in his moral constitution, the sources of that anti-sociality and universal antagonism from which so many evils arise, but which again stimulate a fresh reaction of the faculties, and by consequence more and more aid the development of the primitive tendencies, all tend to betray the adjusting hand of a wise Creator, not that of an Evil Spirit that has bungled in the execution of his own designs, or has malevolently sought to perplex them with evil.

### PROPOSITION THE FIFTH

*The highest problem for the Human Species, to the solution of which it is irresistibly urged by natural impulses, is the establishment of a universal Civil Society founded on the empire of political justice.*

Since it is only in the social state that the final purpose of Nature with regard to Man (viz. the development of all his tendencies) can be accomplished,—and in such a social state as combines with the utmost possible freedom and consequent antagonism of its members the most rigorous determination of the boundaries of this freedom, in order that the freedom of such individual may co-exist with the freedom of others,—and since it is the will of Nature that this as well as all other objects of his destination should be the work of men's own efforts: on these accounts a society in which freedom under laws is united with the greatest possible degree of irresistible power,—*i.e.* a perfect civil constitution,—is the highest problem of Nature for Man: because it is only by the solution of this problem that Nature can accomplish the rest of her purposes with our species. Into this state of restraint Man, who is otherwise so much enamoured of lawless freedom, is compelled to enter by necessity, —and that the greatest of all necessity, viz. a necessity self-imposed; his natural inclinations making it impossible for Man to preserve a state of perfect liberty for any length of time in the neighbourhood of his fellows. But, under the restraint of a civil community, these very inclinations lead to the best effects: just as trees in a forest, for the very reason that each endeavours to rob the other of air and sun, compel each other to shoot upwards in quest of both, and thus attain a fine erect growth,—whereas those which stand aloof from each other under no mutual restraint, and throw out their boughs at pleasure, become crippled and distorted. All the gifts of art and cultivation which adorn the human race,—in short, the most beautiful forms of social order,—are the fruits of the anti-social principle, which is compelled to discipline itself, and by means won from the very resistance of Man's situation in this world to give perfect development to all the germs of Nature.

### PROPOSITION THE SIXTH

*This problem is at the same time the most difficult of all, and the one which is latest solved by Man.*

The difficulty which is involved in the bare idea of such

a problem is this :—Man is an animal that, so long as he lives amongst others of his species, stands in need of a master. For he inevitably abuses his freedom in regard to his equals ; and, although, as a reasonable creature, he wishes for a law that may set bounds to the liberty of all, yet do his self-interested animal propensities seduce him into making an exception in his own favour whensoever he dares. He requires a master, therefore, to curb his will, and to compel him into submission to a universal will which may secure the possibility of universal freedom. Now, where is he to find this master ? Of necessity, amongst the human species. But, as a human being, this master will also be an animal that requires a master. Lodged in one or many, it is impossible that the supreme and irresponsible power can be certainly prevented from abusing its authority. Hence it is that this problem is the most difficult of any ; nay, its perfect solution is impossible : out of wood so crooked and perverse as that which man is made of, nothing absolutely straight can ever be wrought. An approximation to this idea is therefore all which Nature enjoins us. That it is also the last of all problems to which the human species addresses itself is clear from this,—that it presupposes *just notions* of the nature of a good constitution, great *experience*, and above all a *will* favourably disposed to the adoption of such a constitution : three elements that can hardly, and not until after many fruitless trials, be expected to concur.

### PROPOSITION THE SEVENTH

*The problem of the establishment of a perfect Constitution of Society depends upon the problem of a system of International Relations adjusted to law, and apart from this latter problem cannot be solved.*

To what purpose is labour bestowed upon a civil constitution adjusted to law for individual men, *i.e.* upon the creation of a Commonwealth ? The same anti-social impulse which first drove men to such a creation is again the cause that every commonwealth, in its external relations,—*i.e.* as a state in reference to other states,—occupies the same ground of lawless and uncontrolled liberty ; consequently each must anticipate from the other the very same evils which compelled individuals to enter the social state. Nature accordingly avails herself of the spirit of enmity in Man, as existing even in the great national corporations of that animal, for the purpose of attaining through the inevitable antagonism of this spirit a state of rest and security: *i.e.* by wars, by the immoderate exhaustion of incessant preparations for war, and by the pressure of evil consequences which war at last entails upon any nation even through the midst of peace, she drives nations to all sorts of experiments and expedients; and finally, after infinite devastations, ruin, and universal exhaustion of energy, to one which reason should have suggested without the cost of so sad an experience,—viz. to quit the barbarous condition of lawless power, and to enter into a federal league of nations, in which even the weakest member looks for its rights and for protection not to its own power, or its own adjudication, but to this great confederation (*Fœdus Amphictyonum*), to the united power, and the adjudication of the collective will. Visionary as this idea may seem, and as such laughed at in the Abbé de St. Pierre and in Rousseau (possibly because they deemed it too near to its accomplishment),—it is notwithstanding the inevitable[1] resource and mode of escape under that pressure of evil which nations reciprocally inflict; and, hard as it may be to realize such an idea, states must of necessity be driven at last to the very same resolution to which the savage man of nature was driven with equal reluctance—viz. to sacrifice brutal liberty, and to seek peace and security in a civil constitution founded upon law. All wars therefore are so many tentative essays (not in the intention of Man, but in the intention of Nature)

[1] During the two last centuries (*i.e.* from the date of the scheme for organizing Christendom for some common purpose, no matter what, by the first of the Bourbons, Henry IV of France, down to the late Congresses at Aix-la-Chapelle and Verona) the human species have been making their first rude essays—putting forth their feelers as it were—towards such an idea.—The reader must not confound (as too generally is done) that St. Pierre to whom Kant refers,—viz. the visionary who speculated on the means of abolishing war,—with the sentimentalist of our own century, author of *Paul and Virginia*, *Studies of Nature*, &c. The first was at work early in the 18th century, say 1720; the other was patronized by the first Napoleon during his Consulate, consequently entered the 19th century.—*Tr.*

to bring about new relations of states, and by revolutions and dismemberments to form new political bodies. These again, either from internal defects or external attacks, cannot support themselves, but must undergo similar revolutions ; until at last, partly by the best possible arrangement of civil government within, and partly by common concert and legal compact without, a condition is attained which, like a well-ordered commonwealth, can maintain itself in the way of an automaton.

Now, whether (in the first place) it is to be anticipated from an epicurean concourse of efficient causes that states, like atoms, by accidental shocking together, should go through all sorts of new combinations to be again dissolved by the fortuitous impulse of fresh shocks, until at length by pure accident some combination emerges capable of supporting itself (a case of luck that could hardly be looked for) ; or whether (in the second place) we should rather assume that Nature is in this instance pursuing her regular course of raising our species gradually from the lower steps of animal existence to the very highest of a human existence, and *that* not by any direct interposition in our favour, but through man's own spontaneous and artificial efforts (spontaneous, but yet extorted from him by his situation), and in this apparently wild arrangement of things is developing with perfect regularity the original tendencies she has implanted ; or whether (in the third place) it is more reasonable to believe that out of all this action and reaction of the human species upon itself nothing in the shape of a wise result will ever issue,—that it will continue to be as it has been, and therefore that it cannot be known beforehand, but that the discord which is so natural to our species will finally prepare for us a hell of evils under the most moral condition of society, such as may swallow up this very moral condition itself and all previous advance in culture by a reflux of the original barbaric spirit of desolation (a fate, by the way, against which it is impossible to be secured under the government of blind chance, with which liberty uncontrolled by law is identical, unless by underlaying this chance with a secret nexus of wisdom) :—to all this the answer turns upon the following question : Whether it be reasonable to assume a final purpose of all natural processes and arrangements in the parts, and yet a want of purpose in the whole? What therefore the objectless condition of savage life effected in the end,—viz. that it checked the development of the natural tendencies in the human species, but then, by the very evils it thus caused, drove man into a state where those tendencies could unfold and mature themselves, namely, the state of civilisation,—that same service is performed for states by the barbaric freedom in which they are now existing,—viz. that, by causing the dedication of all national energies and resources to war, by the desolations of war, and still more by causing the necessity of standing continually in a state of preparation for war, it checks the full development of the natural tendencies in its progress, but, on the other hand, by these very evils and their consequences, it compels our species at last to discover some law of counterbalance to the principle of antagonism between nations, and, in order to give effect to this law, to introduce a federation of states, and consequently a cosmopolitical condition of security (or police) corresponding to that municipal security which arises out of internal police. This federation will itself not be exempt from danger,—else the powers of the human race would go to sleep; it will be sufficient that it contain a principle for restoring the equilibrium between its own action and reaction, and thus checking the two functions from destroying each other. Before this last step is taken, human nature—then about half-way advanced in its progress—is in the deepest abyss of evils under the deceitful semblance of external prosperity; and Rousseau was not so much in the wrong when he preferred the condition of the savage to that of the civilized man at the point where he has reached, but is hesitating to take, the final step of his ascent. We are at this time in a high degree of *culture* as to arts and sciences. We are *civilized* to superfluity in what regards the graces and decorums of life. But to entitle us to consider ourselves *moralized* much is still wanting. Yet the idea of morality belongs even to that of *culture*; but the use of this idea, as it comes forward in mere *civilisation,* is restrained to its influence on manners, as seen in the principle of honour, in respectability of deportment, &c. Nothing indeed of a true moral influence can be expected so long as states direct all their energies to idle plans of aggrandizement by force, and thus incessantly check the slow motions by which the intellect of the species is unfolding and forming itself, to say nothing of their shrinking from all *positive* aid to those motions. But all good that is not engrafted upon moral good is mere show and hollow speciousness—the dust and ashes of mortality. And in this delusive condition will the human race linger, until it shall have toiled upwards in the way I have mentioned from its present chaotic abyss of political relations.

### PROPOSITION THE EIGHTH

*The History of the Human Species as a whole may be regarded as the unravelling of a hidden Plan of Nature for accomplishing a perfect State of Civil Constitution for society in its internal relations (and, as the condition of that, by the last proposition, in its external relations also) as the sole state of society in which the tendencies of human nature can be all and fully developed.*

This proposition is an inference from the preceding. A question arises upon it—whether experience has yet observed any traces of such an unravelling in History? I answer—some little: for the whole period (to speak astronomically) of this unravelling is probably too vast to admit of our collecting even the form of its orbit or the relation of the parts to the whole from the small fraction of it which Man has yet left behind him; just as little as it is possible from the astronomical observations hitherto made to determine the course which our sun together with his whole system of planets pursues amongst the heavenly host; although, upon universal grounds derived from the systematic frame of the universe, as well as upon the little stock of observation as yet accumulated, enough is known to warrant us in asserting that there *is* such a course. Meantime our human nature obliges us to take an interest even in the remotest epoch to which our species is destined, provided we can anticipate it with certainty. So much the less can *we* be indifferent to it, inasmuch as it appears within our power by intellectual arrangements to contribute something towards the acceleration of the species in its advance to this great epoch. On this account the faintest traces of any approximation in such a direction become of importance to us. At present all states are so artificially interconnected that no one can possibly become stationary in its internal culture without retrograding in power and influence with respect to all the rest ; and thus, if not the progress, yet the non-declension, of this purpose of Nature is sufficiently secured through the ambition of nations. Moreover, civil liberty cannot at this day any longer be so arrested in its progress but that all the sources of livelihood, and more immediately trade, must betray a close sympathy with it, and sicken as *that* sickens; and hence a decay of the state in its external relations. Gradually, too, this liberty extends itself. If the citizen be hindered from pursuing his interest in any way most agreeable to himself provided only it can co-exist with the liberty of others, in that case the vivacious life of general business is palsied, and in connexion with that again the powers of the whole. Hence it arises that all personal restriction, whether as to commission or omission, is more and more withdrawn ; religious liberty is established ; and thus, by little and little, with occasional interruptions, arises *Illumination* : a blessing which the human race must win even from the self-interested purposes of its rulers, if they comprehend what is for their own advantage. Now, this Illumination, and with it a certain degree of cordial interest which the enlightened man cannot forbear taking in all the good which he perfectly comprehends, must by degrees mount upwards even to the throne, and exert an influence on the principles of government. At present, for example, our governments have no [1] money disposable for national education, because the estimates for the next war have absorbed the whole by anticipation. The first act, therefore, by which the state will express its interest in the advancing spirit of the age will be by withdrawing its opposition at least to the feeble and tardy exertions of the people in this direction.

[1] "*No money disposable,*" &c. :—The reader must remember that this was written in Germany in the year 1784, and in the midst of petty courts (which are generally the most profligate). In England, and even elsewhere, there is now the dawn of a better system.—*Tr.*

Finally, war itself becomes gradually not only so artificial a process, so uncertain in its issue, but also in the after-pains of inextinguishable national debts (a contrivance of modern times) so anxious and burthensome, and, at the same time, the influence which any convulsions of one state exert upon every other state is so remarkable in our quarter of the globe,—linked as it is in all parts by the systematic intercourse of trade,—that at length those governments which have no immediate participation in the war, under a sense of their own danger, offer themselves as mediators, though as yet without any authentic sanction of law, and thus prepare all things from afar for the formation of a great primary state-body, or Cosmopolitic Areopagus, such as is wholly unprecedented in all preceding ages. Although this body at present exists only in rude outline, yet already a stirring is beginning to be perceptible in all its limbs, each of which is interested in the maintenance of the whole. Even now there is enough to justify a hope that, after many revolutions and remodellings of states, the supreme purpose of Nature will be accomplished in the establishment of a Cosmopolitic State, as the bosom in which all the original tendencies of the human species are to be developed.

## PROPOSITION THE NINTH

*A philosophical attempt to compose a Universal History,*[1] *in the sense of a Cosmopolitical History, upon a plan tending to unfold the purpose of Nature in a perfect Civil Union of the Human Species (instead of the present imperfect union), is to be regarded as possible, and as capable even of helping forward this very purpose of Nature.*

At first sight it is certainly a strange, and apparently an extravagant, project, to propose a History of Man founded on any idea of the course which human affairs would take

[1] The reader must remember what Kant means by a *Universal History.* In the common sense, as the history of the whole world in its separate divisions, such a history exists already in many shapes that perhaps could not be essentially improved. But in Kant's sense, as a history of the whole *as* a whole, no essay has been made towards it.—*Tr.*

if adjusted to certain reasonable ends. On such a plan it may be thought that nothing better than a romance could be the result. Yet, if we assume that Nature proceeds not without plan and final purpose even in the motions of human free-will, this idea may possibly turn out very useful; and, although we are too short-sighted to look through the secret mechanism of her arrangements, this idea may yet serve as a clue for connecting into something like *systematic* unity the great abstract of human actions that else seem a chaotic and incoherent *aggregate*. For, if we take our beginning from the Grecian History, as the depository, or at least the collateral voucher, for all elder or synchronous History; if we pursue down to our own times its influence upon the formation and malformation of the Roman People as a political body that swallowed up the Grecian state, and the influence of Rome upon the Barbarians by whom Rome itself was destroyed; and if to all this we add, by way of episode, the political history of every other people so far as it has come to our knowledge through the records of the two enlightened nations above mentioned [1]; we shall then discover a regular gradation of improvement in civil polity as it has grown up in our quarter of the globe, which quarter is in all probability destined to give laws to all the rest. If further we direct an exclusive attention to the civil constitution, with its laws and the external relations of the state, in so far as both, by means of the good which they contained, served for a period to raise and to dignify other nations, and with them the arts and sciences,—yet again by their defects served also to precipitate them into ruin, but so that always some germ of illumination survived which, being more and more developed by every revolution, prepared continually a still higher step

[1] A *learned public* only that has endured unbroken from its commencement to our days can be an authentic witness for Ancient History. Beyond that, all is *terra incognita*; and the history of nations who lived without that circle must start from time to time as they happened to come within it. This took place with the Jewish people about the time of the Ptolemies, and chiefly through the Septuagint translation of the Bible; apart from which, but little credit should be given to their own insulated accounts unsupported by collateral evidence. From this point we may pursue their records upwards; and so of all other nations.

of improvement,—in that case, I believe that a clue will be discovered not only for the unravelling of the intricate web of human affairs, and for the guidance of future statesmen in the art of political prophecy (a benefit which has been extracted from History even whilst it was regarded as an incoherent result from a lawless freedom of will), but also such a clue as will open a consolatory prospect into futurity, in which at a remote distance we shall discover the human species seated upon an eminence won by infinite toil, where all the germs are unfolded which Nature has implanted, and its destination upon this earth accomplished. Such a justification of Nature, or rather of Providence, is no mean motive for choosing this cosmopolitical station for the survey of History. For what does it avail to praise and to draw forth to view the magnificence and wisdom of the creation in the irrational kingdom of Nature, if that part in the great stage of the supreme wisdom which contains the object of all this mighty display,—viz. the history of the human species,—is to remain an eternal objection to it, the bare sight of which obliges us to turn away our eyes with displeasure, and (from the despair which it raises of ever discovering in it a perfect and rational purpose) finally leads us to look for such a purpose only in another world?

My object in this essay would be wholly misinterpreted if it were supposed that, under the idea of a Cosmopolitical History which to a certain degree has its course determined *a priori*, I had any wish to discourage the cultivation of *empirical* History in the ordinary sense. On the contrary, the philosopher must be well versed in History who could execute the plan I have sketched, which is indeed a most extensive survey of History, only taken from a new station. However, the extreme, and, simply considered, praiseworthy, circumstantiality with which the history of every nation is written in our times, must naturally suggest a question of some embarrassment. In what way will our remote posterity be able to cope with the enormous accumulation of historical records which a few centuries will bequeath to them? There is no doubt that they will estimate the historical details of times far removed from their own, the original monuments of which will long have perished, simply by the value of that which will then concern themselves,—viz. by the good or evil performed by nations and their governments in a *cosmo-political* view. To direct the eye upon this point as connected with the ambition of rulers and their servants, in order to guide them to the only means of bequeathing an honourable record of themselves to distant ages, may furnish some small motive (over and above the great one of justifying Providence) for attempting a Philosophic History on the plan I have here explained.